Nobody's Nation

NOBODY'S NATION

READING DEREK WALCOTT

Paul Breslin

The University of Chicago Press
Chicago and London

Paul Breslin is professor of English at Northwestern University. He is the author of *The Psycho-Political Muse: American Poetry since the Fifties*, published by the University of Chicago Press, and *You Are Here*, a collection of poems.

The University of Chicago Press, Chicago 60637
The University of Chicago Press, Ltd., London

Printed in the United States of America
10 09 08 07 06 05 04 03 02 01   5 4 3 2 1

ISBN (cloth): 0-226-07426-9
ISBN (paper): 0-226-07427-7

Library of Congress Cataloging-in-Publication Data

Breslin, Paul.
Nobody's nation : reading Derek Walcott / Paul Breslin.
p. cm.
Includes index.
ISBN 0-226-07426-9 (alk. paper) — ISBN 0-226-07427-7 (pbk. : alk. paper)
1. Walcott, Derek—Knowledge—History. 2. Literature and history—West Indies—History—20th century. 3. Postcolonialism—West Indies. 4. Decolonization in literature. 5. West Indies—In literature. I. Title.
PR9272.9.W3 Z545 2001
811′.54—dc21

2001002128

♾ The paper used in this publication meets the minimum requirements of the American National Standard for Information Sciences—Permanence of Paper for Printed Library Materials, ANSI Z39.48-1992.

CONTENTS

ACKNOWLEDGMENTS

First of all, I want to thank Derek Walcott himself for talking with me several times during the course of my work, for putting me in touch with his friends in St. Lucia, and for permitting me to read and photocopy archival materials at the University of the West Indies in Mona, Jamaica and St. Augustine, Trinidad. And I am grateful to him and Sigrid Nama for their hospitality during my 1995 trip to St. Lucia, when I interviewed him at their house.

Several people—Dunstan St. Omer, John Robert Lee, and the Williamses, Gregor, Deirdre, and their daughter Abbie—not only shared their insights into Walcott's life and work, but took me to important places. Dunstan showed me his church murals at Jacmel, Monchy, and Gros Îlet, concluding the day with a stop at Pigeon Island. Gregor took me the length of the island, with stops and detours along the way, sharing his knowledge as he drove. Abbie took me to Dauphin, no easy trip. During my four trips to St. Lucia, I benefited greatly from conversations with MacDonald Dixon, Hunter François, Kendel Hyppolyte, Arthur Jacobs, Jane King, John Robert Lee, Richard Montgomery, and George Odlum. I also am grateful to Robert Deveaux for his assistance in my research at the St. Lucia National Trust Archives, and to Lady Suzette Simmons for showing me several paintings by Harold Simmons from her own collection.

In Trinidad, my thanks to Kenneth Ramchand for his

hospitality and informative conversation on Walcott and Trinidadian culture during my first visit in 1990. Albert Laveaux gave a memorable account of his experiences in the Trinidad Theatre Workshop. Oswald "Moti" Motilal, whom I had met by chance in St. Lucia, took me through the Caroni region down to San Fernando, with stops in several Indian communities along the way. Carlton G. Davis of the University of Florida helped me get in touch with people; his contacts led me to Margaret Walcott, who took time to speak with me. The historian Bridget Brereton gave me insight into Trinidadian politics and culture in the period of decolonization, and Gordon Rohlehr discussed Walcott in relation to folk culture and other West Indian poets. I am grateful, also, to the staff of the UWI Library's West Indiana Collection, Sherrie Singh, Ernest Joseph, and Gloria Baptiste, for their help in threading the maze of the Walcott Archive during the limited time of my stay in 1993.

In Jamaica, thanks to Patricia Dunn, who helped me find what I needed in the materials at UWI, Mona; to Velma Pollard, for a conversation at her home; and to Lorna Goodison for an afternoon at her home in Kingston, talking about Walcott, West Indian literature, and much else with her and with Archie Hudson-Philips.

I have benefited greatly from an e-mail correspondence with Bruce King that began in February 1996. He has been generous in sharing the knowledge gained from his research on his biography, *Derek Walcott: A Caribbean Life,* and in supplying the proofs so I could cite it in my study. Paula Burnett was kind enough to e-mail a chapter from her forthcoming book, *Derek Walcott: Politics and Poetics* so that I could take account of it. Thanks also to Jahan Ramazani for a sympathetic but critically demanding response to the first version of the manuscript; to Laurence Breiner for a critique of two early chapter drafts; and to my editor at the University of Chicago Press, Alan Thomas, for much good advice along the way. Three colleagues at Northwestern have offered valuable critiques of part or all of the book: Christine Froula, Mary Kinzie, and Lawrence Lipking.

Portions of chapter 10 appeared in *Poetry,* vol. 178, no. 1, as "Tracking *Tiepolo's Hound.*"

Of course there are personal debts as well: to my wife Jeanne, for her love and patience, thanks (again!).

ABBREVIATIONS

The following abbreviations are used in the text to refer to Derek Walcott's works.

25 P	*25 Poems*
AL	*Another Life*
AT	*The Arkansas Testament*
B	*The Bounty*
CP	*Collected Poems, 1948–1984*
DC	*Drums and Colours*
DMMOP	*Dream on Monkey Mountain and Other Plays*
EY	*Epitaph for the Young*
FC	"The Figure of Crusoe: On the Theme of Isolation in West Indian Writing, with a Reading of His Poems"
FT	*The Fortunate Traveller*
G	*The Gulf*
GN	*In a Green Night*
HC	*Henri Christophe: A Chronicle in Seven Scenes*
IFN	*The Island Is Full of Noises*
M	*Midsummer*
O	*Omeros*
P	*Poems* (1951)
R & P	*Remembrance & Pantomime: Two Plays*
SG	*Sea Grapes*
TH	*Tiepolo's Hound*

INTRODUCTION

My title comes from "The Schooner *Flight*," by consensus (and the poet's own reckoning)[1] one of Walcott's finest poems. The sailor-poet Shabine, in a much-quoted passage, says, "I have English, Dutch, and nigger in me, / And either I'm nobody, or I'm a nation."[2] By refusing to choose between these alternatives, Shabine implicitly sees himself as both extremes at once: precisely by his inchoate lack of identity, he is representative of a people and carries its latent nationhood by synecdoche within himself. "Nobody" might seem a harsh self-dismissal, echoing colonialists like James Anthony Froude, who claimed that "there are no people" in the West Indies "in the true sense of the word, with a character and a purpose of their own," or disaffected West Indians like V. S. Naipaul, who has described "mimic men of the New World" playing at real life.[3] And yet sometimes the evasion of defined identity can be a deliberate strategy. Odysseus, a character with whom Walcott has more than once implicitly identified himself, escapes the Cyclops by giving his name as "No man." When he blinds Polyphemus, the giant cries out that "no man" has injured him; his neighbors, unwilling to give chase to a nonentity, go on about their business. Odysseus, in this episode, is a little bit like Ralph Ellison's invisible man. In Ellison's novel, invisibility, though it results from a refusal on the part of white people to acknowledge the black person's existence, becomes a strategic resource as well as a limitation. Walcott's figure of "nobody" acquires a similar mobility and ease of escape. To be nobody is to elude imposed definitions of one's identity while deferring the question of what definition to claim in their stead. As Walcott has remarked, "It takes a West Indian a long time to say who he is."[4]

In calling my book "Nobody's Nation," I intend several meanings. First, that a West Indian identity has had to emerge in the face of judgments like Froude's and Naipaul's, that any such identity is empty, derivative, the desperate attempt of nobodies to be somebodies. Second, that the West Indies, since the collapse of the Federation at the end of 1961, has literally been "nobody's nation" in the political sense, although Walcott and many others still believe in the cultural unity of the scattered territories. "The West Indies" exists as an imagined community, but one that has not achieved political embodiment. The remaining two senses concern Walcott's response to this situation. In many of his works, the indeterminate identity of an Odyssean "nobody" becomes a source of strength, a way of eluding definitions imposed by others. The figures he offers as types of Caribbean identity—Adam, Robinson Crusoe, Philoctetes, Odysseus—metamorphose into forms of each other if we follow them through his work. The truest type of all may be Proteus, the shape-shifting Old Man of the Sea. So "nobody" is the Protean hero whose fluidity allows him to shed any fixed identity attributed to him. And finally, Walcott has played on the idea of "nothing," the imputed absence of history and tradition, as an open space for creation rather than impoverishment. "If there was nothing, there was everything to be made,"[5] he recalled, describing the West Indies of his youth. Being a nobody from nowhere, he has argued, circumvents the Anglo-American burden of literary influence, allowing the freshness of an Adamic vision, coming to terms with one's world as if for the first time. Eluding the names given by others, the Caribbean Adam is free to name things for himself. To these ideas, and to their complications and self-contradictions, Walcott has returned again and again.

If a poet needs to define the speaking "I" whose way of experiencing the world will shape the poem, a poet (and still more a playwright) also needs to imagine, as Robert Pinsky says, a society in which the poem or play can take place.[6] The successful definition of an authorial "I" and the imagining of a society in which the poem can take place are part of the same process, informing and enriching each other. The imagined society need not literally exist, but it has to be derived from one that does, as a potential latent within it. Language and form must suggest not only what sort of person might be speaking, but what sort of person might be reading or listening.

Walcott's authorial persona has always been, by his own description, contradictory. He comes before us in the autobiographical *Another Life* as "The Divided Child"; that child would grow up to be the young poet of "A Far Cry from Africa," "divided to the vein" by his English and African ancestry. In "What the Twilight Says: An Overture," he depicts himself as "the mulatto of style" whose art developed by "making creative use of his schizophrenia." And some of his best Caribbean readers have taken Walcott at his word, arguing that profound self-contradiction is the irritant that has hurt him into poetry. Victor Questel, a Trinidadian poet and critic whose untimely death in 1982 cut short a promising career, left behind a dissertation in which he argued that "throughout Walcott's work there is a line of inconsistency and paradox consistent with his confessed 'split' and reflective of the contradictory stance to be expected from a person born in a polyglot society such as the Caribbean." He cites the Barbadian writer George Lamming's description of Walcott as "a model of the ripened ambivalence that makes impossible demands of the heart, tears it to pieces by a contradiction of origins, and finally offers it to the dubious consolation of a livable despair."[7]

Another Caribbean scholar, Gordon Rohlehr, remarks that "Whatever [Walcott] warns against, he is on the verge of attempting it." And like Questel, Rohlehr sees Walcott's self-contradictory imagination as culturally representative: "The law of dialectic, so crucial for an understanding of aesthetic code-switching in the Caribbean, makes us confront our imagined opposite which, in the process of trying to negate, we come somewhat to resemble. Thus Walcott is obeying an inbuilt Caribbean necessity."[8] Questel remarks that "the area that best reflects Walcott's inconsistency is his treatment of the theme of history." As Rohlehr's term "code-switching," borrowed from sociolinguistics, suggests, part of the Caribbean necessity involves reconciling "standard" and "dialect" forms of language and culture. In language it means negotiating the gap between the varieties of West Indian speech and standard English. In culture it means mediating between what Edward Kamau Brathwaite, in his study of creole society in Jamaica, calls "the 'great' and 'little' traditions." He notes that "under slavery there were two great traditions, one in England, the other in Africa, and so neither was residential. Normative value-references were made outside the society," although the synthesis of creolization "mediated the development of local institutions, and an Afro-creole 'little' tradition among the slave 'folk.'" But "the Euro-creole élite" would prove "unable or unwilling to absorb in any central sense the 'little' tradition of the majority." Brathwaite's study covers the years 1770–1820, but he claims that the "dichotomy" still remains, contributing to "the agonistic pessimism of writers like Derek Walcott, Orlando Patterson, and Vidia Naipaul."[9]

The way a West Indian writer tries to resolve Brathwaite's dichotomy involves an interpretation of history. Walcott's quarrel with what he calls history is in part a quarrel with other historical interpretations, including that of Brathwaite, who has emphasized recovery of that second, African "great" tradition suppressed under colonial conditions and has sometimes uncritically celebrated the emergent creole 'little' tradition.[10] But history is also the central arena of his conflict with himself, for his self-definition as a poet and playwright requires some stance toward the past he understands himself to inherit, even if the stance is a rejection of that past as unusable.

When he published his first book of poems in 1948, Walcott aspired to enter the "great" tradition of English literature, the value judgments of which were indeed "made outside the society." There was, he recalls,

> no publishing house in St. Lucia or in the Caribbean. There was a Faber collection of books that had come out with poets like Eliot and Auden, and I liked the type-face and how the book looked. I thought, "I want to have a book like that." So I selected a collection of twenty-five [poems] and thought, "Well, these will look good because they'll look like they came from abroad; they'll look like a published book."[11]

At the same time, he belonged to a generation stirred by West Indian cultural nationalism, with independence and federation expected imminently. In 1947, the year before Walcott assembled those twenty-five poems, detailed coverage of the Montego Bay conference on federation had dominated *The Voice of St. Lucia,* the island's main newspaper, for two months. West Indian writers were beginning to seek—in fiction at first, more than in drama or poetry—characteristically West Indian experience and language. Walcott's own early plays, especially *Henri Christophe* (1949) and *The Sea at Dauphin* (1954), made important contributions to that quest.

In choosing Walcott's war on history as my central theme, I have followed my intuitive sense that here all that is most vexed, inspired, and problematic in his writing converges, so that both the implications and the buried sources of Walcott's self-division are to be traced in this Quixotic campaign. History is a realm of necessity, *ananke* to the poet's *eros,* something to be struggled with, contested, or remade. Or, as Walcott put it when I interviewed him in April 1989: "The poet is the knight, and history is the dragon." The dragon does not choose sides in Brathwaite's split between "great" and "little" traditions: it can rear its head in colonialist historical narratives that consign the "little" tradition to utter nonbeing, or in narratives of protest that dismiss the "great" traditions of the colonizer as not worth assimilating, while reducing the "little" tradition to a reiteration of moral outrage. In either case, "history" becomes a dogmatic either-or choice that constrains rather than frees imagination.

And yet, to achieve his quest, the knight requires the dragon; without one, his occupation is gone. In the most dismissive accounts, such as Naipaul's or Froude's, the colonial knight lacks even a worthy adversary: there simply is no history, and therefore no dragon to be slain. According to such assessments, the absence of history leaves a vacuum in which real people (let alone heroic knights) cannot emerge, but only empty simulacra of their historically embodied counterparts on the other side of the Atlantic.

Some Caribbean writers have made it their life's work to refute such judgments, pointing to Brathwaite's "little" tradition as evidence of an indigenous cultural synthesis, something created in the West Indies by West Indians. But cultural invention is not entirely synonymous with historical agency. It is one thing to show that even under conditions of unfreedom West Indian people found ways to shape their own culture; it is quite another to show that, under colonialism, let alone under slavery, the culture they made could typically exert much influence on events. The Martinican writer Edouard Glissant, though writing of French-speaking Caribbeans, describes their English-speaking neighbors also when he says that "Our historical consciousnesses could not be deposited gradually and continuously like sediment . . . but came together in the context of shock, contraction, painful negation, and explosive forces. This dislocation of the continuum, and the inability of the collective consciousness to absorb it all, characterize what I call a nonhistory."[12] Instead of culture and history going forward together and producing each other gradually by continuous interplay, there were sudden reversals of policy imposed from abroad, old usages suddenly discontinued and new ones put in their place. For Walcott's native St. Lucia, which changed hands thirteen times between France and England before settling into English possession through the treaty of 1814, even the colonially imposed religion and language were subject to change without notice, depending on who won the most recent battle. So even the sense of being without a history turns out, in Glissant's analysis, to be historically produced. Or, as Walcott put it in a characteristically perverse aphorism, "In time, the slave surrendered to amnesia. That amnesia is the true history of the New World." In the same essay that offers this reading of history as amnesia, however, Walcott claims that "the great poets of the New World," far from being hampered by their amnesia, achieve an "Adamic vision," seeing "everything as renewed." And "it is this awe of the numinous, this elemental privilege of naming the New World which annihilates history in our great poets, an elation common to all of them."[13]

To begin to sort out the self-canceling ironies of these pronouncements is to appreciate the lacerating contradictions at the core of Walcott's work. Among these is the problem of Adam's amnesia. In *Genesis,* Adam truly has no history, no past. To have amnesia is to have the same subjective lack of a past; in this case, however, the lack of memory is not the result of having no past to remember, but the sign of a trauma, a psychic wound. Walcott's New World poet feels himself to be Adam in an elemental, ahistorical world precisely because a brutal history, shaped by the Middle Passage, has struck him so hard he cannot remember what hit him. Walcott is fully aware of the implications of "amnesia," as he shows (to select one instance among many) in the closing lines of his poem "Laventille," which describe the West Indian psyche as stunned by "some deep amnesiac blow" that leaves it "bound" in "swaddling cerements."[14] The newborn Caribbean Adam arrives in the burial clothes of the past. He has experienced what Glissant calls a nonhistory, but he must turn it from a wound into an enabling privilege, from *blessure* to blessing. Walcott advocates for the artist a deliberately sustained forgetting, an audaciously sweeping act of psychological denial. "The children of slaves," he writes in "What the Twilight Says," "must sear their memory with a torch."[15] Why does Walcott enjoin this cauterization of memory, this "return through a darkness whose terminus is amnesia," as a discipline for actors who would "keep the sacred urge of actors everywhere: to record the anguish of the race"? How can it be that in order to "record" (*O.E.D.* I.1a, "to get by heart, to commit to memory") one must rigorously forget? And if recording the anguish of the race is not a form of "history," what is it?

It is tempting to read and reread obsessively, expecting some "deep" understanding at last to resolve Walcott's paradoxes, but after some years spent on this endeavor, I have abandoned it as a fool's errand. I have come to believe that the works in which the conflict between the desire to remember and the desire to forget, the desire to retrieve history and the desire to annihilate it, is sharpest, most tangled and unresolved, are by and large the most powerful in Walcott's large *oeuvre.* But the urgency of that conflict, the sharpness and complexity, would not exist if the longing to resolve it were not so deep. Walcott is poised on the cusp between a modernist aesthetic, which takes desperate measures to salvage some sort of artistic order from what it perceives as mere "anarchy and futility" (Eliot), and a postmodern one that accepts brokenness and disorder as the way things are, abandons the ambition to make them whole, and tries to be cheerful about it.[16] The paradox Questel and Rohlehr have noted in his work bears some relation to the "language of paradox" that Cleanth Brooks thought definitive of most true poetry and central to the modernist poetics Brooks espoused. Walcott shares with the New Critics a suspicion of poetry committed to a straightforward political agenda. But whereas Brooks, like John Crowe Ransom and Allen Tate, sees paradox as a way of ensuring Kantian distance from the pressure of warring interests, Walcott's paradox becomes, as Questel argues, an iconic representation of tensions in West Indian society. Walcottian paradox may be resistant to political position-taking, but it is often an extremely effective way of dramatizing, rather than sublimating, social conflict. It may decline to make a political argument, but it is not disinterested in the sense that Brooks recommended; it is rather a metaphor for an agonized state of unresolved conflict.

Within the first day of my first visit to St. Lucia, I had two conversations that seem, in retrospect, to define the polarities of Walcott's imagination. On the tennis court next to the beach cottages where I was staying, the poet's lifelong friend, Dunstan St. Omer, was finishing a set. St. Omer is St. Lucia's leading painter, the "Gregorias" of *Another Life.* He lingered to talk about Walcott, whom he immediately described as "an elemental man." He indeed saw his friend as Adamic, drawing his strength from St. Lucian folk culture and landscape and from a direct connection to the natural world, unattenuated by the historical self-consciousness of metropolitan cultures. And as we sat on the sea wall overlooking Choc Bay while the sun descended toward its reflection in the Caribbean Sea, I could forget my own assumptions for an hour and entertain the possibility of an elemental man.

The next day I met Richard Montgomery, the English-born stage designer who has worked on many of Walcott's plays since the 1970s. He was on the island in preparation for a revival of *The Haytian Earth,* to celebrate the tenth anniversary of St. Lucian independence. At some vague hour past midnight, we had our first Walcott conversation, which he opened by saying: "Derek is a lot more like the Earl of Oxford than Simple Will from Avon." He went on to describe parties in which Walcott moved at ease among prime ministers of island states, intellectuals and politicians, representatives of American foundations. His Walcott is a cosmopolitan, at home in the inner circles of West Indian society—a marginalized society, perhaps, from a North American point of view, but one with its own complexities and hierarchies of power. And as Walcott's fame has grown, as he has become more acclimated to the United States and more widely traveled, he has become a cosmopolitan in the largest sense, not just within the Caribbean. Where St. Omer sees an elemental man, intact through every change of circumstance, Montgomery sees a player of social roles, a many-minded Ulysses. Not an Adamic man somehow escaped from history, but someone who has enjoyed a front-row view of history in the making. Could these contradictory views, offered by two men who know Walcott very well, both be right? One can quote Walcott himself on both sides of the question. As Questel remarked in his dissertation, Walcott attacked as "pastoralism" the "sentimental notion of some original 'pure' or genuine state . . . particularly when such pastoralism is married to ideas about the 'African presence' in the Caribbean, or Black Power, its political corollary." And yet, he "shares in this pastoralism in so far as he does believe in 'green beginnings,' or the 'primal' or concepts of 'Adamic man.'"[17]

After I met him in St. Lucia for a last round of interviews in March 1995, Walcott told me that he had little use for biographical criticism. But, he added, "if you can show how a place like this produced someone like me, or Dunstan, then you will have done something." What follows is my attempt to read some of the most interesting among Walcott's poems, plays, and essays in the context of what I've been able to learn about the place (or places) that "produced" him and the traditions, oral and literary, by which he sought to create poems and plays in the spirit of that place. The chapters explore key phases of his career in roughly chronological sequence from the earliest work to his first book of the new millennium, *Tiepolo's Hound.*

Although I have read extensively in postcolonial theory, I have referred to theoretical work sparingly. The theoretically engaged works most useful to me have usually proven to be those that also attempt a general account of Caribbean culture and literature, such as J. Michael Dash's *The Other America: West Indian Literature in a New World Context* or Antonio Benítez-Rojo's *The Repeating Island: The Caribbean and the Postmodern Perspective.* Most of the time, the theorists are arguing about the general definition of "postcolonial," whereas I am trying to locate a particular poet in relation to a regional history. But when my account of this particular history turns up evidence contrary to widely held theoretical beliefs about postcolonial literatures, I try to sketch the theoretical implications of such findings.

In the first four chapters I address Walcott's question: "How a place like this produced someone like me." I begin with a biographical sketch, in which I have emphasized events that have a bearing on my interpretation of the writing. Bruce King's biography, *Derek Walcott: A Caribbean Life,* is recommended to anyone who seeks a more detailed account. Then I attempt to trace the emergence of Walcott's style from the interplay of influences in both West Indian culture and the canon of Anglo-American literature as he encountered it from the 1940s to the early 1960s. Next I turn to the first mature plays, written during his years in Jamaica (1950–1957). And, in a more thematic chapter, I trace the development of his preoccupation with Robinson Crusoe in relation to his Adamic poetics and rejection of "history," from the early 1960s to the late 1970s.

The remaining chapters trace Walcott's further development through what I regard as his best, or in some cases his most revealing, works. I devote four of these to studies of major works: *Dream on Monkey Mountain, Another Life,* "The Schooner *'Flight,'*" and *Omeros.* Others, necessarily more compressed, attempt to distill the central mood and style of a period in his career: the restless years between his departure from the Trinidad Theatre Workshop and his acquisition of a house in St. Lucia, and the further course of his poetry since the publication *Omeros.* The book ends with a brief evaluative discussion of Walcott's strengths and weaknesses. Throughout, I trace his continuing effort to "say who he is," even in the guise of an elusive Odyssean "nobody," and his attempt, in that saying, to house nobody in a "nation," be it St. Lucia, the West Indies, a transnational diaspora, or a place that exists only in the mind, "no nation but the imagination."[18]

1

Biographical Sketch

> It takes a West Indian a long time to say who he is.
>
> —Derek Walcott

Derek Alton Walcott was born in Castries on January 23, 1930, and grew up just a few blocks from the home of St. Lucia's other Nobel laureate, the economist Sir W. Arthur Lewis, born on the same date in 1915. His parents, Warwick and Alix Walcott, welcomed two children into the world that day: Derek and his fraternal twin, the late Roderick Aldon. A daughter, Pamela, had been born two years earlier. Walcott's immediate grandfathers—a Dutchman from Saint Martin on his mother's side and an Englishman from Barbados on his father's—were white and relatively wealthy, and his immediate grandmothers primarily of African descent and poor. He was, as he would later put it in his most famous early poem, racially "divided to the vein."[1]

Warwick Walcott died on April 23, 1931, after surgery for a mastoid infection. Although the future poet, only a year old at the time, could have no direct memory of him, the father's presence remained in the house. His paintings—he had been a skillful amateur watercolorist—and other "revered, silent objects" (*Another Life*, in *CP*, 153) hung on the walls and stood on the shelves, meticulously cared for by his widow. He also left behind him a circle of artistically inclined friends who remained close to the family. They included, as his son Derek would later recall, "a violinist, an ex-merchant seaman, an inveterate reciter who had seen Barrymore's Hamlet, and a professional painter named Harold Simmons."[2] His profession had been the Civil Service; he was Clerk of the First District Court when he died, and was to have become Acting Deputy Registrar. Alix Walcott was the Head Teacher of the Methodist Infant School, also serving occasionally as Head of the Methodist Primary School. She encouraged the talents of her sons, who often put on plays in the house, and was to live a long life, in contrast to the sad brevity of her husband's. She died in 1992 at the age of ninety-four.

The Walcotts' Methodism was a minority religion in St. Lucia. The dominant religion was Catholicism, a legacy of the strong French influence in the island. St. Lucia changed hands between France and England thirteen times before an 1814 treaty awarded it to the English, who kept it until it became an independent nation in 1979. The English, as a rule, wanted to make their money in the West Indies and go home, whereas the French took more trouble to inculcate their culture and religion. The folk idiom is still a French-lexicon creole; it is heard at least as frequently as English in the Castries marketplace and more frequently out in the countryside. Walcott was relatively "middle-class," mulatto rather than "black," Methodist rather than Catholic. Because Alix Walcott would often invite her pupils and their families to the house, the family was less distanced from poorer St. Lucians than might be expected.[3] Nonetheless, Walcott felt estranged, by his Methodist upbringing, "from the common life of the island."[4]

At the time of Walcott's birth, the population of St. Lucia was less than 80,000, perhaps as little as 60,000.[5] Even today, its population is estimated at just slightly over 150,000. Castries, its largest town, had a population of 17,500 in 1961, and by 1990 had grown to about 45,000.[6] The island is twenty-seven miles long and fourteen miles wide, small compared to Trinidad or Jamaica, let alone Cuba or Hispaniola. Its mountainous terrain makes travel a slow progress through continuous switchbacks, with vertiginous drops to the side of the two-lane road enjoining caution more eloquently than any signage. Despite the recent improvements on the roads along the leeward coast, a trip from Castries to Vieux Fort, at the island's southern tip, takes nearly half a day. The windward side has a flatter and faster highway, but some parts of the coastline are inaccessible. To get to Dauphin, the setting of one of Walcott's plays, one must simply abandon the car and walk the last two miles or so. Before 1963, the island's main product was sugar, with bananas gradually increasing in importance until, in that year, "bananas emerged as the premier cash crop, a position they have not since relinquished."[7] In Walcott's childhood, Castries Harbor still served as a coaling station, though its coal trade had been declining since the 1920s.[8]

By the usual criteria of modernization or "progress," as well as by that of size, St. Lucia does not match the larger islands, or even some of the smaller ones such as Barbados. According to the 1946 census, 43.4 percent of St. Lucians "spoke only [francophone] Creole," although in Castries only 9 percent were entirely without English, whereas "in the North East districts" (i.e., the sparsely populated countryside around Monchy) the percentage rose to 56.5. When Walcott began his career, more than 40 percent of his countrymen could not speak the language in which he wrote. To be sure, the percentage of non-English speakers had already declined from more than 60 percent in 1911,[9] and has continued to decline since. But as of 1980, only 50 percent of St. Lucian adults had attained literacy.[10] In that year, St. Lucia's per capita income was $850 U.S., which was far behind that of Trinidad and Tobago ($4,370) and Barbados ($3,040) and significantly behind Cuba ($1,407) and Jamaica ($1,030). To speak of a St. Lucian "middle class" is to speak of a small elite, and under the colonial rule of Walcott's childhood and youth it was smaller still, comprising mainly the class of civil servants to which his father belonged, a "brown bourgeoisie"[11] allowed to climb just so high and no higher in the hierarchy of colonial administration.

Middle-class St. Lucians sometimes regarded local folklore and folk traditions as embarrassing crudities to be left behind, but this was not so in Walcott's family. His great-aunt, Sidone Wardrope, would recite folk tales for the two brothers when they visited her in the country;[12] Harold Simmons, who taught Walcott and St. Omer painting, was also a folklorist, one of the first educated St. Lucians to take the island's vernacular culture as worthy of serious study.

Any sketch of Walcott's life must pause and pay tribute to Simmons, who became in many respects a father to the fatherless Walcott. Edward Baugh writes that "it was he, more than anyone else, who inspired Walcott to love and care for the common people, as he had opened the eyes of Walcott and St Omer and others, like the amateur photographer Leo St Helene, to the beauty of the St Lucian Countryside." Not only did Simmons teach Walcott painting, he encouraged the boy's interest in poetry. Book 1 of *Another Life* recalls that Simmons introduced the young Walcott to the poems of the Jamaican poet George Campbell; it was Simmons who brought Walcott's poetry to the attention of Henry Swanzy, who soon afterward invited the eighteen-year-old poet to read on his "Caribbean Voices" BBC program; and it was Simmons's review in 1950 of a joint exhibit of paintings by Walcott and St. Omer that encouraged Walcott to choose poetry as his vocation: "Words and imagery are Derek's forte, the brush with discipline will be Dunstan's citadel."[13]

Born in 1914, uneducated beyond high school, Simmons entered the Civil Service in 1946 and did rather well for himself. He rose to the post of District Officer for the Southern District of St. Lucia and edited *The Voice of St. Lucia* from 1957 to 1959. And yet, despite these successes, he remained something of a pariah. Simmons "epitomized the romantic idea of the artist. He was unconventional in dress[14] and habits, contemptuous of middle-class pretentions,"[15] and such attitudes were ill tolerated in the tight colonial society of St. Lucia. Feeling his own isolation keenly, he committed suicide in 1966.

Simmons argued for the necessity of "a distinctive West Indian art," which would come when artists stopped following academic prescriptions for color combination, which "create an atmosphere that is foreign to the tropics," and made color "approximate truth."[16] "Art in itself could not be called art unless it springs from the people," he insisted, "unless it records those things felt and experienced."[17] He believed strongly in the ideal of a unified West Indian culture, urging at the inaugural meeting of the St. Lucia Arts and Crafts Society that its efforts be moved by "a desire to forge a link in the cultural chain that can bind the islands together."[18] He wrote essays about West Indian traditions of cooperation and self-help; about the Carib Petroglyph at Dauphin;[19] about any aspect of local history and tradition that caught his interest.

In 1995 I visited Simmons's widowed sister-in-law in her secluded house on the "Back of the Morne." She showed me several of Harry's paintings, which demonstrate great technical skill, if not a strongly developed individual style. The most visible influences are Van Gogh and Gauguin, but the use of color follows his own demand for truth to West Indian landscape. Simmons's memory is still green for those who were close to him; during that first talk late in the afternoon by Choc Bay, Dunstan St. Omer said, apropos of nothing, "this is Harry's hour."

In *Another Life* Walcott recalls that "about the August of [his] fourteenth year," as he was wandering in the countryside "somewhere above a valley / owned by a spinster-farmer, [his] dead father's friend," he "dissolved into a trance," moved by "a pity more profound / than [his] young body could bear."[20] The earliest fruit of this epiphany was apparently the blank verse poem "1944" that appeared in *The Voice of St. Lucia,* August 2,

1944 (the following summer, the August of his fifteenth year). It was his first publication. In it, the young poet wished that he had never been "taught of God, / By mortal mouth, or man's dry means of lesson," but been left to learn of God from the experience of nature: "Then would my wanderings among the quiet woods / Be my first lesson from the Holy Book." It anticipates the mature poet's desire for an "Adamic" New World poetics in its exclamation:

> Oh! in what happy state I would then be
> As an acknowledged friend to bird or beast
> As our first father was—alive and free,
> And who would not, happy in that condition
> Rejoice he lived?[21]

Aside from showing a precocious competence in versification, the poem would be of little interest had its author not become Derek Walcott. Its sentiments seem conventional and inoffensive.

They were not conventional and inoffensive enough, however, for C. Jesse F.M.I., the most powerful Catholic priest in St. Lucia, whose letters to the *Voice* over the years show him to have been a tenacious fighter for conservative religious values. The fledgling poet found himself chastised in Father Jesse's thirty-line rebuke, "Reflections on Reading the Poem '1944,'" published in the *Voice* just three days after his innocently heterodox meditation. As Walcott would recall the incident in his first notebook for *Another Life,*

> The priest wrote a mechanically witty reply, in heroic couplets [actually, in a six-line pentameter stanza rhymed *ababcc,* with every foot in lock-step iambic], accusing me of pantheism, of animism, in short of heresy. It was a painful shock to a fourteen-year-old boy to be told that he loved what he thought were the natural manifestations of a God in a wrong way; and an equal horror to find that the metre at which he had labored could be so facile a form of argument.[22]

Father Jesse would take up the blunt instrument of his verse again in September to bludgeon down curricular reform in the St. Lucian schools:

> Yes, I must be quite emphatic,
> And declare your scheme aquatic
> Since it fails to cater Doctrine for the mind,

True religion is dogmatic,
Neither fluid nor erratic—
So your syllabus my favour ne'er will find![23]

Father Jesse's poetry could certainly have done with more fluidity and less "Doctrine," but it is of a piece with his pedestrian *Outlines of St. Lucia's History,* which is *faut de mieux* the closest thing to a history of the island that yet exists. It reveals a mind retentive of empirical detail and utterly incurious about motive, cause, or consequence. Nonetheless, this was the most powerful and respected priest in the St. Lucia of his day, and the influence of the Church was potent.

Walcott's troubles with the Church would continue into his mature literary career. His first collection, *25 Poems,* was "savaged in a review in the *Port of Spain Gazette* by the Catholic Archbishop."[24] When his play *Henri Christophe* was first performed by the Arts Guild of St. Lucia in 1950, St. Joseph's Convent provided the hall. To obtain use of the premises, Walcott had to cut the fourth scene, in which the two murderers of Dessalines utter blasphemies like "Ask God why He killed His Son, and what good it did us since." The program booklet included an apology from the producer: "Haiti has had a bloody history and Christophe and Dessalines are products of an age of blood. This play may be offensive in its heretical expressions, its smell of cruelty and carnage, but it cannot half express the facts of the case."[25] In 1956, when the Arts Guild chose *The Sea at Dauphin* and Roderick Walcott's *Banjo Man* as the island's drama entries in the West Indian Arts Festival, Father Joseph Vrignaud led the clergy into action against both plays. Despite vigorous protest from, among others, Harold Simmons, both had to be withdrawn.[26]

And yet the Catholic influence was not in all respects a stifling one. Because there was no Methodist school beyond eighth grade, Walcott attended St. Mary's College. In 1947, as Baugh informs us, "the Presentation Brothers of Cork took over the running of St. Mary's," and Walcott, then in the sixth form, became friendly with one of the priests, Brother Liam, who "was full of the tragic-romantic history of Ireland and its literature."[27] As he would later recall,

> The whole Irish influence was for me a very intimate one. When the Irish brothers came to teach at the college in St. Lucia, I had been reading a lot of Irish literature: I read Joyce, naturally I knew Yeats, and so on. I've always felt some kind of intimacy with the Irish poets because one realized that they were also colonials with the same kinds of prob-

> lems that existed in the Caribbean. They were the niggers of Britain. Now, with all of that, to have those astounding achievements of genius, whether by Joyce or Yeats or Beckett, illustrated that one could come out of a depressed, deprived, oppressed situation and be defiant and creative at the same time.[28]

Walcott's own position, as a Protestant in a Catholic culture, could also furnish Irish analogues. But as Baugh remarks, Walcott's first love, Andreuille Alcée, and his closest friend, Dunstan St. Omer, were both Catholic. A society in which these relationships could openly flourish "was no Ireland in respect of Catholic-Protestant differences and conflicts."[29]

Walcott's wide reading in modernist literature is obvious in *25 Poems* (1948) and *Epitaph for the Young* (1949), both written before he left St. Lucia to attend the University of the West Indies (UWI) in 1950. The influences of Pound, Joyce, Yeats, Eliot, Auden, Thomas, and Spender appear as unassimilated borrowings and explicit allusions. As St. Lucian journalist George Odlum has remarked, "it is in itself surprising that Walcott was aware of the movements taking place in the mainstream of 20th Century European literature at a time when most of his colleagues in the sixth form of St. Mary's College . . . were desperately grappling with 19th Century romanticism."[30] While at St. Mary's, Walcott was also writing plays; two of the scripts survived until recently in the collection of Errol Hill, a playwright and director who has known Walcott from his arrival at the university in Jamaica in 1950.[31]

Walcott has described his first venture into publication:

> I went to my mother and said, "I'd like to publish a book of poems, and I think it's going to cost me two hundred dollars." She was just a seamstress and a schoolteacher, and I remember her being very upset because she wanted to do it. Somehow she got it;—a lot of money for a woman to have found on her salary. She gave it to me, and I sent off to Trinidad and had the book printed [by the Trinidad *Guardian*, one of the two major Trinidadian newspapers]. When the books came back I would sell them to friends. I made the money back. In terms of seeing a book in print, the only way I could have done it was to publish it myself.[32]

Simmons introduced Walcott and his work to Frank Collymore, the editor of *Bim* in Barbados, one of the first literary magazines of distinction in the Anglophone Caribbean. Collymore assisted and encouraged Walcott in preparing the second edition of *25 Poems*, published in Barbados in April

1949, and a Walcott poem appeared in *Bim* for the first time in the December 1949 issue.[33] Soon after Simmons recommended Walcott to Henry Swanzy, Walcott's poetry made its first appearance on "Caribbean Voices" on March 20, 1949. At nineteen, Walcott was already becoming widely known within the Caribbean; in 1952, Errol Hill's London production of *Henri Christophe* would extend his reputation to England as well.

Three historical events had a large impact on St. Lucian life during Walcott's adolescence. The first was World War II, which was more directly felt in the Caribbean than one might have supposed. As part of the empire, St. Lucia participated; as Gregor Williams notes, "conscription was contemplated but so many volunteered that conscription was not necessary."[34] The U.S. Marines had a base on the northern end of the island, at Gros Islet, and the Army set up at Vieux Fort, on the southern end.[35] But it was in Walcott's home town of Castries, with its large harbor, that "the warriors met. British Navy, West India Regiment, U.S. Navy, Marines, Air Force and Army, French emigrees and refugees."[36] After the Germans occupied France, the neighboring island of Martinique came under the jurisdiction of the Vichy government. Martinicans would cross the twenty-one-mile channel to St. Lucia in small boats, under cover of night, to join the Free French. On March 9, 1942, the war came to St. Lucia's doorstep when "a German submarine boldly entered Castries Harbor and torpedoed two ships tied alongside the Northern Wharf. . . . Several lives were lost. "[37]

In the first notebook for *Another Life,* Walcott recalls the American wartime presence on the island:

> The damage done by the Occupation was felt long after they had left. They left behind roads, some buildings, the two air-bases, and a morally shattered economy. Also, like any other Army, they left behind a generation of bastards. They will us a new taste for life, based on an unappeasable discontent. They were warriors and gods, but somehow too accessible. Their friendship was transient, but this was cruel because they made being liked a virtue, and their love affairs were like their buildings, devised to last for a limited period, perfectly constructed within limits, then to be scrapped. I find them no different to those conquistadors who are attracted to meekness and naivete, but who, when the orders require can annihilate affections, and discover a greater sternness. Instead of beads the native race were drawn closer by the hot-dog, the hamburger, the Coca-Cola bottle, canned beer, comics, candy and paper backs, machines and legendary tales of great white cities to the North, etc. For us, this was the new democracy.[38]

Nonetheless, it was to America's "great white cities" that Walcott would go to make his literary career—unlike George Lamming, Samuel Selvon, or V. S. Naipaul, who had gone to England.

The second major event was the planning for independence and federation of the British West Indies. The plan of federating the scattered British West Indian territories under a single government had begun in the seventeenth century as an administrative scheme in England, resisted by the colonists who wanted local control. But by the twentieth century, West Indians themselves had taken up the idea. By the 1940s, the islands had long since ceased to be the profitable colonies they had been in the days of the slave sugar plantations, and the Colonial Office was already sympathetic to plans for federation and independence before the war.[39] With the end of the war, England began to dismantle its empire, starting with the independence of India in 1947. The movement for West Indian unification and independence reached its climax in autumn 1947, when delegates from the various islands met with representatives of the British Colonial Office at Montego Bay, Jamaica, for the First Conference on British West Indian Federation. This assembly "by a majority vote . . . accepted the principle of political federation and set up a Standing Closer-Association Committee to study the possibility of federation and to draft a federal constitution."[40] *The Voice of St. Lucia* devoted most of its space between September 12 and November 4 to coverage of the conference, including transcriptions of the delegates' speeches. Despite the enthusiasm of the conference, the Federation did not come into existence until 1958, and by the end of 1961 it had fallen apart, leaving the islands to proceed separately to independence, beginning with Jamaica and the two-island state of Trinidad and Tobago in 1962.

The ideals of the Federation lived on after its political demise. In contrast to the belligerent assertions of microethnicity that are splitting small nation states into even smaller ones today, they were a throwback to what Peter Alter calls the "Risorgimento Nationalism" of the nineteenth century, rooted in the universalism of the French Revolution.[41] Those ideals were eloquently summed up in a speech by Norman Manley at the Caribbean Labour Conference in Kingston, just before the conference at Montego Bay:

> I say that we in the West Indies can prove one great thing to the world—and that is that a people, none of whom are native to these territories, all of whom have for one reason or another been torn from their countries and brought here, partly willingly, partly by compulsion by distress in their own homelands, that we with our many strands, from Af-

> rica, from India, from China, from an assorted variety of European territories—we are capable of welding the power of that diversity into a united nation.
>
> I pray, before God, if we can prove that to the world, we would have accomplished something which would write West Indian history large across the pages of history for all times. It is a problem to stir and inspire every man who knows anything about the long and bloody history of the common humanity beset and perplexed and torn by artificial divisions without any real meaning in the face of the purpose of life.[42]

To this faith in an underlying shared humanity that transcends racial and regional differences, and to the belief that the West Indies paradoxically exemplify that transcendent unity in a regionally particular culture, Walcott has remained true in virtually all of his writings.

The last of the three events framing Walcott's youth was more local and accidental, but its immediate impact on the emerging poet was perhaps greatest of all. On June 19, 1948, a fire destroyed about four-fifths of Castries. Although "there was no loss of life in the fire . . . 809 families comprising at total of 2,293 persons were rendered homeless. . . . Temporary housing was provided by using the old military barracks and buildings at Vigie and Morne Fortuné."[43] People of different classes were thrown together by necessity. In his early poem, "A City's Death by Fire," Walcott called the fire a "hot gospeller" that "levelled all but the churched sky";[44] the leveling was social as well, striking at the class structure as well as the infrastructure of the city. On the Vigie promontory there developed, as he would put it in *Another Life,* "an atmosphere resembling what they had read of war," in which "lives" were "casually tangled like unsorted laundry," while "some pact / of common desolation had begun."[45]

Walcott finished his studies at St. Mary's in 1947. At that time, St. Lucia was allotted one Island Scholarship per year, sending its best student to Oxford or Cambridge. Walcott recalls that he "had failed to win the Island Scholarship because of [his] poor math" and did not continue his education until 1950, when he "was at last given a Colonial Development and Welfare Scholarship, for which [he] had mechanically applied,"[46] and entered the University of the West Indies, Mona, Jamaica, as one of twenty members of the first graduating class in Liberal Arts.[47] During the interim, he served as assistant master at St. Mary's and worked at his poetry and painting. On March 23, 1950, the Walcott brothers were among "a band of fifteen young art loving enthusiasts" who founded the St. Lucia Arts

Guild. The Guild's "first public appearance" was as sponsor of a joint exhibit of paintings by Walcott and St. Omer in early September 1950. The exhibition "met with luke-warm response" but was thoughtfully reviewed by Harold Simmons, who concluded that "St. Omer . . . was the artist" and "Walcott was the poet." The following week, the Arts Guild premiered *Henri Christophe* under the author's direction, with the blasphemous Part I, Scene iv trimmed to placate the Church, which had provided the performance venue. This production was more successful than the art exhibit.[48] Then school began.

That Walcott attended the newly-opened University of the West Indies rather than an English school may have been more by accident than by design, as his own account would suggest. But if so, it was a very significant accident, allowing him, atypically, to receive his education within the Caribbean. The university was both a product and an inculcator of West Indian cultural nationalism. The planning of the university was closely linked to planning for federation; both envisioned the creation of a unified West Indian identity. The Irvine Committee (a subcommittee of the Asquith Commission on development of education in the colonies) stressed this purpose in its report of 1945. It argued that "if West Indians could work together . . . living in community with each other and with teachers of the highest intellectual ability . . . they would develop fully, not only as individuals, but as West Indians." As they did so,

> [m]any of them might thus so strengthen their desire to serve their own people that it would not weaken when they went on to complete and broaden their experience overseas. This is, perhaps, the only means by which the present divisions and insularities can be broken down. It must be remembered that barriers exist not only as between the colonies but as between races within some of the colonies. . . . There is, perhaps, no atmosphere in which inter-racial co-operation and friendship is more possible than that of a residential university, and the association thus formed might powerfully influence for good the future development of some of these composite societies.[49]

In a lecture that Walcott might have read when it was reprinted in *The Voice of St. Lucia,* Eric Williams made similar connections: "the West Indian university must serve the needs of the West Indian community. Our community is moving, and moving increasingly, in the direction of federation. In my view, what was an ideal and the aspiration of a few enlightened spirits 30 years ago has now become an economic necessity. . . . The West Indian University will have to act, and in my opinion act very consciously, as the rally center for the entire Caribbean, from Cuba to French Guiana."[50] Williams's statement extends the pan–West Indian mandate beyond the Anglophone territories to embrace the French- and Spanish-speaking regions.[51]

The university opened in 1948, but a degree program in liberal arts became available only two years later, for Walcott's entering class of 1950. As S. O. Asein remarks, "during his Jamaica Years, Walcott was able to establish contacts with several of the leading personalities in the Jamaican, and indeed, West Indian, literary scene. There were people like Noel Vaz, the Reckord brothers, Keggie Carter, Errol Hill, Archie Hudson-Philips, Slade Hopkinson, Rex Nettleford, Jimmy Lee Wah."[52] The Jamaican scene was especially strong in painting and theater. In Asein's judgment, "never before . . . had there been a comparable concentration of talents drawn from various parts of the West Indies in any one location; and not even during the brief life span of the defunct Federation was there a repetition of the same pattern of movement of West Indian performing artists with the same degree of professional training and varied experiences and backgrounds."[53] Walcott participated in the Literary Society and took the lead in founding a student newspaper, titled *The Barb* for its first two issues and thereafter *The Pelican*.[54] (A pelican appears on the crest of UWI.) When an Art Society was formed in 1953, he joined that as well. He found opportunities to produce his plays through the university's Dramatic Society, of which he became president before the end of his first term, and the Federal Theatre Company (which was not part of the university, but included among its founders a UWI faculty member, Errol Hill, and a student, Slade Hopkinson). Walcott was already regionally known as a poet, through the "Caribbean Voices" broadcasts and his early publication in *Bim*, before he arrived at the university. Some of his fellow students regarded him with awe. Archie Hudson-Philips recalls that in his youth, several of his brightest friends wrote. "We were gifted. But Derek was different. Even then, we recognized that he was a genius."[55] Nor was the genius shy about asserting himself concerning the production of his plays. He would drink beer at the student union and then look in on rehearsals, Hudson-Philips recalls. On one occasion,

> We doing *Ione* down at the Ward [Theatre], and one morning, Sunday morning, I saw him. He came in and sat down in the back. He was drinking, and Errol [Hill] was there, directing and taking a part. Errol said,

> "No, no, no! That isn't how Derek wanted it done." And he [Walcott] just [switching to a deep, mock-threatening voice]: "DON'T TALK SHIT!"[56]

This exchange would date from the first productions of *Ione* in 1957, when Walcott had been out of school a few years.[57] Still, not every recent graduate would address his former tutor so freely.

Already, as a second-year student at the university, Walcott had a play performed in London:

> *Henri Christophe* was produced in London 25–27 January 1952, at the Hans Crescent House, Colonial Students' Residence by the West Indian Student Association with a cast that included many names that would soon become famous in Caribbean literature, culture, and politics. Those involved in the production were Errol Hill, the novelist George Lamming, the dramatist Frank Pilgrim, Maurice Mason and Kenneth Monplaisir from the St Lucia Arts Guild, the future Prime Minister of Trinidad A.N.R. Robinson, the dramatist Errol John, Roy Augier, Noel Vaz, and the Trinidadian artist Carlisle Chang. The group, with V. S. Naipaul taking the part of Hounakin, performed Walcott's *Sea at Dauphin.* It also read *Henri Christophe* (1951), *Harry Dernier* (1952), and other plays on the BBC Caribbean Voices programme.[58]

This production of *Henri Christophe,* which Hill directed, met with generally favorable reviews.[59]

Walcott's receptivity to the West Indian nationalist fervor around him is evident from his editorials for *The Pelican.* "How many of us are there," he asked in a "Letter from the Editor" of 1951, "who realize what a testing ground for our beliefs and prejuidices [*sic*] this here Campus is?" There can be no portrait of "the average U.C.W.I. [University College of the West Indies] student," because "the West Indian is not one man, but is a composite, a new mixture of races and creeds."[60] The assertion recalls Manley's speech of 1947, quoted earlier, in which he hoped the diverse people of the West Indies would prove "capable of welding the power of that diversity into a united nation." In Trinidad, at the other end of the archipelago, Eric Williams would declare in 1955 that "man in the West Indies is more than white, more than mulatto, more than Negro, more than Indian, more than Chinese. He is West Indian, West Indian by birth, West Indian in customs, West Indian in dialect or language, West Indian, finally, in aspirations."[61]

Walcott's essay goes on to compare the West Indies to ancient Greece: "there are some people who believe that this harbour between the two Americas resembles that antique situation of another vigorous and adolescent people."[62] Another Walcott editorial, on the formation of a campus society for West Indian culture, ends with the hope that the new group would "teach us to see the West Indies as not a nation, but even what is more exciting as an embryonic nation. Yours nationally, The Editor."[63]

Seen through these editorials and through Asein's account, UWI in the early 1950s sounds like an exciting place. Walcott's own recollections of the university, as Nobel Laureate and keynote speaker for a "Gathering of Graduates" at the university in 1993, place it in a less romantic light. "[F]or most of my sentence here," he confessed, "I despised the place, its jaded, predictable curriculum, for not being the University of the West Indies, as I watched Englishmen guide the direction in which I should go." He described it as

> a system that, from Vice Chancellor to Principal to Professors and Lecturers echoed the Kiplingesque pattern of serving Time in the outer provinces, most of its staff recruited from the decent, the dependable, and usually the second rate touchy and humourless men, who might as well have been teaching bellworks in Lagos or Singapore. . . . Next to them, waiting with a conspicuous patience, were the provincial geniuses waiting to administer the same system under a changed flag.
>
> What we thought might have been creation or discovery, by which I mean the exploration of our special bewilderment about being West Indians, was really transition.

What this transition "had to do with was a rapid loss of delight, a sense of afternoon replacing the elation of beginning—of dawn—of a real Light Rising.[64] Fairly soon, we all fell into the habit of playing 'bishe' the Trinidadian for 'cutting classes' . . . walking in a daze of disconnection, towards the Students' Union; a disconnection unable to relate the village of Papine to the rhyming feat [*sic;* "feet"?] of Pope or the sweet asperities of Jane Austen to the rasp of a bleating goat."[65]

However disenchanted Walcott was with his classes, however desultory his efforts and extravagant his exploits with "drinking companions who approached the consumption of beer as another field of research," he "connected with Danny Campbell and Slade Hopkinson and Val Rodgers and Don Bogle and Vernon Smith and Dunstan Champagnie and Bill Brooks and Ronnie Llanos, unrepentant reprobates, all of them."[66] With fellow students who shared his "disconnection" and his love of the arts, he conducted the most important part of his education. Some of those early friends, including Hopkinson and Llanos, became important figures in West Indian theater and continued to work with Walcott after he left Jamaica.

To some extent, Walcott's retrospective disenchantment may arise from the later disappointment of the federalist aspirations of his youth. Near the end of his address, the tone turns elegiac, as he concedes that there was "joy" along with the cynicism, the "false insults and mockery of this institution that was welding the archipelago of our different islands"; there was after all

> a veritable revelation, the only connection of the lonely connection that this gathering celebrates among shaggy hills the white walls and red gowns of nearly half a Century ago, with the shattering of the first federation, eroding our union back to separate Islands, with perhaps only the memory of Gibraltor Hall and Taylor Hall, Irvine Hall, the whole of that time together—the hope of those years as a plaque holds and seizes names in its bronze face or cemetery head-stones.

It would fall to Walcott's generation to see the "islands loosen their ropes from a common and solid mooring to drift again into their own absurdities of isolation, rocks and islets mounting separate flags and even armies." In sad hindsight, he can say

> In our treachery, our chafing at the curriculum we were all Federalist[, an] ecstasy denied our children to whom that radiant union like early morning when the Jamaican mountains is only connected by our nostalgia, a last joy like a cloud losing colour, and impractical, an intransigent vision that hardens in the light of day (political reality, statistics, laws, nations, prime ministers, armies).[67]

But that explanation of his youthful "treachery" must have come long after the fact.

I have already noted that West Indian federalism was a universalizing nationalism, aiming to merge smaller identities in larger ones. Two other features of it deserve attention, because they too seem compatible with, or even sustaining of, Walcott's poetic vision of West Indian identity. First of all, though nationalist movements typically claim that "the nations to which they give political expression always loom out of an immemorial past," often creating "invented traditions"[68] to make the present seem a continuation of that mythical past, the nationalism of West Indian federalists seldom did; the appeal to Africa as the source of ancient traditions belongs to a later moment. Rather, the federalists looked ahead, acutely aware that what they had to work with was "the direct result of the modern post-Columbian history of the region, which witnessed migrations of peoples and population replacements of a scale and complexity perhaps unsurpassed in any other period of equivalent duration in human history."[69] When West Indian historians began to fill in the gaps of Glissantian "non-history," they realized that they were recovering, in Brathwaite's phrase, a "submarine" coherence,[70] not passing on unbroken traditions. The federalist sense of starting afresh may have encouraged Walcott's "Adamic" stance, in which the present is a blank canvas to be filled rather than the outcome of earlier events. As late as 1977, when federation had long since come and gone, Walcott could still tell Robert Hamner that "what has not yet been created or is actually being created by its absence, by the chaos, by the necessity for it to be created—is a West Indies, a West Indian literature."[71]

The second congruence between Walcott's writing and the federalist movement is the uneasy sense of a debt owed from the artists and intellectuals to the unlettered West Indian folk. The very first paragraph of chapter 1 in Sherlock and Nettleford's history of the university reads:

> The chief characters in our story appear only incidentally. They are the West Indian folk. From their positive response to the challenge of change and of penalisation flowed the dynamic forces that shaped our history. They sounded the great ennobling themes of freedom, justice and equality that make our story an inspiring chapter in world history.[72]

Such invocations of the folk are familiar from European nationalism; as Hobsbawm remarks, "more often than not the discovery of popular tradition and its transformation into the 'national tradition' of some peasant people forgotten by history, was the work of enthusiasts from the (foreign) ruling class or elite."[73] But for educated West Indians, the relationship to peasant culture was especially vexed. While the new university could offer the most intellectually talented lower-class youth a chance at social mobility, even Sherlock and Nettleford concede that "the folk" are largely absent from the story they have to tell. Given how small and precariously established the West Indian elite was, and given the temptations of emigration or colonial co-optation with which it was faced, the need to keep faith with "the folk" was especially pressing.

While in Jamaica, Walcott made the transition from student life to the postgraduate challenge of getting a living, which showed him how limited the opportunities for a writer were in the Jamaica of the 1950s. He was married now, for at the University, he had met his first wife, Faye A. Moyston. She was working as a secretary in the administrative office, where Walcott would often come to type his poems. He courted her by leaving love poetry in the typewriter for her to find when she returned from lunch. He graduated in 1953 and married her the following year, after spending the 1953–54 academic year teaching at Grenada Boys' Secondary School in St. George's, Grenada. After a brief return to St. Lucia to teach at St. Mary's in the first term of 1954–55, he settled in Jamaica, making his living first by teaching at Jamaica College in Kingston, and then, from the end of 1956 through 1957, as a feature writer for the magazine *Public Opinion*. If he wanted to earn a living by writing, journalism was the only available way.

Walcott's articles for *Public Opinion* anticipate many of the themes to be found in his writings for the *Trinidad Guardian* a few years later. One of them is his growing annoyance with the abuses of nationalism as an excuse for chauvinism in the arts. "All over the West Indies right now," he wrote in a review of a Federal Art Exhibition, "I think that there are many bad amateurs who are getting a great many fancy notions about national art without getting rapped on the knuckles. They are dangerous and superfluous."[74] Less than two months later, he replied to a letter that had charged the Institute of Jamaica "with prejudicial presentation of Jamaica History." The letter had complained that "the true heroes of Jamaican history, meaning the leaders of the slavery rebellions and the earlier political leaders, were not displayed in portraits anywhere in the building." The reason, Walcott replied, is that serious Jamaican painters had not been moved to paint such portraits. He quoted Bernard Lewis, the Institute's director: "'When our painters are inspired to do portraits of national heroes then these will quite naturally be shown.'" The Institute had also been accused of "loading the staff . . . with people who are non-Jamaican," to which Walcott answered that "it is the usual problem of qualification." He closed by deploring the "sense of inverted prejudice, which for some time in the West Indies may pass under the guise of nationalism, but which is as ignorant as political oppression was."[75] Nonetheless, his estimate of Jamaican art remained high. "The most encouraging aspect of the Annual

Art Exhibition . . . is the emergence of a group of younger Jamaican painters, all under 30, who are showing a firmer interest in painting itself, rather than excursions into literature and haphazard imagination."[76] He wrote appreciatively of Ralph Campbell, "a very energetic painter who has lost much of his former pretentiousness and confusion. . . . His still lives now have a joy-of-living air about them, and his landscapes are clearly seen and cleanly-painted. He has cleaned the greyish tones and neutral wish-washness [*sic*] of his uncertain phase. His colours are fresh and alive."[77]

Walcott thought highly of Jamaica's poetry as well as its painting. He ended the second of a two-part series on Jamaican poets with a declaration that they "have done the most towards evolving a West Indian poetry which is not slavishly imitative or too secure, but they are members of a country which has matured more quickly than any other island in the British archipelago."[78] His criticisms show him already concerned that a dualism pitting white and European against black and African influences in West Indian culture will lead to false choices and dishonest art. "One of our fatal historical inheritances is the problem of racial prejudice. It is not false to say that it takes the West Indian a long time to admit that what is black can be beautiful." Once that possibility is admitted, however, it may be "falsified in an aesthetically aggressive style," swerving all the way to "the opposite course . . . the prejudice that only what is black can be beautiful." But as of 1957, "we have not yet got to that form of African prejudice." Against the dualism of writing that anxiously imitates white metropolitan models and writing that obsessively protests its blackness, Walcott upholds the Federalist ideal of a transracial West Indian identity: "The raceless anonymity of our poets, which is what West Indian means, cannot permit any of our writers, whether black, brown or white to allow themselves to subscribe to 'Poems of the Negro.'" There is a "tradition complex" among "those who think of Western Literature as white writing, or white thinking, and those who think that there should be some distinctive style in our writers. Both attitudes are complicated and dangerous."[79]

In "West Indian Writing," Walcott gave his own sketch of the regional literary tradition. Not long ago, that tradition had been in "a phrase [*sic*] through which every colonial culture passes, when its poets prefer to look like poets rather than to write poetry, and when its theatre consists of accurate reproduction of the accents of its metropolitan country." Recently, however, "in the West Indies, we have just begun to emerge from that period of incubation of intelligence and originality." He dates the beginnings of "something rooted in West Indian writing" from "the Thirties, a period of great political unrest." Although "much of the verse of that period is politically powerful, but artistic junk," he praises the work of Jamaican poets George Campbell and M. G. Smith and the novelist Roger Mais. Perhaps because he was writing for a Jamaican audience, he does not mention their Trinidadian contemporaries, Alfred Mendes and C. L. R. James.[80] In his judgment, however, the full maturity of West Indian literature came in "the late forties," which "saw the appearance of the first true West Indian writers and artists. They were not guilty or bitter about race, not actively concerned with politics, but complete practitioners of their talent."[81] As he would do even more sharply in the late 1960s and early 1970s, Walcott distinguishes between the practice of art and the pursuit of a political agenda, especially one driven by racial guilt or bitterness. In 1957, such a notion of art as separate from and even incompatible with political engagement was commonplace. But Walcott continued to maintain that notion long after it had become heterodox and in some circles discredited.

Walcott praises A. J. Seymour, John Hearne, George Lamming, Samuel Selvon, Edgar Mittelholzer, V. S. Naipaul, E. M. Roach, Wilson Harris, and Martin Carter. But he concedes that "the verse is not practised as seriously as the prose," and that "in the theatre things still run a little wild."[82] The novelists, in short, were more mature than the writers of poetry and drama, the genres in which Walcott himself had ambitions.

Walcott's literary reputation had already reached beyond the West Indies before his move to Trinidad in 1958. There had been the London performances of two of his plays, and his poem "Ruins of a Great House" was included in *New World Writing* for 1956, published in New York by American Library.[83] But for the most part, the poems appeared in regionally-based journals such as *Public Opinion, Caribbean Quarterly,* and *Bim,* while such early plays as *The Sea at Dauphin, Ione, Ti-Jean and His Brothers,* and *Malcochon* were published by the Extra-Mural Department of the University of the West Indies, either at Mona or at the new St. Augustine, Trinidad campus.[84] His first English publication did not come until 1960, when he placed several poems in *London Magazine.* His international reputation was secured when Jonathan Cape published *In a Green Night: Poems 1948–1960,* in 1962.

The year 1957 marks a turning point in Walcott's career, both artistically and personally. The University of the West Indies, supported by a Rockefeller Grant, commissioned him to write a pageant play for the inauguration of the West Indies Federation, which was to hold its first parliament in Trinidad in 1958. In connection with this project, he, Noel Vaz, and Errol Hill "were delegated to undertake a journey to North America at the instance of the Rockefeller Foundation to seek the assistance of Mr. Tyrone Guthrie of London's Old [Vic] Theatre fame."[85] Soon thereafter, he received a Rockefeller Foundation Fellowship to go to New York to study directing with José Quintero at The Circle and the Square and scene design with Stuart Vaughan of the Phoenix Theater.[86] The commission provided Walcott with his first North American travels, but the experience was as frightening as it was exciting. He would later recall how, daunted by the difficulty of his assignment and its "incredibly short deadline," visiting New York for the first time, he had stayed in a "friend of a friend's" apartment overlooking "Central Park in the East Seventies," and, afraid to go out for "sheer terror of the place," had holed up and written *Ti-Jean and His Brothers* in the first four days of his five-day stay.[87] While studying on his Rockefeller Fellowship, he was "isolated" and "felt very alone in the United States. I knew I did not want what was going on. Not on Broadway, but in a way, not off-Broadway as well."[88]

Walcott finally did write his pageant-play, *Drums and Colours,* which was performed as part of the ceremonies for the first parliament of the Federation on April 25, 1958, under the direction of Noel Vaz. Errol Hill was one of two "Guest Producers" and played the part of the Haitian general Dessalines. Ronald Llanos played Calixte, nephew of the French general Le Clerc. And in the role of Emmanuel Mano, organizer of the play within a play, was Errol Jones, later to become the leading actor of the Trinidad Theatre Workshop. The play got a mixed review from its author's own brother, Roderick, who found that it "suffered primarily because of its length" and thought its parts were not entirely "in cohesion with the whole." Nonetheless, he praised it as "an undertaking which had never been attempted before in the history of the theatre."[89]

Walcott has been surprisingly reticent, in his various interviews, about the precise circumstances of his move to Trinidad. Even his essay, "On Choosing Port of Spain," is more of a lyrical description of the city than an autobiographical account of the choice. It begins with a short poem, "For Mildred," which tells us that he "settled on this city casually / . . . by a commission." In the essay that follows, Walcott hints that "one grew to love this city before one loved one of its women" and recalls that when he first "met" Port of Spain, he "was homeless and shell-shocked from the attrition of a failed marriage."[90]

By 1957, Bruce King notes, "Walcott was dissatisfied with his life in the West Indies." His marriage to Faye Moyston (which had produced a son, Peter) would not be formally dissolved until 1959, but it was already going sour. As for his career, his

> likely future was that of an alienated teacher or newspaper writer living on a poor salary, complaining about provincial, colonial life, and corrupt local politicians. His disaffectation was no different from that, say, of V. S. Naipaul or other West Indian writers of the time. Emigration to England seemed likely.[91]

When he went to Trinidad in early 1958 to help prepare *Drums and Colours,* he did not plan on staying. He returned to New York on his Rockefeller Foundation Fellowship. But, as he recalls,

> Sooner or later, I had to decide whether to go back to the West Indies at all. Luckily, my brother was still with The Arts Guild [of St. Lucia]. They went to Trinidad, and he asked me if I would come and help him, so I went down there. I used it as an excuse. I didn't finish my Fellowship. I was very tired and was feeling very depressed about New York theatre and about any chance I might have of ever doing anything there. Plus, of course, at that time in '58, plays about the West Indies, or black actors—well, there wasn't much of a chance of getting anything going. There was no such thing in New York as a company of black actors. So I went back to Trinidad and began the Trinidad Theatre Workshop.[92]

With that decision, a new phase of Walcott's career began.

The workshop began as an expansion of the Little Carib Dance Company, which Walcott joined in May 1959 "and thus created the drama section of the group."[93] He envisioned a West Indian theater in which dance and music would be an integral part of dramatic performance: "I had a company in mind who would be both dancers and actors."[94]

At first, the Theatre Workshop did not give full-scale public performances, only "Showcases," the first of which was staged on December 11, 1959, "before a small private audience."[95] Walcott's program note on that occasion explained that "the Theatre Workshop is simply a studio where the members of various local companies are invited to widen their knowledge in the practice of theatre, with emphasis on acting."[96] The showcase included a dramatic adaptation of a short story by the Trinidadian writer Samuel Selvon and scenes from plays by Tennessee Williams, Bernard Shaw, Arthur Miller, and the Trinidadian Errol John.[97] The first public performance, of Samuel Beckett's *Krapp's Last Tape* and the Jamaican poet and playwright Dennis Scott's *The Caged,* did not occur until May 1962. And only in October 1966, after separation from the Little Carib, did the Workshop begin its first repertory season, housed in the "Basement Theatre" of the Bretton Hall Hotel, a cramped space of "about 50 feet by 25 by ten with a 'stage' 18 feet by eight just six inches off the floor." It could just squeeze in an audience of 95.[98]

In addition to founding the Workshop and continuing to write poems and plays, Walcott made occasional forays into journalism. He reviewed a watercolor exhibition by Noel Vaucrosson for the *Sunday Guardian* on August 24, 1958. He wrote four pieces for the *Guardian* in 1959, three of them appearing in November and December. Then, in January 1960, he resumed his journalistic career, joining the *Trinidad Guardian* staff as a feature writer. Between January 3, 1960, and October 25, 1967, he produced more than five hundred articles on subjects including West Indian painting, theater, and literature, movies, theater productions from abroad, and the annual carnival and calypso season.[99] The success of the Theatre Workshop, which by 1967 had begun to tour outside of Trinidad, obliged him (or freed him) to abandon his journalistic position.[100]

In 1960, Walcott married a Trinidadian, Margaret Maillard. Victor Questel remarked on the contribution of her "dynamism in so far as she assisted with the managing of the Workshop, particularly in areas such as publicity and front of house duties."[101] Letters in the archive at Trinidad suggest that she was primarily responsible for holding the practical end of the Workshop together and that she functioned as Walcott's social secretary as well.

It is hardly surprising that a man working simultaneously as journalist, poet, playwright, and theater director would be spread too thin to be a reliable correspondent or organizer. But it appears, from the letters in the Trinidad archive spanning the early 1960s to the mid-1970s, that he was never much at answering letters, even after he gave up the journalistic work. "How many time I wriet [*sic*] to you and get no answer," begins a letter of October 10, 1961, to Walcott from Alfred Leslie. The same note is still sounding ten years later. Daniel Halpern, following up an unanswered letter requesting work for *Antaeus,* writes on September 21, 1971, "Still no word from you—mum." It appears that a letter from Selden Rodman was finally answered not by Derek but by his wife. "Dearest Margaret," Rodman wrote on December 4, 1970, "It's a bleedin' good thing *one* of you blokes answers letters!" He closed with "Love from us all, and that goes for your incommunicado husband too."[102]

Remarkably prolific and chronically overcommitted, Walcott sometimes planned works that he was unable to finish, such as "Vangelo Nero" (sketched in a notebook about 1972, and partly completed in draft), which is furnished with a "proem" that reads like a prospectus with an escape clause: "This work, which I began with doubt, may suddenly dry up if I find it deceitful. We agreed on this." There is a wonderful letter from Frank Collymore, August 5, 1960, affectionately upbraiding Walcott for nondelivery of poems for *Bim*. It is hand-written, and the choice of red ink is perhaps significant:

> Dear Derek,
> Said Mr Walrus
> The time has come
> To curse him effectively and loathesomely
> By bell, book, and banana
> By principalities powers and emblems of Styx
> By all that is in the water under the bottom of the sea
> And where the flaming hell are those poems
> without which
> Issue 32 will not be complete??
> And kindly send as soon as possible
> IF NOT
> Boils blains and balls
> Light upon you
> Smite you
> And totally ignite you
> and I hope you read poem wh. I forwarded you and why haven't you written and what the hell.
> Yours,
> Coll.
> "Get up and do it now" Post it!
> *Ecc. Ch. xxxxviix.* *T. S. Eliot*
> NOW! *Shakspere: Where were you V.iii*[103]

The Walcott who emerges from these letters (and numerous others like them) is intensely absorbed in his work, generously engaged with friends, workshop members, and other writers when they are present, but apt to let those out of sight slide out of mind as well.

During Walcott's first three years in Trinidad, the West Indies Federation ran its brief course. It was perhaps doomed from the start by the extraordinarily weak powers vested in its central government; critics referred to it as the "ghost federation." It fell apart in 1961 when Norman Manley, under vigorous attack from the opposition party's antifederalist leader, Alexander Bustamante, agreed to a referendum on Jamaica's continued participation. Just before federation, Jamaica had begun to prosper on its own. Many Jamaicans did not want to cede any economic control to a federal government or to allow the smaller, poorer islands to make claims on that prosperity. Manley's referendum failed to win majority support, and Jamaica withdrew. Trinidad's Eric Williams, who had already warned that "ten minus one is zero," now felt that Trinidad must withdraw as well. Both Manley and Williams, as we have seen, had been strong supporters of the federalist ideology, but the economic self-interest of their islands did not coincide with their ideals. One sticking point for Trinidad was free movement to any territory within the Federation: already, people tended to move from Grenada, St. Vincent, and even the more prosperous Barbados to seek jobs in Trinidad. If access were unimpeded, Trinidadians feared, the labor market would be flooded with small-island immigrants. "They beating Grenadians down in the square, / Mm, I'm gonna get my share," snarled one xenophobic calypso of the day. Early in 1962, Trinidad and Tobago became a separate independent nation, as did Jamaica. Ten minus two left eight, and the remaining territories struggled on, with Barbados as the federal capital. But this arrangement collapsed in 1966, as Barbados too received its solitary nationhood.

Walcott himself was a small islander, and according to Questel, he was sometimes resented for it. He had moved to Port of Spain and almost immediately started writing articles that held local art and literature to demanding standards. Whenever possible, he considered particular books, art exhibits, or plays in a wider context of the future of West Indian culture. Among his very first pieces for the *Guardian* in 1958, before he became a staff writer, were negative reviews of two Trinidadian productions: the Phoenix Players' of *Seven Year Itch* and the Community Education Workshop's of *Our Town*. He urged the Workshop players to spend a year improving their acting before mounting another production.[104] (The advice seems less condescending in retrospect, since Walcott's own workshop would spend three years working at its craft before attempting a public performance, whereas at the time of the review thc Trinidad Theatre Workshop was only seven months old.) In 1960, he began calling for more government support for the arts and the creation of a national theater, pointing out that Jamaica's government had done much more for its artists than had Trinidad's. In the years from 1963 through 1965, he returned to these issues with increasing bitterness. "There is," he wrote in 1964, "something wrong-headed in a national vision which spends millions on sewerage, but offers nothing on art."[105] Late in 1965, he could for once applaud, rather than scold, the government for allocating $70,000 (TT) for a Cultural Arts Center, but less than six months later he was again insisting on the need for a national theater.[106]

Even as he was seeking greater support for the arts, Walcott cautioned, as he had in his articles for *Public Opinion* in Jamaica, against low standards and chauvinistic praise for bad art: "The West Indian artist can be overpatronized, smothered with kindness."[107] Patronage was needed, but it must be discerning patronage. As we have seen, some of Walcott's *Public Opinion* articles linked the overpraise of bad work with political and racial chauvinism, "fancy notions of national art" or "the prejudice that only what is black can be beautiful." At first, Walcott's Trinidadian articles criticize the acceptance of poor art simply as a sign of provincial standards, but the issues of politics and race soon reemerge as motives for such indulgence.

With independence came an attempt at cultural self-assertion, inevitably rather self-conscious at first, and particularly an attempt to legitimize and reclaim that which is "black" or "African" in the intricate hybrid of West Indian culture. In Trinidad this was an especially touchy issue because a large minority of the population (which has since grown to a plurality) was descended not from the creole mixture of African and European populations, but from the indentured workers brought from India after emancipation. The attempt to supply West Indian identity with a purely "African" core had already provoked a skeptical response from the Martinican Frantz Fanon, who noted in 1955 that after World War II, "the West Indian . . . changed his values"; instead of trying to be white, he "discovered himself to be not only black, but a Negro." The trouble with this identification is that "there is as great a difference between a West Indian and a Dakarian as between a Brazilian and a Spaniard. The object of lumping all Negroes together under the designation of 'Negro People' is to deprive them of any individual expression." One illusion has been exchanged for another: "[i]t thus seems that the West Indian, after the great white error, is now living in the great black mirage."[108] But throughout the 1960s, emphasis on blackness and Africanness increased, in the West Indies as in the United States. Indeed, some critics of this trend considered it just another instance of insecure colonials importing the latest fashion from abroad, but although the U.S. Black Power movement had some influence on its Caribbean counterpart, one could plausibly argue that the influence ran both ways. Stokely Carmichael was Trinidadian by birth, and Marcus Garvey, coming from Jamaica to Harlem, had been an early champion of black separatism and return to Africa.

By the mid-1960s, Walcott's journalism had become increasingly preoccupied with encroachment of racial and national chauvinism on the arts. In late 1964 he wrote that he "pick[ed] up the newest West Indian novel with a weary fear" that it would turn out to be "another banal, woodenly skilled construction about race, exile, and the search for an identity," another publisher's sample of "the outpourings of black angry young men."[109] "It is time," he urged in 1966, "that we start separating racial or political enthusiasm from good verse." In the same article, he criticizes a poem by P. M. Sherlock "because it propounds the 'philo-Negro enthusiasm,' the ennoblement of fishermen and peasants into dethroned kings of Africa that makes so much West Indian verse 'grand.'"[110] At the time he wrote this, Walcott was still refining *Dream on Monkey Mountain,* his own portrait of the peasant as dethroned king of Africa, which, though it deflates the grandeur with a sharp prick of irony, nonetheless treats Makak's aspirations with considerable respect. Here as elsewhere, Walcott's art often reveals a misgiving sympathy with ideas and myths that his criticism rejects. It is also to his credit that he could respect plays such as Le Roi Jones's *Dutchman* and *The Slave.* Even though Walcott criticizes Jones for allowing his language "to go out of control" and thus diminishing "the merit of his work," he nonetheless concedes that Jones "is writing with a driving, frightening fury," and that given the situation of the Negro in America, "writers like [James] Baldwin and Jones may have no other choice than to dramatise that struggle in the most violent terms."[111]

Walcott's most favorable response to a West Indian novel concerned with race was his review of the Guyanese novelist Denis Williams's *Other Leopards* (1963), which he calls "the most complex and brilliant book I have read on this theme. . . . our pivotal book about race." He notes that "the West Indian mind, because of its past, is helplessly schizophrenic. It rejects Africa, India, or China at its own convenience. It is culturally and socially drawn to Europe, but with the inherited fear of being repulsed or snobbed [*sic*], so it cultivates snobbery." And yet

> Schizoids, in a perverse way, have more personality than the "normal" person, and it is this conflict of our racial psyche that by irritation and a sense of loss continues to create artists, most of whom have chosen exile.

> More than Ireland, even, we are deprived of what we cannot remember, or what, when we visit its origins[,] never existed the way we imagined. . . .[112]

Although Walcott reviewed most of the significant novels or poetry books published by Anglophone West Indians during his years with the *Guardian* and did the bulk of the paper's theater reviewing, much of his journalism concerned American and English literature. Most of the repertory of Trinidadian theater companies was of necessity imported, and the Trinidad Theatre Workshop itself made a point of combining West Indian plays not only with British and American works such as Pinter's *The Lover* or Albee's *Zoo Story,* but with a broad sampling of world theater: Chekhov's *The Seagull,* Genet's *The Blacks,* Ionesco's *The Lesson,* Soyinka's *The Road.* (The Workshop's West Indian repertory was largely supplied by Walcott himself, but it also included work by Eric Roach, Edward Kamau Brathwaite, Errol John, and Dennis Scott, as well as an adaptation for the stage of fiction by Samuel Selvon.) Walcott reviewed books by Muriel Spark, Vladimir Nabokov, Mary McCarthy, Ernest Hemingway, James Baldwin, Norman Mailer, Le Roi Jones, and even one of Ian Fleming's James Bond novels. He wrote an account of his first meeting with Robert Lowell, later to become a close friend, when the Bostonian visited Trinidad in 1962, and he provided the *Guardian*'s obituary for T. S. Eliot. He reviewed movies, including *Never on a Sunday, La Notte* (Antonioni), *The Leopard* (Visconti), *Dr. Strangelove, Cheyenne Autumn* (Ford), *Diary of a Chambermaid* (Buñuel); also a James Bond movie, *Thunderball;* the Beatles' *A Hard Day's Night;* and film versions of *Miss Lonelyhearts* and *Suddenly Last Summer.* This list, already long, is far from complete, but it gives an idea of the range of Walcott's assignments.

Confronted with such a hodgepodge of unlike occasions, Walcott inevitably responded with varying degrees of interest. But he kept a sharp eye out for qualities in art from abroad that could suggest West Indian parallels. Many of his early plays openly synthesize borrowed plots with West Indian materials. Just as *The Sea at Dauphin* remakes Synge's *Riders to the Sea* in a West Indian idiom, *Malcochon* is a West Indian transformation of Kurosawa's *Rashomon,* as *Ione* is a St. Lucian village *Iliad.* Even *Dream on Monkey Mountain,* though not constructed as a sustained parallel, evokes Don Quixote and Sancho Panza in the partnership of Makak and Moustique and makes an obliquely ironic commentary on Robert Graves's *The White Goddess.* Walcott has claimed that his autobiographical poem, *Another*

Life, is indebted to Pasternak's *Safe Conduct,* and *Omeros* advertises its debts in its very title. When a touring Kabuki company visited Trinidad in 1964, Walcott emphasized Kabuki's suggestiveness for West Indian drama.

Along with the simultaneous death of the Federation and birth of the Republic of Trinidad and Tobago, the year 1962 brought publication of Walcott's first mature book of poems, and his first to be widely circulated outside the West Indies. No longer did he have to settle for a book that merely looked as if it had come from abroad; this was the real thing. The manuscript was complete by the end of 1960, but Alan Ross, who was to have brought it to Jonathan Cape in England, suffered a breakdown, which delayed publication by a year or so.[113] With the appearance of *In a Green Night,* Walcott acquired an international reputation. He had already received the Guiness Award for Poetry in 1961 (for "A Sea Chantey," published in *London Magazine* the previous year), and since then, honors from beyond the West Indies have repeatedly come his way, including second prize in the First World Festival of Negro Arts (Dakar, 1966), a Royal Society of Literature Award for *The Castaway* (1966), the Cholmondeley Award (1969), an Obie for *Dream on Monkey Mountain* (1971), the Order of the British Empire (1971), induction as Honorary Member of the American Academy of Arts and Letters (1979), the Welsh Arts Council's International Writers Prize (1980), a MacArthur Fellowship (1981), and the 1992 Nobel Prize for Literature. Nor has he been a prophet without honor in the West Indies, having received Trinidad's Gold Hummingbird Medal (1969), an honorary doctorate from the University of the West Indies (1973), and the St. Lucia Cross (1993), the "nation's highest honour."[114]

Ironically, although Walcott was a prolific writer of poetry and essays during his directorship of the Trinidad Theatre Workshop, which spanned the years 1959 to 1976, his output as a playwright slowed almost to a stop. As Laurence Breiner notes, he had an "extraordinarily productive" stretch from 1957 to 1959, just before his move to Trinidad, but "[a]fter 1959 it appears that Walcott was not writing new plays."[115] *Dream on Monkey Mountain,* however, evolved significantly from its early version; it was not produced until 1967 and not published until 1970. As Leroy Clarke, a member of the Workshop, told Victor Questel,

> the Theatre Workshop was a kind of spawning ground for some of the ideas that Derek had in his plays. And one of the principal plays—*Dream on Monkey Mountain*[—]pulled together the acting, the dancing, the drumming and the singing. All the workshop ideas came together when he brought the "script[,]" and when I say a script—it was not a script

> just yet. The script of *Dream on Monkey Mountain* was written in the theatre.[116]

Since *Dream on Monkey Mountain* still stands as Walcott's finest play, that process of shaping and revision must be counted as significant activity in playwriting, slow and tentative though it may have been.

To examine the scripts in the Trinidad archive is to realize that Walcott has generally treated plays as much more fluid texts than poems. Although he has sometimes revised poems significantly after their magazine publications, he has seldom made changes after their first appearance in a book, and then only minor ones. The plays, in contrast, seem endlessly open to expansion, contraction, and tinkering. *Franklin: A Tale of the Islands* began as a one-act play and ended up with three acts, after passing through a two-act version along the way. Since Walcott did not date his drafts, it is hard to say how long this process took. Tucked into Wilbert Holder's actor's script of *Ti-Jean* are two additional songs and a few extra lines for the scene where Ti-Jean orders the field workers to burn the canes.[117] A surprisingly large number of Walcott's plays have been produced but never published: e.g., *The Haytian Earth, The Isle Is Full of Noises, Steel, The Ghost Dance,* and *To Die for Grenada,* to name five that are well-known but, as of 2000, still unavailable in print. When I asked if he would furnish a script of *Steel,* produced in Boston in 1993, he declined, explaining that he was "still working on that one."[118] And, when visiting Hartwick College to attend the premier of *Ghost Dance,* I learned that Walcott had kept expanding the speeches of his lead character up to the last rehearsals, so that memorization was a bit of a problem. During—or even after—production, a Walcott play may be considered work in progress.

Despite his frustrations at the lack of government support for the arts, Walcott's move to Port of Spain was on the whole a success through the 1960s. He built the workshop into a touring company, acclaimed for its excellence both abroad and (by a small but appreciative audience) at home. Though his work as a playwright slowed, he steadily produced new poetry. But the Black Power revolt of early 1970, which brought the island's racial and ideological tensions to a boiling point, upset him deeply. The political turmoil coincided with a period of great personal strain, and 1970 marks a crisis point in Walcott's career. He turned forty in January, usually a difficult birthday under any circumstances. In late February, at the end of carnival, a part of Trinidad's army defected, siding with the Black Power movement, and launched a brief revolution that was quickly squelched after East Indian labor leaders, unpersuaded that they were "black," refused to join the cause. (Ironically, the Prime Minister, Eric Williams, was himself black, but was accused of favoring a white and mulatto elite.)

As the draft of an unpublished essay, "The Shouting in the Square," reveals, Walcott felt personally threatened by the Black Power movement: "My own paleness excluded me already, but I thought of my children. They were not black enough for the Revolution." He was appalled at the movement's racially based ideology, yet compelled to respect it for providing his "first experience of collective bravery in Trinidad." A diary from that year, preserved in the UWI archive, shows his anxious state at the time: entries juxtapose exasperation with the ideology of the revolt, self-reproaches for excessive drinking and quarreling with Margaret, and frustrations concerning the Trinidad Theatre Workshop. The Revolution and the Workshop were not entirely separate realms. Slade Hopkinson not only joined the Black Power movement, he led an attack on Walcott's leadership at a Workshop meeting and eventually left the company. For Hopkinson, the Workshop was elitist, ignoring the peasant classes.[119] Walcott's diary entry for May 3, the date of Hopkinson's outburst, begins "FINIS?" and continues:

> At last it came, and I write this respecting my own panic, my own paranoia, the disintegration which you have felt, waited for in the workshop. A letter from Slade which is deeper than his illness, the wild, unconfirmed suspicions of malice and discontent which burst and suppurated in the air of a "meeting," and of course, uncontrolled drunkenness culminating in abuse, coarseness before wife, son, friends, etc.[120]

The language of this entry shows how deeply Walcott had embedded the Workshop in his own sense of himself: it switches abruptly from "I" to "you," and it does not make clear who is reproached for "uncontrolled drunkenness," Hopkinson or—as elsewhere in this diary—himself. What he has done and what others have done to him seem hardly separable here. On May 10, Walcott wrote a letter of resignation from the Workshop, although he eventually decided to stay.

Much of Walcott's work throughout the 1970s has a polemical edge to it, excoriating Afrocentric demagoguery in politics and art. Not until *Omeros*, completed only in 1990, did he strike a balance, allowing African influences a prominent role in the West Indian cultural synthesis. In other work of the 1970s, most notably *Another Life* and the poem "Sainte Lucie" in *Sea Grapes,* we see him returning from Trinidadian to St. Lucian settings and seeking to ground his own development there rather than in Trinidad.

At the end of 1976, Walcott finally did resign from the Workshop, under circumstances hinted at in the veiled autobiographical plot of "The Schooner *Flight,*" which he began writing shortly afterward. Walcott was openly conducting an affair with Norline Météevier, a dancer in the company who would later become his third wife. The company split between those who sympathized with Margaret and those who condoned the affair.

After 1976, Walcott continued to live in Trinidad, but he began spending more time than previously in the United States. These years are marked by travel and a sense of uprootedness. His third marriage (1982) was brief, in contrast to the sixteen-year span of the second, and until about 1986 he had no long-term attachment. When I asked Bruce King for help in tracking Walcott's movements in the early 1980s, he replied with a quasi-telegraphic e-mail:

> Unsettled and flying non-stop all over, not possible to do a summary really. Ex. Jan 1980 Trinida[d], Feb 1980 NY, March Virgin[i]a, April Trinidad and NY, May NY, June Trinidad, September NY, Fall 1980 living in NY teaching at NYU and Columbia, Poetry Olympics in London late September, then NY, then back to UK for Welsh prize in October, NY, back to Trinidad at x-mas. 1981: NYU and Columbia next semester, mostly, late April 1981 Trinidad for Beef, back to USA (NY base, but commuting between Chicago and Washington for productions), late May Trinidad, June MacArthur, July St. Thomas, Fall 1981, part-time at Columbia and Harvard, became assist prof at Boston in Jan 1982. The main point is that he was really a NYer at this period and still trying to make it in the USA until the MacArthur and Boston U (mid-1981/ Jan 1982) changed his life.[121]

Still, Walcott in the United States was a more fortunate traveler than most. He obtained teaching assignments first in New York (sharing a course with Joseph Brodsky at NYU in 1980), then at Harvard. Then, in the wake of the sexual harassment charge at Harvard (no formal resolution was ever reached), he joined the faculty of Boston University, where he continues teaching to this day.[122] The MacArthur Award in 1981 meant, as King remarks, that "he no longer had to worry as much about money or about having a roof over his head."[123] In 1980, he traveled to London on an invitation to the "Poetry Olympics," held in the Poets' Corner of

Westminster Abbey, where he had imagined himself rebuffed in early drafts of "The Schooner *Flight.*" Soon after, he traveled to Wales to received the Welsh Arts Council International Writers' Prize. Although he had been to England briefly in 1964, possibly in the late 1960s, and again in 1975, to assist with the abortive Royal Shakespeare production of his play *The Joker of Seville,* only from 1980 on did the UK became a regular part of his itinerary.[124] Given his expanded territory and his friendships with other transplanted poets such as Brodsky and Heaney, it is not surprising that he had begun to refuse "to consider himself a Commonwealth writer," but instead "felt himself an international writer . . . who expected universal understanding."[125] Since 1980, he has traveled extensively in Europe. Although poems with non-Caribbean settings, especially North American settings, are scattered through his earlier work, they are much more common from *The Fortunate Traveller* (1981) onward.

Walcott had known Robert Lowell from the time of Lowell's visit to Trinidad in 1962 to the American poet's death in 1977. Walcott's first attempts to render North American experience often recall Lowell in language and theme. With residence in Boston came friendships with other North American poets and with two distinguished foreigners, Seamus Heaney and the late Joseph Brodsky, who became his closest literary friends. In addition to friendship and admiration for their poetry, Walcott has taken from them a quickened sense that his own West Indian experience has parallels elsewhere in the world, in Heaney's Ulster and Brodsky's Russia. And he has realized the limits to these parallels also: since knowing Brodsky he has been reluctant to describe himself as an "exile," knowing that it was one thing to leave the West Indies to make a literary career, another to flee the Soviet Union.

Walcott's production of plays increased somewhat after his resignation from the Workshop. As King's biography reveals, he spent much time and energy from the late 1970s onward trying to establish a foothold in the U.S. theater scene, staging plays in St. Croix and elsewhere in the U.S. Virgin Islands, and securing productions in New York and Los Angeles. He also made occasional attempts to cross over to the popular genres of film and the musical, culminating in his ill-starred collaboration on Paul Simon's 1998 Broadway bomb, *The Capeman.* Of the plays written since Walcott's departure from the Trinidad Theatre Workshop, the best known, and probably the best, are *Remembrance, Pantomime* (1979), *A Branch of the Blue Nile* (1983; revised 1985), and a stage adaptation of *The Odyssey* (1993). A good many of the post-1976 scripts, however, remain unpublished long after their production (e.g., *The Haytian Earth, Ghost Dance, The Isle Is Full of*

Noises, To Die For Grenada); some, such as *Steel,* Walcott regards as work in progress.[126]

The cumulative effect of Walcott's experience during the late 1970s and most of the 1980s was to push him toward a more liminal, cosmopolitan conception of his identity. The poems range farther in their settings and analogies than formerly: "Egypt, Tobago," the title of a love poem in *The Star-Apple Kingdom* (1979), nicely suggests the sense of geographical dislocation in this phase of his career. But by the time of *The Arkansas Testament,* certain poems express a sharp nostalgia for St. Lucia, as well as self-reproach for having left the island behind; most notable among these is "The Light of the World." Walcott, returning to the island, rides one of the sixteen-seat vans that carry passengers between Castries and Gros Îlet, and feels moved by but estranged from the communal friendliness of the other riders. He gets off at the Halcyon, a tourist hotel "full of transients like [him]self," then walks off into the night alone. The Derek-Sans-Terre, cosmopolitan stance of *The Fortunate Traveller* no longer sustains him.

From the late 1970s through the 1980s, Walcott described himself, on the dust jackets of his books, as living in Trinidad and Boston, but when *Omeros* appeared in 1990, it bore the information that he "lives in Boston and St. Lucia." After receiving the Nobel Prize in 1992, he purchased land at Cap Estates, on the leeward side of the north tip of St. Lucia, just above the land bridge to Pigeon Island. There he has built a house, a studio, and a guest cottage. As early as 1988, there were signs of Walcott's increasing sense of himself as a St. Lucian first and last. After receiving the Queen's Medal for Poetry in that year, he returned to the island, where he was to be honored in recognition of this achievement. He got wind of a development plan for the Jalousie Estates, located between the two Pitons, the most celebrated glories of the St. Lucian landscape. One version of the plan proposed to flatten the peaks of the Pitons to allow tourists to ride to the top on a cable-tram something like a ski lift; even without this desecration, the development would still disfigure the landscape. He used the occasion to denounce the plan, which was subsequently scaled back. The tips of the Pitons remain intact, and the development is much less obtrusive than the initial plans had indicated. This was, according to George Odlum,[127] the first time in many years that Walcott had involved himself in St. Lucian local politics. The year after Walcott's Nobel Prize, St. Lucia finally bestowed its own highest award, the Cross of St. Lucia, on its celebrated poet. In addition, Columbus Square in Castries was renamed Derek Walcott Square in 1994, and the government has leased Rat Island, a former quarantine station off Choc Bay, to Walcott for development into a center for the arts. This project, as of last report, is still in the early stages (and I have met St. Lucians who doubt it will be realized, given what it would cost to make the place—treeless and without water and electricity—usable for the purpose).

Walcott's personal life has again become more stable during this period. He has lived since 1986 with Sigrid Nama. Only his relationship with Margaret Walcott was of comparable duration. He no longer drinks, and a diagnosis of diabetes a few years ago has forced relative moderation upon him. Since coming to New York in 1998 to work with Paul Simon on *The Capeman,* he has shifted his U.S. residence from Brookline, Massachusetts to Greenwich Village, returning to the scene of his first visit in 1957. There have been losses: his mother's death in 1992, and his brother Roderick's in April 2000. It seems appropriate that in this stage of his life, the story of Odysseus, returning home to Ithaca and Penelope after twenty hard years, has engaged his imagination.

His finest work of this phase, *Omeros,* uses material from both the Homeric epics, with a conspicuous debt, in the story of the expatriate Dennis Plunkett's search for a son, to James Joyce's *Ulysses.* He followed it with *The Odyssey: A Stage Version* (1993), continuing the Homeric trend. Published in the year Walcott turned sixty, *Omeros* marks the occasion by gathering and synthesizing, in a single long poem, the most central preoccupations of his work to that point. It has the look of a watershed in the poet's career, and the two books of poetry that have appeared since take different directions. *The Bounty* (1997) continues to use the tercets and some of the metaphors developed in *Omeros,* but both in its subjects (an elegy for Alix Walcott, various poems of place) and in its stylistic manner it recalls his books from the 1980s such as *MidSummer* and *The Fortunate Traveler. Tiepolo's Hound* (2000) is concerned with the vocation of art, and with Walcott's second career as a painter, in some of the same ways the "Homage to Gregorias" portion of *Another Life* is. The two recent books move from the concern, in *Omeros,* with collective identity and myth, toward a more intimate engagement with individual feeling and the look of the physical world. Walcott's poetry since *Omeros* strikes me as exploratory, still in the process of defining a new phase of his career. At seventy, he still keeps diligently at his writing (and, increasingly, at his painting too). His admirers have reason to hope that much of his best work is still before him.

2

"Fishing the Twilight for Alternate Voices": The Early Poems and *Henri Christophe*

Tradition, Voice, and Audience

A reader searching Walcott's early, privately printed collections for poems like the ones we know will for the most part be disappointed. The plays *Henri Christophe* (1949) and (more strikingly) *The Sea at Dauphin* (1954) are more fully realized than the poems of the same period. Not until 1956, when "A Far Cry from Africa" and "Ruins of a Great House" first appeared, did the poetry begin to catch up. One reason for this disparity may be the difference in the means by which the plays and the poetry sought their audiences. As Walcott himself recalls, books of poems were objects that came from abroad; he wanted his early collections to resemble the Faber editions of modern English poets. Although, through *Bim* and the "Caribbean Voices" broadcasts, he was seeking a West Indian audience for the poems, their form and diction comes out of Anglo-American modernism. A book, even an obscure colonial book printed in a run of two hundred copies, can eventually find its way to distant readers. The plays, on the other hand, had to be performed. They had to be actable by West Indians and to hold the interest of a West Indian audience. Walcott could evade, for a time, the challenge of imagining a society in which his poems could take place, but the plays forced him to deal with his society as it actually was.

Walcott's engagement with the "little tradition"—its heroes and legends, its language and form—begins in *Henri Christophe,* with its choice of postrevolutionary Haiti as subject and with its incorporation (as yet tentatively and in "low" characters only) of creole vernacular speech. Five years later, he would write *The Sea at Dauphin* entirely in vernacular—so much so that outsiders had trouble understanding the dialogue.[1] The early poems, in contrast, may describe West Indian places and experience, but the form and language of the representation come "from abroad." Not until 1958, with the first version of "Tales of the Islands," did Walcott attempt sustained vernacular in his poems. But the early volumes repay attention if read as the record of a young colonial poet's struggle to find his relation to the Anglo-American tradition. This struggle, difficult for any young poet, might seem especially daunting for a black poet growing up in a small island of the West Indies, and one in which, moreover, the most widely spoken idiom is not a form of English at all, but a French-lexicon creole.

Walcott himself, however, has refused to label it a struggle of any kind. His "early education," he claimed in retrospect, "must have ranked with the finest in the world. The grounding was rigid—Latin, Greek, and the essential masterpieces, but there was the elation of discovery. Shakespeare, Marlowe, Horace, Vergil—these writers weren't jaded but immediate experiences."[2] English, despite its historical connection to British colonialism, never loomed before him as the language of the colonizer, as French had confronted Fanon and Césaire. He describes himself as having been "[a]t nineteen, an elate, exuberant poet madly in love with English."[3] After all, he told Edward Hirsch, "the English language is nobody's special property. It is the property of the imagination; it is the property of the language itself."[4] Even colonialism itself, he insists, provided opportunity: "I feel absolutely no shame in having endured the colonial experience. There was no obvious humiliation in it. In fact, I think that many of what are sneered at as colonial values are part of the strength of the West Indian psyche, a fusion of formalism with exuberance, a delight in both the precision and the power of language."[5]

Walcott supplemented his education with readings in Eliot, Pound, Auden, Joyce, and [Dylan] Thomas, all of whom broke in one way or another with the conventions of the earlier verse he was taught in school. But unlike the tradition-saturated literary world of the metropolis, the colonial world made its young writers "yearn for structure as opposed to wishing to break away from it because there was no burden, no excess of literature in our heads," and so he had "never felt inhibited in trying to write as well as the greatest English poets."[6] He recalls "the elation of discovery"[7] just where Harold Bloom would lead us to expect anxiety.

Nonetheless, if the tale told by the early poetry may be trusted, "the elation of discovery" cannot have been the whole story. Colonial marginalization seems not to have shielded Walcott entirely from "the remorseless and intimidating legacy of the past" that Walter Jackson Bate called "the greatest single problem of modern art,"[8] and that Bloom calls the "anxiety of influence." His St. Lucian origins at once complicated that anxiety and provided him with a means to resist it. Like most young poets, Walcott imitated the styles he admired. The attendant anxiety—the theme, as it happens, of several poems in the first collection—is the one described by Bloom, the fear of proving no poet at all, of never passing beyond imitation into an art of his own. But simultaneously, for Walcott, there was a uniquely colonial anxiety, pushing in an opposite direction: that of being separated from legitimate aspiration itself, of being barred even from the first step of imitation. The first anxiety demands a break with the past, the second a filial embrace of it. But if one is not acknowledged by one's father, how is the filial embrace possible? As Walcott put it,

> [M]y first poems and plays expressed this yearning to be adopted, as the bastard longs for his father's household. I saw myself legitimately prolonging the mighty line of Marlowe, of Milton, but my sense of inheritance was stronger because it came from estrangement. I would learn that every tribe hoards its culture as fiercely as its prejudices, that English literature, even in the theatre, was hallowed ground and trespass, that colonial literatures could grow to resemble it closely, but could never be considered its legitimate heir. There was folk poetry, colonial poetry, Commonwealth verse, etc., and their function, as far as their mother country was concerned, was filial and tributary. I sighed up a continent of envy when I studied English literature, yet, when I tried to talk as I wrote, my voice sounded affected or too raw.[9]

It is one thing to say that imitation is a stage of apprenticeship to be transcended by the mature writer, another to say that it is the inherent sign of a derivative culture, never to be outgrown.

To be sure, outgrowing imitation is difficult even for the metropolitan poet. As Bloom points out, the young aspirant is in a "double bind. 'Be like me' and 'Do not presume to be too much like me,'"[10] the master poet says to the apprentice. To be too much like the predecessor is to remain only an apprentice. And yet to be altogether unlike the predecessor is to be merely incompetent. For a West Indian writer, the literary double bind has its cultural and political counterparts. The literary "master" is all too easily identified with the colonial one. The problem for Walcott was to accept literary apprenticeship without experiencing it as an extension of colonial oppression. Imitation had to be disentangled from the familiar disparagement of colonial culture as mimicry of a metropolitan original.

As Laurence Breiner points out, in an article that adjusts Bloom's speculations to a West Indian context, "the fear of being mimic men" is a "very Bloomian" form of anxiety. Homi Bhabha remarks, in his suggestive if cryptic essay "Of Mimicry and Man: The Ambivalence of Colonial Discourse," that the colonial situation condemns the imitator to be "the subject of a difference that is *almost the same, but not quite.*"[11] This language parallels the Bloomian master poet's "'Be like me' and 'Do not presume to be too much like me,'" but it takes in the general case of cultural assimilation, not just the more specialized domain of poetic influence. Whereas the poet may hope to move beyond imitation to mastery, colonial "mimicry" is a permanent mark of inferiority, an unbridgeable gap between the 'authentic' culture of the colonizer and its specious, slightly askew replication among the colonized. When the apprentice is denied access to mastery, the difference between the literary and the political sense of "master" collapses.

Bate and Bloom describe the burden of the past as constantly growing with each generation. Anxiety is most acute among belated inheritors of a long tradition, its moments of greatest originality far in the past. The West Indian case might seem to be a politicized version of that same anxiety, compounded by the fear that one is not even a legitimate inheritor of the distant past. But latent within the charge of "mimicry" is an opposite implication. If the veneer of imitated culture is so thin, its connection to the underlying experience of the mimic so tenuous, then perhaps there is really an absence, rather than an intimidating presence, of tradition. Unlike the belated English poets, whose overwhelming consciousness of past achievement leaves almost no space for new invention, the West Indian poet suffers not from too much past but from too little, or from a sense that such past as there is may not be truly one's own. Naipaul's dismissal of Caribbean culture as "mimicry" is not separable from his claim that "nothing was created in the West Indies," but is only a different way of saying the same thing.

Walcott's insistence that "there was no burden, no excess of literature in our heads," that his literary initiation was all freshness, exuberance, and open possibility, may be understood as a way of turning the Naipaulian diagnosis into a strength. "If there was nothing," he wrote in "What the Twilight Says: An Overture," "there was everything to be made."[12] In "The Caribbean: Culture or Mimicry?" he explicitly engages Naipaul and through wordplay on "nothing" reverses its derisive implications: "Nothing will always be created in the West Indies, because what will come out of there is like nothing one has ever seen before." Indeed, "cultures can only be created out of [the] knowledge of nothing, and in deeper than the superficial, existential sense, we in the Caribbean know all about nothing."[13]

But sometimes Walcott's claim of indifference to anxiety of influence strains credibility. On the need for originality he has been of different minds at different times. In his 1979 interview with Edward Hirsch, he found it "important . . . to find a voice that was not inflected by influences," and conceded that he was "still working on this."[14] By the mid-1980s, he seems to welcome other voices. In the Hirsch interview for *Paris Review* (1985), he praises Robert Lowell for his "openness to receive influences," for a "multifaceted imagination . . . influenced even in his middle-age by William Carlos Williams, or by François Villon, or by Boris Pasternak, all at the same time." He found it impossible to "separate [his] affection for Lowell from [Lowell's] influence on [him]."[15] Two years later, he told David Montenegro: "I have been very flattered, as opposed to being insulted, when I've been told that I sound like someone else who was great. I always considered that to be an honor and not an accusation. . . . If I was an apprentice to Leonardo, I would feel terrific if someone said, 'This is as good as Leonardo' or 'You got this from Leonardo.' Obviously, I'd say, yes, thanks very much." The truly serious "poet of any modesty hopes to make just a small contribution to the sound of the world's hum, and does not by any means wish to be individual or to be praised for his style or whatever."[16] In my first conversation with him, Walcott compared the great poets of the past to "lighthouses."[17] When I observed that although one steers by a lighthouse, no one tries to become the lighthouse, he indicated that I had understood. (It has since occurred to me, however, that if one steers too close to the lighthouse, one shipwrecks on the rocks, meeting precisely the fate the lighthouse was built to warn against. The metaphor is perhaps more Bloomian than Walcott meant it to be.)

Breiner, reading Walcott's openness to influence in Bloomian terms, calls it an instance of "Apophrades," the return of the dead, which is Bloom's name for the last of his six "revisionary ratios," the maneuvers by means of which poets defend themselves against precursors. Or more precisely, as Breiner says,

> this is not actually the name of a manoeuvre, but the name of an event which Bloom sees as characteristic of a late stage in a poet's career, and to which his manoeuvre is a response. The return of the great precursors is a kind of second childhood for the poet, since he associates their presence with the first sense of vocation that came through his naive response to them. If all has gone well, he is now strong enough to pay his respects: "the poem is now held open to the precursor, where once it was open." Bloom theorizes that sometimes the poet is drowned again in influences, but that where apophrades is successful, the dead seem to speak again, but in the voice of the living.[18]

But, as Breiner admits, the notion of "the return of the dead" combines oddly with Walcott's insistence on an Adamic poetics, resulting in "a radically compromised Adam," an "Adam with a past," an "Adam inhabited by presences, virtually a shaman full of ancestral spirits."[19]

From a Bloomian perspective, Walcott's Adamic stance, despite Breiner's best efforts, can only seem a desperate whistling in the dark. And to many North American critics, Walcott's apophrades, which has persisted throughout his entire career rather than being overcome in youth and then reappearing late in life, has seemed more a fault than a strength. Helen Vendler, for one, remarked that "[h]e is still, even as a fully developed writer, peculiarly at the mercy of influences,"[20] which suggests not a voluntary holding open of the work but helpless submission.

As long as we hold to the notion of influence as a lonely wrestling between outsetting bard and the mighty dead, accomplished in some literary dream-space, Walcott's response to influence is bound to seem odd and unsatisfactory. (It is perhaps relevant that Bloom considers some of the poets most important to Walcott—T. S. Eliot, Ezra Pound, and Robert Lowell—to be overrated minor figures.) Bloom's version of influence may suppose a situation that was not Walcott's, in which a long-established and relatively well-defined tradition has settled its weight on the present, rather than the more volatile circumstances of the West Indies about to emerge from colonial rule.

But there are, and have been, other ways of imagining influence. Walcott himself, in the David Montenegro interview, says "maybe I have a medieval mind—I'm really part of a guild."[21] Not only in the medieval period, but well into the eighteenth century, imitation was considered a legitimate form of poetic invention, as in Samuel Johnson's "The Vanity of Human Wishes," imitated from Juvenal. For understanding Walcott's response to influence, Mikhail Bakhtin may prove more useful than Bloom, even though he applies his description of the individual writer's relation to the already said to the novel and not to the supposedly "monologic" or single-voiced genre of lyric poetry. But the Caribbean, with its mingling of languages and cultures, has a way of relaxing boundaries—and genres too are boundaries. Bakhtin helps us to see that Walcott's best poems are to some extent "novelized," and that maturation for this poet has to some degree meant relaxing the demand for monologic consistency, a single "voice" to be heard in all of his poems. Bakhtin also recognizes that the literary tradition is only a part, though for a writer an important part, of the cultural history that precedes any new utterance: the linguistic environment is social as well as literary. But unlike death-of-the-author theorists, Bakhtin emphasizes the role of desire, choice, and conflict in shaping available language to new uses:

> Any concrete discourse (utterance) finds the object at which it was directed already as it were overlain with qualifications, open to dispute, charged with value, already enveloped in an obscuring mist—or, on the contrary, by the "light" of alien words that have already been spoken about it. . . . The word, directed toward its object, enters a dialogically agitated and tension-filled environment of alien words, value judgments, and accents, weaves in and out of complex interrelationships, merges with some, recoils from others, intersects with yet a third group: and all this may crucially shape discourse, may leave a trace in all its semantic layers, may complicate its expression and influence its entire stylistic profile.[22]

Language in this account is charged with the intentionality of those who use it. Any new intention meets resistance from the intentions of those who have already spoken their countervailing "alien words" about the same object. When the influence of one writer on another is "deep and productive, there is no external imitation, no simple act of reproduction, but rather a further creative development of another's (more precisely, half-another) discourse in a new context and under new conditions."[23] The ambience of the already said may seem obstructive, hindering each new utterance from passing in a straight line, through open space, to its object. But by a metaphor of refraction, Bakhtin suggests that this interference can sustain as well as hinder. Eventually, the refraction of the new utterance in the dense medium of the already said reveals its spectrum of connotative meanings:

> If we imagine the *intention* of such a word, that is, its *directionality toward the object,* in the form of a ray of light, then the living and unrepeatable play of colors and light on the facets of the image that it constructs can be explained as the spectral dispersion of the ray-word . . . in an atmosphere filled with the alien words, value judgments and accents through which the ray passes on its way toward the object; the social atmosphere of the word, the atmosphere that surrounds the object, makes the facets of the image sparkle.[24]

In this passage, the "atmosphere of the word" is explicitly "social," and only through the interaction of the new utterance with all the others does language achieve its luminosity. What resists also completes. Bakhtin's approach admits, no less than Bloom's, that the relationship between any new utterance and the already said entails conflict. But whereas Bloom thinks of the strong poet as one who succeeds in laying claim to the literary dream-space of his own imagination and thus in achieving an autonomous voice, Bakhtin asks us to think of even the most original literary utterance as taking into itself many others, which may be adapted to new contexts rather than simply imitated or rejected. The resulting work must reckon not with a single overbearing precursor, but with a whole range of possible voices, many of which may be heard in the street rather than through the speakers of other poems.

If we concede, with Bakhtin, that poetry is social as well as literary, then any emerging poet must find a relationship not only to earlier poetry, but to possible readers. Even if we grant Walcott's claim that his colonial situation exempted him from the English poet's burden of the past, it left him without a socially located audience. American readers who have studied the earlier literature of their own country will begin to have a sense of déja vu as they read of Walcott's predicament. Here, too, there was said to be a lack of history, a social texture too "thin," as Henry James put it in his study of Hawthorne, to sustain literary creation. Here, too, books produced at home were suspect. Our own authors tried the "Adamic" stance long before Walcott did. North American Adamicism of the 1840s and 1850s produced some of the same contradictions as Walcott's, but what rings true in it is the sense of having to create, as opposed to being born into, a national literature—and a national audience. Some of what has been said about the formative years of American poetry may also be said of the West Indian situation in Walcott's youth.

In "Freneau, Whitman, Williams," Robert Pinsky argues that in Freneau, the earliest of his three poets, the sense of a social context has yet to be formed. Freneau's satire against slavery, "To Sir Toby," though "skillful in execution and truly admirable in feeling, falls short because it fails to imagine a society—which is to say, an American society—in which the poem itself can take place." Freneau takes his couplets and balanced syntax from the style of Pope, who uses formal parallelism to point up subtle incongruities. "In puns, or politics, or tales, or lies, / Or spite, or smut, or rhymes, or blasphemies," writes Pope, and in that list, says Pinsky, "the ironically out-of-place element—'rhymes' among smut and blasphemies, 'politics' among puns and lies—is like a knowing social joke between reader and writer." But this is an aristocratic, urbane mode, presuming an aristocratic, urbane reader. "Freneau's list, 'Snakes, scorpions, despots, lizards, centipedes,' frames the term 'despots' in the same way, but lamely," because "the Popean rhetorical forms contradict any sense of who addresses the poem to whom." As a result,

> there is no place in Freneau's poem for the implied social understanding between him and his reader, the vibration that would animate the twisted parallelism. The truest political component of poetry, the sense of whom the poem belongs to, is pale and overpowered by Freneau's enumerated horrors on one side and by his Popean ironies of balance and imbalance, evenness and disproportion on the other side.[25]

In Bakhtinian terms, one might say that the "social atmosphere of the word" has not yet been constituted: there is Pope at Twickenham, Sir Toby's slave plantation somewhere in Jamaica, and nothing but ocean between them. The voices that enter the new utterance have not yet been placed in a field of intelligible relations to each other. Walcott encountered similar difficulties.

Walcott's attempt to imagine a society in which his poems could take place would later receive help from an emergent West Indian cultural nationalism that looked forward to federation and independence. As Benedict Anderson claims in his much cited *Imagined Communities,* nations must first be imagined before they have a chance to become politically embodied; people who have never met each other face to face must come to think of themselves as joined together by common experience and loyalties. But before his departure for Jamaica, Walcott had traveled only to Barbados, and that only briefly. The idea that St. Lucians were part of a larger West Indian people appealed to him, but it must have remained something of an abstraction. The growth of print culture and a large, literate middle class, which Anderson believes enabled the imagining of national communities in early nineteenth-century Europe, were not features of the predominantly oral and peasant culture of St. Lucia in the 1940s. It is not surprising, then, that the early poems sound so uncertain as to who is speaking to whom.

Exuberance and Anxiety: *25 Poems*

Despite Walcott's recollection of himself at nineteen as "an elate, exuberant poet,"[26] there is little elation or exuberance in the tone of his first book, and a great deal of anxious fretting about the future. Several of the poems concern poetic vocation. The most elate and exuberant of these is "As John to Patmos," one of the four that Walcott retained in his *Collected Poems 1948–1984*. But most of the others are far less sanguine. They are not announcements of excited discovery so much as grimly determined resolutions not to fail.

"Inspire Modesty by Means of Nightly Verses," which Walcott placed first in *25 Poems*, indeed makes a modest beginning. It is a prayer addressed to an unspecified being, and in this as well as its language of oracular paradox it brings to mind Auden's "Petition." It envisions a future beset with dangers. It uses a mixed sonnet form, following two Shakespearean quatrains (*abab cdcd*) with a variant Petrarchan sestet linked by one of its rhymes to the second quatrain (*cecece*). The poem has no major turn, and syntactically it breaks 9–5 rather than the traditional 8–6. Its indecisiveness of form seems of a piece with its guarded requests:

> Inspire modesty by means of nightly verses,
> Defer hands that construct a selfish end
> By rope; disintegrate all that perverse is
> In arms that circumscribe a private friend.
> Render those faithful whom we least suspect
> Of friendship; and those whom we know betray,
> May they confirm our better judgment. Wreck
> Maps for our murder, but our iron hate
> Make secure as telegraph poles are strict.

Provoke the nervous beams in foreign lovers,
Our ultimate disaster make circumspect,
Strengthen the fraud that white and black are brothers,
Give us the wisdom that does not expect
More from ourselves than we expect of others.

(*25 P,* 5)

Some of the contradictions in this poem merely remind us that the "language of paradox" was standard equipment in Anglo-American poetry of the 1940s, but others suggest the young Walcott's uncertainties about his vocation and his cultural community. Why does this poet who "saw [himself] legitimately prolonging the mighty line of Marlowe, of Milton," pray for modesty and the wisdom not to expect too much? Just who are "we," and who are "those" who stand outside this collective identity?

Such uncertainties reverberate throughout the poem. Whose are the "hands" of line two: do they belong to enemies ("those whom we know betray," the makers of "Maps for our murder") or to the speaker himself? Is the danger ensnarement by others, or is it suicide? That question, one might speculate, derives from a larger one: do the constraints on the poet come from external sources, such as colonial domination and the killing embrace of "foreign lovers," or from the internalization of self-doubt? The realm of the trustworthy appears quite narrow, a private rather than public sphere. "In arms that circumscribe the private friend" the perverse dissolves, but outside that boundary all is treachery.

Several other poems in the first volume take up, rather conspicuously, the theme of poetic vocation threatened with failure. "Inspire Modesty" is followed by "The Gay Plague," in which the dread of failure becomes quite explicit:

Words we correct all the night
In morning are no longer neat.
And giant Fear his citadel
Appoints in us from head to heel. . . .

(*25 P,* 5)

Fear's "citadel" occupies the entire interior space of the body, rather as if Browning's Childe Roland, upon finding the dark tower at last, had swallowed it. Other poems that dwell on the threat of failure include "Letter to a Painter in England," in which one may choose to go abroad and "rot under the strict grey industry / Of cities," or to stay home and see one's "gifts rotting under this season"; "Elegies," in which, meditating on the untimely deaths of promising poets such as Thomas Chatterton, Walcott writes "I am as young as they died, and am proud in a trade of fames, / I fear death, inmate of my hand, leaps wall to join their names"; and "In a Year," where the poet laments that "these are brown and dead words that I now talk." But perhaps the most interesting among these broodings on poetic failure is "Carnival for Two Voices," because it thematizes what elsewhere appears only as stylistic symptom: the absence of a common social space enclosing poet and audience.

"Carnival for Two Voices" takes its title from the West Indian folk tradition of carnival but then strikes up its dialogue in voices that speak, once again, the language of Anglo-American modern poetry. "Children playing near the pond's mirror / In their cries the impatience of terror" (*25 P,* 29)—these are not the accents of the Calypso tent. This first voice, "A," and its companion, "L," are revealed, in the course of the poem, to be "Art" and "Life." "L" at times sounds somewhat earthier than "A," but more typically, they are indistinguishable. The only distinctively West Indian speech here—indeed in the entire book—is found in neither voice, but rather in the interjection of the "Crowd," which ends the poem by interrupting the dialogue with "Jour Ouvert . . . beat it out baby . . . beat it baby" (*25 P,* 32). Even this rendering of the patois cry that announces the opening of carnival is a bit stiff. The phrase is usually rendered as "j'ouvert," "j'ouvet," or even "jouvay," any of which more nearly approximates its East Caribbean pronunciation than Walcott's standard French orthography.

The early poems often affect the language of the alienated poet, which is a legacy of metropolitan avant gardes engaged in critique of middle-class values. As Renato Poggioli pointed out long ago, avant-garde artists are often persons of middle-class origins who deliberately declass themselves and seek community in an alternative "*milieu artiste.*"[27] But in the St. Lucia of the 1940s, there was no bohemian *milieu artiste,* as Harry Simmons was so painfully aware, and only a small and unconfident middle class, itself subservient to colonial authority. Walcott's adopted idiom, like Freneau's, was incommensurate with the circumstances.

While some of the *25 Poems* declare a rift between artist and middle class, the split in "Carnival for Two Voices" is between poet and the common people of his island. "The Fishermen Rowing Homeward . . . ," retained in *Collected Poems 1948–1984* under the title "The Harbour," reveals a similar rift. "The fishermen rowing homeward in the dusk, / Do not consider the stillness through which they move," the poem begins. The unlettered fishermen row, unaware that anyone observes them. Since they do not "consider the stillness," the poet must do so for them. They do the fishing and rowing, he does the reflecting and writing. He turns their literal progress over the water into a metaphor of his own "progress outward / To a sea which is crueller than any word / Of love." He contrasts himself not only with the fishermen, but with "the secure from thinking"—presumably tourists—who "may climb safe to liners, / Hearing small rumours of paddlers drowned near stars." The fishermen in their boat and the tourists in their cruise ship are secure, while the poet on his figurative "voyage" is most at risk to drown. Thirty years later, in "The Schooner *Flight,*" Walcott would invent a speaker, Shabine, who is both a figurative and a literal seafarer, a sailor sprung from the folk who is also able to write of them in phrases "soaked with salt." But in 1948, his language had yet to be marinated.

"Travelogue" is the only poem in the first book that makes explicit reference to the plan of Federation. The ideal of "the federated archipelago" is central to its resolution, coming into the poem after forty-five lines of vacillation about the prospects of the island (presumably St. Lucia) and the poet's relation to it. He concedes that "the people are small," their ambitions limited (*25 P,* 17). Then, into this scene of limitation, comes "History" to speak the closing lines:

> But History asks, "Do not exhort men to build worlds
> Shallower than their slow ebbing loves and fortune,
> Or taller than sky or the bird-frightening chimney.
>
> Let all on islands of the heart construct the day
> Of the federated archipelago, black
> And white live apart, if so, but dream the same dreams.
>
> Then might God and his wise machines elect to cross
> With a shower of blossoms, and make if no Eden
> Then such a peace as traveller expects of islands."
>
> (*25 P,* 18)

"History"—soon to become a far less beneficent presence in Walcott's poetry—arrives with a program. First of all, ambition must have an appropriate scale. The ambitions of the islanders are stunted, but those of the colonizers were too grandiose and turned murderous, destroying "lost red and black tribes" (*25 P,* 18). Ambition should have the size and depth of human passion, but it should not become imperial.

History addresses not only "all on islands," but all on metaphorical "islands of the heart." The relation of island to archipelago becomes generalized as a metaphor of the relationship between individual aspirations and collective identities. Elsewhere in his earliest poetry, Walcott repeatedly uses the metaphor of islands to describe human separation, while aspiring also to connect across that distance. "We, being all islands in air ourselves, should not / From sickness of another's heart feel better," begins another poem from the first collection (*25 P,* 16). A few years later, "The Pursuit of April—A Letter," in *Poems* (1951), will describe a bridge that "joins the sleeping limbs of banks with music / As love can vault us in our separate islands" (*P,* 29).

The movement from the islands of the Caribbean to "islands of the heart" is a universalizing trope, and in this it is of a piece with the rhetoric of West Indian nationalism. Walcott's language is also distinctly "federalist" in proposing something less than the effacement of all differences in unity. "History" seems ready to continue the arrangement that "black / And white live apart," as long as they "dream the same dreams" (*25 P,* 17). They can participate in the same imagined community, yet "occasion" will bring them together as seldom as formerly (*25 P,* 17). Finally, the nationalism of this poem seems unusually skeptical, provisional, and cautious.

"I With Legs Crossed Along the Daylight Watch," later titled "Prelude," gained a belated significance when Walcott placed it at the opening of *Collected Poems 1948–1984.* The title and gateway placement of this poem suggest that Walcott sees it in retrospect as an early harbinger of what was to follow. It would be foolish to claim too much for this early lyric. Nonetheless, it develops a step farther than other poems in the first book toward the interplay of voices characteristic of his later work. In "Prelude," the voices are not yet West Indian. But the poem marks one of Walcott's first attempts to reinterpret for his own purposes a quarrel within Anglo-American modernism about the relationship between skeptical intelligence and what might be called the Dionysian, the corporeal, or the "primitive."

Elsewhere in *25 Poems,* the language of Dionysian celebration of the sensuous world, indebted to the style of Dylan Thomas and the lyrical side of Auden, has been cordoned off from a language of analysis, satire, and self-doubt, indebted to Eliot, Pound, and the more caustic side of Auden. But in "Prelude" the languages of abandon and critique enter into debate with each other. It is a step toward what would become Walcott's characteristic way of assimilating influences. Rather than seeing himself as the overshadowed son of a giant precursor, unable to claim his place except by a Promethean act of misreading or denial, Walcott invites various ancestors to the house, sets them arguing among themselves, and turns them into voices for his own internal symposium, each bearing one line of a polyphony that is more than the sum of its parts. A number of English and American modernists, including Stevens, Hardy, and above all Auden, for whom it is almost a stylistic signature, had developed the habit of playing off a lyrical, passionate voice against a deflating, analytical and ironic counter-voice. "Prelude" begins to turn this internal debate into a dramatization of Walcott's own cultural dividedness.

The poem's opening evokes a vigilant preparation for conflict:

> I with legs crossed along the daylight watch
> The variegated fists of clouds that gather over
> The uncouth features of this my prone island.
>
> (*25 P*, 23)

If the meaning of these lines connects them to Walcott's satirical mode, their metaphorical compression and obliquity connects them to the more irrational, Dylan-Thomas-like style of "As John to Patmos" or "A City's Death by Fire." One is also reminded of Césaire's depiction of his town as "*plate-étalée*," and of his soul as "*couchée. Comme cette ville dans la crasse et dans la boue couchée*,"[28] although Walcott had not yet read the *Cahier*.[29]

Walcott's next stanza moves toward a more transparent, discursive style, sounding more like Auden than Thomas:

> Meanwhile the steamers that disturb our lost horizons prove
> Us lost.
> Found only
> In tourist booklets, behind ardent binoculars;
> Found in the pale reflection of eyes
> That know cities, and think us here happy.
>
> (*25 P*, 24)

These lines depict the tendency, analyzed by Memmi and Fanon, of colonized peoples to see themselves as they are seen, as secondary reflections in another's eye.

As the poem moves from the collective to the individual, from the problem of colonial identity to the challenge of poetic vocation, the language becomes increasingly self-deprecating, its irony turned on the speaker in the manner of Eliot's "Love Song of J. Alfred Prufrock." Like the speaker of "Prelude," Prufrock fears being defined by another's gaze. But in "Prelude," the language of self-consciousness that, for Prufrock, was prompted by fears of sexual rejection takes on a new context. The anxiety in "Prelude" is that of a black, colonial poet preparing to assert himself on equal terms with his metropolitan contemporaries. He needs to find out what his relationship, as poet, will be to the people of his "prone island," and to the strangers from beyond the horizon with "eyes / That know cities, and think us here happy" (*25 P*, 24).

Walcott subtly lightens Eliot's tone, modulating to the insouciance of "the living images / Of flesh that saunter through the eye." The carnal world enters the eye alive, bringing its body with it. In the poem up to this point, there has been an undeclared struggle for the poet's allegiance between an Eliotic voice of self-denying submission to the discipline of art and a more assertive, less diffident gaiety. Now the speaker's attention turns outward, from the difficulties of self-definition to the sensuous plenitude of the surrounding world.

The closing stanza brings the poem to its turning point, an entry into poetic vocation:

> Until from all I turn to think how
> In the middle of the journey through my life
> O how I came upon you, my
> Reluctant leopard of the slow eyes.

The allusion to Dante's leopard seems to continue the Eliotic mode, since it is through Eliot that a young poet in the 1940s would first be led to Dante. But Dante's leopard (*lonza*) is an obstacle to the poetic quest. Walcott's leopard, in contrast, seems downright attractive, a muse or a lover. It is more like the leopard in Hart Crane's "The Wine Menagerie," which Walcott had not yet read, or the beasts surrounding Dionysus in Pound's second canto, which he had. The assertion of imaginative potency, the leap across the gap between mind and world, is registered in style as well as meaning. It returns the poet to the center.

In "A Far Cry from Africa," written eight years later with a similar antiphonal play of analytic and Dionysian styles, the warring discourses more fully disclose the implications of their conflict. "A Far Cry from Africa" defines the colonial poet's dilemma more explicitly, in more fully imagined symbolism. Even the title serves notice that close attention will be rewarded: it plays on the idiom "a far cry from," thus evoking the poet's awareness of cultural as well as physical distance from Africa, even as he is moved by its cry across the Atlantic.

The opening of the poem announces its violent subject, the "Mau Mau rebellion" of 1952–1960, in which the Kikuyu fought a guerrilla war against the British colonists and a loyalist faction among themselves. Walcott portrays the conflict in animal—and animistic—metaphors. He figures the violence as a wind "ruffling the tawny pelt" of the continent, extending the metaphor when he likens the Kikuyu to "flies" feeding on the Africa-lion's "bloodstreams," the rivers of the veldt. The comparison to a disease-carrying insect, as much a byword for vileness as the lion is for nobility, hardly flatters the Kikuyu. After the next line, "Corpses are scattered through a paradise," one begins to notice a ventriloquism of colonialist attitudes. "Paradise" is a familiar European description of "backward" places like Africa—or the Caribbean, for that matter. When the final line of the first stanza refers to the Kikuyu as "savages," it echoes the claims of the prosecutors in the trial of Jomo Kenyatta in 1952–53 that no one "looking at Mau Mau objectively" could deny that it is "a purely barbarous movement . . . accompanied by circumstances of revolting savagery."[30] It is hard to say at this point whether Walcott is satirizing colonialist judgments of the Kikuyu or to some degree endorsing them. As one follows the further turnings of the poem, one gathers that he does both—the colonizer's response is smugly ethnocentric, and yet it is truly "savage" to butcher children in their sleep.

The poetic style in which Walcott portrays the violence of the Kikuyu comes from the repertory of modernist neoprimitivism: its animism is reminiscent of Hart Crane (whom, by now, he had read) or D. H. Lawrence, and its density of metaphor follows the high modernist rejection of discursive statement in favor of image and analogy.[31] This language seems allied to the British interpretation of the rebellion as atavism. As Walcott's indictment begins to shift from the Kikuyu to the colonists, his style shifts also, becoming more abstract, akin to Auden whose discursive mode in part represented a reaction against high modernist irrationalism:

> Only the worm, colonel of carrion, cries:
> "Waste no compassion on these separate dead!"
> Statistics justify and scholars seize
> The salients of colonial policy.[32]

The stylistic quarrel within modernism itself, between loyal and disloyal Europeans, has been reenacted within the poem, where it becomes an iconic representation of the poet's own ambivalence. The first line of this passage serves as transition, continuing the animism of the opening but moving from symbolist suggestion to the baldly allegorical "colonel of carrion," while also deflecting the poem's anger from the Kikuyu to the English. The appeal to "statistics" and "policy" parodies—as does Auden's language in poems such as "The Unknown Citizen"—the bureaucratic, speciously "objective" style of modern political explanation. The end of the stanza erupts with impatience at such temporizing: "What is that to the white child hacked in bed? / To savages, expendable as Jews?" The phrase "expendable as Jews" reminds us that Africans have no monopoly on savagery, and that savagery, European style, begins with a reduction of its victims to something "expendable" in service to a calculated end.

The façade of detachment collapses abruptly when the last stanza moves into the first person. The poet introduces himself as one "poisoned with the blood of both," alluding to the racially mixed ancestry that divides him "to the vein," but also implicating himself in the guilt of each side for shedding the "blood" of the other. The events slice the poet in half and "batten upon" his own "lifeblood." The poem ends in a flurry of unanswered questions:

> I who have cursed
> The drunken officer of British rule, how choose
> Between this Africa and the English tongue I love?
> Betray them both, or give back what they give?
> How can I face such slaughter and be cool?
> How can I turn from Africa and live?
>
> (*CP,* 18)

Walcott's profit on the colonizer's language goes beyond knowing how to curse, as he proves by the very act of writing the poem. To accept an "English" poetic inheritance while sympathizing with the Kikuyu is to "Betray them both," whereas to "give back" both the English and the African parts of his identity would be to cancel his own existence. In any case, such a giving back is impossible, as he would later point out: "The language I used did not bother me. . . . [I]t was irretrievably given, I could no more give it back than they could claim it."[33] The dilemma can only be endured, not resolved. To "face" the conflict in Kenya is to lose all composure, torn by irreconcilably divided loyalties, yet to "turn from" it is to rip away half of the divided identity, an amputation the psyche cannot survive. Walcott would explore this dividedness more fully in later works, but "A Far Cry from Africa" is his most memorable early account of it.

"Let me fare forward / towards . . .": *Epitaph for the Young*

Walcott's second early volume, *Epitaph for the Young* (1949), is a long poem in "XII Cantos"—as this formal description suggests, the engagement with influence here shifts away from Auden and Thomas toward Pound, Eliot, and, as it happens, Joyce, whose Stephen Dedalus becomes an analogue for the young poet, discouraged by the provincialism of his culture yet bound to it even in his antagonism. In this poem, a more West Indian perspective begins to mitigate insular preoccupations, although the satirical passages direct much of their energy against conditions specific to St. Lucia. *Epitaph for the Young* would remain Walcott's longest poem until the completion of *Another Life*, for which he later considered the earlier effort "sort of like an *Urtext*."[34] In 1989, when he was finishing *Omeros*, he connected that poem, too, with *Epitaph for the Young*.[35] Both of these mature long poems are set primarily in St. Lucia, and both, like *Epitaph*, take up the ambition of the epic poem in their attempt to define the identity of a people.

The larger, West Indian perspective appears first of all in the overarching conceit of the poem as a sea voyage; this is its largest debt to Pound's *Cantos*. The aim of Walcott's voyage, however, remains tentatively defined: "Moving in the kind wind, by thoughtless islands, / Towards . . ." (*EY*, 3). To bring thought to the thoughtless islands, and to arrive at the unnamable destination pointed at by the ellipsis, is the task of the poem (Cantos II, III, IV, VIII, and XI also trail off with "Towards . . ."). At the beginning of the second Canto,

> Voyaging,
>   In the first strong wind, gathering purpose,
> We observed the wreckage drifting at morning,
> Signifying
>   Land, and the flotsam of other purposes. . . .

As the sun rises, "A rim of fragile islands, virginal," becomes plain to the sight (*EY*, 4). These lines suggest not only that West Indian consciousness is "fragile," but also that although it is "virginal," it is formed of "the flotsam of other purposes"—the leavings of a history fragmented, as Glissant has remarked, not only by the mixing of languages, races, and cultures, but by the volatile caprice of metropolitan colonial policy.

The fourth Canto, bearing the epigraph, "There is not a West Indian

Literature," is preoccupied with the obstacles to creating one. It indicts (with parodic echoes of Pound's *Hugh Selwyn Mauberley* and Eliot's *The Waste Land*) the timidity of the colonized, clerical middle class: "Died most as Suppressor of His Majesty's Conscience in the Colonies, / Inspector of Civil Service lavatories. . . . / Voucher and Report undid them" (*EY,* 11). The aspiring youth, visiting "pontifical, morning-gown solemn Professor Eunuch," asks him why he gave up writing. "I was a blind bat, my boy," the professor replies, "Fishing the twilight for alternate voices. / Taking arms against a whole tradition . . . you'll stop too, / You are just young" (*EY,* 11). The encounter recalls the "Mr. Nixon" section of *Hugh Selwyn Mauberley,* in which an older writer advises a young man to "give up verse, my boy, / There's nothing in it." But Professor Eunuch's description of himself as "a blind bat" also recalls Pound's description, in Canto II, of "poor old Homer blind, blind, as a bat, / Ear, ear for the sea-surge, murmur of old men's voices." If even Homer was a blind bat, then Professor Eunuch may have given up too easily.

The young poet sets out anyway:

> So I began to write, to take up arms,
> Fitting out vaguely for a pitiless sea,
> Willing to drown under impersonal stars . . . [Walcott's ellipsis]
>
> (*EY,* 12)

The omens for the voyager are not auspicious. To succeed, he must overcome not only the despair of "Professor Eunuch" but also his lack of ready access to any sustaining tradition:

> Veiling your inheritance, you kneel before
> The sessile invocation of the thrush, the sibilant yew trees,
> By broken and flaked languages, near a drying river,
> You practice the pieties of your conquerors,
> Bowing before a bitter god.
> *Marassa carrefour,*
> *Adoré nan pié Damballa.*
>
> (*EY,* 10)

The two lines of creole (which stand out as an isolated swerve into the vernacular) evoke *loa* of vodoun.[36] Walcott apparently regards Vodoun as submission to the "pieties" of the "conquerors"; only later would he come to see it as a "cunning submission," so that in the end, "what was captured from the captor was his god."[37] Similarly, he describes creole vernaculars as "broken and flaked languages." Although he offers, in Canto X, to "drink to any West Indian who / Strips speech of tie and socks" (*EY* 31), he himself was not yet ready to do so.

In *Epitaph for the Young,* the "unity" with "distant others" remains largely hypothetical. The community of the single island is all too tangible: with "They shall / Motor to Vigie on Sundays" (*EY,* 19), we are back in St. Lucia among the stifled middle class. The inhabitants of other islands, as depicted in this poem, share the same socially unformed condition. The closest thing to a shared community is a shared lack of community. At first, the prospect of connection with distant others seems charged with possibility, a yearning for wider experience and shared aspiration. But then it turns out that these others can only be imagined as living in societies just as constricted as one's own, so that the same satirical pin that punctures the others for their nationalistic delusion of "country forming" (*EY,* 19) also deflates the poet's own federalist intimations. "Who gives a darn," he puns in Canto X, "For the threaderation of the Vest Indies?" (*EY,* 31). The poem's satire on subservient, narrow-minded Catholic moralism addresses a St. Lucian rather than broadly West Indian problem. "We have had enough of the Lady on the promontory," he writes, parodying Eliot's "The Dry Salvages" (*EY,* 14).[38]

Near the end of Canto VII, Walcott offers a blessing "with a maker's hands," praising "those who see a world among these islands / Where we shall try to live in peace and fail, / The failure nothing." Of greatest interest here, for Walcott's later work, is the tension between the need to climb "ladders to see the wide world" and the imperative "to live near in humility." The passage continues with praise for

> The little men, reciters at parties, quadroon bohemians,
> The fisherman trailing the sun in his darkening net,
> And the workman in overalls putting up the ladder of the sun,
> All those who dream against reason, who will make us
> More powerful than stones in the Atlantic tributary,
> But powerless, permanent, lovely and human,
> Proud not of overcoming complexion,
> But climbing poet and labourer nearer the tireless sun.
>
> (*EY,* 21)

The last line presents the poet and laborer as equal sharers in the quest, climbing the ladder together to approach the sun. But the metaphorical linkages of the passage do not entirely support that affirmation. At first, climbing the ladder meant leaving the island in order "to see the wide world"; one must, presumably, then climb back down to the island "to live near in humility." The workman puts up "the ladder of the sun," but at this point it would seem that he prepares it for someone else to climb. In his desire to bring poet and laborer together on the ladder, Walcott describes each as a version of the other: the poet has a "maker's hands," while the fisherman and workingman are included among "those who dream against reason," a noble folly usually reserved for poets. The "reciters at parties" and "quadroon bohemians" mingle, among the "little men," with fishermen and carpenters—or perhaps they *are* the fishermen and carpenters, released from their daytime labors. Despite Walcott's desire to effect this union, however, the passage shows him uneasily aware of differences of class and education within his own island. Not only has the West Indian community with "distant others" proved virtually impossible, as yet, to imagine, but even the small community of the island contains distances that have to be bridged.[39]

A Creole Sonnet Sequence: "Tales of the Islands"

"From very early on," Walcott has said, "I knew what I wanted my poems to sound like."[40] In "Tales of the Islands," he at last "strips speech of tie and socks," as the switching between standard and creole English that had long been his practice in the plays emerges within a sequence of ten sonnets. Although his subsequent poems have not always used both registers, both have been available to him ever since.

"Tales of the Islands" manages to imply, in its 140 lines, a vast labyrinth of communal memory, of which the brief "chapters" yield only a tantalizing glimpse. Chapters II and III, along with VII, VIII, and IX, are condensed accounts of eccentric characters who have all been, doubtless, the subject of many a "curious tale that threaded through the town" (*CP*, 26). The central grouping of Chapters IV, V, and VI provides a contrast, juxtaposing to the traditions of the town a more restless milieu occupied by young men with artistic or intellectual aspirations, including the poet himself. As in his later autobiographical poem, *Another Life*, the "chapters" do not follow linear narrative conventions. The sequence has no clear-cut progression, but evokes rather a pluralistic situation in which many divergent lives exist simultaneously; each sonnet might be likened to one of the "islands" of the title.[41] The extremely free handling of sonnet form, which follows neither traditional divisions nor traditional rhyme schemes, augments the sense of unhierarchical pluralities, incomplete closure. And yet connecting motifs gradually emerge, most notably the tension between Christianity and an almost pagan vitalism, along with the disparity between the restless self-consciousness of the young writers in Chapters IV through VI and the torpid resignation of old recluses like Cosimo de Chrétien, Miss Rossignol, and the Jew "who fought / The Falangists *en la guerra civil*" (*CP,* 26). Long since returned from whatever adventures they once had, these have settled into the local way of life and seek no other.

Chapters I and X frame the vignettes between with a prologue and epilogue. The French epigraph, "la rivière dorée," promises an enchanted landscape recalling both the language of myth or fairy tale and the more literal quest for gold that drew colonists to the New World. The opening lines evoke a dreamlike scene in which real and imagined sounds blur into each other:

> The marl white road, the Dorée rushing cool
> Through gorges of green cedars, like the sound
> Of infant voices from the Mission School,
> Like leaves like dim seas in the mind. . . .
>
> (*CP,* 22)

The sound of the river is compared both to the human voices of the children and to the natural voices of rustling leaves, then finally to the sound of "dim seas in the mind," nature internalized by imagination. And yet this dream world is also a very particular place, "*ici,* Choiseul."

The murmurous sound of the river echoes in "the stone cathedral." The redoubled sound, like its primary source, evokes multiple analogies—the cathedral "echoes like a well, / Or as a sunken sea-cave, carved, in sand." One might read this prodigality of metaphor as imaginative plenitude, flowing inexhaustibly from the voices of river and schoolchildren. Alternatively, one might read it as the defeat of imagination by *sensuous* plenitude, as the stunned poet casts about for tropes. The island poet enjoys the inspiration of a sensuously magnificent landscape but also incurs the risk of writing a merely sensuous poetry.

The sound of the river has echoed not in a natural well or cave but in a "cathedral." Religion echoes nature, and so the image of a female saint represents a female body also:

Touring its Via Dolorosa I tried to keep
That chill flesh from my memory when I found
A Sancta Teresa in her nest of light;
The skirts of fluttered bronze, the uplifted hand,
The cherub, shaft upraised, parting her breast.

(*CP,* 22)

The poet, thinking of Bernini's *Ecstasy of St. Theresa,* cannot help responding sexually as well as religiously, as the phrase "skirts of fluttered bronze" attests. However "chill" the metal, it still images "flesh," and the words "shaft" and "breast" have erotic overtones. St. Theresa herself, moreover, described religious experience in erotic language ("the sweetest caressing of the soul by God"),[42] and Bernini's sculpture makes "the saint's ecstasy . . . palpably physical."[43] The sonnet closes with a prayer and an image, run together with no transition but a semicolon:

Teach our philosophy the strength to reach
Above the navel; black bodies, wet with light,
Rolled in the spray as I strolled up the beach.

(*CP,* 22)

Island philosophy must strengthen itself against the overwhelming sensuality of the place. No sooner is the resolve "to reach / Above the navel" uttered than it is tested by the image of "black bodies, wet with light." If the primary force of this image is erotic, the recurrence of "light," again at the end of the line, strongly links these bodies with St. Theresa. Although light reveals sensual beauty, it is also a spiritual illumination, revealing what the senses cannot perceive.

After the opening warning against a poetics—and ethics—of pure sensuality, Walcott follows with portraits of a man and a woman who have rejected sensuality too completely. Cosimo de Chrétien may have "controlled a boarding house," but "His maman managed him." Concerned with his real or imagined noble descent, he finds no suitable marriage partner, remaining "fairly chaste" lest "*un sang impur*" pollute the lineage. (The allusion to "La Marseillaise" ironically reminds us that "impure blood" can be imputed to aristocrats as well as commoners.) This "count of curios" is burdened by his own snobbery. His concern "Never to bring the lineage to disgrace" (*CP,* 23) is especially absurd in the West Indies, with its mixture of races and nationalities.

The third sonnet concerns Miss Rossignol, Cosimo de Chrétien's female counterpart. She was once beautiful, as the poem's epigraph, from Villon's "*Ballade de dames du temps jadis,*" suggests, and has, like de Chrétien, an aristocratic air: "she had white skin, / And underneath it, fine, old-fashioned bones." Miss Rossignol has taken her refuge in the church, but she has known a richer life: "that flesh knew silk / Coursing a green estate in gilded coaches." She is compared to the "Magdalen of Donatello," as if to imply that she does penance for a former career of sexual excess. Neither her self-mortification nor the count's timidity offers the kind of "philosophy" sought in the first sonnet. It is one thing "to reach / Above the navel," another to reject the body from the navel down.

After the two portraits of enervated resignation come three sonnets depicting ambitious young men, full of energy if somewhat pretentious. The first of these bears the epigraph "'Dance of Death,'" hinting that the conversation to follow, for all its apparent vitality, is only a ritual in which the "college boys" talk like artists and intellectuals to impress each other and themselves. The poem begins with an argument about painting already in progress. The speaker replies heatedly to one of his companions, as they approach a bar: "Outside I said, 'He's a damned epileptic / Your boy, El Greco! Goya, he don't lie'" (*CP,* 23). His colloquial language implies a sense of familiarity with these masters and a refusal to be intimidated by European high culture. Weary of aesthetic talk, "Doc" laughs and suggests "'Let's join the real epileptics'" inside the bar:

> Two of the girls looked good. The Indian said
> That rain affects the trade. In the queer light
> We all looked green. The beer and all looked green.
>
> (*CP,* 23–24)

The speaker prefers Goya, but the "queer light" is a mannerist like El Greco. Its painting includes the young intellectuals along with "the real epileptics" inside the bar, the seemingly available "girls" and the drinkers of beer. The philosophical resolve "to reach / Above the navel" yields to a bohemian stereotype of the artist's life, in which alcohol and sex are the wellsprings of inspiration. As the group starts in, one companion "drape[s] an arm around" the speaker, "like a wreath." Given the epigraph "dance of death," "wreath" carries its funereal connotations. The speaker's next words, too, are morbid:

> 'Our mother earth'
> I said. 'The great republic in whose womb
> The dead outvote the quick.'
>
> (*CP,* 24)

The remark implies a cynicism about political change, an awareness of the power of the past to influence the present. At the same time, however, it also suggests an organic continuity with previous generations, despite the common belief that no such continuity exists in the West Indies. The last words, however, belong to the speaker's two companions. "The Indian," speaking creole, cuts the posturing speaker down to size: "Y'all too obscene," he says in objection to the womb metaphor, and besides, "Y'all college boys[44] ain't worth the trouble." At this point, the group finally enters "the bare room." The rhyme of "room" with "womb" hints that the group's fraternizing is also "bare" or barren, unable to assist at the birth of true creation. Sensing this, perhaps, the speaker grows "worried," but Doc reassures him: "'Don't worry, kid, the wages of sin is birth.'" The reversal of St. Paul's warning (*Romans,* 6:23) affirms the bohemian portrait of the artist after all—through "sin" the poetic career is born. (At an earthier level, of course, Doc's remark is also a joke about fathering illegitimate children.)

The tension between Christian and bohemian impulses becomes, in the fifth and sixth sonnets, a more complicated tangle of Christian and African traditions with modern historicism, literary bohemianism, and island hedonism, all of which may contend within a single person. Chapter V, with its epigraph from the title of Montaigne's essay "Of Ancient Customs," describes the reenactment of an animal sacrifice[45] "For the approval of some anthropologist." The priests objected to "such savage rites / In a Catholic country," but "one of the fathers was himself a student / Of black customs; it was quite ironic."[46] The irony extends further if one believes, with the anthropologist James Frazer, in a connection between such Catholic rites as communion and this "savage" one, in which participants "take turns drinking the blood."

Although critics point to Chapter VI as Walcott's first great success in the use of creole, the first linguistic heterogeneity within the speaker's own voice (as opposed to other voices in Chapter IV) occurs in the last eight lines of Chapter V. Mervyn Morris interprets the apparent switch to present tense in lines 7 ("They lead sheep . . ."), 12 ("They tie the lamb up, then chop off the head"), and 13 ("And ritualists take turns . . .") as a switch to creole, which does not change the verb form to register past tense.[47] To hear the lines as creole sets up an ironic juxtaposition with such phrases as "Great stuff, old boy" in line 14 or the entirety of line 10: "The whole thing was more like a bloody picnic." This is the speech of the "Oxbridge" chap in the following section. The contrast effectively registers the tension between the "absolutely natural grace / Remembered from the dark past whence we come" and the academic self-consciousness with which the ceremony has been reconstructed. "Bloody picnic" is both an irritated dismissal of the ritual and a reminder of its disturbing origins.

Chapter VI opens with a burst of energy,[48] as if in protest against the antiquarianism of Chapter V. The syntax of Chapter V grows tighter as the sonnet progresses. Of the last six lines, five are strongly end-stopped, the other partially so. Chapter VI, however, drives forward through eight enjambments before coming to rest a line beyond the traditional placement of a sonnet's turn. The paratactic connective "and," entirely absent in Chapter V, appears seven times. Not only does the speaker switch into broad creole (much further from the acrolect than the modest departures in Chapters IV and V); he suddenly seems to be addressing the reader more intimately: "Poopa, da' was a fête," he begins, and later injects, "don't name me"—this is privileged gossip, just between us. Even the "Black writer chap, one of those Oxbridge guys" gets drunk and forgets himself enough to "quote Shelley" in creole.[49] The affectations of Chapters IV and V fall away.

This "fête" is a real event, not an anthropologist's reconstruction. It too grows out of a violent past, but it has evolved into a joyful tradition sustained by a living culture. And yet, just as one prepares to affirm this chapter as the vital center of the sequence, one remembers the opening sonnet's warning about unreflective sensuality and the critique, in Chapter IV, of the bohemian artist as hell-raiser. To say that the West Indian writer has no "*angst*" may be only another form of the old libel, that West Indians do not participate in history. And it obviously isn't true: the "Oxbridge chap" is anxious enough about his own self-presentation to slip from standard English into creole. He does not know how to place himself in relation to the vital but coarse tradition manifest all around him.

The fête shows up the anthropologists' stuffiness, but an anthropological perspective reveals the blindness of its energies:

> And it was round this part once that the heart
> Of a young child was torn from it alive
> By two practitioners of native art,
> But that was long before this jump and jive.
>
> (*CP*, 25)

However innocent the fête may seem, Walcott juxtaposes it with a disturbing precedent. The last four lines allude to a murder case of 1902 in rural St. Lucia, near Monchy. One Montoute Edmond, who had come to St. Lucia from Haiti, found that his crops were failing. He believed that a human sacrifice would regenerate the land, and with the help of two accomplices, he kidnapped and killed a twelve- or thirteen-year-old boy. His case provides the plot for Roderick Walcott's play, *Malfinis, or The Heart of a Child.*[50] "Long before this jump and jive," perhaps, but recent enough to cast a shadow on the St. Lucian present.

Despite the distance between the Shelley-quoting writer and the Afro-Caribbean traditions of the islands, the murder is motivated by the same magical suppositions as the myths Eliot had imported into *The Waste Land* from Frazer's *The Golden Bough.* Brathwaite's "great" and "little" traditions run eerily parallel here. And if one remembers Edward Trelawny's account of Shelley's cremation, the distance between the English Romantics and Montoute Edmond becomes suddenly bridgeable: "What surprised us all, was that the heart remained entire. In snatching this relic from the fiery furnace, my hand was severely burnt; and had any one seen me do the act I should have been put into quarantine."[51] But the middle sections of the sequence describe a dilemma, not a synthesis. One can neither go back to the unreflective carnality of the fête nor trade one's identity for a new-minted Oxbridge self: after a few drinks, "have" will slide back to "has," and the repressed origins will return.

Chapters VII, VIII, and IX are more insular, less amenable to generalization, than the first six. The only connection among the three is that all represent further varieties of entrapment; Chapter IX, with its depiction of witchcraft and lycanthropy, seems juxtaposed with the Christian "Via Dolorosa" of Chapter I and the self-mortifying piety of the "witch"-like Miss Rossignol in Chapter III. The epigraph of Chapter VII is "lotus eater . . .," as if to suggest that its protagonist has been seduced by the island from his responsibilities elsewhere. The dominant symbol of the poem is "that pool blocked by / Increasing filth that piled between ocean / and jungle," called "'Maingot'" by the local fishermen. It images the stagnation within Franklin, the malaria-ridden expatriate haunted by "memories / Of his own country where he could not die," and even its "sighing grove / Of dry bamboo" mirrors his sadness and desiccation. The bamboo roots are "freckled with light / Like feathers fallen from a migratory sky." As it twice did in Chapter I, the word "light" occurs at the end of a line. Here it offers the only hint of brightness in Franklin's situation, but since it has been casually dropped like the feathers of a migratory bird, it offers little hope: light comes from elsewhere and is bound elsewhere, passing the island by. (The West Indian term for a foreigner temporarily living on the island is "bird of passage.") In the closing lines, spoken from Franklin's point of view, stagnation seems inherent in the place itself:

> In the tea-coloured pool, tadpoles
> Seemed happy in their element. Poor, black souls.
> He shook himself. Must breed, drink, rot with motion.
>
> (*CP*, 25)

The tadpoles become like the European stereotype of the island blacks, "happy in their element" of blind animality. To "breed, drink, rot with motion" is to live without any philosophy at all, let alone one that will "reach / Above the navel." But one cannot dismiss the possibility that stagnation—like the stereotype of the "happy" black—is in the prejudiced eye of the beholder.

Chapter VIII depicts a veteran of the Spanish Civil War who has sunken into a listless old age—or perhaps has actually just died. One cannot be entirely certain, which may be the point. The hour is that "Of bleeding light and beads of crimson dew"; the man is "sunwashed" in the evening light. Everything in the portrait suggests enervation and decay: dust covers the old political pamphlets, a nearby "dish of olives has turned sour," and the veteran's "body, past the age of sweat / Sprawls like a hero, curiously inert." "An ant, caballo, rides" down his nose while "fleas explore a seam of dirt." The "glacial" eye is presumably open, and it is this that suggests death rather than mere unconsciousness—along with the fact that insects walking on one's face are not conducive to sound sleep. Walcott describes this man as an "exile," thus connecting him with the aspiring "college boys" of Chapters IV through VI. He "has the wry face of a Jew," seeming Jewish both in his irony and in his status as racial outsider. Is this the old age that awaits "Doc," "the Indian," and the "Black writer chap" once their youthful energy wanes?

If Chapter VIII may be read as a *memento mori* for the aspiring young, Chapter IX suggests that the terrors hidden beneath the gaiety of the fête have not faded entirely from modern island life. The story is reported indirectly, as "A curious tale that threaded through the town / Through greying women sewing under eaves"—one needn't necessarily believe it, but there are those, even now, who do. "Greed," the story runs, "had brought old Le Brun down"—he had made a "bargain" with "fiends," receiving the power to change himself into an animal. "One night," having "changed himself to an Alsatian hound," he is killed by "his own watchman." The story arouses curiosities that it does not gratify—why did Le Brun strike the bargain, what "scent" was he tracking when he changed himself into a hound? One gathers that the "greying women" already know the tale intimately, so that the barest allusion is enough. They repeat the story to each other in order to share a communal memory, not out of eagerness to inform the uninitiated. One imagines, too, that there must be many other stories like this one, waiting to be retold.

The closing chapter finds the poet on an airplane, bound from St. Lucia toward "the final north." The re-use of this sonnet in Chapter 17 of *Another Life* locates the moment as Walcott's departure in 1950 for the University of the West Indies in Jamaica. He watches the scene below him, where the island is "narrowing the fine / Writing of foam around the precipices." The vivid text of the island's tales grows smaller as the plane rises, much as the lines of foam grow smaller approaching the shore. The island's roads, from this perspective "small and casual as twine / Thrown on its mountains," figuratively recall the legend that "threaded through the town." The fascinating tangle of island lore recedes into the distance. At last, "all that I loved / Folded in cloud," and the flight pushes into estrangement, "each mile / Dividing us and all fidelity strained / Till space would snap it." Just then, the poet's consciousness suddenly empties: "Then, after a while, I thought of nothing." "Nothing" is already a loaded word for Walcott; as he puts it in "Nearing La Guaira," "Nothing is bitter and is very deep" (*GN*, 21–22). Even as he leaves St. Lucia, he prays that nothing "would change," so that he can recover everything upon his return—but also, perhaps, for the opposite reason, that the state of nothingness will change into a sustaining presence. To leave is to break faith but also to gain a more detached perspective. The poet's distance was necessary for him to write these "tales," which end by narrating the departure that made them possible. The epigraph for this section is itself an affirmation of allegiance. Whereas most of the others quote European literature, "*adieu, foulard*" names a West Indian song, traditionally sung on occasions of leave-taking.

The sequence closes in a tone of reportorial objectivity: "When we set down at Seawell it had rained." The fact that "it had rained" must be inferred from the fact that the ground is still wet. To come to a new place is to step at random into a continuing process of local weather and local history, as intricately nuanced, doubtless, as the one just left behind, but as yet unfamiliar. Nor has he yet reached his destination, for Seawell was the name of the old airport in Barbados. There, the young poet is presumably changing planes for the longer flight to Jamaica. The new surroundings will be learned slowly, through countless small inferences analogous to "it had rained." The newcomer, as yet uninitiated, clings to the unadorned data of the senses. The emotional richness of Walcott's poetry needs the sustenance of the milieu he has left behind—the clipped declaration of this sentence contrasts starkly with the language of the poem it closes. And yet by remaining behind, he would risk the fate that has closed in on virtually all of the characters depicted in the sequence—de Chrétien, Miss Rossignol, Franklin. His mind concentrated on "nothing," the poet turns his back on his origins.

From Black Jacobins to Black Jacobeans: *Henri Christophe*

Henri Christophe: A Chronicle in Seven Scenes was the first work of Walcott's to achieve success in England, thanks to Errol Hill's London production of 1952. A Reuters article called Hill's staging of the play "a remarkable achievement which might be said to have laid the foundations . . . of a genuine West Indian drama," and Hill himself called *Henri Christophe* "the finest West Indian play ever written."[52] The play was published in 1950 but finished, according to Walcott's note at the end of the script, in September 1949. Apart from the small private printing by the Barbados Advocate and a mimeograph circulated by the Extra-Mural Department of the University of the West Indies, Mona, the text has been unavailable. But Walcott devoted several paragraphs in "What the Twilight Says: An Overture" to a reconsideration of this early effort, and his remarks serve well as an introduction. Driven by "precocious rage" and "a fear of that darkness that had swallowed up all fathers," he recalls,

> I was drawn, like a child's mind to fire, to the Manichean conflicts of Haiti's history. The parallels were there in my own island, but not the heroes: a black French island somnolent in its Catholicism and black magic, blind faith and blinder over-breeding, a society which triangulated itself medievally into land-baron, serf and cleric, with a vapid, high-brown bourgeoisie. The fire's shadows, magnified into myth, were those of the black Jacobins of Haiti.
>
> They were Jacobean too because they flared from a mind drenched in Elizabethan literature out of the same darkness as Webster's Flamineo.[53]

He had been "in awe of their blasphemy," and although in retrospect "one may see such heroes as squalid fascists who chained their own people," nonetheless "they had size, mania, the fire of great heretics. . . . [T]he Jacobean style, its cynical, aristocratic flourish came naturally to this first play—the corruption of slaves into tyrants." The play's "theme has remained: one race's quarrel with another's God."[54]

As Walcott's wordplay on Jacobin and Jacobean suggests, *Henri Christophe* begins where C. L. R. James's *The Black Jacobins: Toussaint L'Ouverture and the San Domingo Revolution* (1938) ends. James's narrative is concerned primarily with the complex interaction of the Haitian revolution with the French revolution and its international consequences. The central figure is Toussaint, who led the Haitian revolt until his arrest by the French on June 7, 1802. With the achievement of Haitian independence in January 1804, James ends his story, reflecting in a brief epilogue on the implications of the revolution for later years. At the opening of Walcott's play, the news of Toussaint's death in his cell at Jura on April 7, 1803, has just reached Haiti. The play quickly moves to Dessalines's assumption of the title of emperor in October 1804, his assassination (with Henri Christophe's secret approval) in 1806, and the ensuing power struggle between Christophe and Alexandre Pétion, whose republic controlled the southern and western parts of Haiti while Christophe ruled in the north. It ends with Christophe's suicide in 1820, as rebellious army troops were marching on his palace at Sans-Souci. To Walcott's credit, the seventeen-year fictional span goes by quickly. There is a temporal leap between Christophe's coronation (1811) in scene 5 and the final days of Christophe's life in scenes 6 and 7. The play collapses time near its end, so that the death of Archbishop Corneille Brelle in 1817 seems to occur a few hours, rather than three years, before that of Christophe himself. As soon as Christophe, in scene 3, conspires with Pétion to assassinate Dessalines, the pace accelerates, so that Christophe's downfall happens, like Antonio's demise in Webster's *The Duchess of Malfi,* suddenly, "In a mist."

Walcott's postrevolutionary *tristesse* contrasts with James's revolutionary fervor. For James, the Haitian revolution is a sign of hope for the future, pointing the way for the colonies in Africa. For Walcott, the event is one of many in Caribbean history that can be understood as both a birth and a death, or as a still-unfinished beginning. It is but one part of the ambiguous heritage in whose "swaddling cerements" West Indian consciousness is "still bound." Toussaint's generals were able to finish the work of revolution, but without their leader's moral suasion to bind them together, they fell into a struggle for power. "The corruption of slaves into tyrants" is indeed the theme of Walcott's play, though qualified with recognition of a heroic courage in Christophe.

"Christophe is a two-sided mirror," remarks one of his generals. For Christophe is torn between his own ambition and loyalty to the principles of Toussaint, whose memory haunts the action. The fallen leader's "democratic" teachings rebuke Dessalines's monarchic aspirations. Christophe, accordingly, justifies his conspiracy against Dessalines on republican principles: "Kings rule and grow corrupt, / Absolute authority can only disrupt / The church and state" (*HC,* 16). He says to the king's face "In this rule there is an end / Of democracy" (*HC,* 17), criticizing the policies of forced labor ("You keep your own people in virtual slavery") and racial revenge: ("You kill offenders because of their complexion" [*HC,* 18]). In overthrowing Dessalines, however, Christophe becomes very much like him. Driven on by his trusted secretary Vastey, he seeks and receives a crown of his own; he embitters his people by forcing them to labor in the construction of his palaces and his fortress at Ferriere; and, when Vastey deceitfully persuades him that the white Archbishop Brelle harbors racism and treason, he tells the cleric "I am tired of your complexion" (*HC,* 51) and kills him in a fit of suspicious rage.

The events that Walcott leaves out are perhaps as significant as those he emphasizes. Christophe's finest moments as king came in 1814. The Treaty of Paris did not mention Haiti among the Caribbean properties to be divided among the colonizers, leaving the implication that if France chose to reclaim its former colony, England would not protest. The French negotiated with Pétion a payment of compensation for the dispossessed planters and then tried to persuade him "to renounce independence in return for the assurance of being retained as lieutenant-governor."[55] But Christophe, concerned about the possible loss of independence, arrested the French envoy Médina and found papers that proved the French intended not only to repossess the country, but to restore slavery. Pétion and Christophe, from this point, closed ranks to resist a French takeover. Christophe "conceived the macabre plan of giving Médina a state funeral—with the condemned man attending in person."[56] This last anecdote is indeed "Jacobean," reminiscent of such psychological tortures as Flamineo's ruse of the unloaded pistols in *The White Devil* or Ferdinand's gift of a dead man's hand to the Duchess of Malfi. But Walcott omits the incident, unlike Aimé Césaire, who staged it effectively in *La tragédie du Roi Christophe.*[57] Césaire, admiring Christophe less ambivalently than Walcott, prefers to emphasize his hero's fierce defense of Haitian liberty rather than his despotism and self-deceit.

Walcott turns James's Jacobins into Jacobeans partly as an experiment in style, recreating the texture of Jacobean dramatic verse remarkably well at times. But the postrevolutionary Haiti the play depicts also resembles the intrigue-ridden courts of Jacobean plays. In Walcott's play as in those of the Jacobeans, power is everywhere corrupt, and even the clergy is either too ineffectual or itself too corrupt to provide a moral resistance. In such conditions, the temptation of revenge proves irresistible. T. S. Eliot, whose criticism Walcott "cherished" in his youth, describes Webster as "an interesting example of a very great literary and dramatic genius directed toward chaos,"[58] and there was chaos enough in postrevolutionary Haiti. For Eliot, the most influential guide to seventeenth-century literature for Walcott's generation, the Jacobean period marked the last wrenching moment before "a dissociation of sensibility set in, from which we have never recovered,"[59] as England slid toward its own "internal, cormorant war" (*HC,* 3).

In *Henri Christophe,* one can find the beginnings of Walcott's quarrel with "history." The word occurs frequently in the play, especially in scene 2 (when Vastey is urging Christophe to oppose Dessalines), scene 5 (when Christophe is tempted to assume kingship), and scene 7 (when Christophe, facing his imminent death, reflects on the meaning of his career). What "history" means in this play depends largely on who is speaking. For Vastey, history is a game of chess; his metaphor ambiguously positions Christophe as both player and chesspiece:

> My personal advice is: in your talk,
> Do not be too smooth, show your discontent
> At being brushed off the chessboard of history;
> But play the pieces on the board with duplicity,
> Until you are king by the hand of history.
>
> (*HC,* 12)

In only five lines, Vastey has completely tangled the question of agency: first he describes Christophe as a piece swept off the board by Dessalines; then he appeals to him as a cunning strategist directing the game; finally he imagines history itself as playing with no opponent. If the hand of history makes kings, then Christophe's complicity in the killing of Dessalines must be excused. Such treacheries become, as Dessalines says of his slaughter of the whites, "a necessary horror" (*HC,* 23). Here, already implicit, and implicitly condemned, is the "idea of history which justifies and explains and expiates" (*MH,* 27).

Brelle, the Archbishop, speaks of "history" three times as he presides over Christophe's inauguration. He, too, envisions a historical power shaping human purposes: "Let us live like servants / To the inspired intentions history frames today," he tells the assembled people. But one must choose to serve those intentions. Moreover, the word "inspired" implies another power still higher than history's. A few moments later, he links "history" to memory:

> Hold this life precious
> To tell history and children remembering us in queer languages
> By cracked columns, in dusty aisles where weeds
> Are memory's signatures: our breed shall learn
> How men like you [Christophe], Toussaint, Brelle, Dessalines, dead
> Led their own people from embarrassment to insolence,
> Breaking their former masters on their knees.
> Rise and rule well, but never give cause
> To turn these children against themselves and you. . . .
>
> (*HC,* 33)

In this usage, history is less a causal agent than a retrospective interpretation and judgment. When Christophe (at first) refuses the crown, Brelle says "Return my mitre, it has made history." Here, the mitre stands metonymically for Christophe's decision: we make the history we live in, rather than submitting to a power that manipulates us like pieces on a chessboard.

Dessalines, the champion of "necessary horror," is presented throughout with scant sympathy. As the play opens, he complains of the crowd outside the Government Palace waiting for the news from France. "They want, as is only natural, to hear / About Toussaint," explains Pétion, to which Dessalines snarls, "If they are rabble, make them orderly" (*HC,* 2). The messenger is shocked at Dessalines's impassive response to word of Toussaint's death: "I expected to move iron men to tears; / You look as if I had discussed the weather" (*HC,* 2).

One might argue that by making the white archbishop Brelle a strong voice of moral clarification, and by portraying Dessalines as a coldhearted tyrant with almost no mitigating virtues, the young playwright had capitulated to racial stereotypes. Nonetheless, this impression is balanced by the moral authority of the old black general Sylla, the evenhanded portrayal of Pétion, the wisdom of anonymous common people in crowd scenes, and the internal divisions of Christophe himself—and above all, by the memory of Toussaint.

Sylla remains loyal to the values of Toussaint, whose example provides a standard of justice by which others are found wanting. He had hoped the revolution would create "a federation / Of complexions" (*HC*, 31). His presence insures that whites do not have a monopoly on rectitude within the play. Moreover, there is moral intelligence within the folk. When a hired shill agitates the crowd to proclaim Christophe king, a voice calls out "We saw what the sceptre did to Dessalines; / Do we want that repeated?" (*HC*, 38) and warns "that power changes the powerful" (*HC*, 39). The people are not as easily manipulated as Dessalines might wish.

Early in the play, Christophe takes the same positions as Brelle and Sylla, in his suspicion of "Absolute authority" (*HC*, 16), his desire to avoid civil war, his disapproval of racial revenge. He also criticizes the callous Dessalines, who "wastes money like blood" (*HC*, 15) while his people starve. But only when he has convinced himself that "this king is not [his] friend" (*HC*, 23) can he endorse Pétion's call for assassination. His motives are not pure; in addition to his moral outrage, he harbors the same ambitions as Dessalines, for "They want to sit upon an only throne" (*HC*, 23). He begins to agree with Dessalines and Pétion's notion that the end justifies the means. After becoming king, he gives way to grandiose dreams of power and revenge:

> Let us build white-pointed citadels,
> Crusted with white perfections over
> This epilogue of Eden, a prosperous Hayti,
> My kingdom, where I, a king rule,
> Mine, mine Vastey! Once slave,
> Then after that, Napoleon can envy,
> With the Antilles mine, the whole archipelago overturning
> Cauldrons of history and violence on their master's [sic] heads,
> The slaves, the kings, the blacks, the brave.
>
> (*HC*, 41)

Racially, he will turn the tables, attended by "yellow haired serving boys" (*HC*, 41). But as the phrase "white perfections" suggests, he remains caught in the European association of whiteness with civilization and achievement, blackness with savagery. The imagery of light and dark at the close of the play underscores this dualism. As the coronation scene draws to its end, Vastey says: "Let us go in. / It is beginning to get dark" (*HC,* 41). Vastey keeps lighting candles in a vain attempt to relieve the gloom, while Christophe goes down to moral paralysis and suicide.

Perhaps the most significant scene, as a harbinger of Walcott's future development, is the fourth, although it is the shortest and slightest of the seven. Most of it is given to the conversation of the two murderers sent to dispatch Dessalines. Like the "low" characters in Shakespeare, they speak mostly in vernacular prose rather than verse; as noted earlier, theirs is the first use of creole in Walcott's writings.[60] Here, as in many of Walcott's later works, these speakers engage in a sort of "code switching," mixing creole phrases with a higher, more literary diction.[61]

Finally, this impressive early play may raise the question of whether its author may have been too harsh in his judgment of Dessalines and even Christophe while idealizing the memory of Toussaint. Perhaps so, but it is instructive to read what James, much more sympathetic to Dessalines and critical of Toussaint than Walcott, has to say of Dessalines's 1805 massacre of the whites. After pointing out that the French had already "resolved on a war of extermination," to which Dessalines's actions were only a defensive reaction, he nonetheless concludes:

> The massacre of the whites was a tragedy; not for the whites. For these old slave-owners, those who burnt a little powder in the arse of a Negro, who buried him alive for insects to eat, who were well treated by Toussaint, and who, as soon as they got the chance, began their old cruelties again; for these there is no need to waste one tear or one drop of ink. The tragedy was for the blacks and the Mulattoes. It was not policy but revenge, and revenge has no place in politics. The whites were no longer to be feared, and such purposeless massacres degrade and brutalise a population, especially one which was just beginning as a nation and had had so bitter a past. The people did not want it—all they wanted was freedom, and independence seemed to promise that. Christophe and other generals strongly disapproved.[62]

Finally, on this crucial point, James and Walcott are very close, even to the striking parallelism between James's dictum that "revenge has no place in politics" and Walcott's later insistence, in "The Muse of History," that revenge has no place in literature.

Henri Christophe, though not on the level of Walcott's mature writing, is nonetheless an extraordinary accomplishment from a nineteen-year-old who had yet to attend university. Many of the characteristic ideals and stylistic traits of his later work appeared first in this play. Its dramatic verse is sometimes stilted or long-winded (one unimpressed Trinidadian reviewer called it "fustian").[63] But it gives us an Henri Christophe of considerable moral complexity, a character indeed impressive for "size, mania," and "fire."

3

The Young Playwright in Jamaica

When Walcott arrived at the University of the West Indies, he had already achieved precocious success both as a poet and as a playwright, but he had yet to evolve a fully mature style in either role—notwithstanding the promise evident in the best moments of the two earliest books of poetry and of *Henri Christophe*. In 1951, he put together a third locally published collection of poems that remains by and large in the category of juvenilia. Walcott retained only one of its poems, extensively revised, for *In a Green Night* (he reprinted six from *25 Poems*), and neither the *Selected Poems* nor the *Collected Poems 1948–1984* contains any work from the 1951 volume. For the most part, Walcott's greatest accomplishments during his Jamaican residence came in his plays. By the time he moved to Port of Spain and started the Trinidad Theatre Workshop in 1959, he had written two of his best: *The Sea at Dauphin* (1954) and *Ti-Jean and His Brothers* (1957). Especially productive was the transitional period of 1957–1959, from the first Rockefeller-sponsored trip to the United States and Canada to his decision to live in Trinidad. Laurence Breiner remarks that

> [t]he first versions of nearly all the major plays completed by 1970 date from those years, among them *Ione, Ti-Jean and His Brothers, Journard, Malcochon, Franklin*[:] *A Tale of the Islands, Drums and Colours*, and *Dream on Mon-*

> *key Mountain.* After 1959 it appears that Walcott was not writing new plays. In the decade of 1960s he concentrated on poetry. . . .[1]

In this chapter, I shall be mainly concerned with *The Sea at Dauphin* and the official and unofficial products of the Rockefeller commission: *Drums and Colours* and *Ti-Jean and His Brothers.*

Walcott, throughout his career, has often drawn allusive parallels between his writings and notable works from elsewhere in the world. He acknowledges the debt of *The Sea at Dauphin* to Synge's *Riders to the Sea* and of *Malcochon* to Kurosawa's film *Rashomon.* We have already seen how *Epitaph for the Young* recalls both the *Odyssey* and the modernist appropriations of the *Odyssey* in Pound and Joyce. The parallel to the *Iliad* in *Ione* (1957), anticipating the one in *Omeros* by more than thirty years, is hard to miss: two villages erupt in murderous quarreling after the beautiful Helene, daughter of the headman of one village, is caught *in flagrante delicto* with the son of the headman of the other village. Her outraged husband is named Achille.

One might think that Walcott's parallels are simply a way of claiming universality for his West Indian materials. But some of his models, such as Synge, themselves come from a colonial tradition, and some of them, such as Kurosawa, come from outside the European tradition altogether. And both Synge and Kurosawa, like Walcott himself, were interested in parallels between their own traditions and those of the European classics. *Riders to the Sea* was itself likened, first and most notably by Yeats, to Greek tragedy.[2] In 1898, Synge had "attended Professor H. D'Arbois Jubainville's lectures at the Sorbonne in which the ancient Irish civilization was compared with that of Homer's Greece, a comparison he never forgot."[3] Emphasizing the Hellenic parallel runs the risk of reading Synge's play as "an imitation Greek tragedy in little, dressed up in peasant outfit,"[4] just as emphasizing the parallel to *Riders* risks turning *The Sea at Dauphin* into an exotic derivative of an Irish original. But to read either work as merely an attempt to dignify the local garb by hanging it on a prestigious model does serious injustice. Rather, the adopted model changes as it assimilates different cultural energies and circumstances.

The Sea at Dauphin indeed owes much to Synge. We have already seen that Walcott's Irish teachers at St. Mary's impressed upon him the similarity between St. Lucia's colonial situation and Ireland's. Both countries, moreover, are predominantly Catholic and still rooted to an extent in a village, peasant culture that no longer exists in many parts of the world. Walcott's own account of the borrowing stresses the role of language:

> When I read Synge's *Riders to the Sea* I realized what he had attempted to do with the language of the Irish. He had taken a fishing port kind of language and gotten beauty out of it, a beat, something lyrical. Now that was inspiring, and the obvious model for *The Sea at Dauphin*. . . . If you know very clearly that you are mutating such and such a work, it isn't that you're adopting another man's genius, it is that he has done an experiment that has worked and will be useful to all writers afterwards. When I tried to translate the speech of the St. Lucian fisherman into an English Creole, all I was doing was taking that kind of speech and translating it, or retranslating it, into an English inflected Creole, and that was a totally new experience for me, even if it did come out of Synge.[5]

Synge's main "inspiration" to Walcott was his success in "translating" vernacular speech into a heightened dramatic language that brought out its "beauty" and its rhythms. But the beauty had to be made as well as found: random transcription of conversation among Irish or St. Lucian fishermen would not generate either play.

In Walcott's account, the words "mutating," "translating," and "retranslating" all point to the necessity of departing from what is already given—either in Synge's play or in St. Lucian speech—in order to write *The Sea at Dauphin*. Moving the setting from the Aran Islands to St. Lucia meant not only a change of language but a change of cultural milieu. There is no one like Afa or Hounakin in *Riders to the Sea*. These characters could exist in St. Lucia but not in the Aran setting.

Because the most commonly used form of St. Lucian creole has a French rather than an English lexicon, Walcott's first task of translation was a literal one. But an English creole also exists in St. Lucia, so Walcott did not have to invent one entirely from scratch. To help linguistic outsiders, Walcott often makes his characters paraphrase their French creole phrases with English creole equivalents. He builds the repetitions into the cadence of their speech with remarkable skill, so that one almost never has the feeling that the gloss is an extraneous imposition. For the extended patois song of the "chorus of Dauphin women" (*DMMOP*, 69–70), he simply follows each stanza with a more or less standard English version. This is the only part of the play where, in a production, one would have to choose between creole and a mediating translation.

Not only an English or American audience, but an audience from other islands of the West Indies too, might struggle with the language of *The Sea at Dauphin*. As Walcott remarked to Edward Hirsch, "[e]very island in the Caribbean has its own syntactical structure: a Trinidadian is not going to understand a Jamaican the first time off."[6] The idiom of the play struck Slade Hopkinson, reviewing a Jamaican production, as "a little difficult for the non-St. Lucian," although it "is clarified for the spectator through dramatisation."[7] The version of the script that appeared in 1970 in *Dream on Monkey Mountain and Other Plays* goes noticeably lighter on the patois than the version published ten years earlier in *Tamarack Review.* The difference is evident in the opening moments of the play, where "vent raide, eh?" has been changed to "Wind hard, eh?" and the question "Ko Debel?" becomes "Where Debel?"; other patois phrases ("kai veni," "Trop rhum pas bon") have simply been dropped.[8] Apparently, Walcott had concluded in the intervening years that foreign readers needed a few more concessions than the earlier version had given them.

Walcott is no more literal in adhering to Synge than in adhering to spoken patois. *Riders to the Sea,* though it concerns the dangers besetting fishermen, tells its story largely through the women who survive them. Bartley, the only male among the four characters, is offstage for the last ten of the script's fifteen pages and is none too garrulous in the first five. In *The Sea at Dauphin,* women appear briefly and anonymously, entering as a chorus and speaking only a few individual lines assigned to "a woman," "another," and "first woman." Like so many of Walcott's plays since, *The Sea at Dauphin* depicts a predominantly male realm of experience.

The characters in *Riders to the Sea,* however deeply they mourn their losses, accept them stoically as inalterable fate. Yeats, in fact, preferred *In the Shadow of the Glen,* finding *Riders* "too passive in suffering."[9] There are, at most, brief flickerings of rebellion, as in Maurya's flash of resentment against the "young priest" who counsels trust in God but fails to stop Bartley from going on his fatal errand:

> Nora. Didn't the young priest say the Almighty God wouldn't leave her destitute with no son living?
>
> Maurya (*in a low voice, but clearly*). It's little the likes of him knows of the sea.[10]

Maurya senses something unjust, even unnatural, about the brevity of the fishermen's lives: "In the big world the old people do be leaving things after them for their sons and children, but in this place it is the young men do be leaving things behind for them that do be old."[11]

A distance almost as wide as the Atlantic itself separates such furtive muttering from the blasphemous and anticlerical tirades of Walcott's Afa:

> God is a white man. The sky is his blue eye,
> His spit on Dauphin people is the sea.
> Don't ask me why a man must work so hard
> To eat for worm to get more fat. Maybe I bewitch.
> You never curse God, I curse him, and cannot die,
> Until His time.
>
> (*DMMOP,* 61)

As for priests, white men from abroad who are forever "saying *bettise* about God" (*DMMOP,* 71), they are parasites on a land too poor to afford them. "Dauphin people build the church and feed you, not their own people, and look at Dauphin!" says Afa to Père Lavoisier:

> *Gadez lui!* Look at it! You see? Poverty, dirty women, dirty children, where all the prayers? Where all the money a man should have and friends when his skin old? Dirt and prayers is Dauphin life, in Dauphin, in Canaries, Micoud. Where they have priest is poverty. (*DMMOP,* 73–74)

Through Afa's railings, Walcott gives his play a political edge absent in Synge's: the church appears as an exploitative instrument of colonial domination, and Père Lavoisier is not merely naïve like Synge's young priest, but willfully blind. It should surprise no one that this play got Walcott into more trouble with the church than anything else he ever wrote, while *Riders* became the "only safe play" by Synge to produce after the *Playboy* riots had made him notorious.[12]

Other characters regard Afa as embittered, lacking compassion or the capacity for love: he is a magnificent pariah. Yet anger and bitterness are not his alone. Augustin, Afa's fishing partner or "mate," quarrels with him, curses him as "*cooyon*" and "*salop,*" and finally rushes forward, ready to strike him with a stone until Hounakin intervenes (*DMMOP,* 50, 55–56). Gestures in *Riders to the Sea* express grief or agitation but not anger. In *The Sea at Dauphin,* however, gestures become increasingly charged with barely restrained violence. Afa "*shakes* [Hounakin] *roughly*" until Augustin threatens him with a cutlass (*DMMOP,* 63–64); in his climactic denunciation of Père Lavoisier, Afa hurls a bucket of fish to the sand and says "That is God! A big fish eating smaller ones." Then he tears the scapular from his own neck and throws it down as well, disavowing the faith it represents (*DMMOP,* 73–74). From this point onward, the play becomes gentler, but one could hardly fault it, as Yeats did Synge's, for being "too passive in suffering."

Walcott likes to tell on himself the story of how, upon asking a group of fishermen to suggest suitable names for his hero, he misheard the creole pronunciation of "Arthur" as the exotically African "Afa."[13] One might take this story as his wry acknowledgment that although he is St. Lucian, he too remains slightly removed from the Catholic, peasant culture of his characters. But even if he is no fisherman's son, his play shows considerable insight into the milieu of its characters, as a North American reader may confirm by reading Jane C. Beck's extensive interviews with a St. Lucian fisherman, the late Alexander Charles. Her informant, like Afa, fishes on the windward side of the island and prides himself on courage in the face of danger: "you've got to have sense to fish, and to fish up to windward of the land you've got to be a hero." Like Afa, he is stubbornly independent: "when you're fishing you follow no man." He is, again like Afa, no orthodox Catholic. He is not only a fisherman but an obeah man, and people attribute his fishing prowess to the assistance of the devil. He has some of Afa's bitterness too, and is well aware of the hardness of his life: "Ah, this thing you call a fisherman—it's a terrible job." And, on another occasion: "You think the ocean is nice? The ocean has got no friend." Before settling on fishing, he had engaged in other occupations that bring to mind other Walcott characters: he began as a charcoal-burner like Makak in *Dream on Monkey Mountain,* and like Shabine in "The Schooner *Flight,*" he has engaged in smuggling.[14]

Walcott's imagined fisherman departs from Beck's literal one first of all in his enhanced powers of language, his syntactical control and metaphorical invention. Charles's language has the vividness of its idiom, but Afa's combines, as Walcott intended, the playwright's "own individual poetic sensibility with the strength of the root, the mass racial sensibility of expression."[15] Second, Afa has a critical distance from the culture that has produced him. He arrives by his own observation at something like the familiar Marxist critique of religion as the opiate of the people: the church teaches the poor to accept this world and postpone hope to another, and in so doing it makes effective protest unthinkable. This insight makes Afa an exceptional character rather than simply a representative instance of his class.

Aside from Afa, the most memorable character in *The Sea at Dauphin* is Hounakin, the East Indian, "more old than Dauphin self," who remembers a time "when it didn't have no Dauphin, only cane, and a green river by the canes" (*DMMOP,* 66–67). It is from those canes, rather than fishing, that he once got his living. Now, old and poor, still mourning the death of his wife and too proud to beg, he asks to join Augustin and Afa in their boat. They refuse to take him. The disappointed Hounakin promises Augustin that he "will not kill himself" (*DMMOP*, 69), but when the fishermen return they find that, whether by choice or chance, he is dead: "he fall down from the high rocks by Point Side. His face mash up" (*DMMOP*, 73). Père Lavoisier's attempt to cheer the villagers up by assuring them that Hounakin "had God" triggers Afa's blasphemous tirade.

Afa's harsh treatment of Hounakin expresses the scorn of a fisherman for a landlubber. But it is not depicted as an instance of hostility between creoles and East Indians. As Augustin's godfather, Hounakin has been brought into a creole family across racial lines. And Hounakin's death elicits whatever compassion Afa is capable of, even though it takes the form of anger at the priest's empty consolation rather than overt tenderness. In depicting the bond between Augustin and Hounakin as stronger than their differences of race, culture, and occupation, Walcott affirms his ideal of a West Indian identity that subsumes difference.

As Walcott's own commentary suggests, *The Sea at Dauphin* is first and foremost a language experiment. James Joyce thought *Riders* had substituted lyrical language for sound Aristotelian plot construction (in this respect it was not Greek enough), and one might make a similar complaint about *The Sea at Dauphin*—which would survive the objection, as Synge's play survived Joyce's. What carries both plays is the surge of their language, the sense of releasing lyrical possibilities in the speech of people whose lives might seem, to an unsympathetic observer, as hard and barren as the rocks of Aran or Dauphin themselves.

Walcott's verbal music, like the gestures of his actors, is harsher than Synge's. It displays what he described to Hirsch as "the sort of extravagant care that the West Indian takes in cursing someone else."[16] It becomes a human countervoice to the seething of wind and water, a Stevensian violence from within pressing against the violence from without. Some of the *patois* vocabulary concerns implements used in fishing—*nasse* (net), *calabasse* (calabash)—but the staples of conversation are *cooyon* (fool), *garce* (bitch), and *salop* (slut; these last two may apply to men as well as women).[17] And yet the same fishermen who address each other by these terms of abuse prove capable of a gentleness that is the more poignant for their concealment of it. Even the flinty Afa, stone-hearted as the Dauphin land itself, knows that he denies his feelings because he could not bear the pain they would bring:

> And this new thing, compassion? Where is compassion? Is I that put
> rocks where should dirt by Dauphin side, man cannot make garden

> grow? Is I that swell little children belly with bad worm, and woman to wear clothes white people use to wipe their foot? In my head is stone, and my heart is another, and without stone, my eyes would burst for that, would look for compassion on woman belly. (*DMMOP,* 53)

Afa's response to the futility of Dauphin life is to narrow his attention to the practical tasks of survival from one moment to the next. Whereas *Riders to the Sea* ends with a resigned bow to necessity—"No man at all can be living forever, and we must be satisfied"[18]—*The Sea at Dauphin* ends with Afa's request to Gacia for help in furling the sail. Afa means to go on living, if not forever, then at least for another day.

"Derek's 'Most West Indian Play'": *Ti-Jean and His Brothers*

Just before he embarked on his travels in preparation for *Drums and Colours,* Walcott finished *Ione,* produced in March 1957 at the Ward Theatre in Jamaica. This play shares some features with *Ti-Jean and His Brothers* and *Drums and Colours,* the plays that emerged from his commission. In *Ione,* as in *Ti-Jean,* the play emerges from a folk narrator's introduction; *Drums and Colours* is framed by the opening scene of its own organization as a carnival pageant. In all three plays, the frame connects the dramatic performance to folk traditions of performance, but it also has something in common with Brecht's attempt to create a new "epic theatre" that does not aim at "the engendering of illusion" and thus "will stop pretending not to be theatre." Instead of "implicat[ing] the spectator in a stage situation," it "turns the spectator into an observer," demanding ethical judgment of, rather than empathy with, the proceedings on the stage.[19] Walcott has cited Brecht as one of the influences behind *Ti-Jean* (especially its "distancing of characters"),[20] but by framing the plot of *Ione* as a storyteller's narration, Walcott already reminds his audience, in Brechtian fashion, that what it sees is "a demonstration" only, and not "the actual event."[21] To that objectification of the narrative, *Malcochon* and *Ti-Jean* would add the extensive and stylized use of dance and music that Brecht (and Brecht's appropriation of Japanese and Chinese theatrical conventions) suggested to Walcott. The play also has links to still later works, in its use of a parallel to Homer (two villages fight over a woman named Helene, and her husband is named Achille) and in its presentation of a somewhat different version of the *conte* of Ione that would appear nineteen years later in the poem "Sainte Lucie." As Walcott writes in a note for the poem, the song was "heard on the back of an open truck travelling to Vieuxfort, some years ago" (*CP*, 314).

Bruce King quotes Roderick Walcott as crediting the 1957 Summer School for Dance and Drama at UCWI, Mona—at which time *Ione* had already been written—with a key contribution to his brother's conception of West Indian drama. Beryl McBurnie, the Trinidadian dancer whose Little Carib Theatre would become the first home of the Trinidad Theatre Workshop, was its dominant presence. Through her work, "Derek saw the possibilities of using the West Indian body rhythms, movements, and gestures that the dancers had developed as the basis for an acting style."[22] Perhaps it was McBurnie's example that accounts for the increased presence of song and stylized representation of action in Walcott's next play, *Ti-Jean*. He had already recognized that something within West Indian tradition resembled the nonrealistic conventions of Brechtian drama or Noh theater; McBurnie showed him another possible convergence of these foreign influences with West Indian traditions.

In an article for the *Trinidad Guardian* in 1970, Walcott recalled, as the editorial note put it, "how he created what he calls his 'most West Indian play,' and the source of its creation."[23] One might have expected that play to be *Drums and Colours*, commissioned for the inaugural ceremonies of the West Indies Federation in 1958. Yet it was not the commissioned epic pageant, but a play that sprung from him unbidden, that seemed to him most deeply grounded in West Indian experience. In 1957, after going to Stratford, Ontario to seek help from Tyrone Guthrie with the commissioned play "still hugely indistinct in [his] head," he went to New York:

> I had not yet begun "Drums and Colours." Yet, in spite of an incredibly short deadline, but during a five day stay in New York, my first visit there, out of sheer terror of the place, and a fierce but illuminating nostalgia for the untheatrical simplicities of Saint Lucia, the island where I was born, I had written "Ti-Jean and His Brother[s]," and I mention the swift but gushing place [*sic*] of the play's creation because most of my plays have taken me ten years to get into satisfactory shape.

"The epic history," Walcott continues,

> was written under commission to intense pressure, which is another good day of working if you are a professional playwright, but the small geyser of joy which was "Ti-Jean and His Brothers" is an experience which I remember with amazement and delight . . . and the reason why

> I record this is that it ejects, like all springs, a clear and natural truth: it was the least forced, the most spontaneous, the least laboured of my plays so far, both in rhythm and in concept. It was the most West Indian thing I had done and it was created under the pressure of sudden loneliness and exile.

Walcott depicts his most West Indian play, created under the least West Indian circumstances, in language that reminds one of Wordsworth's definition of poetry as "the spontaneous overflow of powerful feelings."[24] It is elemental, informed with a "natural truth" rather than a merely cultural one, and like a spring it wells up from beneath the ground, from "the African art of the story-teller . . . whose mode goes as far back [as] and even past the tribal memory." The origin of the play is simultaneously tied to a particular place (St. Lucia) and tradition (African storytelling) and to something more primal, antedating the identity of any "tribe." Ultimately, the story belongs to a "world peasant mythology" whose "source is Protean and universal." *Drums and Colours,* in contrast, was a project built to specification.

Drums and Colours attempts to gather many eras and many islands in its pan–West Indian sweep, as opposed to the insular specificity of *Ti-Jean,* which draws on St. Lucian creole and folklore. Whereas the commissioned play deals with historical events, *Ti-Jean* renders history indirectly, as myth and parable. *Drums and Colours* is grandly theatrical, drawing on the pomp of the inaugural ceremony itself and the style of Trinidad carnival; *Ti-Jean,* so Walcott claims, looks nostalgically back to "the untheatrical simplicities" of the smaller, less worldly St. Lucia.

In parts of his retrospective essay, Walcott seems uneasy with his own idealization of *Ti-Jean.* "Later such simplicities seemed childish, primitive, too artless, and for several years later I avoided and almost despised the play for its folksiness," he confesses. As "the sort of self-torturing, convoluted, multiple-draft writer who is contemptuous of speed," he felt that "this play had leapt to life too fast." He reconciles his ambivalence about *Ti-Jean* by crediting it with a synthesis important to his development. Though its accentual lines of two or three beats seemed "almost moronic in their lilt," that "metre . . . was more instinctual yet more formal than prose, and one comes across such revelations not by accident, but because somewhere, under intense pressure, under the pain of the folk memory a formal and rigorous training in all aspects of metric will fuse into truth." Here, motifs associated with *Drums and Colours*—"pressure," hard work, professional skill—join those associated with *Ti-Jean:* instinct, folk memory, and childlike simplicity. "Formal and rigorous training" must fuse with "folk memory" and dissolve the dualism that separates them.

The success of a play like *Ti-Jean,* which attempts to join the resources of sophisticated literacy to those of West Indian storytelling, folk song, and dance depends first of all on finding performers who know their way around in both contexts: they have to be at home in both the conventions of creole folktale and those of world theater (the essay mentions Brecht and Noh plays as influences). Though it need not respond at all levels, ideally, the audience too would be at home in both traditions.

The "Prologue" immediately establishes the double frame of reference. The first speakers are a frog and a cricket, as one might expect in a folk tale. The first words from the frog, "Greek-croak," initiate a series of puns on "crik crak," the formulaic phrase by which West Indian storytellers signal the beginning and the end of a narrative. The play, true to the folkloric convention, repeats the formula at its end, closing with the frog's "Messieurs, creek. Crack" (*DMMOP,* 166). But the wordplay makes classical as well as folkloric allusions. "Greek-croak" recalls not only "crick-crack" but also the onomatopoeic chorus in Aristophanes' *The Frogs.* And when he sneezes, the frog puns: "Aeschylus me!" (*DMMOP,* 86). The audience needs to know both West Indian oral conventions and Western literature to get the jokes.

Of Walcott's efforts to fuse "formal and rigorous training" with "folk memory," this one concedes most to folk tradition. In contrast to *The Sea at Dauphin* and *Malcochon,* there is no attempt to "mutate" a text from another culture into a West Indian shape. There are a few passages of elevated diction, most notably at the beginning and the end, when Walcott is framing the narrative. The few classical allusions, except for the poor mother's Sophoclean "Look, perhaps it is luckiest / Never to be born, / To the horror of this life" (*DMMOP,* 96), are mostly comic rather than sententious, as in Mi-Jean's remarks on Socrates:

> In Chapter Five from para-
> Graph three, page 79,
> This book opines how Socra-
> Tes would have been better off blind.
> God gave him eyes like all of we,
> But he, he had to look.
> The next thing, friends, was jail, *oui!*
> Hemlock and him lock up.
>
> (*DMMOP,* 122)

The character in *Ti-Jean* who puts most faith in books and learning is Mi-Jean, whose intellectual pride leads only to defeat at the hands of the Devil.

The political allegory of the play is effective, simple, and therefore not in great need of commentary. Walcott has given the Devil two masks: he can appear, as in the folk tale, as Papa Bois, the Old Man of the Woods, or as a white planter. One might take these as the general and historically particular avatars of evil: though the Devil can take any shape and any complexion, in the St. Lucian context he is the colonizer. The successive encounters of the three brothers, then, may be taken as the story of successive attempts to respond to colonial oppression. The eldest, Gros-Jean, trusting his "arm of iron" to bring him success, labors mightily for the Planter, only to find that his sole reward is further exploitation. Mi-Jean trusts only his book learning; he might be said to represent the first generation of colonial intellectuals, overeager to prove their equality. Ti-Jean, however, trusts his instincts and succeeds; unlike his brothers, he is not alienated from himself. They have objectified one part of themselves—physical strength or intellect—and deemed it all-sufficient. Ti-Jean responds as a feeling rather than a calculating person, and he knows that neither he nor his own abilities can be self-sufficient. He alone speaks courteously to the animals, and the bird reciprocates by providing important help in his victory over the Planter. Walcott gets some good comic theater out of Mi-Jean's pretentious language, rather like the Robber-Talk of Carnival, except that the Midnight Robber knows he is speaking meaningless rant, whereas Mi-Jean thinks he is saying something profound.

The allegorical role of the three brothers seems straightforward enough, the humor at the expense of Mi-Jean immediately accessible. But two other prominent features of the play provoke further thought. One is the peculiar wager the Devil makes with each of the three brothers in turn, and the other is the role of his familiar spirit, the Bolom. A bolom, in West Indian folklore, is the spirit of a foetus that did not succeed in being born. It is kept by an obeah adept, who must feed it in order to keep it alive. It lives in corners or under beds and can move with great speed, and it can harm the living at the command of its master.

It is the Bolom, speaking on behalf of the Devil, who announces the terms of the wager. He explains that the Devil "is dying to be human," so that he can "enjoy / Those vices he created" (*DMMOP,* 99). Therefore, if anyone can make him feel anger, that person will be rewarded, but anyone who tries and fails will be eaten. Moreover, if one of the sons succeeds in making the Devil angry, the Bolom too "shall feel life" (*DMMOP,* 100). The linkage of the Bolom, as an image of the unborn West Indian soul, with the Devil suggests that West Indians are still serving the wrong master, not yet free of internalized colonial ideas. More curious is the notion of a Devil who *wants* to lose his bet, yet works as hard as he can to win, and then, when he finally does lose, tries to renege on the terms. The Devil thus becomes a divided being, weary of his own role as tormentor. One might read into this portrait an oblique recognition of the fact that Britain was planning to relinquish the islands voluntarily, whether out of bad conscience, diminished profits, or some impure combination of both. In addition, one might read it as a commentary on the perversity of evil: although the Devil yearns to escape his role, it is the law of his being to play it, though it gives him no satisfaction—or because it gives him no satisfaction: part of his damnation is his imprisonment in an essential emptiness, a privation of even diabolical good.

The other curious feature is the role of anger in the terms of the bet. In the Bolom's initial announcement, the brothers must make the Devil angry in order to win, and will lose if they fail to do so. But within the play, the terms become implicitly different: whoever gets angry first loses. From the Devil's point of view, then, anger is a humanizing emotion. If he can feel it, he will be that much less a devil, more nearly a man. But from the human point of view, anger represents a temptation to be resisted. It is a loss of self-control that makes one vulnerable to enemies and exploiters, and perhaps also a diminution of one's own moral stature as well. We have seen that even in the early *Henri Christophe* Walcott distrusts revenge or revolutionary anger. His characteristic stance, as he says in his essay on *Ti-Jean*, is "self-torturing." His anger is released in an internal quarrel, not directed outward. In this respect, the character most like Walcott's lyric persona is the Devil himself!

Certainly, Walcott has not shied away from depicting anger in his poems and plays: Afa rages eloquently in *The Sea at Dauphin;* Lestrade delivers bitter tirades in *Dream on Monkey Mountain,* and Walcott unleashes fury in poems such as "The Schooner *Flight,*" "The Spoiler's Return," or the nineteenth chapter of *Another Life.* But in his work, anger is seldom a liberating emotion.[25] Formal resolution arrives only when anger has been overcome, so that Shabine can make his peace with the sea, or Makak can go back to "the green beginnings of this world." In *Ti-Jean,* the emotion that finally humanizes the Devil is not anger but sorrow:

> What is this cooling my face, washing it like a
> Wind of morning. Tears! Tears! Then is this the

> Magnificence I have heard of, of
> Man, the chink in his armour, the destruction of the
> Self? Is this the strange, strange wonder that is
> Sorrow? You have earned your gift, Ti-Jean, ask!
>
> (*DMMOP,* 162–63)

The Devil is weeping not for himself, but in response to the beauty of Ti-Jean's singing, inspired by grief at the death of his mother. As in the poem "Ruins of a Great House," "All in compassion ends."

Immediately after the Devil achieves humanity, the Bolom chooses to be born, though warned by Ti-Jean "what it bring" (*DMMOP,* 162). The Bolom has described himself as

> a child which was strangled
> Who never saw the earth light
> Through the hinge of the womb,
> Strangled by a woman
> Who hated my birth,
> Twisted out of shape,
> Deformed past recognition. . . .
>
> (*DMMOP,* 97)

Ti-Jean's mother addresses it as "Child of the Devil" (*DMMOP,* 94) and asks it "What does your white master / The Devil want from us?" (*DMMOP,* 98). If it is indeed the Devil's child, and the Devil is, in one of his avatars, a white Planter, one might infer that it is the child of a coerced union between a Planter and a black woman, who has killed it as slave mothers sometimes killed their babies to spare them a life of bondage. More generally, and with surer warrant, one may read it as an emblem of cultural strangulation and deformation of identity ("deformed *past recognition*"). It is the motif of death in birth, or birth in death, that we have encountered in "Laventille" with its image of the West Indian people "still bound" in "swaddling cerements" (*CP,* 88). To be still bound is to be stillborn as well. Only when the Planter Devil has been defeated can the cerements become cradle clothes. If the Devil can make you angry, Walcott implies, he still has power over you. As the Planter himself says, "the Devil comes in through apertures" (*DMMOP,* 126), and to be angry is to create an opening.

Federalist Pageantry: *Drums and Colours*

Drums and Colours, the job of work that Walcott escaped from in writing *Ti-Jean,* is his most public play, designed for an important occasion. Whether constrained by the terms of the commission or fired with hope for the West Indian Federation, Walcott in this play trusts more than elsewhere in a political ideal, the federal vision of a pan–West Indian unity that would overcome regional and racial tensions. "The stage," Walcott's directions tell us, "is set with a centrepiece of regimental and African drums, with the flags of Britain, France, Spain and Holland."[26] Out of the African presence, symbolized by the drums, and the four principal European colonizing nations, the new West Indian state will emerge. *Drums and Colours* begins with the spectacle of its own organization, as an event in Trinidadian carnival. Mano, the organizer of the revels (and also, like those he summons, a character within the play), calls "Ram, Pompey, Yette, Yu" to help him with his "plan": "we going change round the carnival. / They bound to pass this alley, like I hear them approaching, / Position yourself, we going ambush this roadmarch!"

Just seven lines into the play, Walcott has already evoked the racial history of the Caribbean, and especially of Trinidad. Mano and Yette are Afro-Caribbean; Ram and Yu, as their names suggest, are Indian and Chinese. Later in the play we encounter a Jew who has fled to the New World from Spanish persecution; Paco, who is half Spanish and half Taino; and Anton, the illegitimate son of a slave woman and a Haitian planter, passed off as a racially ambiguous "nephew." The pageant includes events in Trinidad (Raleigh's last expedition), Jamaica (scenes set in 1830 and 1833, on the brink of abolition, with the Morant Bay rising of 1865 as the main action), and Barbados (a comic encounter between a dignified Barbadian steward and a disorderly English sailor). Thus he touches on the three most populous and economically powerful territories of the new Federation. A fourth island, Hispaniola, though not part of the Federation, is crucial as the site of both Columbus's settlement and the Haitian Revolution, "the only successful slave revolt in history."[27] These plots are discontinuous, part of the disjointed "non-history" that Glissant describes, but in a larger sense part of a single process of colonization, creolization, and decolonization, extending over the vast time span of the action. Introducing the play to the audience, Pompey sings:

Now you men of every creed and class
We know you is brothers when you playing mass,

White dance with black, black with Indian,
But long time, it was Rebellion[.]

We are asked to look back from a present characterized by harmony of the races and classes to an angrier era, "The painful birth of democracy" (*DC,* 3).

In adopting Carnival as the emblem of West Indian unity, Walcott was merely borrowing a commonplace. But many observers of Trinidad in the late 1950s remarked that the commonplace was somewhat tendentious. Ivar Oxaal ascribed this attitude to Trinidadian "middle class Creole ideology," which tended "to regard Carnival as a 'national' festival when it in fact is almost exclusively a Creole event."[28] Quite apart from its idealization of the present, the play runs into problems of dramatic organization in the attempt to bring its disparate events, widely separated in space and time, into relation with each other. In his "Author's Note," Walcott says that "the scenes are so arranged that interested producers can excise shorter, self-contained plays from the main work" (*DC,* 2). But do they make a unified work when performed together? How does one narrate and stage a Glissantian nonhistory, whose unity, if it has one, is hidden, "submarine"?

The main form of connection is the transatlantic voyage, linking the various West Indian episodes to the European metropolis where the fate of the islands has been decreed. The "strait-stitching schooners" that "thread archipelagoes" in the poem "A Sea Chantey" also stitch this play together. Significantly, the action begins not with Columbus's arrival in the New World, but with his departure, in chains, for Europe. With him sails Paco, son of a Spaniard and a Taino; he is an early product of New World *mestizaje.* From Cadiz Paco wanders to England, and in his embittered old age he encounters the young Walter Raleigh.[29] His malicious confirmation of the fable of Eldorado sends Raleigh, years later, on his fool's errand to the Caribbean. Mano, the leader of a Jamaican band of maroon rebels, gets his faith that "God on the side of the right cause" from "an old Jew long time gone" who "teach that to my great great grandfather" (*DC,* 86). The audience recognizes that Mano is descended from the enslaved boy whom the Jew bought, in an act of compassion, on the wharf of Cadiz in 1510, and raised as his own son in the New World. The connecting threads of the play, in order to stitch the archipelago together, must include Europe in their crewel-work.

Walcott provides a symbolic motif, appearing at the beginning of the play and again at the end, in the gold coin that Quadrado, an officer loyal to Columbus, gives Paco as a memento. First given in 1499, this coin turns up 366 years later in the possession of Calico, a ruined Jamaican planter who defects to the rebels. Like the gold doubloon nailed to the mast in *Moby-Dick,* it suggests multiple meanings. It is, first of all, the visible sign of colonial greed: it was the rumor of gold that brought the Spanish to the New World in the first place, and that lured Raleigh to his ruinous search for Eldorado. Quadrado acknowledges the moral, though he universalizes it instead of applying it specifically to the Spaniards: "The true stamp of acquisitive man is here, / Compounded in his image, not his maker's." Conventionally a symbol of purity, gold becomes for Quadrado a "pus-crusted metal" (*DC,* 11). At the same time, he reminds Paco "[t]hat gold outlasts the wearer." The coin is a reminder of the transience of human power but also of the persistence of human greed: generations come and go, but the quest for gold continues. As he hands the coin over, Quadrado says, "Here keep our God" (*DC,* 12). Gold, then, is also an idol. The worship of gold, unfortunately, is Columbus's most lasting legacy to the New World, though his name means Christ-bearer. And finally, as money, the unit of exchange, the coin suggests that the unifying fact of colonial history is commodity exchange extended to all parts of human life, with slavery as its most extreme and violent example.

In the Morant Bay episode that closes the pageant, the ruined planter Calico wanders into Mano's camp of rebels, ready to go over to their side. When Mano demands that he contribute to their treasury, Calico offers the coin. As he surrenders it to Ram, Mano shouts, "Well, ain't it an Indian you giving it to, and ain't it an Indian them did wrangle it from?" (*DC,* 88). Symbolically, Calico's donation puts paid to the account of colonial exploitation. Amerindian and East Indian, conflated in Mano's witticism, fuse in a composite West Indian identity.

Although Walcott's play does not ignore the violence of the colonial past, it focuses on ruined or penitent colonizers. We meet Columbus and Raleigh at the moment of their undoing; we do not see Calico as a whip-wielding planter, but as a hapless bankrupt throwing in his lot with the newly emancipated slaves. Columbus recalls that he "was a weaver's son," and "could not guess the web of destinations / That [he] would weave within the minds of men" (*DC,* 16). "Hypocrites and malefactors have wrecked my work," he laments, insisting that he "did all for God, and the lion of Castile" (*DC,* 17). Las Casas blesses him with "this hand that fights for the Indians' cause" (*DC,* 6). Columbus, according to the new governor Bobadilla, has been removed because he dares "to contradict their majesties' edicts / Against these Indians who are their native subjects," and because he has permitted "indiscipline" (*DC*, 6). The worst brutality, we infer, will come under Columbus's successor, while the discoverer is punished for being too humane. In the next episode, though Raleigh clings to his delusions, his captive, the Spanish governor of Trinidad de Berrio, realizes that "there is no El Dorado," and knows "the terrible expense / When men or nations turn to beasts for gold" (*DC*, 47). He sees the colonizing mission as "of a finished age, the age of conquest, cruelty. / The gold is veining out" (*DC*, 46). After the battle in the Jamaican episode, an English sergeant regrets having killed Pompey:

> I had nothing against the little fellow but my job,
> And that I can't think about. I'm sure you'll win through.
> There's many in England, and all over the world
> Who wish you the best.
>
> (*DC*, 97)

Walcott's colonizer, in this play, seems almost as reluctant as his Devil in *Ti-Jean*.

There are reluctant rebels too, most notably Toussaint L'Ouverture. When Dessalines exclaims "It is a new age, the black man's turn to kill" (*DC*, 72), Toussaint replies, "Then we are no better, revenge / is very tiring" (*DC*, 73). He is tormented by the turn of events he has unleashed: "I hate this now it is all finished" (*DC*, 74). When he encounters his former master, Calixte, the two men accuse each other of the cruelties wrought by each side. "I was never cruel. It was the times," Calixte exclaims, complaining of the "slaughtering of children" by "a rabble, turned savage as wild pigs" (*DC*, 74–75). Toussaint replies by recalling "those years / when we were whipped and forced to eat our excrement, / Were peeled alive, pestered with carnivorous ants." "All of a sudden . . . / You have grown a delicate orchid called a conscience / And blame the times." But in the end, both men confess bewilderment. "What is happening to the world, to Haiti?" asks Calixte, and all Toussaint can say is, "O God, I do not know, Monsieur Calixte. I do not know, / I am pushed forward, lifted on the crest of the wave, / Then I am abandoned among the wreckage" (*DC*, 76). Toussaint must bow at last to Dessalines and to pragmatic necessity: "Shoot him. Mr. Calixte, it is the times" (*DC*, 77).

Although *Drums and Colours* makes good on Pompey's promise to the audience to show "*the rod of correction, till rebellion*" (*DC*, 4), both those who wield the rod and those who rebel against it are full of misgivings. As in

Ti-Jean, anger is not a cleansing fire consuming the past away, but a temptation to be resisted because it repeats past cruelties, although oppressed and oppressor may change places. That emphasis on reconciliation certainly fits the occasion of the play, but it is also emblematic of Walcott's abiding distrust of "revenge."

4

Adam's Amnesia: The Uses of Memory and Forgetting

For many years, Walcott has closely associated the idea of the New World Adam with what he called, in a 1965 lecture, "The Figure of Crusoe." In the poem "Crusoe's Journal" (1965), the journal is a West Indian "first book, our profane Genesis / whose Adam speaks that prose / which, blessing some sea-rock, startles itself / with poetry's first surprise" (*CP,* 92). In "Crusoe's Island" (1964), the conflation is still more explicit: Walcott refers to Crusoe as "The second Adam since the fall" (*CP,* 69). The lecture invokes "Crusoe the namer," and of course the naming of the creatures is one of Adam's most important privileges.

After 1965, the Adamic motif begins to appear on its own, while the Crusoe figure lies dormant through the late 1960s and early 1970s, reemerging in the play *Pantomime* (1978). And finally, it combines with yet another myth, that of the wounded archer Philoctetes, in the unpublished play *The Isle Is Full of Noises* (1982), and, less overtly, in *Omeros* (1990). The Adamic motif receives strong emphasis in precisely the years when Crusoe is in abeyance, as Walcott inveighs against the obsession with race and "history" in Trinidad during that period. In Walcott's nomination of Crusoe as "The second Adam" lies the elusive significance of his claims for a New World Adamic poetics, most explicitly put forward in "The Muse of History: An Essay" (1973).[1] For if the defining trait of Adam was his temporal priority to all other men, then the second Adam, on the face of it, would seem no Adam at all. And Robinson Crusoe, though sundered from his previous life after the shipwreck, is nonetheless a man with a past, whose responses to island solitude depend both on the economic rationalism he had learned in England and on the objects he has salvaged from the wreck. In "The Muse of History," Walcott poses Adamic poetics as the alternative to an obsession with the colonial past, and yet its outcome is not erasure of that past, but "the assimilation of the features of every ancestor." What does it mean to speak of an Adam with ancestors? Or, for that matter, to revive the Adamic notion of poetics, prominent during the "American Renaissance," late in the twentieth century? Not only Adam, but Adamic poetics as well, has a past.

The notion of a Second Adam may have been suggested by theology: Christ is the Second Adam in that his incarnation and sacrifice inaugurate a radically new beginning. The term evokes soteriological interpretation of the Bible (which, as Sacvan Bercovitch argued,[2] still influenced the New England writers of the American Renaissance), in which the past is not so much erased as reinterpreted. Old Testament types receive their meaning retrospectively, as they are fulfilled in New Testament antitypes. Similarly, past historical events turn out to have been prefigurations, recognizable as such when the events they shadowed forth arrive. I do not mean to suggest that Walcott derived his New World "second Adam" from the trope of Christ as Second Adam (though his Methodist upbringing might well have acquainted him with it) or from the Adamic metaphors of Emerson and his contemporaries in the United States. Rather, I point to these other uses of the myth of Adam as analogues: in both cases, there is an attempt to redefine the role of Adam in some way that allows us, his belated descendants, to inhabit it and so break free of old constraints. The New World Adam might be seen as a secular adaptation of the theological topos of Christ as the Second Adam, come to restore a fallen world. The first Adam literally had no history, but those who would become the second Adam must shed theirs. Knowing that they are not first-comers, they must learn to experience the world as if they were. The problem for Walcott is how to accomplish that change. Can one reinterpret the West Indian past in some way that disarms its power to blight the present? Or would it be better to discipline oneself to a voluntary amnesia?

In "What the Twilight Says: An Overture," he urges actors who would "record the anguish of the race" to "return through a darkness whose terminus is amnesia." The usual cause of amnesia is a traumatic blow, and, as if to reinforce the harshness of that metaphor, he adds: "The children of slaves must sear their memory as with a torch."[3] Here, the implied metaphor is the cauterization of a wound, and by the logic of that metaphor, memory is infection that must be burned away. To record anguish, it is somehow necessary to expunge the memory of anguish. But only by a new anguish, the touch of flame on one's own flesh, can it be expunged.

The U.S. version of Adamic poetics, in addition to anticipating by some hundred years Walcott's more expansive and pluralistic version, provides its own evidence of amnesia. Nowhere is that amnesia more startlingly evident than in this passage from R. W. B. Lewis's *The American Adam,* which was, in the palmy days of myth criticism, the standard treatment of the subject:

> Natty Bumppo is the first full-fledged fictional Adam. He is born with all due ceremony during an incident that has every self-conscious quality of a ritual trial. The incident, which is one of the greatest moments in all Cooper's fiction, is in the seventh chapter, when Deerslayer kills his first Indian.[4]

Lewis, writing in the academic culture of 1955, apparently saw no need for irony or indignation in this observation. Nowadays, we might ask why it is the American Adam, rather than the American Cain, who is born in that moment. Natty's assumption of Adamic identity involves not only the forgetting but the displacement of a first-comer, and not only a forgetting of past violence but an originary act of violence by the Adamic figure himself. Walcott's Adamicism differs from Cooper's, or from Lewis's account of Cooper's, because it acknowledges from the outset that Adamic innocence, if it remains possible at all, emerges from violence and must somehow come to terms with the guilt or rage past violence has provoked.

Some twenty years after splicing Adam to Robinson Crusoe in the 1960s, Walcott adds two more figures to his composite myth: Philoctetes and Odysseus. For Walcott, access to the Adamic state requires abandoning the "Muse of History," under whose spell there can be only "a literature of revenge written by the descendants of slaves or a literature of remorse written by the descendants of masters."[5] Walcott's Adamic figure must somehow incorporate slave and master (Crusoe and Friday), exploited and exploiter (Philoctetes and Odysseus), into a single mythical figure. But his imagining of such a figure usually begins with, or else circles back to, a bitter conflict. There is seldom a direct, untroubled path to Adamic "exuberance," "wonder," and "ancestral . . . praise of the earth."[6]

Walcott's merger of Adam and Robinson Crusoe is at once a classic instance of creolization and an implicit acknowledgment of the New World

Adam's inevitable status as a second-comer. The shipwreck suddenly divides Crusoe from his former life. He has been engaged in typical colonial adventurism (including the slave trade) and brings his English attitudes with him. But he is suddenly without the social support that used to sustain them, an Englishman without an England. The island, uninhabited, presents him with no trace of a human past. And yet, he is not thrown back altogether on his unaided resources. He is able to salvage some tools and supplies from the ship, and these prove invaluable to his survival. The story parallels West Indian experience, in which fragments of European (or African, or Indian) culture, torn from their origin, have to be put together by an ad hoc *bricolage* and made to function in their new context.

With the coming of Friday, the story takes on an additional resonance, reenacting the master-slave relationship of New World colonization. Friday is a Carib, native to the region, but in Walcott's appropriation he may appear as a black creole. In the end, for Walcott, the Crusoe and Friday figures join in a composite identity, just as African and European lineage join in his own ancestry. Their fusion enacts Walcott's belief that the integration of racial identities into a West Indian identity is the only viable alternative to debilitating fragmentation and angry obsession with past injustice. As Walcott puts it in the lecture, "It is his [Crusoe's] and Friday's children who have generated this disturbing society."[7] In this chapter I consider Walcott's appropriation of the Crusoe myth in the three Crusoe poems of the 1960s, the 1965 lecture, some poems from *Sea Grapes* (1976), and the play *Pantomime* (1978). I shall defer its transformations in *The Isle Is Full of Noises* (c. 1982) to the chapter on *Omeros,* to which the unpublished play is linked by its joining of Adam-Crusoe to Philoctetes.

In his early treatments of Crusoe as isolated maker of West Indian consciousness, Walcott presents a man vulnerable, in his isolation and his protean incorporation of contradictory identities, to the psychic wound of madness. The speaker of "The Castaway"[8] (1964) may be "Godlike" as the solitary consciousness in his world, but he is also engaged in "annihilating godhead, art / and self." "I abandon dead metaphors," he proclaims. The poem closes with a string of similes and metaphors, as if to exemplify what has been abandoned, and yet one of them describes the very consciousness that has been generating the abandoned metaphors in the first place: "[t]he ripe brain rotting like a yellow nut / Hatching / Its babel of sea-lice, sandfly, and maggot" (*CP,* 58).[9] Whether the speaker has arrived at an exhilarating discovery or ruinous self-destruction remains an open question.

At the opening of "The Castaway," isolation is pure lack, as "The starved eye devours the seascape for the morsel / of a sail" (*CP,* 57). The speaker desperately awaits the approach of a ship, bringing the sustenance of a wider world. But no sail appears; instead, "the horizon threads it [the eye] infinitely." The line where sight terminates has become a thread, the eye a needle that stitches no fabric. Alone in this blankness, the speaker fears his own activity, unchecked by dialogue with another consciousness: "Action breeds frenzy." At the same time, he fears the intrusion of some unknown other into his solitude, "[a]fraid lest [his] footprints multiply," joined by those of another person. Defoe's Crusoe was afraid of hostile Caribs, but Walcott's, as a nascent West Indian, has more to fear from the ships of Europe, since rescue would interrupt his creolization: this castaway both desires and fears the approach of that sail on the horizon.

If the castaway's isolation threatens him with solipsistic self-aggrandizement or self-annihilating madness, it has also taught him "contemplative evacuation," a negative discipline that teaches him to accept that "We end in earth, from earth began. / In our own entrails, genesis." With the distractions of metropolitan culture stripped away, he returns to primal beginnings and the bond with nature. But the second of these lines complicates the first: genesis is within ourselves, in our "entrails." This word returns us to the metaphor of starvation and eating posed in the opening lines. The self ingests the world, and of that food it creates human consciousness. The sparse fare of his environment refines the castaway's perceptions: "If I listen I can hear the polyp build, / The silence thwanged by two waves of the sea" (*CP,* 58). But if the "entrails" draw nutriment from the earth, they also leave a spoor of excrement: "In the sun, the dog's feces / Crusts, whitens like coral" (*CP,* 57). The comparison of coral and feces casts a troubling shadow on the image of the building polyp. In his listening, the speaker becomes aware of epochal time in the growth of the coral reef. But does he find the deeper "history," "subtle and submarine / through colonnades of coral" ("The Sea Is History," *CP,* 365), that Walcott later seeks to recover? Are the coral polyps building a rich historical unconscious, or mere waste? The castaway's situation transforms him, but whether the result is visionary sublimity, solipsistic madness, or an unstable compound of both, the poem cannot judge with certainty. The final tercet, concluding the list of abandoned metaphors, reads:

> That green wine bottle's gospel choked with sand,
> Labelled, a wrecked ship,
> Clenched sea-wood nailed and white as a man's hand.
>
> (*CP,* 58)

Is the "gospel" the *veritas* in the already consumed *vino*, irretrievable now that the wine is exchanged for sand? Despite the line break, it seems to be the bottle that is "[l]abelled," not the "wrecked ship"; or is the wrecked ship itself a trope for the bottle? Metaphor too is a "labeling" process, and the fluidity of Walcott's syntax in these lines unsettles it. We cannot be sure which figurative "label" is affixed to what. The last line could be a trope for the wrecked ship, which itself may be a trope for the sand-choked bottle. Or it could be an additional image of a fragment of driftwood, ultimately traceable to a wrecked ship. In either case, the last metaphorical turn likens the object to a human hand—a white human hand, which makes it racially distinct from the persona of the poet. The comparison at once anthropomorphizes, blending the human body with human artifacts and the natural environment, and suggests an incomplete identification between perceiver and object: the hand, whoever's it may be, is not his own.

In "Crusoe's Island" (1964), the speaker is no longer literally alone in the landscape. This island (as we can infer from the names of the parishes) is Tobago.[10] In contrast to the metrical and syntactic fluidity of "The Castaway" (and, for that matter, of "Crusoe's Journal"), "Crusoe's Island" adopts a more formal, almost oratorical stance, and the trimeter of its third section recalls that of Yeats and Auden in such public poetry as "Easter, 1916" or "September 1, 1939." Crusoe and Friday are gone, having left "progeny," as in the essay, without the mediation of any woman; it is as if this male interracial couple has replaced Adam and Eve in the Genesis story, producing a culture with fathers but no mothers. The last figures glimpsed in the poem, however, are young girls in their communion dresses, who represent the unselfconscious innocence of the island's culture, from which the poet is estranged by his education. The folk culture, then, appears as a feminine domain, beautiful and enviable for its faith, but untenable for a young male poet struggling with the legacy of various fathers. He has wandered outside the islands' Adamic (or Evaic?) consciousness, and upon his return he is moved by it but cannot reenter it completely.

"Crusoe's Journal," more fully than "The Castaway" or "Crusoe's Island," shows us how the Adamic Crusoe might be reconciled with the historical "contaminations" Defoe's protagonist also evokes. It opens with the crossing of a demarcation in space and time: "Once we have driven past Mundo Nuevo trace" (*CP*, 92). This place name is as figurative as it is literal. Among the meanings of "trace" are "way or path," "the track made by the passage of any person or thing," "vestiges or marks remaining and indicating the former presence, existence, or action of something," "a mark or impression left . . . on the mind," "a quantity so minute as to be inferred but not actually measured," and "a non-material indication or evidence of the presence or existence of something" (*O.E.D.*). So this name immediately recalls the antinomies of Walcott's Adamic poetics: we are entering the New World, but a New World haunted by vestiges of former presence, with paths already laid down before our arrival. Or we are encountering only a faint sign of an already vanishing New World, its barely persisting residue. The local Trinidadian meaning of "trace" may also be relevant: "a pathway between a row of houses which are generally backing on each other" (*Dictionary of Caribbean English Usage*). The New World stands, then, with its back to the Old World, and the poem follows the trace to reach the New, then drives beyond.

Even if this Mundo Nuevo is but a trace of its former self, it remains habitable as a state of mind, where the intellect, liminally "perched between ocean and green, churning forest," can again contemplate a world stripped to its bare essentials, as Crusoe, similarly perched at the shore of his island, was compelled to do. In Crusoe's creation of a West Indian "first book,"

> even the bare necessities
> of style are turned to use,
> like those plain iron tools he salvages
> from shipwreck, hewing a prose
> as odorous as raw wood to the adze. . . .
>
> (*CP,* 92)

The language is at first prose, not poetry. It cannot afford the luxury of a style that is not also useful; it is plain like the tools that fashion it. If it is "raw" in the sense of crude, it is also raw in the sense of fresh, "in a natural or unwrought state; not yet subjected to any process of dressing or manufacture" (*O.E.D.*). So the language that Crusoe has "wrought" retains the unspoiled naturalness of the materials from which he fashions it. At some point his prose "startles itself" with the "surprise" of poetry and gives the Caribbean its "first book, our profane Genesis" (*CP,* 92). He is both the author of this "profane Genesis" and the Adam whose emergence it narrates.

Thus far, the "we" of the poem seem wholly allied to Crusoe, his grateful descendants. But in the ensuing lines, "we" become the "savages" he has converted and subjugated (*CP,* 93). In this passage Crusoe is compared to Christofer, to Columbus the bearer of Christ and colonial domination.

His speech, originary and fresh when he is presented alone, becomes "mnemonic as a missionary's," the boilerplate of dogma, of the already said. And yet it is this passage that suggests how Adamic freshness can emerge from the contaminations of history. This missionary Crusoe "bears . . . // the Word to savages,"

> its shape an earthen, water-bearing vessel's
> whose sprinkling alters us
> into good Fridays who recite His praise,
> parroting our master's
> style and voice, we make his language ours,
> converted cannibals,
> we learn with him to eat the flesh of Christ.
>
> (*CP,* 93)

The passage pivots on the double meanings of words: "good Friday" identifies not only the converted cannibal, but the remembrance of the crucifixion in the communion service. "Alters" evokes as well the "altars" of a church. A summary rejection of Crusoe's categories is not necessary, for a playful reinterpretation of them can "make his language ours." Friday's "parroting" may begin as colonial mimicry, but he gradually changes what he imitates, and in so doing becomes no longer a mimic, but an originator of creole speech. So although "All shapes, all objects multiplied" from the mind of Crusoe, "Our ocean's Proteus," his Protean indefiniteness leaves the assimilating Friday room for maneuver, for multiplications of his own devising.

There is, however, a passage in the essay that may provoke us to complicate this reading of the poem. Walcott offers, as an image of Crusoe,

> a lonely man on a beach who has heaped a pile of dead bush, twigs, etc., to make a bonfire. The bonfire may be purposeless. Or it may be a signal of his loneliness, his desperation, his isolation, his symbol of need for another. Or the bonfire may be lit from some atavistic need, for con templation. Fire mesmerizes us. We dissolve in burning. The man sits before the fire, its glow warming his face, watching it leap, gesticulate and lessen, and he keeps throwing twigs, dead thoughts, fragments of memory, all the used parts of his life to keep his contemplation pure and bright. (*FC,* 34)

In this image of the hermit and the bonfire, Walcott finds "in the case of the West Indian poet . . . the metaphor of tradition and the colonial talent" (FC, 3). He notes that West Indian writers have "brought from England, from India, or from Africa, that dead bush" (FC, 7). To take the bonfire metaphor seriously is to see everything that comes from the Old World—and not just Europe, but Africa and India as well—as dead wood. It is necessary to the West Indian writer only as firewood is necessary to the fire: by burning away the vestiges of the Old World, the West Indian imagination gives heat and light. Instead of assimilating old forms, the imagination must consume them in order to release its energies. Here, the writer as Crusoe begins to resemble the actors of "What the Twilight Says: An Overture," who must journey to darkness and amnesia, stripping away all mimetic aspects of their art.

As "Crusoe's Journal" builds toward its ending, its language insists paradoxically on a creation *ex nihilo,* but also on the availability of Crusoe's journals as material for that creation:

> So from this house
> that faces nothing but the sea, his journals
> assume a household use;
> we learn to shape from them, where nothing was
> the language of a race. . . .
>
> (*CP,* 94)

The lack of a comma after "was" is significant, for it allows the reading that "nothing was the language of a race"; before Crusoe's coming this people spoke Nothing, but now they have acquired English. The beach house faces nothing but the sea: a large exception, to be sure, but one that, as Wallace Stevens wrote in "The Idea of Order at Key West," "never formed to mind or voice"; without "the maker of the song," it is only "meaningless plunges of water and the wind."[11]

Crusoe's journal, then, appears simultaneously as the first New World writing and a salvaged raw material, still needing to be shaped into a New World language. Crusoe is a liminal figure in whom the vestiges of Old World forms are burned away like the dead wood in his bonfire, kindling by that same fire the nascent West Indian imagination. The Old World traditions are necessary as fuel, but they are consumed away in the act of creation, even as they lend their light to the flame. The key to the transformation is the discovery of the unforeseen, the moment when prose startles itself with poetry's surprise, or, as Walcott rephrases it at the close of the poem, "when the clear voice / startled itself saying 'water, heaven, Christ,' / hoarding such heresies as / God's loneliness moves in His smallest creatures" (*CP*, 94).

These final lines evoke once more the threshold where mimicry (the repetition of the English words) gives way to the unexpected and heretical. Walcott's sparse punctuation leaves open two very different ways of construing the last two lines. Either "God's loneliness moves in His smallest creatures" is itself an example of the kinds of heretical statements Crusoe hoards, or else the voice is hoarding whatever heresies God sets in motion within even His smallest creatures. In this second reading, God Himself initiates the heretical thoughts of the beings He has created, and it is His own loneliness that moves in Crusoe's, prompting the hermit's own lesser creation, in accordance with Coleridge's definition of the Imagination as "a repetition in the finite mind of the eternal act of creation in the infinite I AM."[12] If so, all creation except the deity's is mimicry. And all creation, for the deity Himself as well as for Crusoe, first arises from loneliness, from lack and absence. The engagement with building materials, traditions, things available for use, is a later moment in the process. And what is available is never the absent thing one had, in one's loneliness, desired. It is already here, waiting to be transformed or consumed in use.

Transformation can be accounted for by the idea of creolization, but burning away evokes the other polarity of willed amnesia, annihilation of the past as a necessary precondition of entering the present. The early poem that seems to me most deeply honest about the contradictions between these two outcomes, most reluctant to declare them fused by elegant paradox or virtuosic wordplay, is "Laventille," named for a hillside slum at the edge of Port of Spain.[13] At the top of the hill is a church and shrine, Our Lady of Laventille, from which one can see the town below and the sea stretching beyond it. The speaker climbs the hill to attend a christening at that church. Since the poem's occasion is a ceremonial affirmation of a child's birth and naming, it evokes a meditation on that child's prospects. The speaker's upward path is also a path of decline. Socially, "To go downhill / from here was to ascend," this high place being only "the height of poverty / for the desperate and black" (*CP*, 86). The poem does not evade the squalor of its setting, "where the inheritors of the middle passage stewed, / five to a room, still clamped below their hatch" (*CP*, 86). In this image, the horrors of slavery are superimposed on the present, in a grim version of Eliot's "historical sense," through which the entire legacy of the past "composes a simultaneous order."[14]

The poem ends by combining imagery of birth and burial, in the lines already discussed briefly in the introduction:

> Something inside is laid wide like a wound,
>
> some open passage that has cleft the brain,
> some deep, amnesiac blow. We left
> somewhere a life we never found,
>
> customs and gods that are not born again,
> some crib, some grille of light
> clanged shut on us in bondage, and withheld
>
> us from that world below us and beyond,
> and in its swaddling cerements we're still bound.
>
> (*CP,* 88)

Some internal wound, invisible and of the spirit, is reopened. "Open passage" suggests some conduit from outside to the inside of the brain that will not close, but it also resonates with "middle passage" as if to suggest that this indeed was the "deep, amnesiac blow." In these lines, the pastlessness that Walcott has elsewhere celebrated as Adamic vision becomes a wound, the telltale sign of a violent history. Where there is amnesia now, we can infer a past trauma.

Walcott's mingling of images of birth and death underscores the ambiguous consequences of amnesia. The bars of the infant's "crib" become "some grille of light / clanged shut on us in bondage," a barred window in the prison-hold of the slave ship. The infant's swaddling clothes are also a corpse's cerements. The West Indian psyche, then, remains "bound" long after emancipation, newly dead and newly born at once. The poem leaves open the question of whether the way out of this impasse will come from memory—the retrieval, at last, of the "life we never found"—or forgetting, a rebirth into Adamic pastlessness that will unwind the "swaddling cerements" holding the infant prisoner.

Another poem of about the same period implies that the Caribbean Adam's Eden is without a past because it devours all traces of its past; it is not a peaceable kingdom but a locus of constantly recurring primal violence, which leaves no trace on the landscape. "Air" (1965) takes as epigraph James Anthony Froude's notorious dismissal of the West Indies:

> There has been romance, but it has been the romance of pirates and outlaws. The natural graces of life do not show themselves under such conditions. There are no people there in the true sense of the word, with a character and a purpose of their own. (*CP,* 113)

The rain forests of the islands "devour all," including the genocidal history of colonization. Into them have vanished "two minor yellow races, and / half of a black," all lost in "that gross un- / discriminating stomach" (*CP,* 113). The islands are full of an annihilating "nothing"

> which eats gods, which devoured
> the god-refusing Carib, petal
> by golden petal, then forgot,
> and the Arawak
> who leaves not the lightest fern-trace
> of his fossil to be cultured
> by black rock. . . .
>
> (*CP,* 114)

The rain forest, like the swamp in the poem of that title (1964) or the serene beach of "The Almond Trees" (1965), is a place of "widening amnesia" (*CP,* 60), with "no visible history"[15] because the fierce tropical climate has dissolved all trace of past events. As Walcott told Edward Hirsch in his *Paris Review* interview, "[T]here are always images of erasure in the Caribbean."[16] A thoroughly erased surface is indistinguishable, to the eye, from one never written upon. But to describe it as erased is to reveal one's awareness of the past; a truly Adamic consciousness would describe an erased surface as blank. In Walcott's poems, the erased history has to be acknowledged, since it invisibly haunts the present. But in acknowledging it, the poem usually aspires to exorcise it and thus erase it in a more complete sense.

The figure of Adam, no longer paired with Crusoe, appears prominently in several poems toward the beginning of *Sea Grapes* (1976), which is an unusual book for Walcott not only in its large number of short, almost gnomic poems, but in the bitterness of a good many of them, especially—and surprisingly—those in which Adam's name appears. When Adam is mentioned in *Sea Grapes,* the serpent is usually at his side. In "New World," the two endure the Middle Passage together and conspire to corrupt the Eden in which they have arrived:

So when Adam was exiled
To our New Eden, in the ark's gut,
the coined snake coiled there for good
fellowship also; that was willed.

Adam had an idea.
He and the snake would share
the loss of Eden for a profit.
So both made the New World. And it looked good.

(*SG*, 12)

The "coined snake" suggests that the tempter is money, and the implication seems to be that the oppressed of the New World have cooperated with their oppressors in despoiling "Eden for a profit." Adam and the snake, the formerly colonized and their former colonizers, cut a deal, and through that corruption the New World is made. "New World" envisions a postlapsarian Adam who has sold his paradise. In the next poem, "Adam's Song," "men still sing the song that Adam sang / against the world he lost to vipers." It is not a song of fresh beginnings, but the one "he sang in the evening of the world // with the lights coming on in the eyes of panthers / in the peaceable kingdom / and his death coming out of the trees" (*SG*, 13). "The Brother," after excoriating the "treachery" of those "who never have change / but exact thirty pieces of silver / in the name of a cause," concludes with this riddle:

And, when your love is spent,
In Eden, who sleeps happiest?
The serpent.[17]

(*SG*, 16)

In these poems, Eden has become a snakepit. But in "Names" and "Sainte Lucie," Walcott returns to the prelapsarian Adam the Namer, Adam the founder of "my race." These poems follow rather than precede the embittered ones, as if to suggest that Adamic consciousness remains possible even after the betrayals of history.

"Names" is dedicated to Edward Brathwaite, who both as historian and as poet has sought to trace the continuity of West Indian identity backward through its many displacements and wanderings. The poem imagines a moment of origin: "My race began as the sea began, / with no nouns, and with no horizon." In this state, prior to naming, prior to a sense of boundary or limit, there is neither "memory" nor "future." There is only the pure experience of the present, which can look neither backward nor forward. Nonetheless, having so begun, the speaker "looked for that moment / when the mind was halved by a horizon" (*SG*, 32). The horizon divides, separating one part of the mind from another, breaking the unity of the primal state. It also evokes the separation of past from present, and of Old World from New. Though the "race" must have begun prior to the memory of a past or the anxious projection of a future, it no longer inhabits that beginning. When, the poem asks, did the transition occur? The speaker has "never found that moment," despite his searching. For the West Indian, brought from Benares, Canton, or Benin, "the horizon sinks in the memory." One cannot remember the moment at which one began to remember. It is as if one had "melted into a mirror" (*SG*, 32).

The first act of the unformed, oceanic "race" is the naming of the self in a cry of naked assertion:

> A sea-eagle screams from the rock,
> and my race began like the osprey
> with that cry,
> that terrible vowel,
> that I!
>
> (*SG*, 33)

The cry is sound in the process of becoming language. The bird's scream is a "terrible vowel," a noise heard for the first time as the morpheme and phoneme "I." There are still "no nouns," only a pronoun that locates but does not yet name the being who utters it. The effort to name then moves from speech to writing, and from singular to plural, as the nascent "race" seizes a "stick / to trace our names on the sand / which the sea erased again, to our indifference" (*SG*, 33).

If the first part of the poem deals with the Caribbean people attempting to utter their own identity, only to have the names erased, the second part deals with the names that have remained on the maps. These were given by the colonizers, in remembrance of the places they left behind, whether in affection or bitterness: "And when they named these bays / bays, / was it nostalgia or irony?" More irony than nostalgia, according to this poem; the names are "belittling diminutives," so that "little Versailles / meant plans for a pigsty, / names for the sour apples / and green grapes / of their exile" (*SG*, 33). Nonetheless, "the names held," and despite the irony of those who gave them, the place dignifies them in its own way, with its own unexpected beauty: "Valencia glows / with the lanterns of oranges, / Mayaro's / charred candelabra of cocoa" (*SG,* 34). That the names were first given in contempt finally does not matter, for they undergo metamorphosis. The colonizers, "Being men . . . could not live / except they first presumed / the right of every thing to be a noun." Naming is not a choice, it is what "men" of any sort must do in order to live as human beings. But while they have "held," names do not necessarily keep their original form or intention; they are subject to continuous renegotiation. Thus, "the African acquiesced" and "repeated" the names spoken by the European but also "changed them" (*SG,* 34).[18] The poem ends by depicting a colonial scene of instruction:

> Not Orion, not Betelgeuse,
> Tell me, what do they look like?
> Answer, you damned little Arabs!
> Sir, fireflies caught in molasses.
>
> (*SG,* 34)

The instructor's abuse, though playful and even affectionate, is abuse nonetheless. Yet by asking not what the stars *are,* but what "they look like," he leaves the student room to invent. The student, though answering to a taskmaster, becomes an initiator rather than an imitator, giving, instead of received names or definitions, his own evocative simile.

"Sainte Lucie," which follows "Names" in the collection, extends the topos of naming and unnaming. It begins with a litany of St. Lucian village names, and its first section closes with a declaration of loyalty in two lines of creole French—a language created when "[t]he African acquiesced [to], / repeated, and changed" the language of the French colonists—followed by one line of creole English, made from the language of their rivals:

> *moi c'est gens Ste. Lucie,*
> *C'est la moi sorti;*
> is there that I born.
>
> (*SG,* 39)

It includes also a French creole *conte,* transcribed from memory and then translated, and closes with an homage to Dunstan St. Omer's extraordinary altarpiece at Jacmel, hidden in an unprepossessing church atop a small knoll, amid the banana groves of Roseau. This section explicitly evokes a West Indian laborer as a New World Adam, and a discussion of it, in relation to the altarpiece itself, sheds further light on Walcott's West Indian Eden.

The altarpiece was St. Omer's first church commission after Vatican II. Before that time, it had not been acceptable to present a black Holy Family. St. Omer's depiction of Joseph and Jesus in the Church of St. Joseph the Worker in Gros Îlet, for instance, shows father and Son as blond Caucasians. In smaller panels to the side of the church, he includes a few black faces in crowd scenes, discretely relegated to the background. But Vatican II encouraged vernacular interpretation of religious symbols, freeing St. Omer to paint as he wished. Almost all of the figures in the Jacmel painting were done from local St. Lucian models (including a self-portrait in which St. Omer, in a blue robe, looks back at us over his shoulder). Joseph's head, in profile, was taken from a photo of an American basketball player (apparently Wilt Chamberlain, though St. Omer says he does not recall). The infant Jesus has what St. Omer called "an antelope face," of a kind seen in African art. He pointed out that the Scriptures say nothing about the race of Christ. It would not be inconsistent with the Gospels, then, to imagine Joseph and Mary as Ethiopian Jews.[19] The painting itself is an example of how an imposed tradition ceases to be an imposition as those who have accepted it move beyond acquiescence to reshape it anew.

The landscape depicted in the altarpiece is indeed Edenic; it is as crowded with banana trees as the valley outside the church, and the prevailing hue is a leafy green. On the left, a barefooted, shirtless man links arms with a woman in a simple dress; they are the couple who, says Walcott, "could be Eve and Adam dancing" (*SG,* 47). Like Makak, released from his noble delusions in *Dream on Monkey Mountain,* they have returned "to the green beginning of this world" (*DMMOP,* 326). Walcott claims for the altarpiece a union between art and its source in the collective life of the St. Lucian people, so that the chapel is "the pivot of this valley," and the painting, "signed with music,[20] / . . . turns the whole island." It is a vernacular analogue of Eliot's "still point of the turning world" in *Four Quartets.*

And yet, this St. Lucian Eden combines unfallen and fallen realities. No sooner has the poem declared that "'This is a rich valley, / It is fat with things" (*SG,* 46) than it adds:

This is a cursed valley,
ask the broken mules, the swollen children,
ask the dried women, their gap-toothed men,
ask the parish priest, who, in the altarpiece,

carries a replica of the church,
ask the two who could be Adam and Eve dancing.

(*SG*, 46–47)

If the valley's "roads radiate like aisles from the altar towards / those acres of bananas" (*SG*, 46), extending the sacral order of the painting into the lives of the people outside, those people also bring their sorrows into the church. The priest is well aware of their troubles, both in his actual life as their clergyman and as a figure in the imagined world of the painting. This Adam has already heard the words God spoke in expelling him from the garden: "In the sweat of thy face shalt thou eat bread" (Genesis 3:19). He has "known" Eve (Genesis 4:1), and has bruised the serpent's head, with his machete if not with his heel. Walcott imagines

A Sunday at three o'clock
when the real Adam and Eve have coupled
and lie in rechristening sweat

his sweat on her still breasts,
her sweat on his panelled torso
that hefts bananas,
that has killed snakes
that has climbed out of rivers,

on a Sunday at three o'clock
when the snake pours itself
into a chalice of leaves.

(*SG*, 47–48)

Walcott here mixes images of Adam's fate after the fall—his carnal sexuality, his need to labor for the means of life—with sacramental language ("rechristening," "chalice"). The "chalice of leaves" suggest that nature is sacred, a vessel of communion. But the chalice contains the snake, the image of the Tempter himself. The West Indian Adam, then, is unfallen in his primal, unselfconscious bond with the world around him and in his ability to name and possess that world. But he is also fallen; he knows that he is poor and must work hard to survive, and he cannot help knowing something of the islands' bitter history of colonization and slavery.

Walcott explores the Crusoe figure most fully in *Pantomime*. In this play, conflict arises from an English expatriot resort owner's attempt to enlist his handyman, a retired Calypsonian, for a pantomime—in the British music-hall sense, not Marcel Marceau's—on the Crusoe theme. The play's edgy comedy turns on the resort owner's idea of reversing roles, playing Friday to his black employee's Crusoe. *Pantomime* negotiates a precarious balance between the good-humored slapstick of the genre its title evokes and a more corrosive kind of satire. Walcott's remarks on the play to Edward Hirsch caution against overemphasis on the racial bitterness between the Englishman, Harry Trewe, and the Trinidadian Jackson Phillip:

> The point is very simple. There are two types. The prototypical Englishman is not supposed to show his grief publicly. He keeps a stiff upper lip. Emotion and passion are supposed to be things that a trueblood Englishman avoids. What the West Indian character does is to try to wear him down into confessing that he is capable of such emotion and there's nothing wrong in showing it. Some sort of catharsis is possible. That is the main point of the play. It's to take two types and put them together, put them in one arena and have that happen. I have never thought of it really as a play about racial conflict. When it's done in America, it becomes a very tense play because of the racial situation there. When it's done here, it doesn't have those deep historical overtones of real bitterness. I meant it to be basically a farce that might instruct. And the instruction is that we can't just contain our grief, that there's purgation in tears, that tears can renew. Of course, inside the play there's a point in which both characters have to confront the fact that one is white and one is black. They have to confront their history. But once that peak is passed, once the ritual of confrontation is over, then that's the beginning of the play. I've had people say they think the ending is corny, but generally that criticism has come when I'm in America. The idea of some reconciliation or some adaptability of being able to live together, that is sometimes rejected by people as being a facile solution. But I believe it's possible.[21]

Nonetheless, speaking of the play soon after its first performances, Walcott described it as much more intense than farce. He told Christopher Gunness that behind Trewe's "stolid façade" of English reserve, "there is much horror and fear and trembling. The cracks appear and it is where these cracks appear that Jackson darts in and widens. The play is about Jackson besieging and darting in and out until the whole thing crumbles, the wall is broken down and we look into his room and see Trewe naked and exposed. This is how confessional psychodrama works."[22] The play vacillates between the poles of farce and confessional psychodrama, and a good production must somehow balance the claims of each. So too must a good commentary. When Patrick Taylor, for instance, writes that Jackson's "killing of the parrot is . . . a symbol of the violence inherent in the situation, of the violence that may be necessary at any time to further the liberation process and preserve it from the aggressor,"[23] he seems to be reading some imaginary rewrite of Walcott's script by Amiri Baraka.

The American production I saw at the Court Theatre, Chicago, in April 1993 confirmed Walcott's sense that the play becomes "tense" when done here; it slighted the farce in favor of the psychodrama. Bruce King recalls watching rehearsals that same month for a production in Boston, with Trinidad Theatre Workshop players Nigel Scott and Claude Reid. He "was struck by the way Walcott continually shifted exchanges between comedy and threat, between text and subtext. Within seconds the play could move from vaudeville farce to near violence, from tragedy to froth."[24] Walcott, dissatisfied with American performances that overplay the conflict, was also dissatisfied with Helen Camps's production at the Little Carib in 1978, in which "the play lost its bite and became jokey," while Horace James "transformed Jackson into a 'kindly nurse-companion Friday humoring a senile Crusoe.' Walcott was incensed at James's lack of respect for the text."[25] Neither a toothless nor an overly fierce *Pantomime* would do.

The power of Walcott's play arises from Jackson's agility in "darting in and out" not only of the cracks in Harry Trewe's façade, but of the farcical conventions of pantomime, which provide him with a license to speak home truths that might otherwise have to be suppressed. In this respect, pantomime combines well with the creole traditions of Calypso, Jackson's former métier. In Calypso, too, picong and *sans humanité* protect mordant satire behind the shield of convention. The comic conventions of the play, and of the developing play within the play, help Jackson cross the barriers of class and race that, in a less ritualized situation, he might not think it wise to disturb. Farce turns out to be Adam-Crusoe's ally against the social conventions that prevail outside the theater. On stage, they dissolve in laughter, creating for him a sheltered space where he can shed the constraints of colonial history.

If, as Walcott has said, the action of the play is Jackson Phillip's slow dismantling of Harry Trewe's "façade," Jackson himself must present, if not a façade, a mask, or rather several masks. He performs sometimes as Friday, sometimes as Crusoe; and, at the end of the play, he impersonates Harry's ex-wife, whose picture he literally holds before his face as he speaks. Theatricality and role-playing in *Pantomime* are not evasions of truth, but a means of exposing it. What the two men discover, in the give-and-take over the creation of their Crusoe panto, is that they were acting anyway in their real-life roles, but in a bad script neither wishes to play. "You see," says Jackson, "we both acting a role here we ain't really really believe in, you know. I ent think you strong enough to give people orders, and I *know* I ain't the kind who like taking *them*" (*R & P,* 138, emphasis as in Walcott's original). The conventions of art, which encourage flexibility and invention, contrast with the more rigid conventionality of social roles.

Harry, like Jackson, is a retired performer, a veteran of the stage and music hall. The trouble with his idea for a Crusoe pantomime is not that it is too theatrical, but that it is not theatrical enough: it is timidly conventional, and he is unwilling to let Jackson's improvisational style disrupt the clichés of his plot. Jackson reaches behind Harry's façade and pulls him gradually into the theatrical energies his own plan has unleashed, forcing him to enter fully into the roles he has proposed and experience their implications. Jackson rouses the dormant actor within Harry to come out from behind his British reserve and perform. In doing so, he also rekindles his own belief that Calypso is his "God-given calling" (*R & P,* 170) to which he must return.

In *Pantomime,* we can begin to appreciate the sense in which the actor's seeming "mimicry" becomes something originary and transforming. As the Crusoe skit evolves, it becomes more than a reenactment; it becomes a struggle between the two men for control and interpretation of the Crusoe script. Both men refer to their work together on the play as a "game" (*R & P,* 106, 118), and through most of the play, each is trying to win.

The charge of "Mimicry" has usually been aimed by Europeans at colonials, and in an angry moment after Jackson has killed Harry's parrot for repeatedly squawking the name of its late German owner, one "Heinegger," the Englishman says, "You people create nothing. You imitate everything" (*R & P,* 156). In which he sounds like—imitates, if you will—Froude and Naipaul. So the charge of mimicry boomerangs, as it does elsewhere in the play. The parrot, stock emblem of mimicry, is identified not with West Indians but with Europeans.[26] As an unreasoning creature, it cannot know that "Heinegger" sounds like a racial insult. "[H]ow can a bloody parrot be prejudiced?" Harry asks, and Jackson replies, "The same damn way they corrupt a child. By their upbringing" (*R & P,* 100). This exchange suggests that European racism is itself a form of mimicry, a mindless acceptance of received attitudes rather than active malice.

The tension between "classical acting" and "*Creole* acting"—a term that reduced Jackson to laughter when he first heard it at an audition (*R & P,*

131)—informs the sudden shifts of tone in the play. Though he wonders "what kind o' acting" (*R & P*, 131) creole acting might be, he later gives a good definition, provoked by the speech Harry has written for Crusoe. That speech might be taken for a parody of the more "classical" side of Walcott's own style. "O silent sea, O wondrous sunset that I've gazed on ten thousand times, who will rescue me from this complete desolation," it begins. "The ferns, the palms like silent sentinels, the wide and silent lagoons that briefly hold my passing, solitary reflection" (*R & P*, 142; 144). And then it brings in, as if in further self-parody, the figure of Adam:

> Adam in paradise had his woman to share his loneliness, but I miss the voice of even one consoling creature, the touch of a hand, the look of kind eyes. Where is the wife from whom I vowed never to be sundered? How old is my little son? If he could see his father like this, mad with memories of them. . . . Even Job had his family. But I am alone, alone, I am all alone. (*R & P*, 145)

That, Jackson concedes, is "[t]ouching, yet there is something missing," namely, the goats. "The goats? So what?" says Harry (*R & P*, 146). "[M]y point," replies Jackson, "is that this man ain't facing reality. *There are goats* all around him." Harry's Crusoe "is not a practical man *shipwrecked.*" "I suppose," Harry observes, "that's the difference between classical and Creole acting?" To which Jackson assents: "If he is not practical, he is not Robinson Crusoe. And yes, it is Creole acting, yes."

Creole acting (and acting like a creole) involves practicality, assertiveness rather than elegiac passivity, and "faith" (*R & P*, 147) that despite the shipwreck, he will come out all right. "He not sitting on his shipwrecked arse bawling out . . . 'O silent sea, O wondrous sunset,' and all that shit. No. He shipwrecked. He desperate, he hungry." Since "Robbie is the First True Creole,

> he watching the goat with his eyes narrow, narrow, and he say: *blehhh,* eh? You muther-fucker, I go show you *blehhh* in your goat-ass, and vam, vam, next thing is Robbie and the goat, *mano a mano,* man to man, man to goat, goat to man, wrestling on the sand, and next thing we know we hearing one last faint, feeble *bleeeeeehhhhhhhhhhhh,* and Robbie is next seen walking up the beach with a goatskin hat and a goatskin umbrella, feeling like a million dollars because *he have faith!* (*R & P*, 148)

The creole identity grows from the unaided self confronting hunger, shipwreck, and solitude and creating what it needs. It thrives on improvisation. When Harry encourages Jackson to "improvise," his enthusiasm is rekindled:

> Jackson: You mean we making it up as we go along?
> Harry: Right!
> Jackson: Right! I in dat!
>
> (*R & P,* 113–14)

Confronting lack and emptiness, the creole response is to improvise. For Crusoe as for Walcott, if there is nothing, there is everything to be made.

We need to remember that Harry Trewe is not really a "classical" actor any more than Jackson Phillip is. His own tradition is English music-hall comedy, which like Calypso requires spontaneity and energy rather than precisely rehearsed nuance. He has seen Jackson perform for the guests in a "little Carnival contest for the staff" and "artist to artist, I recognized a real pro" (*R & P,* 110). Before he can recognize Jackson "man to man," as the Calypsonian demands as the price of his continued participation in the pantomime, he recognizes him artist to artist, and that is the first step in the leveling of the master-servant relationship. The two traditions really have much in common.

At the same time, Walcott has his classical ambitions, and "classical" acting has its contribution to make. When Harry sees Jackson uncovering the more serious and potentially "offensive" (*R & P,* 125) implications of their reversed Crusoe plot, he tries to call the play off. But Jackson will not have it: "You see, it's your people who introduced us to this culture: Shakespeare, *Robinson Crusoe,* the classics, and so on, and when we start getting as good as them, you can't leave halfway. So, I will continue. Please?" (*R & P,* 124). What unnerves Harry is that the play they are creating together has spilled over, by the logic of their own improvisations, beyond his original intention to "keep it light" (*R & P,* 112). Just as Crusoe and Friday have been reversed, Harry's role as director, producer, and writer of the play has been usurped by Jackson's assertive challenge. The creole actor begins to push beyond light entertainment to the complexity and seriousness of "classical" theater. As Harry says, "if you take this thing seriously, we might commit Art, which is a kind of crime in this society." It would make people "think too much" (*R & P,* 125). Committing Art, of course, is what Walcott sets out to accomplish. But to do it, he needs to fuse the energy of "Creole acting" with the resources he brings from "classical" literature.

As Jackson wrests the Crusoe pantomime out of Harry's control, he also begins to draw Harry out of his tight control of himself. Just once, early in the first act, Harry touches on his past: "My son's been dead three years, Jackson, and I'vn't had much interest in women since, but I haven't gone queer, either" (*R & P,* 103). But before the shock of these offhand revelations has a chance to register, the dialogue pushes on as if nothing important had been said. It's only in the second of the two acts, after Harry offers to "have a drink, man to man" (*R & P,* 134), that the two men begin to talk about their personal lives, and Harry does most of the talking. The initiator of change in this play is Jackson, but we measure the change primarily through his effect on Harry.

As Harry gradually drops his reserve, we learn of his loneliness, and most particularly of his failed marriage. Already within the opening minutes of the second act, attempting to apologize to Jackson for the morning's events, he can admit that his Crusoe mania arose from boredom and solitude, sitting "in an empty boarding house" (*R & P,* 135) on a slow Sunday afternoon. "I daresay the terror of emptiness made me want to act." As the two men begin to open up further, Harry asks Jackson if he is married, then mentions his ex-wife's remarriage. The sign of their growing trust is this talk about women. It emerges that Harry has come to the West Indies in the wake of a personal disaster. Not only did his wife leave him, she is responsible for the death of their son, killed in an auto crash while she was driving drunk. On top of that, she has become a theatrical star, completely outshining him. Indeed, the Crusoe panto has already been played before, in England, with his ex-wife Ellen as Crusoe, to Harry's Friday. She "wiped the stage with [him]. . . . Why not? I was no bloody good" (*R & P,* 164). Harry, then, resembles the sort of colonialist anatomized by Albert Memmi, the mediocre European with an inferiority complex who comes to the colonies to shore up his self-respect.[27] Paradoxically, Jackson restores Harry's self-respect not by playing the role of the colonized inferior, but by refusing to play it, and by offering, instead, his creole Crusoe as a model of tough, practical will to survive. After Harry's verdict that he "was no bloody good," Jackson summons him back into the play to resume his part: "Crusoe must get up, he must make himself get up. He have to face a next day again" (*R & P,* 164). After Jackson's speech, Harry feels the burden of his past lift and quotes Coleridge's "Rime of the Ancient Mariner": "'The albatross fell off and sank / like lead into the sea'" (where, doubtless, it will join the silenced parrot).

Does Crusoe remain a Caribbean Adam in this play, as Walcott had envisioned him in the 1960s? Some of the same paradoxes are still in force: the sense of emptiness in the present caused by a trauma in the past; the conversion of that emptiness into an open space of possibility through liberation from the burden of the past; the sense that to name is the most powerful assertion of being (as Jackson, in renaming himself "Thursday" and improvising an imaginary language to force on Harry's Crusoe, well knows). There is also the curious elision of the couple Adam and Eve with the same-sex couple, Crusoe and Friday.

Watching the closing minutes of *Pantomime,* as Jackson plays the role of Ellen so that Harry can vent his bitterness on her, one recalls Jackson's earlier gibe at Harry's ambiguous "sexual taste" (*R & P,* 105); his protest that "if anybody should happen to pass" and see him beside the undressed Harry, his "name is immediately mud" (*R & P,* 103); and Harry's defensive denial that he has "gone queer" (*R & P,* 103). And one might well conclude, with Eve Kosofsky Sedgwick, that "homophobia directed by men against men is misogynistic,"[28] at least in this instance. For Walcott, must the restoration of Adamic freedom and manly self-assertion entail the banishment of Eve, her vilification as a "melodramatic bitch" (*R & P,* 163)? Perhaps, but it is important to enter a few qualifications. First of all, the practice of a male actor portraying a woman is commonplace in English pantomime comedy, so what we are seeing is in part an allusion to a theatrical convention. The staging of the scene, moreover, points up the degree to which Harry has conflated his self-contempt, his conflict with Jackson, and his anger at his wife. In his role as Ellen, Jackson climbs to the same spot on which Harry made a mock suicide attempt in Act I and threatens to jump, and Harry chases "her" with the same ice pick he had used to try to intimidate Jackson. To some extent, Harry's anger at Ellen is a displacement of other feelings that playing the scene out allows him to acknowledge and redirect more justly.

It is also crucial that Harry does not sustain his anger all the way through the scene. If he needs to vent his rage at Ellen, he also needs to forgive her, and Jackson, sensing this, makes sure that she asks him to do so. When he does, Jackson can drop the wife impersonation. And instead of emerging with his male pride reaffirmed, Harry admits finally that Ellen eclipsed him on stage. "That's the real reason I wanted to do the panto. To do it better than [she] ever did" (*R & P,* 164). If he is still driven by the urge to compete with her, that seems in context less a matter of a macho refusal to be bested by a woman than of a humiliated actor's desire for a second chance. Just as the interplay between Harry and Jackson evokes the dynamic of colonizer and colonized but improvises a new script that gives the two a second chance at "reconciliation or some adaptability of being able to live together," so the interplay between Harry and Jackson-as-Ellen allows the resolution, at least on Harry's part, of a longstanding bitterness.

At the end of the play, each man has given something to the other. Jackson's contribution is the more obvious one: he has been the catalyst in exorcising Harry's bitterness at his ex-wife and in breaking down his characteristically English emotional inhibition. But Harry has also revived in Jackson, who at the beginning of the play was "finish with show business" (*R & P,* 102), the recognition that "Caiso is [his] true work" (*R & P,* 170). Each has kindled the theatricality of the other, and theatricality reveals itself as a transforming power. Through the mythical reenactment of the traumatic origins of West Indian colonial history, Jackson and Harry are able to change the script and throw the burden of the past from their shoulders. Starting with familiar roles, familiar masks, they improvise until they find ways to shed their historically imposed roles and communicate "man to man."

5

Dead Ends and Green Beginnings: *Dream on Monkey Mountain*

More than thirty years after its first performance, *Dream on Monkey Mountain* remains Walcott's best-known play, and arguably his best as well. Although the idea for the play appears to have come to him before his move to Trinidad in 1959,[1] the UWI archive contains no trail of early drafts by which to follow the evolution of the play from its conception to its premiere in 1967. As LeRoy Clarke of the Trinidad Theatre Workshop told Victor Questel in an interview of 1980, "The script of *Dream on Monkey Mountain* was written in the theatre. . . . Oftimes [*sic*] the actors can lay claim to having written *Dream*. I am not saying this as a put down to anybody. *Dream* was a communal effort."[2] Walcott himself has claimed that in this play, "the strength of the characterization does not come from me, it comes from the imagination of my people."[3] Its central character, Makak, "comes from my own childhood," he recalls.[4]

In "What the Twilight Says: An Overture," his preface to *Dream on Monkey Mountain and Other Plays,* Walcott mentions, among the extravagantly named "derelicts" he knew in the streets of Castries, a certain "Lestrade sallow and humped like a provincial Sherlock Holmes" (*DMMOP,* 23). Gregor Williams, seven years younger than Walcott, recalls Lestrade as an idler on the wharfs of Castries Harbor, dressed in a colonial officer's uniform and carrying a small monkey on his shoulder. Cuthbert Charles, a St. Lucian contemporary of Walcott, confirms this memory.[5] Walcott volunteered in an interview that when he began writing *Dream,* he "remembered an almost inhuman man named Makak Rougier [*sic*]—I suppose his name meant 'Rougier's monkey,' because he worked for a man named Rougier—who used to come into town and get terrifyingly drunk. He'd roar up and down the main street, fling things around, and get arrested."[6] The "Macaque Augier" who turns up in a prose entry in the first notebook for *Another Life* would appear to be a version of the same figure,[7]

> a redskinned, villainously ugly drunkard called "Macaque." "Macaque Augier" stuck to a role. Nature had given him the part, as if the nickname had gone in search of the right horror, the small yellow eyes shot with drink, the bitterness of the western half-breed, the short bowed legs, long jaw and hanging arms, the barrel chest and a voice that roared to burst its staves when he came pitching down the street from Monkey Hill, careering drunk. He smelled of old banana leaves, of country trucks, old crocus bags, white rum and his own reeking anguish of being half-black, half-white, a wild red nigger. He was a habitual felon, and I imagined him dancing and rattling his bars with rage, an animal beyond the law. He always made sure to commit some minor crime that would gaol him for Christmas. The magistrates knew this. He wasn't a dangerous man really, just murderously ugly. Proud of his red skin and green-yellow eyes, and of a criminal record for small offences, something like forty-four convictions; obscene language, assault, theft, house-breaking, vagrancy.
>
> That Christmas season the magistrate decided to do "Macaque" out of his Christmas feast. He had robbed and beaten up someone. As the charge was being read, "Macaque" smiled confidently to the court. The magistrate was young and earnest. He had just come back.
>
> "I see here that you have forty-four previous convictions. This makes your forty-fifth. I also notice that a lot of these convictions, Mr. Augier, happen around Christmas. I see that you are smart enough to keep them minor. We all know why you choose that time of year to go to jail . . ."
>
> Macaque screwed up his face.
>
> "You get well fed there, you get your hams, your rum, Christmas cake . .[.]"
>
> Macaque signalled to the interpreter. The interpreter smiled and came over.
>
> "What the magistrate say?"

> The interpreter told him in patois. Macaque frowned harder.
>
> "But this time you're not going to be indulged, Mr. Augier. Instead, the court is going to impose a fine."
>
> "Un fine?"
>
> "Fine" the interpreter relayed.
>
> "You are fined fifteen dollars and bound over."
>
> "No jail?" Makak [*sic*]
>
> "Non. Pas la g'aole. Un fine." Macaque went blank. There was a long silence. Then he whispered to the interpreter.
>
> "Ask the magistrate if I can say something . . ."
>
> "The prisoner would like to ask one question, your honour."
>
> "Go on, Mr. Augier. You can put your question through the clerk of courts."
>
> "Dis magistrat-," Macaq [*sic*] shouted. "Si c'est en chou-choute ma-ma'i, moi cai 'trapper cinq gourdes l!"
>
> 'The prisoner would . . . the prisoner would like to know if it's in your honour's mother's . . ."
>
> "I understand enough." The gavel banged. "Six months. Contempt of court."
>
> Bon Noël, Macaque.[8]

This account, like the play, emphasizes the divide between English, the language of the colonial courtroom, and patois, the language of the common people. In the course of writing the passage, Walcott plays with different forms of the name, hitting at one point on the spelling he would use in *Dream*. Unlike the dark charbonnier of the play, this Makak is a mulatto; that aspect of his identity, his "reeking anguish over being half-black, half white," is assigned in the play to Lestrade. Moreover, this Makak is a clever trickster, provoking the judge into giving the jail sentence he had meant to withhold (though six months is more than Makak had bargained for). In contrast, the Makak of *Dream* is guileless and vulnerable to manipulation by others.

If *Dream on Monkey Mountain* owes something to the collective efforts of the Trinidad Theatre Workshop and something to Walcott's childhood recollections, its connection to Frantz Fanon, signaled by Walcott's epigraphs from *The Wretched of the Earth,* has been more widely noticed. Patrick Taylor, who grounds his *Narrative of Liberation* in Fanon's social psychology of decolonization, reads the beheading of the moon goddess that ends Makak's dream as "the death of the white colonial world *and* of the black world created in resistance to colonialism." In that moment, "Makak beheads his goddess, he eliminates the white mask, but in so doing he must likewise destroy the black reaction to that mask, all are one, all are the colonizers' image and must be destroyed."[9] Without evoking Fanon, Tejumola Olaniyan reaches a similar conclusion:

> The challenge of resistance is no longer simply to invert the hegemonic discourse, but to radically alter the terrain of production of discourse and the relations of the subordinated to it. With Makak's final act—a rejection of black-white essentializing narratives—the dominant discourse's main supporting pillar, Manichaeism, becomes obsolete.[10]

And indeed it is Fanon who said that "what is often called the black soul is a white man's artifact," who claimed that "the first action of the black man is a *reaction*," and who described a "colonial world . . . cut in two" by racial "Manicheism," through which the image of the black as the white's other is culturally imposed. And it is Fanon too who argued the necessity of "violence as a cleansing force"[11] if the colonized are to reclaim their power to act, rather than to be merely acted upon. Both Taylor and Olaniyan read the play as performing Fanon's insight that the assertion of pure, essential blackness is a reaction, still imprisoned within the dualism of colonial discourse. With the destruction of the myth of white superiority, the need for that reaction disappears as well. And both read Makak's reluctant decision to behead the white moon goddess as a cathartic action, by which he attains his freedom. (Taylor, however, notes that "[w]hat is most significant here is that Makak comes to a consciousness of himself through a symbolic act, the dream, rather than through a real act of murder";[12] art may then replace literal violence as the "cleansing force" Fanon thought necessary for the psychological reintegration of the colonized.)

What Taylor and Olaniyan offer strikes me as perceptive yet incomplete, scarcely acknowledging the elusiveness of this strange play. Indeed, the peculiarity about *Dream on Monkey Mountain* is that although its plot can be read as a clear, even simple political allegory, its attitude toward that simple plot, which becomes enmeshed in multiple ironies and competing mythical parallels, is surprisingly complex—so complex that Errol Hill could judge the play "a tangled, incoherent piece."[13] One might sum up the allegory enacted by the plot in a single sentence by Fanon: "It now seems that the West Indian, after the great white error, is now living in the great black mirage."[14] We have seen that as early as his Jamaican articles for *Public Opinion* in 1957, Walcott was concerned that as West Indians emerged from the white error, a self-defeating black chauvinism would take its place, and the same concern returns in his *Trinidad Guardian* pieces of the 1960s, when the play was taking shape. *Dream* had reached more or less its present form by 1967, three years before the Trinidadian Black Power revolt, but the ideas enacted in 1970 had been brewing for years, and Walcott's distrust of them was a matter of public record.

Hard questions remain. Is the play's enactment of both error and mirage a solemn ritual, necessary for the exorcism of folly, or a bitter satirical farce? Or if it is both, how do the solemn ritual and the satirical farce combine to make a whole? What is the relationship between Makak's identity at the end of the play and the dream he has just enacted? In what sense does he become "free": has he achieved some sort of power or rejected power altogether? Has he "cut through illusion to discover his essential self,"[15] as Robert Hamner claims, or merely retreated from an unfinished struggle? Does he go back to a green beginning or a dead end?

The readings of Taylor and Olaniyan contrast with that of Osy Okagbue, who claims that *Dream* (in common with several other West Indian plays) avoids in its plot

> a linear contiguity of events, and opt[s] instead for a cyclic progression of action. This to a large extent is similar to African traditional theatre in that the basic architectonic patterns and the key metaphor of the mask allow a freedom of coexistence and association between diverse dramatic moments. Meaning in this theatre comes as an experience of totality.[16]

If so, the resemblance extends not only to African traditional theater but also to other nonrealistic traditions such as the Noh (invoked through an epigraph). In "A Note on Production" Walcott warns that this play, like other dreams, "is illogical, derivative, contradictory" (*DMMOP*, 208); we could do worse than to take him at his word.

If the form is nonlinear, we should not expect an allegory of history as dialectic or progress narrative, culminating in decisive closure. The unstable ironies, the rapid veering between blasphemy and reverence directed at the same characters, actions, and values, must be understood as a registration of simultaneous contraries, experienced together in all their jarring contradiction. That unforgettably powerful registration of divided consciousness, rather than a narrative of liberation, may be the greatest achievement of this play.

Taylor and Olaniyan place great emphasis on the *racial* significance of

Makak's decision to behead the Apparition. And certainly the Apparition's lunar pallor stands for racial whiteness, and for the psychosexual hold of white women on the fantasies of black men, as described by Fanon in *Black Skin, White Masks.* But she is also the inspirer of Makak's eloquence. Although, as Lestrade says, he "forget[s his] name" and his "race is tired" (*DMMOP,* 220), under her influence he persuades others to "Believe in [them]selves" (249), so that even the lowliest can say, with the petty criminal Souris, "I believe I am better than I am. He teach me that" (302). If she is indeed a sort of ghost conjured by colonial discourse, she nonetheless elicits Makak's language-making power, which is both a source and a manifestation of his spiritual greatness. Under her tutelage, Makak transforms colonial discourse into poetry, even if in becoming poetry it exhausts and destroys itself. But does Makak also destroy the source of his power when he beheads the muse? Does he go back to his home a free but diminished man?

There is a further twist that connects the Apparition's role as muse to her role as emblem of racial whiteness. In the list of characters for *Dream on Monkey Mountain,* Walcott identifies her as "the moon, the muse, the white Goddess, a dancer." *The White Goddess* is the title of a celebrated speculative book by the poet Robert Graves, who argues that the ancient pagan worship of a moon goddess, obliquely traceable in poetry and myth to the present day, is the source of all true poetic inspiration. Graves, it so happens, was one of the dust-jacket sponsors of *In a Green Night:* "Derek Walcott handles English with a closer understanding of its inner magic than most (if not any) of his English-born contemporaries." This blurb appeared on the jackets of *In a Green Night* and the *Selected Poems* of 1964, but on none of Walcott's subsequent books. It is high praise, but it makes an issue of Walcott's colonial non-Englishness. It is not overtly racialized, but like Breton's praise for Aimé Césaire ("Here is a black man who handles the French language as no white man today can"),[17] it is an ambiguous compliment.

By alluding to Graves in naming Makak's "muse" in *Dream on Monkey Mountain,* Walcott places himself in roughly the same difficult relationship to Graves (and the tradition he exemplifies) that Makak bears to the Apparition. We have seen that Walcott's first aspirations as a poet were inspired by his love of English language and literature, even though his subject has so often been the quest for a language and identity rooted in black West Indian experience.

Walcott may not have ploughed through all of Graves's tome. But if he got through the first chapter, he read the following passage:

> The test of a poet's vision, one might say, is the accuracy of his portrayal of the White Goddess and of the island over which she rules. The reason why the hairs stand on end, the eyes water, the throat is constricted, the skin crawls and a shiver runs down the spine when one writes or reads a true poem is that a true poem is necessarily an invocation of the White Goddess, or Muse, the Mother of All Living, the ancient power of fright and lust—the female spider or the queen-bee whose embrace is death.[18]

When Makak first sees the Apparition, he is similarly transfixed: "my feet grow roots, I could move no more. / A million silver needles prickle my blood, / Like a rain of small fishes. / The snakes in my hair speak to one another" (*DMMOP,* 227). Walcott has given a racial significance to the whiteness of the goddess, but she nonetheless retains her role as muse—and therein lies Walcott's familiar problem of how to accept English language and literature without also accepting English colonialism. There is a parallel irony in the fact that Walcott's epigraphs from *The Wretched of the Earth* come not from Fanon's text, but from Jean-Paul Sartre's introduction. As Laurence Breiner has remarked, "there is the problem that Makak's black consciousness has a white source. Walcott's provocative epigraph from Sartre invites the view that black pride remains less a positive statement than the negation of a negation initiated by Europe."[19]

For Graves, the goddess is changeable, appearing both as beautiful woman and as hag or monster. He describes her as "the black screaming hag Sycorax, 'Pig Raven,' mother of Caliban the ugliest man alive."[20] The goddess, in this guise, appears on the other side of the racial divide, not as Miranda but as Sycorax. One might suspect that the identification of the goddess with racial whiteness is itself a product of colonial discourse. While reading Fanon's chapter on "The Fact of Blackness" in *Black Skin, White Masks,* Walcott would have come across a quotation from Senghor: "But now comes the radiance of the goddess Moon and the veils of the shadows fall / Night of Africa, my black night, mystical and bright, black and shining."[21] Senghor, like Makak, can enlist the white moonlight as emblem of the "Night of Africa." It is Lestrade, in his first phase as psychologically bleached colonial flunky, who offers the diagnosis: "is this rage for whiteness that does drive niggers mad" (*DMMOP,* 228). Makak himself refers to the Apparition as "God who once speak to me in the form of a woman on Monkey Mountain" (*DMMOP,* 226), only moments after Lestrade has reported Makak's claim, during the previous night's drunken outburst, "that with the camera of [his] eye [he] had taken a photograph of God and all that [he] could see was blackness" (*DMMOP,* 225). For Makak, as for Graves, it would seem that the goddess is elusive and changeable, a paradoxically white avatar of a black God. But in a culture where everything is racialized, even the muse does not escape. Can one extricate her from colonial discourse, or is the only way out to chop off her head?

A reader of the play needs to imagine how it would look in performance, for dance and visual symbolism count for a great deal in Walcott's stagecraft. We are told that "[a] spotlight warms the white disc of an African drum until it glows like the round moon above it." Here, the racially black heritage of Africa is visually linked to the moon, for the head of the drum itself is round and white. A moment later, "[r]eversed, the moon becomes the sun" (*DMMOP,* 212). In some respects, the play represents the "Manicheism" of Fanon's colonial "world cut in two," whose "frontiers are shown by barracks and police stations."[22] We are indeed on a frontier, for the set is a prison, and it is divided in half, with "two prison cages on either side of the stage" (*DMMOP,* 212), just as the narrative is divided into two contrasting parts, framed by a prologue and an epilogue. But the first images of the play suggest the convertibility of opposites into each other. Although that mutability may suggest a critique of rigid colonial dualisms, it also invites a mode of understanding akin to dream interpretation, in which opposites so often turn out to be aspects of the same thing, toward which the dreamer has conflicting and simultaneous emotions.

The dividedness of the play appears in its mercurial changeability of mood, its virtuoso juggling of yearning lyricism, solemn ritual, and embittered *picong.* The serious, ritualistic side has received the most attention. Okagbue is perfectly right to liken *Dream* to an initiation rite, and Walcott notes that the character of Basil emerged out of "a death figure from Haitian mythology,"[23] Baron Samedi, an aspect of Ghede the death-god, an important Petro loa in Vodoun ceremonies. As Theodore Colson observes, there are also numerous parallels between Makak and Christ.[24] But along with these sacral overtones, there are obvious links to Trinidadian Carnival. "Monkey See, Monkey Do" is a stock Carnival character, and both Moustique (*DMMOP,* 239–40) and Lestrade (323) assume that the Apparition's mask, left behind with Makak, is indeed for Carnival use. Yet the mask is also a symbol of racial self-alienation. Moustique, when caught impersonating Makak, holds up the mask and says "All I have is this, black faces, white masks," a clear allusion to Fanon's title.

Throughout the play, ritual ceremony alternates with comic deflation. Is Makak a Christ figure, or is he Don Quixote to Moustique's Sancho Panza? Is he the Lion of Africa, ready to put on his "rage" (228)? Or is he only a sham lion of Carnival, as in the poem "Mass Man," where "Through a great lion's head clouded by mange / a black clerk growls" (*CP,* 99)? Then again, just how frivolous is Trinidad Carnival itself? Should we take it as political critique, given its historical association with cultural defiance of colonial repression, its Bakhtinian inversions of hierarchy? Or as a religious ritual, recognized in the church calendar, the farewell to the flesh that its name denotes? The ironies and mutually canceling possibilities of interpretation in this play crowd into our awareness, jostling for attention like the dancers in carnival itself. For Makak and Lestrade, and even for Moustique, identity is complexly determined and very hard to sort out. Although the play evokes a stark dualism, the multiple ironies to which that dualism is subjected turn the play into a hall of mirrors, such that any choice of identity confronts its own mocking negation. Does the play finally arrive at a stable perspective, or, having tracked all possible perspectives to their negation, does it shatter the mirrors altogether?

Mimicry, mirroring, the wearing of masks that may either reveal or conceal the wearer's identity—these motifs dominate the play, especially its first half. In tracing them, I shall concentrate on the various plays within the Prologue and the first act: Lestrade's interrogation of Makak for the audience of Tigre and Souris; Makak's performance as faith-healer; Moustique's attempt to impersonate Makak and repeat the performance for profit; and, in the second half, the scene in which Makak holds court before the "tribes."

Mimicry, mirroring, and masking are the methods of theater itself. The first instance of mimicry appears in Walcott's own imitation, in the Prologue, of oral forms of song, dance, and social ritual. An offstage *conteur,* engaged in a call-and-response with a similarly unseen chorus, mediates between the audience and the characters onstage. Their song addresses a woman whose "son in de jail a'ready," advising her, in a creole idiom, to "Take a towel and / band your belly"[25] (*DMMOP,* 212). The song counsels not protest or revolt, but resignation to things as they are. As the characters onstage begin to speak, Lestrade replaces the *conteur,* conducting his interrogation of Makak as a call-and-response game, with Tigre and Souris as chorus, while Makak responds to each command with numb, perfunctory obedience. This segue suggests that folk stoicism, pragmatic though it may be, is closely linked with the racial self-hatred Lestrade can count on in his prisoners, and with the Fanonian white mask he wears as a defense against that self-hatred.

The opening scene establishes Lestrade as a surrogate playwright, a role for which he challenges Makak throughout the play. He is also Makak's rival as a man of words. To be sure, Lestrade has none of Makak's unconscious eloquence. He is all calculation, an opportunist who boasts in the opening scene "I can both accuse and defend this man" (*DMMOP,* 220) and by the play's end has done "the white man work" (279) and "the black man work" (307) with equally blind zeal. He is the primary voice of colonial false consciousness in the play, yet he raises even this unpromising material to an embittered poetry, beginning with his first abusive words to Tigre: "Dat, you mange-ridden habitual felon, is de King of Africa" (214). Walcott has remarked that his plays draw on "the simple eloquence and delight in polysyllables that you can get in knocking rhetoric, like the robber in Carnival tradition, or in people making speeches, or in the sort of elaborate care that the West Indian takes in cursing someone else."[26] Despite Lestrade's obsequious worship of English and Englishness, his style is West Indian through and through, inexhaustibly inventive in its terms of abuse. If at times Walcott invites the audience to laugh at his bombast ("when the motive of the hereby accused by whereas and ad hoc shall be established . . . " [221]) or occasional malapropisms ("all and Sunday" [220]), more often he endows Lestrade with a mean-spirited verbal brilliance, as in his racist parody of Genesis:[27]

> In the beginning was the ape, and the ape had no name, so God call him man. Now there were various tribes of the ape, it had gorilla, baboon, orang-outan, chimpanzee, the blue-arsed monkey and the marmoset, and God looked at his handiwork, and saw that it was good. For some of the apes had straighten up their backbone and start walking upright, but there was one tribe unfortunately that lingered behind, and that was the nigger. (216–17)

His catalogue of the "tribes of the ape" parallels Adam's naming of the beasts; the comically grotesque "blue-arsed monkey" stands out among the other more scientifically neutral terms. Lestrade's Darwinian scripture ascribes more generosity to God, who at least calls the "ape" a man, than to the colonialist, who denies the humanity of the "nigger."

The prologue is itself a ritual, presided over by Lestrade. All present, except the bewildered Makak, know how to play their roles in it, having been taught them by long experience with the colonial code. Tigre and Souris cheer Lestrade on ("Drill him, constable, drill him" [221]), and they recite in unison with Lestrade his instructions to the prisoner, which they apparently know by heart. The ritual is held together by mimicry: Lestrade impersonates his white superiors in putting Makak through his paces, while the chorus, even as it reviles Makak for his pliability, is itself monkey-like, obediently chiming in at Lestrade's prompting. Alone among the major characters, Lestrade has "no animal's name" (307), but that is only because, in his identification with whiteness, he tries to occupy the position that confers animality on the others.

Makak's narrative of his encounter with the Apparition offers a lyrical counterpoetry to Lestrade's *picong*. Lestrade, Tigre, and Souris interpret his speech as evidence of colonial brainwashing, the rage for whiteness, but in contrast to the mechanical behavior in the rest of the scene, it seems courageously unconventional, a confession that only someone untouched by cynicism would dare to offer. That Lestrade allows Makak to continue his speech for thirty-six lines without sarcastic interruption suggests that its language touches something even in him.

As an instance of the counterpoint between Lestrade's antipoetry and Makak's lyricism, we might compare the corporal's speech (222) to the "lords" of the court (as played by Tigre and Souris) with Makak's verse narrative of his encounter with the Apparition. Lestrade tells his hearers that "as you can see, this [Makak] is a being without a mind, a will, a name, a tribe of its own," the dehumanizing list of negations culminating in the neuter pronoun "its." Like most racist rhetoric, his speech asserts that the inferiority of the other is self-evident ("as you can see") while nonetheless expending a great deal of energy to prove it.

Lestrade announces in English that he "shall ask the prisoner to turn out his hands" and then, in creole, instructs Makak to do so. It is necessary not only to exert power over Makak, but to be seen to exert it. The switch to creole marks the turn from the "lords" to the lowly charcoal-burner, but in the theater we would be overwhelmingly aware that Tigre and Souris are of the same race as Makak and are prisoners, not "lords"; they are no more judges than Lestrade himself is a prosecuting attorney. By accepting their roles in Lestrade's farce, Tigre and Souris can for the moment feel superior. As he continues to demonstrate Makak to his literally captive audience (and, of course, to the play's audience as well), Lestrade offers to "spare" us "the sound of that voice, which have come from a cave of darkness, dripping with horror. These hands are the hands of Esau, the fingers are like roots, the arteries as hard as twine, and the fingers seamed like coal" (222). Makak's voice has been replaced by Lestrade's, yet much of what Lestrade says reappears, its context altered, in Makak's own language. In the account of the Apparition, he says "my feet grow roots" (227), and "coal" will take on symbolic importance in scene 2. Makak's power to speak for himself requires a transformation of Lestrade's terms of abuse.

As Makak begins his speech, "the cage is raised out of sight" (226) as if to suggest that while he is speaking, he achieves a provisional freedom. Although Lestrade speaks in the role of prosecutor, Makak replies not in the role of defense attorney but rather as folk *conteur,* encouraging his auditors to envision the scene he describes. Before recounting the dream, he describes himself with an abjection strangely dignified by its casual frankness:

> Sirs, I am sixty years old. I have live all my life
> Like a wild beast in hiding. Without child, without wife.
> People forget me like the mist on Monkey Mountain.
> Is thirty years now I have look in no mirror,
> Not a pool of cold water, when I must drink,
> I stir my hands first, to break up my image.
>
> (*DMMOP,* 226)

Makak is a sort of anti-Narcissus, so repulsed by his own appearance that he has avoided all mirrors, taking pains to "break up" his reflection in the water before drinking. This is not only a metaphor of self-hatred, but also a refusal of self-recognition or definition. Makak compares himself to the amorphous "mist," and the image of mist begins his account of his "dream":

> make a white mist
> In the mind; make that mist hang like cloth
> From the dress of a woman, on prickles, on branches,
> Make it rise from the earth, like the breath of the dead
> On Resurrection morning, and I walking through it. . . .
>
> (*DMMOP,* 226)

Even before recounting the actual meeting with the moon goddess, Makak proleptically shapes an identity from the mist: the mist is first solidified into the cloth of a woman's dress, as he will be clothed in a new selfhood by the female Apparition; then it becomes the breath of the awakening dead at Resurrection, a sign of immortality rather than a "confusion of vapour" (227). As he describes his movement through the fog, he foreshadows two motifs important later in the play: he breaks "the web of the spider," and as if released by that action, the spider returns as an omen of doom for Moustique (238).[28] By describing the dew-laden web as "heavy with diamonds," brightening his walk to his lowly "charcoal pit," he adumbrates his metaphor in scene 2 of the people as "living coals," transformed by "pressure" to "brilliant diamonds" (249).

Just before encountering the Apparition, Makak has a moment of exaltation: "I feel I was God self, walking through cloud. / In the heaven on my mind."[29] To feel that one is God is the complete opposite of feeling that one is nothing, as dangerously inflated as the feeling of nothingness is self-abasing. The epigraph from an unnamed Noh play—"If the moon is earth's friend, how can we leave the earth?"—might be read as a warning against such delusions of godhood. Makak will adopt the words of this epigraph near the end of the play, when his dream of African splendor collapses, leaving him "a king among shadows" who had "wanted to leave this world" but remains bound to it, just as his patroness the moon goddess is (304). As Makak sees and hears "this woman singing," his "feet grow roots," so that he feels connected to the earth beneath him for the first time. Instead of feeling he "was God self," adrift in the cloud, he recognizes the presence of a divinity that is not himself.

Among other things, the moon is a conventional emblem of madness, and Makak himself prefaces his narrative by saying: "I fall in a frenzy every full-moon night. I does be possessed" (226). Whether it is possession as psychosis or possession by a higher power is left for us to decide. Toward the end of his speech, the Apparition appears to him and to the audience, but not to the other characters on stage. Tigre quickly offers his diagnosis, "[t]he old man mad," and Lestrade offers an etiology: "is this rage for whiteness that does drive niggers mad" (228).

Makak confesses his madness, but in terms that ally it to the frenzy of an inspired prophet:

> Help poor crazy Makak, help Makak
> To scatter his enemies, to slaughter those
> That standing around him.
> So, thy hosts shall be scattered,
> And the hyena shall feed on their bones!
>
> (*DMMOP*, 229)

He has arrived, under the sponsorship of a white deity, at an "Afrocentric" position: he claims to be a Dahomean king in exile, whose mission is the destruction of the white oppressor. At the end of this speech he falls on the floor, reenacting his previous collapse in a dance of possession inspired by the Apparition's voice. At the sound of her voice, he recalls, he "feel [his] spine straighten," alluding to Lestrade's sarcastic version of evolution in which "some of the ape had straighten their backbone," leaving the "tribe" of "the nigger" behind. But even as Makak describes his newfound upright stance, he collapses, his action contradicting his words. With this fit, Makak enters the dream world that rules the play until its epilogue. It is like the moment in a Vodoun ceremony when Legba opens the gate and the gods take possession of the worshippers.

As scene 1 opens, "MAKAK remains on the ground, the mask near him" (231). He has not moved since the end of the prologue, but we have gone back to the morning of the day that ended with his arrest (224). Moustique, familiar with Makak's strange fits, notices that there is "No fever. No sweat" (231–32), as if signaling that this illness is not somatic but mental. When Makak tells him bluntly "I am going mad" (232), Moustique's reply establishes the contrast between the two: "Go mad tomorrow, today is market day" (232). If Makak is the moon's creature, Moustique is the sun's, and only the business done under the sun is real to him. His mocking suggestion that Makak should bring his dream to market (237) foreshadows his own attempt, in scene 3, to do so himself.

The contrasting temperaments of the two men have become defined by the middle of the scene. An analogy linking Makak to Don Quixote becomes obvious when he commands Moustique: "Saddle my horse!" and prepares to "ride to the edge of the world," to which his baffled friend replies: "Saddle your horse? Berthilia the jackass?" (240–41). Berthilia is Makak's Rosinante. When Moustique laughs at Makak's resolve to go to Africa ("We walking?"), Makak throws him aside, shouting "Out of my way, insect!" This outburst is the first sign of a potential in Makak for the blind anger that will emerge in the second part of the play. But he quickly apologizes, and Moustique agrees to accompany him on his journey.

Such abrupt shifts of mood pervade the entire play. Immediately after the tender reconciliation, Moustique launches into a satirical, calypso-like song: "Is the stupidest thing I ever see / Two jackasses and one donkey," he sings, but he concludes with the more melancholy reflection that "A man not a man without misery" (242). As the first scene ends, "[t]he dancer, doing the *burroquite*, or donkey dance, circles the stage and turns the disc of the sun to moonlight. The lights dim briefly, just long enough to establish a change of mood" (242). Through dance, gesture, and lighting, a shift of tone occurs once more, after the last words of the scene have been spoken, preparing for the more lyrical mode of scene 2.

The healing scene that establishes Makak as a folk hero occurs through Moustique's initiative. A sick man, bitten by a snake, is being carried to the hospital. As someone explains that "they putting coals under his body to make him sweat," hoping to get the poison out of his system, Moustique pricks up his ears and offers to summon Makak, who "know all the herbs, plants, bush," in return for something to eat. He envelops Makak in a charismatic aura, proclaiming that "[h]e have this power and this glory" (246) and addressing him, on his arrival, as "Master" (247). And at first, it may seem as if Makak will insist on his own authority: "Let all who want this man to heal, kneel down. I ask you. Kneel!" (247). But he wants the people to kneel as a sign of their concern for the sick man, not of their submission to the healer, and the tone is a mixture of request ("I ask you") and command ("Kneel!").

Although Moustique has presented his "Master" as an adept in bush medicine, it is not through herbs that Makak undertakes his healing, but through burning coals, as if linking the lowly commodity he lives by to his prophetic vocation. He asks "a woman to put a coal in this hand, a living coal. A soul in my hand" (248). By asking the woman to entrust a "soul" to his hand, Makak solicits faith in his powers, but in receiving the coal from a woman, he ritually repeats his reception of his vision from the goddess. As if to confirm his dependence on her, he waits for the full moon to rise before beginning his incantations.

Makak does not claim his powers from Africa; on the contrary, he introduces himself as rooted by divine authority in the soil of his home:

> Like the cedars of Lebanon,
> like the plantains of Zion,
> the hand of God plant me
> on Monkey Mountain.
>
> (*DMMOP,* 248)

The people, in contrast, are "trees, / like a twisted forest, / like trees without names, / a forest with no roots!" (248). He asks them to believe in him, but also to believe in themselves, and describes his own power as the instrument of a higher one.

Since coal is made from decaying trees, and under intense pressure, carbon, the element of coal, becomes diamond, there is a geological conceit linking Makak's metaphor of the people as uprooted trees to his exhortation:

You are living coals,
you are trees under pressure,
you are brilliant diamonds
In the hand of your God.

(*DMMOP,* 249)

Coal in this metaphor is racial blackness; it is also the cheapest and most humble commodity in the marketplace—charcoal burning is the work of those who can get nothing better, the trade of last resort. The "pressure," then, is also oppression. Yet through self-trust, coal can become diamond.[30] When it seems that his efforts have failed, Makak blames self-hatred and lack of faith: "Let us go on, *compère.* These niggers too tired to believe anything again" (250). His words recall his own answer, in the prologue, to Corporal Lestrade's question, "What is your race?": "I am tired." And if the others are "trees without names," has Makak not also forgotten his name, lost between the false identities of Monkey and Lion?

One begins to see why Errol Hill found the play "incoherent."[31] After all, if Makak's great revelation in the epilogue is that "[t]he branches of [his] fingers, the roots of [his] feet," which until that moment "could grip nothing," have now "found ground" (326), then is it not premature for him to claim such rootedness early in the play, rendering his closing speech anticlimactic or dully redundant? Yet if we do not demand a linear unfolding of a consistent allegory, but see the play as a dreamlike eruption of conflicting emotions that have to be sorted out by a slow process of untangling and retangling, recovery and loss, then the illogic will trouble us less.

The motif of mimicry established at the outset continues with Moustique's impersonation of Makak in scene 3, although the object of imitation is no longer whiteness, but a more dignified and powerful black identity. This scene establishes the problem that will dominate the second part of the play: the difficulty of distinguishing false prophets from true ones, or a new truth from a new illusion. Does the "dream" come through the gate of ivory or the gate of horn?

The scene opens with a monologue by Lestrade, still addressing his auditors as "my lords" as he had in the prologue; it is as if, for him, scenes 1 and 2 have never happened and he is continuing where he left off. Moments like this one serve notice, if any is still needed, that we are not dealing with clock time, but with subjective time moving differently in different characters, bringing past and present into sudden juxtaposition. Still claiming to uphold "the high torch of justice through tortuous thickets of darkness to illuminate with vision the minds of primeval peoples," Lestrade offers "the facts" of what happened at Quatre Chemin Market early on "market Saturday," the day that would end with Makak's arrest. Lestrade intervenes as chorus between the action on stage and the audience, setting the scene before appearing as a participant in it. The situation is already tense: the corporal "was armed because the area was on strike" (256) and, as we later learn, there has been "cane-burning taking place in the district" (260).

As people in the market trade tales of the miracles of Makak, their conflicting stories go considerably beyond what we have actually witnessed in scene 2. Makak is becoming the object of a cult, and his exhortation "Believe in yourselves!" (249) may soon be forgotten in favor of Moustique's "All your deliverance lie in this man" (251). Shortly thereafter, Moustique will arrive, hoping to capitalize on this nascent credulity. His pragmatism is widely shared: the villagers are surprised that Makak is "not asking for nothing" (258) in exchange for his services.

Moustique is not the only manipulator on the scene. Passing a vendor, Lestrade compliments the "nice pawpaw" he has for sale; "Oui, mon corporal," replies the vendor, afraid to contradict him, though as Inspector Pamphilion[32] immediately remarks, "[t]hat was a melon." "I know," says Lestrade, "but in the opinion of the pistol, and for the preservation of order, and to avoid any argument, we both was satisfied it was a pawpaw" (260–61). Lestrade explains to the Inspector that he carries a pistol "not to destroy," but rather "to protect people from themselves" (259–60). That remark describes, more precisely than he apparently knows, what he and the system he serves are doing: he protects them not only from harm but from the very recognition of reality. Backed by force, the colonial order can compel assent to any falsehood its stewards wish to impose. The legal "order" upheld by Lestrade is as phantasmagorical as Makak's dream.

Lestrade then offers his judgment of the villagers, whom he calls "my people" even as he despises them.[33] He admits that he "would like to see them challenge the law, to show me they alive." For all his protestations that he is preserving order, Lestrade inwardly hopes for trouble. His diagnosis that the people are "paralyse with faith" (261) reverses Makak's. To him, Makak is merely an "ignorant, illiterate lunatic, who know two or three lines from the Bible by heart, well one day he get tired of being poor and sitting on his arse so he make up his mind to see a vision, and once he make up his mind, the constipated, stupid bastard bound to see it." He goes forth "as if he is God self," and the people are "glad that he will think for them." He raises their hopes, and so "to protect them from disappointment, I does reach for my pistol. History, Mr. Pamphilion, is just one series of breach of promise" (260–61). Faith, for Lestrade, is merely credulity. He sees history as a futile cycle of raised and punctured expectations, as one false prophet, surrounded by gullible followers, succeeds another.

Lestrade, the closest thing to a villain in the play, is nonetheless a complex, intelligent, and occasionally even sympathetic character. To the extent that we suspect Makak's quest of Quixotic delusion, we are forced to grant that the corporal has a point. And when Lestrade says that Makak acts "as if he is God self," he echoes Makak's own words just prior to his vision (227). The possibility that Makak's mission will prove futile has already been raised before Lestrade weighs in with his verdict. Inspector Pamphilion sees Makak as a genuine subversive threat: the rumor of his arrival "like a cane fire," he says (262), thus figuratively linking him to the strikes and cane-burning already in progress. But Lestrade remains unimpressed: "It's the crippled who believe in miracles. It's the slaves who believe in freedom" (262). This second statement paradoxically suggests that to be "free" means to recognize that freedom does not exist; a slave is an unfree person who foolishly imagines it could be otherwise.

In the marketplace, a singer, a vendor, and a dancer begin to enact, with a call-and-response chant in creole, the story of Makak's descent from the mountain. This street play within a play suggests the grounding of Walcott's own drama in just such improvised folk theater; it contrasts with the monkey chant of the prologue in its excited expectation ("*Ous kai weh ou kai weh*" [You'll see it for yourself]) and its political edge ("*Quittez charbon en sac*" [Leave your bags of coal]; "*Negre ka weh twop misere*" [Niggers see too much misery], 263) as it urges charbonniers to join the strike. In the midst of this spontaneous performance, Moustique enters, disguised as Makak, wearing the black hat taken from Basil in the previous scene. The hat joins Moustique with Basil the death god: Moustique's fraudulent mimicry is "killing" Makak's vision.

Moustique addresses the crowd in words roughly similar to Makak's in the prologue, identifying himself as "the Abyssinian lion" prepared to fight "the enemies of Africa." Challenged by Lestrade, he tries counter-intimidation, urging the crowd to join him in a pseudomagical nonsense chorus of "*Abou-ma-la-ka-jonga,*" then turning the monkey chant of the prologue against Lestrade (266). His denunciation of Lestrade and Inspector Pamphilion as "just the usual voice of small-time authority" (267) rings true; so far he is doing rather well. But soon he begins to lose our sympathies. He has listened to Makak carefully, so that he can repeat the metaphor of "pressure bringing light" from coal and the figure of rootedness. But whereas Makak had claimed to be "planted" in the soil of his home, Moustique heightens the emphasis on Africa: "Zambesi, Congo, Niger, Limpopo . . . is the roots of your trees that is the veins in my hand" (267); and it is not the West Indian people, but explicitly "Africa," that "shall make light" (268). Unlike Makak, Moustique solicits donations. When he says, "I cannot cure . . . except you believe I can cure" (268), he subtly shifts Makak's emphasis from self-trust to trust in the healer.

Basil, who denounces the imposter, revises Makak's metaphor of the burning coal: "The tongue is on fire, but the eyes are dead." He compares Moustique's oratory to the mist that rises from "coals put out by water. What comes from that mouth is vapour, steam, promises without meaning. The eyes are dead coals. . . . And the heart is ashes" (269–70). The "vapour" recalls the fog obscuring Makak's sight just before his encounter with the Apparition. Coal can be transformed to diamond or burnt to ashes.

Moustique, abandoning his masquerade, offers a cynical defense: "Makak! or Moustique, is not the same nigger? . . . you all want me, as if this hand hold magic, to stretch it and like a flash of lightning to make you all white? God after god you change, promise after promise you believe, and you still covered with dirt; so why not believe me. All I have is this [*Shows the mask*], black faces, white masks!" (270–71). In this speech, Moustique confirms the nihilism of Lestrade: "History . . . is just one series of breach of promise." He cannot imagine any satisfactory outcome other than becoming white, for the idea of questioning white privilege is beyond his ken. He understands his challenge as survival in the world as it is, rather than transformation of that world. The crowd, unappeased, falls upon him and beats him fiercely. Makak, arriving too late, pleads with the dying Moustique: "Open your eyes . . . and tell me what you see. . . . Tell me and I will preach that." To which Moustique replies, "I see a black wind blowing." As Makak stares into his eyes, "*what he sees there darkens his vision. He lets out a terrible cry of emptiness*" (274). In the second part of the play, Makak abides by his promise to "preach that," riding "a black wind" of racial revenge that is increasingly revealed as an "emptiness."

Spirits appear to claim Moustique's body, and their form reinforces the ambiguity of the Apparition. Among the "*demons, spirits, a cleft-footed woman, a man with a goat's head, imps*" comes "*the figure of a woman with a white face and long black hair of the mask*" (274–75). Is the Apparition indeed a *diablesse* as Moustique had suspected (236)? Or does she take the shape projected by the imagination that sees her? Graves's goddess, too, had the qualities of both muse and witch, beauty and monster. Significant, too, are

Makak's final gestures: "*Makak writhes on the ground in a fit, and the music dies*" (275). Makak's visions have always begun with such fits of madness or possession, so this one signals a new phase of the dream.

As the first scene of Part Two opens, the play may seem to have come back to its starting point. Makak is back in prison with Souris and Tigre, while Lestrade addresses him as "King-Kong" and mutters that he's "got the white man work to do" (279). But the second epigraph from Sartre's preface to *The Wretched of the Earth,* positioned between the two parts, warns us that there will be "two worlds . . . two bewitchings," and the second is about to begin. If the first part has been dominated by Lestrade's subordination to "the white man work" and by Moustique's debased imitation of Makak's leadership, the second will follow the dream of African return. Or, to interpret in a parallel but different way, the nightmare of colonialism gives way to the nightmare of postcolonial corruption. With Moustique gone, Makak's dream is free of constraint, but it also loses its anchorage in the common life of the people. It is, in the terms of the play's Noh epigraph, in danger of leaving the earth.

What Makak saw in Moustique's dying eyes has indeed darkened his vision: "I open my eyes and I see nothing. I see man quarrelling like animals in a pit" (281). If his faith in his mission has waned, so too has that of his antagonist Lestrade: "Once I loved the law. I thought the law was universal, a substitute for God, but the law is a whore, she will adjust her price. In some places the law does not allow you to be black, not even black, but tinged by black" (279–80). Lestrade is inching toward his imminent swerve from the white toward the black pole of his double identity, while Makak, shaken by Moustique's death, has begun to lose confidence in his role as black warrior or African king.

Moustique exploited Makak's legend artlessly and unsuccessfully, but now Makak falls prey to a more skillful and ruthless predator, Tigre. On the supposition that "old men so does have money hide away," Tigre persuades Souris to "help the old bitch escape, track him to Monkey Mountain, then put him out of his misery" (281–82). Then he incites Makak to kill Lestrade and escape. "You know why you must kill him? Because she tell you to, old man, remember, in the dream? Lion, she call you. And lion don't stop to think. The jaw of the lion, that is the opening and closing of the book of judgement" (283). Tigre's insistence that "lion don't stop to think" makes impulse and anger into their own law, which is no closer to justice than the white, English law of Part One.

Sounding for a moment rather like Fanon in his brief for the psychological necessity of violence against the colonizer, Tigre asks Makak: "How else can you prove your name is lion unless you do one bloody, golden, dazzling thing, eh? And who stand in your way but your dear friend, Corporal Lestrade, the straddler, neither one thing nor the next, neither milk, coal, neither day nor night, neither lion nor monkey . . .?" (283). So goaded, Makak chooses between the beasts, stabbing Lestrade and crying: "Blood! Blood! Blood! Lion . . . Lion . . . I am . . . a lion!" (285). Freeing Tigre and Souris, *"near-weeping with rage,"* he commands them to drink Lestrade's blood: "Is not that they say we are? Animals? Apes without law? O God, O gods! . . . . Which God? God dead, and his law there bleeding. Christian, Cannibal, I will drink blood" (286). The Nietzschean "God dead" does not push Makak into a postreligious consciousness, but rather back to polytheism, from God to gods. The two are linked in the parallelism of "Christian, Cannibal," as in the poem "Crusoe's Journal," which observes that in the ritual of communion, "converted cannibals . . . / eat the flesh of Christ" (*CP,* 93).

Makak is embarked on the task Walcott sets for the West Indian actor: "[e]very actor should make this journey to articulate his origins, but for those who have been called not men but mimics, the darkness must be total" (*DMMOP,* 5). He resolves that "if that moon go out . . . I will still find my way; the blackness will swallow me. I will wear it like a fish wears water" (286). Even if the moon, source of his vision thus far, should fail him, he will continue. When Souris asks how they will go to Africa, he replies: "Once, when Moustique asked me that, I didn't know." But he now realizes that the journey takes place in the mind, which "can bring the dead to life, it can go back, back, back, deep into time. It can make a man a king, it can make him a beast" (291). In this speech, he is aware that the unfolding action represents his own consciousness rather than literal events. But that awareness comes and goes as he abandons himself to his inner script.

Makak, who began his journey as a healer, now depicts himself as a bringer of strife. He offers to make Tigre his general, "because he is a man, a man who know how to hate, to whom the life of a man is like a mosquito, like a fly. [*Claps his hands at an insect, and drops it in the fire . . .*]" (292–93). If we recall that Moustique's name means mosquito, the gesture becomes the more ominous. Makak has begun to forget, in his rage at his "enemies," the value of an individual human life, for which, in his tender regard for the dying Moustique, he had previously shown high regard. The play continues to move by violent swings between opposites.

Souris, reentering with a chicken and some garden vegetables he has stolen, breaks the apocalyptic vision of Tigre with mundane banter, only to return, albeit in jest, to the sacred: "O Blessed Saviour, a miracle. Ground provisions, look, potatoes, one yam." The conjunction of "Blessed Saviour" with Souris's petty larceny prompts Makak to recall that Jesus "on the day he dead [*opening his arms*] had two thief by him." Now he is once again the compassionate Christ, having but a moment earlier spoken as a man of vengeance. At this point, Souris and Tigre, who have been fairly confident of their ability to manipulate Makak, begin to fear him. Tigre warns Souris: "That is the eyes of a man who will kill you in your sleep. They are looking at you, and like you not there" (294). And he is right: once Makak begins to see other people as mere insects, fuel for the fire, he no longer acknowledges them as "there."

By this time, Makak has persuaded himself that the forest is full of his "armies"; after all, "you can see their helmets shining like fireflies, you can see their spears thick as bamboo leaves." In his madness, tenor and vehicle have switched places, so that the imagined helmets and spears are literally present, while the actual fireflies and bamboo leaves become mere figures of speech. He calls for "War. Fire, fire and destruction." And with this vow of destruction, Souris says "*eh bien.* We reach Africa" (295). In the dream-logic of the play, Africa means the state of mind at which Makak has arrived, totally rejecting Englishness or whiteness in favor of Africanness or blackness, which states are nonetheless still construed within colonialist discourse, as bloodthirsty, primitive, nihilistic.

As if summoned by Makak's ritual vow of bloodshed, the resurrected Lestrade returns, still reeling from the wound inflicted at the end of Part One. Basil emerges "*out of the bushes,*" and confronts Lestrade just as he had confronted the dying Moustique, giving him a brief chance "to repent" (296–97). Lestrade has been such a despicable colonial flunky that one wants to believe his confession: "Too late have I loved thee, Africa of my mind, *sero te amavi,* to cite Saint Augustine who they say was black." But there is nothing saintly, or Augustinian, in this repentance under duress: "I kiss your foot, O Monkey Mountain. [*He removes his clothes*] I return to this earth, my mother. Naked, trying very hard not to weep in the dust. I was what I am, but now I am myself. [*Rises*] Now I feel better." He should not feel so instantly comfortable. He sings "the glories of Makak! The glories of [his] race," only to remember suddenly: "What race? I have no race!" (299). But his zeal will not pause for such reflections. "Let me sing of darkness now," he exclaims, and then borrows from both his own contemptuous description of Makak as "a being without a mind" (222), and Makak's description of his vision: "My feet grip like roots. The arteries are like rope" (300). At this point he recognizes that "I have become what I mocked. I always was," and, addressing Makak as "old father," begs his forgiveness. Makak immediately accepts him as "one of us" (300). It is hard to say how much of this is repentance, how much expedience, and how much simply another turn in the dialectic of mimicry. As Souris says, "Who is the monkey now, Lestrade?" (301).

Makak, meanwhile, begins to modulate from rage at the colonizer to anger at his own people: "I have brought a dream to my people, and they rejected me. Now they must be taught, even tortured, killed. Their skulls will hang from my palaces. I will break up their tribes" (301). Newly arrived in "Africa," he is turning into a postcolonial African dictator in the style of Mobutu. At this point, Tigre has had enough and abandons his attempt to "dissolve in [Makak's] dream" in favor of a crude grab for the money. In the first part of the play, our sympathy was primarily with Makak and his vision. But now that the dream has evolved to nightmare, it is almost a relief to hear Tigre's bluntly empirical response to Souris's question, "are you sure who you are?": "I'm a criminal with a gun, in the heart of the forest under Monkey Mountain. And I want his money" (303). Just a few moments before, we were entertaining the idea of Makak as Christ offering pardon to the two thieves.

Makak is stunned that Tigre's demand, like Moustique's, is for money (303). Suddenly, his confidence collapses. When Tigre orders him to lead him to the money, he says, "I am lost. I have forgotten the way" (303). Souris protests: "You will bring us so far, then abandon us? You will surrender that dream?" (304). In reply, Makak delivers his most enigmatic speech, playing on motifs of shadow and substance, which remain fatally linked to other paired opposites, light and darkness, black and white. Holding the mask before him, he begins:

> I was a king among shadows. Either the shadows were real, and I was no king, or it is my own kingliness that created the shadows. Either way, I am lonely, lost, an old man again. No more. I wanted to leave this world. But if the moon is earth's friend, eh, Tigre, how can we leave the earth. And the earth, self. Look down and there is nothing at our feet. We are wrapped in black air, we are black, ourselves shadows in the firelight of the white man's mind. (304)

On the face of it, this reply marks a capitulation to "colonial manicheism." To be black is to be a shadow, an epiphenomenon of white thought. But on further consideration, we may decide that Makak and his companions "are" shadows not as an inevitable result of their blackness, but as a result of their enthrallment to his insubstantial dream. Makak sees his mistake as the attempt "to leave this world," instead of finding some way to persevere within it. The dream that emerged from vapor has become an obscuring mist in its own right, from which Makak longs to be free. He is almost ready to return from moonlight to daylight, where the shadows will be corporeal and Lestrade will resume his familiar if odious role. Souris makes one last appeal, recalling Makak's own metaphor of the burning coal as spiritual life: "But your dream touch everyone, sir. Even in those burnt-out coals of your eyes, there is still some fire. Dying, but fire. If a wind could catch them again, if some wind, some breath" (304). But Makak will have none of it: "And these tears will put them out." As before (281), the vision in the fire is foreboding: "[t]he tribes will wrangle among themselves, spitting, writhing, hissing, like snakes in a pit." Like Christ asking to be spared the cup, he asks, "O God, O gods, why did you give me this burden?" (305).

As Makak falters, consumed by his agony of "self-hatred" (305), the newly converted Lestrade takes over. He picks up Makak's spear and closes on Tigre. Formerly the upholder of white rationalism and law, he now has visions, like the superstitious folk: "I seen death face to face, Tigre, look! He's behind you" (305). When Basil calls his name, Tigre turns and Lestrade drives the spear home. Now a servant of "jungle law" (306), Lestrade urges the vacillating Makak forward: "Anywhere! Onward, onward. Progress. Press on" (306). Movement, blind energy regardless of direction or destination, has become self-justifying. From here to the end of the play, Makak is a figurehead: "Put him in front. He's a shadow now. Let him face the moon and move towards it" (306). Souris, reminding Lestrade that "[t]he world is a circle" (307), suggests that the new order will prove much like the old, albeit with the racial hierarchy reversed.

The scene closes with one of those speeches in which Lestrade appears to understand exactly what he is doing and yet finds nothing wrong with it. "Bastard, hatchet-man, opportunist, executioner" (307), he calls himself. He claims to "have no ambition of [his] own. I have no animal's name. I simply work" (307). Lestrade is Walcott's recurring modern figure, the dispassionate servant of History or Progress in whose name all things are permitted. He is proud that he alone of the major characters has no animal name. But Lestrade's lack of animality is finally lack of vitality as well; it renders him soulless and superserviceable.

The "tribes" push the reluctant Makak on to kingship. As "*Bronze trophies are lowered*" and "*[m]asks of barbarous gods appear,*" the chorus celebrates his "conquests," in the manner of an Asante praise-singer. His "eye is the sun," his "plate is the moon at its full": in their wishful thinking, these two symbols, in tension throughout the play, have been united. They find in him a king "Whose blackness is a coal, / Whose soul is a fire, / Whose mind is a diamond" (310), recapitulating the symbolism of the healing scene in Part One. Christlike, he "drew the thief to his bosom, / The murderer to his heart." He is even "brother to God," virtually fulfilling the most megalomaniacal words of his initial vision ("I feel I was God self" [227]). One part of the hyperbolic paean rings true: "Drinker of rivers, / In whom Gods waken, / Die, are reborn" (309). If anything holds through all the dizzying metamorphoses of Makak's vision, it is his role as an agent of transformation, in whom old identities are broken up to make room for the new, as yet still tentatively forming. That is the "burden" the gods have given him.

Despite Makak's self-deprecating insistence that he is now "only a shadow"(311), Lestrade presses on, convening a drumhead court to try a list of "prisoners" drawn from the whole pantheon of Western culture. In contrast to backward places where "the swiftness of justice is barbarously slow . . . our progress cannot stop to think" (311), and Lestrade is proud that it can't. His choice of Basil to read the list of the accused suggests that a death sentence has in effect been imposed already. Basil's heterogeneous list has a comical edge; as he delivers it, *"[t]he TRIBES are laughing."*

The prisoners include the greats of Western literature, science, and philosophy (Shakespeare, Marlowe, Dante; Galileo and Copernicus; Aristotle and Plato). With them are the navigators, explorers, and naval commanders who opened the way for colonizers and empire-builders (Sir John Hawkins, Sir Francis Drake, Sir Cecil Rhodes, Horatio Nelson). Incongruously thrown in among this lofty company are Tarzan and Al Jolson, for their contribution to racial stereotypes. But the list does not spare Abraham Lincoln or William Wilberforce for their efforts on behalf of abolition. "Their crime, whatever their plea, whatever extenuation of circumstances, whether of genius or geography, is, that they are indubitably, with the possible exception of Alexandre Dumas, Sr. and Jr., and Alexis, I think it is Pushkin, white. Some are dead and cannot speak for themselves, but a drop of milk is enough to condemn them" (312). The timing of the first sentence, with its polysyllabic digression into extenuations and exceptions, landing with a long-deferred thud on the monosyllabic "white," is that of a skilled comedian. The audience, as well as the tribes, should be laughing. But why one laughs will depend on one's view of the play.

If one is looking for a narrative of liberation, the inversion of the old "drop of blood" definition of racial blackness is, as it were, the punch line, and the ensuing statement that this drop "is enough to banish them from the archives of the bo-leaf and the papyrus, from the waxen tablet and the tribal stone" is to be taken straight. But if one sees Basil's accusation as simply the obverse of white racism, no less absurd than its opposite, then the continuation is also under the sign of irony. The "tribes" themselves, though they were laughing but a moment before, do not hesitate with their judgment: "Hang them!"

The first prisoner to be summoned is Moustique, who like Lestrade has been revived after his apparent death. When Moustique asks, "How am I guilty?" Lestrade tells him "You have betrayed our dream." That is certainly true, if Makak's dream is understood as it was in Part One, scene 2, and Moustique's impersonation of Makak as the betrayal. But we must remember who is talking: Lestrade, who has developed the betrayal of dreams into a subtle science, is in no position to bring such a charge. Moreover, the dream that Makak represents has devolved since Moustique's death into a quest for power and revenge.

When Moustique pleads with Makak, we must again remember who is talking: by his own admission, he "take the dream [Makak] had and I come and try to sell it" (273). But he is also Makak's oldest friend, indeed his only friend from the days before his fateful encounter with the Apparition. And his words harmonize with much that Walcott has written in his own essays about racial politics:

> Look around you, old man, and see who betray what. Is this what you wanted when you left Monkey Mountain? Power or love? Who are all these new friends? You can turn a blind eye on them, because now you need them. But can you trust them for true? Oh, I remember you, in those days long ago, you had something there [*Touching his breast*], but here all that gone. All this blood, all this killing, all this revenge. (314–15)

Makak, taken aback, promises he "will be different," but Moustique does not believe him: "Now you are really mad. Mad, old man, and blind. Once you loved the moon, now a night will come when, because it white, from your deep hatred you will want it destroyed." With these words, Moustique has predicted the ending of the play. Finally, he denounces Makak as "more of an ape now, a puppet" (315), and sings the monkey song, as if to take us full circle back to the prologue.

After Makak has sent Moustique off to his second death, Lestrade hurries on to the next case, the Apparition herself. Lestrade insists that "[s]he, too, will have to die" so that Makak "can sleep in peace." In a sense he is right, for to sleep in peace would be to sleep dreamlessly, and the Apparition has set the entire dream in motion. But Makak delays the execution: "Before I do this thing, tell me who she is" (318). Lestrade replies that she is "an image of your longing. . . . Nun, virgin, Venus, you must violate, humiliate, destroy her, otherwise humility will infect you. You will come out in blotches, you will be what I was, neither one thing nor the other" (318–19). How far should we trust his words? That she is an image of Makak's longing rings true. But the idea that humility is a disease, indistinguishable from self-abasement, is part of Lestrade's problem. He can imagine only a binary choice between abjection and arrogance.

Lestrade depicts the Apparition as the erotically forbidden white woman, and he confesses that he too has "longed for her":

> She is the colour of the law, religion, paper, art, and if you want peace, if you want to discover the beautiful depth of your blackness, nigger, chop off her head! When you do this, you will kill Venus, the Virgin, the Sleeping Beauty. She is the white light that paralysed your mind, that led you into this confusion. It is you who created her, so kill her! (319)

Just how much the symbolic logic of the play endorses Lestrade's rhetoric is open to question. The Apparition has led Makak into his confusion, but also into his vision, his eloquence. In a sense he has created her, but he seems to have needed this fiction to initiate his transformation. To kill the paralyzing obsession with whiteness, is it also necessary to kill off law, religion, art, even "civilization"? Are these things inherently "white," or is Lestrade's belief that they are part of his still unresolved problem? As Walcott remarks in "What the Twilight Says," it would be "manic absurdity" to "give up thought because it is white" (*DMMOP,* 31).

Makak, finally persuaded, insists that he must perform the execution alone. In preparation, he removes his robe, recalling various other moments of uncovering in the play, especially Lestrade's removal of his clothing during his conversion speech. "Now, O God, I am free" (320), he proclaims; then he strikes off the Apparition's head. With that gesture, the scene ends and the dream is at last broken.

"I am free"— but as the epilogue begins, *"[t]he cell bars descend"* (320), and we are once again back in Quatre Chemin jail. Still, if Makak is not quite out of prison yet, he is about to be. The main sign of his freedom is that, for the first time in the play, he remembers his real name—neither the derisive "Makak" nor the secret name given by the Apparition, but simply "Felix Hobain." Showing an unprecedented gentleness, Lestrade urges Makak to "go home" (323) and offers to "explain everything to Alcindor. Sometimes there is so much pressure . . ." (324; Walcott's ellipsis). The word "pressure" recalls Makak's central metaphor, of coal compressed to diamond; in Lestrade's context, it places the process of soul-formation back in the daylight world. The play turns toward its close under the sober auspices of the sun, with Lestrade's aphorism, "Our life is a prison" (325), as a reminder of the limits of freedom.

Makak's closing speech claims a new rootedness after his travails, "washed from shore to shore, as a tree in the ocean":

> The branches of my fingers, the roots of my feet, could grip nothing, but now, God, they have found ground. Let me be swallowed up in mist again, and let me be forgotten, so that when the mist open, men can look up, at some small clearing with a hut, with a small signal of smoke, and say, "Makak lives there. Makak lives where he has always lived, in the dream of his people." (326)

The claims of prophecy and kingship that dominated his dream give way to a claim of modest stability: instead of "palaces," a small clearing with a hut, a small signal of smoke; instead of a new order of blood and revolution, the persistence of the rooted man in the place where he has always lived. Makak had feared that his "kingliness" might have "created the shadows" (304) of his subjects, but now the causality is reversed: it is the collective imagination of the people that created the myth of Makak, their communal memory that will preserve it. The symbols associated with the Apparition—roots, branches, mist—reappear, with subtle transformations. When he heard the Apparition's singing, Makak's feet "grow roots" (227), but he did not yet claim at that point to have "found ground." Only in the faith-healing scene, where he claims to have been planted like "the cedars of Lebanon" (248) on Monkey Mountain, does he anticipate this final assertion, but the triumph of that occasion initiates its corruption, as first Moustique, then Tigre, and then Lestrade try to turn Makak's intuitive powers to their own advantage. The claim of rootedness in Part One, scene 2 proves to have been premature.

For Makak (or perhaps we should now call him Felix Hobain), going home means going "back to the beginning, to the green beginning of this world" (326). With these words, Makak becomes a solitary avatar of Walcott's Caribbean Adam. This ending presents a serious obstacle to any reading of the play as a progress narrative of political liberation. For the Manicheism of colonial discourse has not dissolved. We have, perhaps, a kinder and gentler Lestrade than we met in the prologue, but he repeats his racist litany as before: "Niggers, cannibals, savages! Stop turning this place into a stinking zoo!" (323–24). Moustique's prayer "for the world to change" (254) remains no closer to realization. Makak is going out into the same world that he left behind; it is no less colonized, racially hierarchical, and poor than it was. What has changed is his sense of his place in that world. He still lives within a colonized world, but he no longer has internalized colonial discourse. His newfound sense of dignity is "small" but firmly grounded, and it is enough to immunize him to the insults that world will doubtless continue to offer. The valedictory language at the end of the epilogue is not political but religious, beginning with Souris's blessing and continuing through the last words of the play: "To me father's kingdom."

What, then, has Makak accomplished in beheading the Apparition? He certainly has not, even within the metaphorical terms of the play, effected a revolution. Rather, he has played out a cathartic drama of consciousness, in which he has followed the hope of salvation through his dream of a secret dignity conferred in the remote past, in a forgotten land across the ocean. If the Apparition was, in part, racial whiteness, urging him in her illusory perfection to construct his own, equally illusory, black perfection, she also seemed to be the source of his poetic language, his newfound charismatic power to move and inspire others, his ability to assert himself in the face of difficulty. Lestrade thinks that art, law, and religion must perish with her, but he also provides the insight that makes such nihilism unnecessary: "It is you who created her" (319). If so, the poetry of Makak's language is his own; if the Apparition was a necessary catalyst for a time, she is needed no longer. Makak renounces his role as prophet or visionary; the play leaves open the question of whether, with his madness, he has also lost his heroic size. He can return to his green beginning because, through the windings of his dream, he has traced an apocalyptic hope to its dead end.

6

Another Life: West Indian Experience and the Problems of Narration

Contexts

From very early in his career, amid the Federalist hope that the West Indian archipelago would emerge as a New World counterpart of ancient Greece, Walcott has been fascinated with analogies between ancient Greece and the West Indies. And out of these analogies came, very early, his aspiration to write a West Indian counterpart of Homeric epic. But his first epic-length poem, *Another Life* (1973), is not so much an epic as an autobiography, albeit of an atypical kind. His second, *Omeros* (1990), certainly looks like an epic, but he has denied that it is, insisting that the poem ultimately disowns its extensive parallels to Homeric counterparts.

Undertaking a long poem for the first time in *Another Life,* Walcott confronted the problems of narration posed by what Glissant would call a "non-history." Yet at first glance, the poem seems more straightforward than its Anglo-American modernist counterparts. In its unhurried pace, it recalls nineteenth-century examples such as *The Prelude, In Memoriam,* or *The Ring and The Book.* It is almost Victorian in its expansiveness and unapologetic delight in elevated rhetoric, extended painterly description, and digressive metaphors.

The unusual qualities of Walcott's autobiographical long poem may partly derive from his interest in prose models.

Walcott claims that Pasternak's *Safe Conduct* was the strongest influence on the style of *Another Life*. His friend Robert Lowell, who had urged him to "put more of [himself] into his poems,"[1] had been working since the late 1950s toward a style that could recover some of the prose virtues—especially flexibility, capacious registration of experience, and immediacy of communication—for poetry. In 1961 Lowell had suggested that "[t]he ideal modern form seems to be the novel and certain short stories. Maybe Tolstoy would be the perfect example—his work is imagistic, it deals with all experience, and there seems to be no conflict of the form and content."[2] In the prose memoir embedded in *Life Studies* (1959), Lowell uses objects as a sort of Perseus' shield in which to contemplate otherwise unbearable or confused memories: "[E]ach [object] has its function, its history, its drama. . . . The things and their owners come back urgent with life and meaning—because finished, they are endurable and perfect."[3] Writing to Walcott about *Another Life*, he thought that the poem's "core is the French novel of recollection, the time caught and lost between childhood and middle age. The must [*sic*] brilliant writing is in the innumerable St. Lucia descriptions, most of them recaptured moments, and so, though not necessarily narrative, [they] are autobiography."[4] He recognized the debt to prose models, having sought them out himself in the period when he was writing *Life Studies*, and also the displacement of "narrative" into "descriptions."

Both *Another Life* and *Omeros* grow out of explorations begun in Walcott's early years. He has referred to *Epitaph for the Young* as something of an "Ur-text" for both of them—which would suggest that both, albeit in different ways, continue the questing "toward" some emerging West Indian identity begun in that effort of 1949. The early stages of composition are more fully documented for *Another Life* than for most of Walcott's poetry, for in 1965 and 1966 he filled two exercise books with notes and drafts, and these have been placed in the archives of UWI, Jamaica. In draft, the poem began as a prose memoir; only toward the end of the first notebook does Walcott shift to verse. Edward Baugh's deeply researched and in many ways excellent monograph has made use of these notebooks, but my interest in Walcott's conception of narrative leads me to different parts of them. Baugh treats *Another Life* almost as if it were an outsized lyric, organized by patterns of imagery and symbolism. The poem's tendency to replace narration with emblematic landscapes or objects partly justifies his approach. But its motifs function metonymically as well as symbolically, acquiring shifting implications as the poem repeats them in different contexts. Like such novelists as Joyce, Woolf, and Faulkner, Walcott finds the meanings of events primarily in a slow accretion of emotional resonances.

Walcott's verse autobiography has drawn comparisons, not least from Baugh, to Wordsworth's *Prelude*. But Walcott told me: "I felt much closer to the prose of Pasternak than I did to any poetry at all at that time. I'd never read *The Prelude;* I'd read bits of it. But because thematically it is the same sort of subject, I imagine, the comparisons are made about 'attempting' a *Prelude;* I had no such intention."[5] And in a 1966 essay for the *Trinidad Guardian*, he wrote: "I cherish at least one minor masterpiece of Pasternak's prose, his autobiography 'Safe Conduct.'" He praises the way, in Pasternak's work, "everything, churches, trains . . . snow, insects are returned with a dulled but fixed sheen," so that "the naming of things, the simplest things, like buckets, sofas, the sound of rain, are [*sic*] merely, by the act of his naming them, reverberations," conveying "the sadness of common things, common occurrences."[6] Walcott begins the first notebook under the aegis of Pasternak by transcribing the last two stanzas of his poem, "The Wedding Party," which already hint at the difficulties of autobiography:

> And life itself is only an instant,
> Only the dissolving
> Of ourselves in all others
> As though in gift to them;
>
> Only a wedding, bursting
> [I]n through the windows from the street,
> Only a song a dream
> Of grey-blue pigeon[.][7]

These stanzas set the problem of the nascent poem: how to narrate an identity that is constantly "dissolving," becoming self-present only in flashes of intense experience.

Safe Conduct appears to have been useful to Walcott in three ways: for its style, which renders the inward experience of events through a painterly description of landscape, setting, and objects; for its digressive musings on the nature of biographical narrative and the vocation of the poet; and also, it may be, for certain parallels between Pasternak's experience and his own. Both works depict a fragile, innocent first love (though that is a standard feature of *Bildung* narratives) and formative artistic influences; more significantly, the suicide of Mayakovsky darkens the ending of Pasternak's memoir as the suicide of Harold Simmons shadows the closing chapters of Walcott's. With both deaths comes an elegiac closure, a suggestion that both men were forerunners, embodying the collective aspirations of a people. Of Mayakovsky, Pasternak writes: "And it occurred to me then . . . that this man was perhaps this State's unique citizen. The novelty of the age flowed climatically through his blood. His strangeness was the strangeness of our times of which half is as yet to be fulfilled."[8] Walcott offers a similar apotheosis of Simmons: "he is a man no more / but the fervour and intelligence / of a whole country" (*CP,* 277).

The kinship of style and of narrative form between the two works is deeper and harder to illustrate concisely. Some of Pasternak's critique of the limits of literal description and linear narration resembles Walcott's. "I think," writes Pasternak, "that only heroes deserve a real biography, but that the history of a poet is not to be presented in such a form. One would have to collect such a biography from [i]nessentials. . . . The poet gives his whole life such a voluntary steep incline that it is impossible for it to exist in the vertical line of biography where we expect to meet it."[9] Walcott, in a long entry for October 11, 1965, expresses a similar impatience: "I can't give facts. I do not know where to find them, how to arrange them. The blonde hair on a young girl's forearm, I should call it 'down,' is more important to me than the precise rearrangement of her features, or the date that I did something. Of course it is merely affectation, building a monument to the self." Later in the entry, he suggests that

> [a]ll biographies should be in the third person. The pretext of confession, whose real purpose is not exploring but ennobling life, is the supreme fiction; there is no style tha[t] can record the diurnal boredom, the fact, interminably longer than any fact, shock or revelation, that we spend life in a state of nothing. I do not mean enervation or lassitude; but any 'life' that told the truth would be too boring, too true.

Pasternak similarly asks: "What does an honest man do when he speaks the truth only? Time passes in the telling of truth, and in this time life passes onward. His truth lags behind and is deceptive. Should a man speak in this manner everywhere and always?"[10]

If the literal record of events, one after another in time, cannot narrate the development of an artist, the emphasis must turn away from what happened toward the imaginatively transformed experience of what happened. The artist, and the artist as autobiographer, must be "[f]ocussed on a reality which feeling has displaced," and "art is a record of this displacement." In that record, "[d]etails attain clarity, losing independence of meaning. Each detail can be replaced by another. Any one is precious. Any one chosen at random serves as evidence of the state which envelops the whole of transposed reality."[11] This method is both more and less subjective than conventional narrative. If it concentrates on the inward registration of experience on the artist's consciousness, it emphasizes that inwardness only insofar as it is part of the artistic process. "The more self-contained the individuality from which the life derives, the more collective, without any figurative speaking, is its story."[12] Both Walcott and Pasternak tell their stories largely as their response to encounters with other artists, and with works of art. We see Pasternak as the composition student of Alexander Scriabin and the admiring friend of the brilliant, enigmatic Mayakovsky. Just as Pasternak tried music and philosophy with some success before turning to literature, Walcott pursued his painting as keenly as his writing. *Another Life,* like *Safe Conduct,* is painterly in its depiction of places and things; it is also full of allusions to European art, which Walcott had discovered as a boy through reproductions in books.

One can trace Walcott's unease about narrative not only to his encounter with Pasternak's autobiography, but to the reflections of such West Indian writers as Wilson Harris, whom he had admiringly reviewed in the early 1960s for *Trinidad Guardian.* Harris's masterpiece, the *Guyana Quartet,* emphasizes the subjectivity of its characters and treats time as repeatable or reversible,[13] so that its first novella, "The Palace of the Peacock," can open with the death of its central character. In "Tradition and the West Indian Novel," Harris argued that "the depth of inarticulate feeling and unrealized wells of emotion belonging to the whole West Indies" challenged writers to develop a "*native* tradition of depth" in place of the "ruling and popular convention" of fiction. "The native and phenomenal environment of the West Indies, as I see it, is broken into many stages in the way in which one surveys an existing river in its present bed while plotting at the same time ancient and abandoned, indeterminate courses the river once followed." Instead of following clock time, fiction must offer a simultaneity of present and past, giving form to indeterminate alternatives, in order to be true to the fragmented, repeatedly interrupted development of West Indian cultures. It required an intensive rather than extensive method, bearing in on "the smallest area one envisages, island or village, prominent ridge or buried valley, flatland or heartland" until it became "charged immediately with the openness of imagination."[14] He speaks of fiction, but what he says could be applied to Walcott's poem.

Another Life "progresses not by narration but by a sequence of tableaux."[15] But the tableaux are informed with the traces of past movement, just as for Pasternak, "[i]nanimate objects . . . were the living models of still-life, a medium particularly endearing to artists. Piling up in the furthest reaches of the living universe and appearing in immobility, they gave a most complete understanding of its moving whole, like any boundary which strikes us as a contrast."[16] Consider, for instance, Walcott's description of the house he grew up in. "Why," he asks, "should we weep for dumb things?" Perhaps because "a house . . . / . . . bears the depth of forest, of ocean and mother," and there is "a radiance of sharing" that "extends to the simplest objects" (*CP,* 155). People and things have a "true alignment," as if composed in a painting, from which they cannot be moved (*CP,* 157). The concentration on objects, landscape, and allusions to painting also gives form to feelings otherwise too inchoate for literary representation.

Not only does *Another Life* render experience as place or artifact, a still life instinct with the lingering traces of violent and contradictory movement; it follows Harris's directive to charge each small thing with "the openness of imagination." One might find its language excessive, seething with an intensity in excess of any apparent motive. And yet, the disproportion between extravagant description and uneventful narrative may register something important in Walcott's early experience. One need only compare the young Pasternak's social mobility and privilege (financially unburdened, wandering freely from Russia to Germany to Italy, encountering great artists such as Rilke, Scriabin, and Mayakovsky) with Walcott's islanded boyhood. In a revealing passage from the first notebook, Walcott meditates on the struggles of the young St. Omer, which he sees as representative of the West Indian artist's predicament:

> This rage, although I couldn't recognise it that early, was the demon that possessed Dunstan ["Gregorias" added in margin]. Its chart is a schizophrenic's: manic depressive with or without the aid of liquor. Then our native drink is more destructive than wine. He would move from a frightening exhilaration in life, whatever surrounded him[,] to an unshakeably silent despair. . . . [h]e see-sawed madly between dreams of fame, money, power and immortality to an acceptance of his calling as a lie, a lay-about's self-deceit. The deterioration set in early because he was the victim of what we had been taught: the rewards of art, of inevitable immortality, of a society—so rapt in his own vision of it

> that it would change. He loved it and thought as love makes a woman radiant, that his country would become beautiful. Platonist victim. . . . So Gregorias virtually attacked each blank canvas as if it were his last chance for immortality. He assaulted its surface, singing loudly to the landscape all the while.[17]

One might say that in *Another Life,* Walcott similarly attacks the blank page as if seeking a last chance for immortality, singing loudly to the landscape all the while.

Art and Divided Consciousness

Painting, in addition to encouraging frozen tableaux as an alternative to narrative, provides the young poet with a cultural mirror in which to recognize himself. When Walcott portrays his childhood persona as "The Divided Child," he means not only the racial divisions of black and white, or the cultural divisions of English and West Indian; he means also the dualism of art and life, as his epigraph from Malraux's *Psychology of Art* suggests. According to Malraux, a young artist is "more deeply moved by the sight of works of art than by that of the things which they portray." However moved the young Walcott may have been by his experience, his deepest motive for writing and painting was the love of poems and paintings themselves.

The opening chapter of Malraux's book, "The Museum without Walls," suggests that with the aid of reproductions, a modern student of art anywhere in the world may make a wider comparison of artworks than even the best-traveled European of earlier days. Walcott, though he did not leave the West Indies until he was twenty-seven, had Thomas Craven's *Treasury of Art Masterpieces* (1939), which Baugh calls "a profound influence on his youth."[18] He could, with Malraux's endorsement, claim an equal footing with any European in his study of painting. But if art was to some extent its own world, it also kept referring back to "life." Whether Walcott's ambition was to confer the universality of art on St. Lucian experience, or to discover a universality already latent within that experience, remains uneasily ambiguous throughout the poem. In Chapter 1, we meet the young Walcott as "the student" of art, sketching a landscape on Vigie promontory. He has "magnified the harbour," as if to confer a heightened significance on it. He waits at sunset for "the tidal amber glare to glaze / the last shacks of the Morne till they became / transfigured sheerly by the student's will, / a cinquecento fragment in gilt frame" (*CP*, 146). The shacks must be "transfigured," but the resulting image remains a "fragment" in a gilded (and guilty) frame. As Baugh points out, the ensuing lines undercut the student's efforts: "The vision died, / the black hills simplified / to hunks of coal," returning us from Renaissance Italy to the coal-carriers and *charbonniers* of St. Lucia.[19]

To a large extent, the racial split and the split between art and life are connected. The art that the young Walcott ardently admired was European, with depictions of white flesh by white artists, in a landscape remote from his own. When he attempts to see himself in the art of Giotto and Cimabue (referred to in the Malraux epigraph), disparities of race and culture exacerbate the inherent split between body and representation. The first clear allusion to a particular artwork occurs on the first page of the poem, when Walcott, describing himself, writes: "The dream / of reason had produced its monster: / a prodigy of the wrong age and colour" (*CP*, 145). He refers to Goya's *El sueño de la razón produce monstruos,* which depicts an Enlightenment gentleman asleep at his desk, his pen lying where it had fallen. Nearby lies a large cat-like creature, about the size of an ocelot. Owls crowd at his back, staring down at him, while indistinct bats hover behind him in the shadows. By allying himself with the cat, the bats, and the owls, rather than with the dreamer, Walcott depicts himself as the feared, repressed other of European civilization. The ambiguity of Goya's title (*sueño* can mean either "sleep" or "dream") is very much to the point: from the Enlightenment point of view, when reason falls asleep, the monstrosity it had subdued breaks free. But to translate *sueño* as "dream" implies that reason produces the very monstrosity it suppresses.[20] Walcott suggests that he is an inevitable product of the very civilization that would reject him. But at the outset of the poem, the monstrous prodigy is still trying to take up reason's work where the sleeper left it, willing a St. Lucian landscape into the conventions of European painting. No wonder that "with slow strokes, the master [Simmons] changed the sketch," or that he would counter his student's yearning "for whiteness, for candour,"[21] by reading from the Jamaican poet George Campbell: "'Holy be / the white head of a Negro, / sacred be / the black flax of a black child" (*CP*, 147, 146, 148–49).

That "new book" seemed to inaugurate "another life" (*CP*, 149), but this beginning has to be constantly reenacted. In the very next section, describing the funeral of a light-skinned St. Lucian girl who had been nicknamed "Pinkie," Walcott superimposes upon her image Thomas Lawrence's portrait, "Pinkie," which depicts "Miss Barrett" in a bonnet and ethereally flowing gown. The portrait, from 1795, predates Goya's *El sueño de la razón* by just four years but belongs to a different world, still clinging to a decorum in which reason is very much awake and in control. Simmons, too, had confronted the struggle for a synthesis of European art with his own heritage, as evidenced by the presence in his studio of both a "plaster-of-Paris Venus" and his own "kerchiefed, ear-ringed portrait: Albertina" (*CP*, 147).[22]

The opening chapter concludes with a reminder that in one sense, at least, "everything whitens": everything dies. Death immediately becomes associated with photography: its arrest of movement in a "still," the whiteness of bones in X-rays, of a flashbulb, of the moon (still abroad to trouble some dreaming Makak). The starkness of the photograph contrasts with the rich amber glaze of the old masters. The contrast may be the old dichotomy between photography that (supposedly) records and painting that "transfigures," but there is also a parallelism: if the legacy of "Europe" includes the painting and poetry that the young Walcott admires, it also includes the objectifications of modern technology, the human body subjected to the unsparing gaze of camera (especially when used by tourists), X-ray, and electric light.

As Baugh remarks,[23] the first six chapters of *Another Life* set forth the social and personal circumstances from which Walcott emerged. After locating the first chapter on Vigie promontory, significant as the site of Simmons's studio, Anna's home, and the emergency housing where all classes mingled after the Castries fire of 1948,[24] Walcott narrows the focus to the house in which he grew up. Taken together, the opening chapters insist on grounding identity not on any principle or abstraction, but on the most immediate and local attachments, a particular house in a particular part of a small island. In this way, the poem declares at once its faith in the power of minute particulars to generate larger, more universal insights, as they are "magnified" in the medium of art. The poem moves outward from this center, which remains somewhat cloistered, keeping the fascinating but frightening peasant lore of the supernatural at a safe distance: "One step beyond the city was the bush. / One step behind the church door stood the devil" (*CP*, 167).

Chapter 3 turns outward toward the streets of Castries, gathering material for the "pseudo-epic" (*CP*, 183) under construction. "The candle's yellow leaf next to his bed / re-letters *Tanglewood Tales* and Kingsley's *Heroes*," just as Walcott will "re-letter" those accounts of the Greek myths in a St. Lucian alphabet, so that "[t]he black lamplighter" of Castries holds "Demeter's torch." In a manner reminiscent of the "Wandering Rocks" section of Joyce's *Ulysses*,[25] Walcott gives a catalogue of persons, places, and things. A few of these ("Helen," "Midas," "Nessus," "Troy town") continue the classical motif, but most are locally named as well as locally observed. The transformation of Helen into "Jamie, the town's one clear-complexioned whore, / with two tow-headed children in her tow" (*CP*, 161) may seem ironically deflating.[26] But as with Joyce's parallelism of the *Odyssey* and modern Dublin, the cumulative effect is less to place the modern analogues in a belittling shadow than to discover a latent mythical potential in unpromising material. And some of these characters harbor a protest against the conditions that have produced them. Weekes, a grocer and solid citizen, is also a Garveyite awaiting Exodus to Africa; even the filthy "Nessus" "rises in sackcloth, prophesying / fire and brimstone on the gilt wooden towers of / offices, odures, on / Peter & Co. to burn like Pompeii, on J. / Q. Charles's stores" (*CP*, 163, 162). The catalogue concludes with a valediction on them all: "These dead, these derelicts, / that alphabet of the emaciated, / they were the stars of my mythology" (*CP*, 164). Here mythology functions as painting has in the first two chapters: it is a mirror in which to see, imagine, and redefine one's world, even if the extreme distance of the mirror from the imaged world turns self-recognition into a leap of faith.

The young Walcott's access to folk tales of obeah and *gens gajés*[27] came through his aunt Sidone, in whose voice, as he put it in *Midsummer*, "shadows stood up and walked."[28] Despite the influence of Catholic or Methodist church, the "atavism" of folk tradition runs deep, for its "tubers gripped the rooted middle class, / beginning where Africa began: / in the body's memory" (*CP*, 167). These lines illuminate Walcott's frequent use of the word "amnesia," which comes into this poem early in Chapter 1 ("Darkness, soft as amnesia, furred the slope"—*CP*, 146). The middle class may have chosen to forget such "atavism," but the body's memory is not the same as the mind's. As we have seen, amnesia for Walcott is the body's form of memory, because the mind's inability to remember is the somatic trace of an old wound.

The tale of the supernatural that follows resembles the story of Le Brun in "Tales of the Islands," though the possessed man is here named Manoir. "He was the first black merchant baron" (*CP*, 170), and precisely because a black man's success in business seemed so implausible in those colonial times, the rumor sprang up that Manoir was one of the *gens gajés* pledged to the devil. As Manoir dies, struck down while prowling in canine form, a priest attempts to exorcise the spirit that has possessed him. The priest calls, in Latin, upon the maker of the world to cast the spirit into

Gehenna (*CP,* 170), but a fly, speaking as a representative of Beelzebub his lord, is also praying "at [Manoir's] ear well," and this prayer is in French. The clash between French and Latin parallels the clash between folk religion and religious orthodoxy, and both parallel the clash between the artificial paradise of European art and St. Lucian experience. But Walcott also connects European art to St. Lucian experience when he likens the fly to a detail of a painting reproduced in the *Treasury:* "Some jewelled insect in a corner of Crivelli" (*CP,* 165). He alludes to a Virgin and Child in which mother and child look down at an exquisitely painted fly in the lower left foreground. Even in a religious painting from Europe, the devil's insect appears. The infernal powers are not confined to the islands.

If the young poet's imagination kindles to folk tales of the supernatural, he is also drawn to "the Jacobean English" he heard in church, "the speech of simple men, / evangelists, reformers, abolitionists," whose "text was cold brook water" (*CP,* 166). He associates the eloquence of the chapel with the figure of Matthew Arnold. "I know those rigorous teachers of your youth," he says, recalling the Victorian poet's "Stanzas from the Grand Chartreuse." Arnold, like the "divided" child of Walcott's poem, felt trapped "between two worlds, one dead, / The other powerless to be born." Arnold's lost paradise is the Catholic faith of the monks, whereas Walcott's is the folk culture. Nonetheless, because of "the passionate, pragmatic / Methodism of [his] infancy," he fears what he longs for as "traumatic, tribal" (*CP,* 166), and malign.

By Chapter 5, Walcott has begun to recapitulate material from the opening sections; he opens with a recollection of Manoir's commercial empire, then evokes the "black hills" that were "simplified / to hunks of coal" (*CP,* 146) in a description of coal carriers at work "on black hills of imported anthracite" (*CP,* 171). Yet returns of this kind are not flashbacks, since no narrative timeline has been established, but rather a network of simultaneous association, the metamorphic convertibility of images into each other. That is why it is possible for Baugh, with considerable success, to read *Another Life* as a giant lyric poem, held together by patterns of imagery. But this circling back also allows a slow, metonymic accretion of context. For instance, Chapter 5's epigraph is the colonial motto of St. Lucia, the Virgilian phrase *Statio haud malefida carinis.* Against this motif of safety stands Manoir's sign, "LICENSED TO SELL / INTOXICATING LIQUOR" (*CP,* 171): his ambition is associated with forbidden intoxications of drink and magic. His anomalous wealth also contrasts starkly with the poverty of the coal-carrying women. The Latin motto sounds increasingly ironic as the stifling poverty and colonized psychology of the island becomes apparent.

A schoolboy, translating the motto in his strongly accented speech, renders it, more aptly than he knows, as "a safe anchorage for sheeps" (*CP,* 172).

In Chapter 7, which closes the first of the poem's four parts, the relation of art and life returns to central importance. "Provincialism loves the pseudo-epic," Walcott begins, "so if these heroes have been given a stature / disproportionate to their cramped lives, / remember I beheld them at knee-height" (*CP,* 183). He apologizes for his unprepossessing characters, yet claims that the perspective of childhood justifies their magnification as a subjective truth.

Walcott's adoration of European art awakens an apparently opposite quest. Schooled by European masterpieces, his aspiring painter's "hand" sought "in the deep country" for

> the natural man,
> generous, rooted.
> And now I yearned to suffer for that life,
> I looked for some ancestral, tribal country. . . .
>
> (*CP,* 184)

As yet, the yearning to suffer remains a willed primitivism, as the increasingly self-mocking continuation of the passage recognizes: "I looked from the bus window / and multiplied the bush with savages" (*CP,* 184). Walcott's heroes among the artists were Gauguin, who went off to Tahiti and the Marquesas to find (and become) the unspoiled natural man, and van Gogh, who believed that rural scenes, caught in the open air, brought authenticity to his art.

Only when an experience of deep identification with the island's poor comes over him unbidden does the self-conscious yearning to suffer for the folk become spontaneous compassion. "About the August of my fourteenth year / I lost my self somewhere above a valley / owned by a spinster-farmer, my dead father's friend." The place links the experience to the legacy of the poet's father, but, as the separation of "my self" into two words emphasizes, it entails not some passage into identity but rather a complete forgetfulness of self. "I dissolved into a trance" (*CP,* 184), the poem tells us, and one might read the pronoun as in implied quotation marks. This experience is completely involuntary: "I was seized by a pity more profound / than my young body could bear"; "uncontrollably I began to weep"; "I felt compelled to kneel" (*CP,* 185). And yet it is still empathy at a distance: "the poor still move behind their tinted scrim" (*CP,* 185), as if veiled for a mysterious ritual. The passage ends, however, with a stronger sense of identification: "in that ship of night, locked in together, / through which, like chains, a little light might leak, / something fastens us forever to the poor" (*CP,* 185). The implied metaphor is the hold of a slave ship, as all of the island's people are connected by the trauma of the Middle Passage. But the slave ship is the vehicle, not the tenor, of a metaphor about the night: it is also as if, in the solitude of night, sleep, and dreams, class differences dissolve in a common uncertainty and fear of death. But there is still a distinction between "us" and "the poor."

Returning from the account of his "trance," Walcott asks himself, "But which was the true light? / Blare noon or twilight?" The question abruptly poses yet another dichotomy. The opposition of twilight and noon remains incompletely defined until Part Two, in which Walcott and "Gregorias" embrace an art of "blare noon," acolytes of "Vincent [van Gogh], saint / of all sunstroke" and "Paul [Gauguin], their heads plated with fire" (*CP,* 198–99). In Part One, art is suffused with vague yearning, a twilight activity. That transitional light is appropriate for the half-awakened vocation of the young artist. But Chapter 7 brings a moment of conversion, in which, "like Saul, unhorsed," he was changed completely. He "fell in love" and at the same time "fell in love with art, / and life began" (*AL,* 186). The conversion occurs, to be sure, under the auspices of Michelangelo, Raphael, and Uccello, but it sends him back to the common life of the island.

Walcott's epigraph for Part Two, "Homage to Gregorias," contrasts with the Malraux quotation of Part One, in which a European writer describes the apprenticeship of famous European painters. Instead, a Caribbean writer, Alejo Carpentier, describes Caribbean people of various races—whites, blacks, and Amerindians—trapped in futile pursuit of a European ideal, "more and forgetful of the sun they had left behind, trying desperately to imitate what came naturally to those whose rightful place was in the net." Having wasted their youth in "unlighted studios," they eventually come home exhausted, having lost the "heart to set themselves the only task appropriate to the milieu that was slowly revealing to me the nature of its values: Adam's task of giving things their names"[29] (*CP,* 189). The European art of Cimabue and Giotto, who according to Malraux loved paintings even more than they loved the natural world, has led to an Adamic poetics, in which the artifice so strenuously acquired must forget itself in a return to primal beginnings. At some times Walcott sees himself as a sophisticate in search of the natural man; at others, he claims citizenship in the Edenic place that Carpentier's protagonist must seek from afar.

The poem quickly establishes the "sun-struck" intensity of open-air painting in its tropical setting: "Days welded by the sun's torch into days!" (*CP,* 193). Gregorias brings a martial resolve to his encounter with heat and the elements, "the easel rifled on his shoulder, marching / towards an Atlantic flashing tinfoil." As he advances, he sings "'O Paradiso'" (*CP,* 194), finding his heaven on the same coast the French priest of Chapter 6 had experienced as hell. The pact between the poet and Gregorias, to pay full homage to the island in their art, follows:

> But drunkenly, or secretly, we swore,
> disciples of that astigmatic saint,
> that we would never leave the island
> until we had put down, in paint, in words,
> as palmists learn the network of a hand,
> all of its sunken, leaf-choked ravines,
> every neglected, self-pitying inlet
> muttering in brackish dialect, the ropes of mangroves
> from which old soldier crabs slipped
> surrendering to slush,
> each ochre track seeking some hilltop and
> losing itself in an unfinished phrase,
> under sand shipyards where the burnt-out palms
> inverted the design of unrigged schooners,
> entering forests, boiling with life,
> *goyave, corrosol, bois-canot, sapotille.*
>
> (*CP,* 194)

The island may be "Paradiso," but an enjambment qualifies the promise not to leave it with "until." Once every feature of the island has been "put down" in their paintings and poems, the young artists will be free to go. Their art is a labor of love, but it also discharges a debt. The language suggests an almost magical faith in the power of art to embody the experienced world: not to depict but to "put down" intact ravines, mangroves, palms, and forests. The artist is like a "palmist" (a pun, linking the fate written in the hand with the fronds of the trees he attempts to capture in paint); he interprets signs that are already given, to be studied rather than transformed. But much of the description implies an incompleteness in the landscape as found: the "ochre track" up the hillside trails off in "an unfinished phrase," the ravines are "sunken" and "leaf-choked," their breath and power of speech stifled. The inlets are "muttering in brackish dialect," quietly and indistinctly. Much of the landscape suggests exhaustion (the aged soldier crabs "surrendering to slush," the "burnt-out palms"), yet the forests of the interior are "boiling with life." To the initiated, this landscape discloses a primal fecundity, suggested by the catalogue of creole plant-names at the end of the passage. The vitality of the landscape reveals itself through the creole speech of those who truly inhabit it. The young Walcott and St. Omer do not fully inhabit it until, through their art, they arrive as "conquerers who had discovered home" (*CP,* 195).

The chapter closes with a reflection on the paradox it has raised: that the landscape is already eloquent in a language that waits to be heard and written down, but in the meantime remains mute, "choked," inarticulate. "For no one had written of this landscape / that it was possible," the last section begins, and the enjambment insists that merely to write of it is not enough; one must write "that it was possible" for art and literature. The place has an oral language, creole, but not yet a written one. Things have names, but the names conceal, or are concealed; the weeds proliferate, "hiding in their names," and "whole generations died, unchristened, / growths hidden in green darkness, forests / of history thickening with amnesia" (*CP,* 195). Weather and geography conspire with cultural trauma to sustain this "amnesia," as "the lost Arawak hieroglyphs and signs / were razed from slates by sponges of the rain," and "the archipelago like a broken root / [was] divided among tribes." The young artists aspire to recover this "life older than geography," deep sources of identity threatened with erasure.

Walcott depicts the painter's work as furious struggle, recalling van Gogh's letters from Arles, where "from seven o'clock in the morning till six in the evening" he often "worked without stirring except to eat a bite a step or two away," painting "landscapes done more rapidly than ever before." For van Gogh as for his St. Lucian disciples, painting was "headlong work."[30] As Baugh says, Chapter 9 of *Another Life* "is a remarkable poetic re-creation of the act of painting,"[31] but it also includes, in its second section, a critique of language as the medium of that re-creation, since the very metaphors used to evoke the act of painting signal the difference between the crablike ambiguity of metaphor and the "linear elation" of Gregorias's brushstrokes.

Walcott's language at once insists on the complete fusion of the energies of art with those of nature and on a stubborn, mocking resistance within nature itself. The painting is latently present before the first brushstroke: "There are already, invisible on canvas, / lines locking into outlines. The visible dissolves / in a benign acid." This auspicious beginning, which grants to art the power to dissolve the given and reshape it, soon generates its own countermovement: "[o]ver your shoulder the landscape / frowns at its image" (*CP*, 197). Nature becomes a disapproving critic of the emerging painting. The energies of art and natural fecundity interpenetrate each other, but the resulting profusion of forms can intimidate as well as inspire:

> April ignites the immortelle,
> the leaf of a kneeling sapling
> is the yellow flame of Lippi's "Annunciation."
> Like the scrape of a struck match, cadmium orange,
> evened to the wick of a lantern.
> Like a crowd, surrounding the frame,
> the muttering variegations of green.
>
> (*CP*, 197)

The yellow of nature and the yellow of Fra Lippo Lippi's palette coincide. But the "variegations of green" crowd around the easel-frame, "muttering" like the inlets (*CP*, 194). What tints will represent the indistinct variegation, what artistic language will translate its muttering? The censorious landscape has now multiplied into a "crowd" of natural presences, under whose inspection the painter must continue his work. As the artist struggles, he sees his strain mirrored in nature: "The mountain's crouching back begins to ache" (*CP*, 197).

The imagery evokes a scene of medieval combat, as "a bird's cry tries to pierce / the thick silence of the canvas" (*CP*, 198). The artist's canvas, initially offered as a field receptive to natural energies, has become impervious, silent, and resistant, like a shield held up in defense. The landscape grows more threatening: "At your feet / the dead cricket grows into a dragon, / the razor grass bristles resentment . . . // and a crab, the brush in its pincer, / scrapes the white sand of canvas." The crab becomes the artist's *Doppelgänger*, painting the natural "canvas" of the beach. The artist too acquires armor as "the sun plates [his] back" (*CP*, 198). He resembles a knight in combat against his carapaced adversaries, the cricket-dragon in its exoskeleton, the crab in its shell. His work grows increasingly violent, as "the sun explodes into irises, / the shadows are crossing like crows, / they settle, clawing the hair, / yellow is screaming" (*CP*, 199). These crows first appear in a metaphor: "From the reeds of your lashes, the wild commas / of crows are beginning to rise" (*CP,* 198). Though subjectively generated, the "crows" are at that point understood as part of the landscape. Now they become a figure for "shadows" and settle in the painter's hair, returning to the head that first conjured them. Subject and object, painter and landscape, like the "Days welded by the sun's torch into days" (*CP,* 193), disappear into the fire that consumes them both: "Nature is a fire, / through the door of this landscape / I have entered a furnace. // I rise, ringing with sunstroke!" (*CP,* 199). The fire consumes the appearances that feed it so completely that only the fire itself remains visible. This moment might seem an apotheosis, but only five lines later, "the mouth is sour with failure" (*CP,* 199).

The artist's labor fails because the subjective experience of fusion with the energies of nature itself has not been transferred to the canvas. The moment of intensity has left no lasting trace: "Nothing will show after this, nothing / except the frame which you carry in your sealed, surrendering eyes" (*CP,* 200). Looking back on the reasons for his failure, Walcott concludes that although he could depict "the visible world that [he] saw / exactly," he was too much given to second thoughts. In contrast to the "circuitous instinct" of his own "poor crab" of a hand, Gregorias "would draw / with the linear elation of an eel / one muscle in one thought" (*CP,* 201).

The crab-painter, casually introduced in the first section, turns out to be an emblem of the young Walcott. The indirection of metaphor and paradox, and the historical self-consciousness of "that style, / this epoch, that school" (*CP,* 201), constrain his efforts. Gregorias, in contrast, "abandoned apprenticeship / to the errors of his own soul." As a result, "[h]is work was grotesque, but whole, / and however bad it became / it was his, he possessed / aboriginal force" (*CP,* 201). Through Gregorias's unswerving "linear elation," the initial dream of a landscape "set down" in paint has come true: "Now, every landscape we entered / was already signed with his name" (*CP,* 201). Walcott's divided, complex temperament will require verbal rather than painted images as its artistic medium.

The energies of painting are self-delighting, as we find in Chapter 10, which describes Gregorias's "first commission" from the young French priest at the church in Gros Îlet, a village just north of Rodney Bay on the leeward coast. In this pre–Vatican II work, St. Omer could not depict the holy family or saints as black, though he did sneak a few black faces into the background;[32] yet his delight in his work shines through the borrowed European styles:

> Above the altar lace
> he mounted a triptych of the Assumption
> with coarse, purpureal clouds, a prescient Madonna
> drawn from Leonardo's "Our Lady of the Rocks."
> He soared on his trestles,[33] the curled days shorn
> by the adze of St. Joseph the Worker,
> till dusk, the tree of heaven, broke in gold leaf.
>
> (*CP*, 205)

When he comes down from his trestles, however, Gregorias faces the same dilemma as the young Walcott: how shall he make a career as an artist in a place that cannot sustain an artistic career? Gregorias faces a difficult future, as a "darkness" gathers within him. Somehow, he will have to negotiate the gap between the "black nudes gleaming sweat / in the tiger shade of the fronds" (*CP*, 203) that he produces in the privacy of his studio and the evocations of Leonardo required for the Gros Îlet commission. And he will be unable to earn a living from his painting. He affects an indifference to the public response to his work: "Man I ent care if they misunderstand me, / I drink my rum, I praise my God, I mind my business!" and he claims that in contrast to Walcott, whose "poetry too full of spiders, / bones, worms, ants, things eating up each other," he "love[s] life" (*CP*, 206). He exclaims of himself, "Ah, Gregorias, you are a genius, yes! / Yes, God and me, we understand each other" (*CP*, 207). There is a compensatory bravado in his gestures, as he portrays Europe as suppliant rather than conqueror:

> As if the thunderous Atlantic
> were a record he had just put on.
> "Listen! Vasco da Gama kneels to the New World."
>
> (*CP*, 207)

But he is aware of his own exaggerations, at once defiant and self-mocking.

The sight of "the insane asylum" (*CP*, 207) across the harbor triggers a consideration of madness. Walcott draws a distinction between Gregorias's "madness" and his own obsession with "our history" (*CP*, 208). As Baugh remarks, the manuscript draft includes an account of Walcott's "experience in boyhood of living through the breakdown of an uncle, his mother's brother, who had lived in their house and died in a mental asylum."[34] Walcott writes:

> Up to now I do not remember where my uncle was buried. Probably in the asylum itself, although I doubt that ignorance could have been vicious and frightened enough to separate the graves of the mad from the graves of the sane, as the Church distinctly separated suicides from the blessed dead.[35]

This passage, though it has no counterpart in the poem, tellingly foreshadows *Another Life*'s association of madness with suicide and both with the figure of the artist. Shadowing the poem is the awareness that the story of the artist's life may be a narrative with a (literally) dead end. In retrospect, the ecstasies of artistic awakening that Walcott shared with Gregorias are at once sacred and premature. "[I]n the beginning, all / Drunkenness is Dionysiac, divine" (*CP,* 219), and it remains forever an article of faith that "Gregorias, lit, / we were the light of the world!" (*CP,* 220). But the time was coming when "we too would resemble / those nervous, inflamed men, / fisherman and joiner, / with their quivering addiction / to alcohol and failure" (*CP,* 220–21). Lit with inspiration, the artist borrows divine energies and may without blasphemy appropriate the words of Christ. But to be "lit" can also simply mean to be drunk. Gregorias had sung "O paradiso," and Walcott had felt himself to be Adam in paradise, but the future will reveal them to be "damned poet and damned painter" (*CP,* 220), akin on the one hand to their tormented heroes, Gauguin, van Gogh, and Baudelaire, and on the other to the common people—this time not in their latent glory but in their frustration and failure. If the artist longs to be one with the fisherman and joiner, in many a fisherman and joiner there is a balked artist: "We saw, within their eyes, / we thought, an artist's ghost" (*CP,* 221).

Despite his quest for the St. Lucian "natural man," the young Walcott had tried to make the history he learned at school into a usable past. In his fantasies, he "butchered fellaheen, thuggees, Mamelukes, wogs" (*CP,* 211) as enthusiastically as any white colonist. At such moments, he remembers, "my head roared with gold. I bled for all. I thought it full of glory" (*CP,* 211). Gold has been the color of awakening artistic vocation, sexual desire, and love for Anna, all of which occurred in the same "golden year" (*CP,* 192). But the same color has also evoked the "golden, bugled epoch" (*CP,* 180) of colonialism at its zenith. The convergence of all of these motifs on the word "gold" suggests the seductive danger of identifying artistic achievement, sexual desire, and even love itself with European ideals of beauty and power. In *Drums and Colours,* we recall, gold was the European "God."

Even within a fantasy of himself as a white eighteenth-century soldier stunned by the heat and hardship of his tropical post, Walcott holds to his own sense of experience as a series of self-erasing gestures followed by new beginnings: "This forest keeps no wounds, this nature heals / the newest scar, each cloud wraps like a bandage / whatever we enact" (*CP*, 212). In this poem, one is always beginning "another life" rather than continuing a course of action. But self-erasure resists narrative: whatever happens is soon rubbed out, and we return to an open beginning.

Ideas of the divine, too, are always being destroyed and remade: "I am pounding the faces of gods back into the red clay they / leapt from the mattock of heel after heel, as if heel / after heel were my thumbs that once gouged out as sacred / vessels for women the sockets of eyes" (*CP*, 213). The run-on syntax and breathless enjambment enacts the furious smashing of forms, unmaking the gods and tracing their manufacture back to its primal origins. God-making is bloodthirsty work from the outset, and it remains so despite the apparent progress from "primitive" worship of clay figures to Christian monotheism, which has sanctioned the butchery of "fellaheen, thuggees, Mamelukes, wogs" (*CP*, 211), not to mention Caribs and Africans. Better to pound all gods "back into what they never should have sprung from, / staying un-named and un-praised where I found them— / in the god-breeding, god-devouring earth!" (*CP*, 213). In the end, the earth survives its gods. With "history" discredited and the gods deposed, the ground of origin recedes in infinite regress: "Where else to row, but backward? / Beyond origins, to the whale's wash, / to the epicanthic Arawak's Hewanora,[36] / back to the impeachable pastoral" (*CP* 217). Once again, this resolution resists narrative form. Pastoral does not move.

After the "Impeachable Pastoral": Love, Departure, and "History"

The transition to the third part of the poem comes with one of those random events that assume such prominence in a Glissantian "non-history" and resist the writer's desire for plot to unfold from what has already happened. And yet, this event, which sweeps the inert social order of the town away, inaugurates something the poet will call "history." With the Castries fire of 1948, the "impeachable pastoral" is over:

> And then, one night, somewhere,
> A single outcry rocketed in air,

> the thick tongue of a fallen, drunken lamp
> licked at its alcohol ringing the floor,
> and with the fierce rush of a furnace door
> suddenly opened, history was here.
>
> (*CP*, 221)

Here is one more permutation of the word "lit," connecting the energies of creation to those of destruction. The lamp, like the two young painters, runs on alcohol. The kindling of the fire is figuratively likened to drunkenness, and the "thick tongue" of the lamp recalls the "tongue of the carpenter's plane" and the "tongues of shavings" that "coil from the moving pen" (*CP*, 216) of the poet. Earlier, "through the door of this landscape" Walcott had "entered a furnace" (*CP*, 199) as he vainly struggled to wrestle a resistant nature onto his canvas. "History," too, is an ungovernable fire, and it leaps through a breach opened by mere chance.

The title of the third part of the poem, "A Simple Flame," emerges from the fiery arrival of "history," diverting fire again from destruction to ardor. The epigraph from César Vallejo braces the poem for change: "All have actually parted from the house, but all truly have remained. And it's not the memory of them that remains, but they themselves. Nor is it that they remain in the house, but that they continue because of the house" (*CP*, 223). Chapter 2 had grounded the future poet's career in the experience of growing up in his mother's house, that "sang softly of balance, / of the rightness of placed things" (*CP*, 157) and preserved the memory of his late father. Now the "house" expands, becoming a figure for the island itself as the nurturing environment of its people. St. Lucians who seek a name in the world must eventually leave the house, but everything they do remains grounded within it. As Vallejo puts it, "[t]he functions and the acts go from the house by train, or by plane or on horseback," but "[w]hat continues in the house is the subject of the act" (*CP*, 223).

The first "flame" that we encounter in Part Three is that of the Castries fire itself, described in a language reminiscent of Pasternak's description of a fire in *Safe Conduct*.[37] It shatters the order of time ("They heard the century breaking in half") and space ("the telephone wires sang from pole to pole / parodying perspective"; "the sea was level with the street"), so that the cosmos itself seems no longer upheld by "the broken axle tree" (*CP*, 225). And yet the fire unifies, as "those who thought their lives strange to their neighbours" (*CP*, 225) find their "lives casually tangled like unsorted laundry." Divisions of class dissolve in "some pact / of common desolation" (*CP*, 226) among the displaced families on the Vigie promontory. Despite the insistent repetition of "burnt" and "broken," images of regeneration begin to appear as "the grid of stars budded with lights" and the stunned "refugees began another life" (*CP*, 226).

Despite the violent eruption of history into Walcott's life, the motions of nature—the moon's rising and setting, or the wind's continuous rippling of the waves—go on as before. To the extent that he aspires to escape from history into primal relation with the natural world, Walcott is tempted to collapse the linearity of narrative into the circling back of natural process, or into a profusion of appositive description that keeps adding and adding, like the lapping of waves on the shore. Actions, as well as words, can appropriate these natural rhythms. In the third section, as Walcott watches the approach of the boat that will take him across the harbor to Anna, he admires the oarsman's stroke, "unstudied, pentametrical, / one action, and one thought" (*CP*, 227). The passage recalls the single-minded purity of Gregorias's painting, "one muscle in one thought" (*CP*, 201). In such approximations of natural force art finds its greatest power as well as its connection to the life of the body.

The fourth section brings the encounter with Anna, portrayed throughout in imagery of sunlight and gold: "The sixteen-year-old sun / plates her with light" (*CP*, 229), just as sun had "plate[d]" Walcott's "back" as he painted with Gregorias, and had once "plated with fire" the heads of van Gogh and Gauguin (*CP*, 198–99). At the moment when he "asked her, 'Choose'" and "she nodded," history seems magically repealed: "that nod / married earth with lightning. / And now we were the first guests of the earth, / and everything stood still for us to name" (*CP*, 230–31). But within a few lines, Eve mutates to "that flax-bright harvester / Judith, with Holofernes' lantern in her hand" (*CP*, 231), foreshadowing the trouble ahead—and foreshadowing, too, its connection with Walcott's artistic vocation, for the image is again out of a painting, Carlo Sarcani's "Judith and Holofernes," which appears in full-page reproduction in Malraux's *Psychology of Art*.[38]

The division of Anna into a vision of angelic innocence and a potentially dangerous Judith becomes more intelligible as Walcott describes a split in his own desire. From the "divided child" has come a divided youth. He portrays Anna, singing with the choir at Christmas, as a "profile of hammered gold, / head by Angelico, / stars choiring in gold leaf" (*CP*, 231). In the sixth section, he undercuts the idealized portrait: "But this as well; some nights, after he left her, / his lechery like a mongrel nosed the ruins, / past Manoir's warehouse" (*CP*, 232). He loves an innocent girl out of Fra Angelico but also seeks an earthier satisfaction on the seamier side of town. The reference to "Manoir's warehouse" recalls the story of Manoir's pact with the devil, lending a sulphurous undertone to Walcott's own lust. It also connects lust with the poorer, blacker side of St. Lucian life, while Anna remains associated with whiteness and European art. Gregorias warns him, "You are creating this, and it will end. / The world is not like this, / nor is she, friend" (*CP*, 232).

The long first section of Chapter 14, "Anna awaking," is written from Anna's point of view, the only sustained excursion into another voice that occurs within the poem. It reminds me of Randall Jarrell's remark about Lowell's "The Mills of the Kavanaughs": that the heroine seems less a real person than a "symbiotic state of the poet," so that "[y]ou feel, 'Yes, Robert Lowell would act like this if he were a girl'; but whoever saw a girl like Robert Lowell?"[39] Even Baugh, more attuned than I to this part of the poem, concedes that Anna is "a metaphor of certain states of feeling which Walcott is temperamentally inclined to cultivate."[40] In her monologue, his ventriloquism is readily apparent. Walcott blames youthful artistic self-consciousness for separating him from Anna, but the wall still appears to be there when the mature poet attempts to speak from her perspective. Perhaps the interiority of other people is intractable within his method of displaced narration through landscape and objects as images of his own subjectivity.

As if aware that Anna has begun to vanish as he tries to depict her, Walcott asks, "Who were you, then?" (*CP*, 239). He is compelled to "wake / to the knowledge that things / sunder from themselves, like peeling bark," leaving no core of identity but only "the emptiness / of a bright silence shining after thunder" (*CP*, 240). This is the closest thing to an underlying vision of experience the poem has offered so far: the one stable truth is that things change, and change entails a painful rupture with a previous self. Hence the perpetual experience of being on the threshold of "another life" that gives the poem its title; hence the suspicion of linear narration, since all stories tell only that "things sunder / from themselves." All narratives are narratives of loss and mutability. In a sense the plot of *Another Life* is the fall from innocence into experience, but its insistence on an Adamic poetics looks not toward an accommodation with that fallen state but toward a paradise regained through defiance of time's narrative, just as the straining after universality (Anna as "all Annas") seeks an abiding wholeness behind the particular loss.

Chapters 16 and 17 conclude the third part of the poem with meditations on the young poet's impending departure from the island. As Castries, the "cement Phoenix," recovered from the fire, "things found the memory of their former places" (*CP*, 245). But things, being sundered from themselves, cannot return to their prior innocence. The war "had infected language," leaving behind its horrifying images of "[t]he shoes / of cherubs piled in pyramids / outside the Aryan ovens," so that the very smell of Castries in sunlight brings to mind "[b]urnt flesh" (*CP*, 246). History has come to Castries, and the young Walcott prepares to go out to meet it.

The young poet begins to attract notice in the wider world, attending "Tea with the British Council Representative," who encourages him, perhaps a bit backhandedly, in his work ("of course you will soon shed your influences" [*CP*, 248]). The talk is of Eliot, Elgar, and Britten, and of future travel ("England then. When?"). At last, the island prodigy is to move among the giants of the metropolis. The prospects of fame and achievement are closely linked with sexual desire, as the young man's attention strays from the conversation of "Mr. Winters" to Mrs. Winters's sexual allure (*CP*, 248). When the next section evokes Anna practicing the piano, supervised by "Sister Annunziata" next to "the convent balcony" (*CP*, 248), the disparity between the two scenes suggests that Walcott will soon part from his virginal first love.

The section closes with Walcott's prayer that when he leaves, "what I have sworn to love [may] not feel betrayed." "Make of my heart an ark, / let my ribs bear / all, doubled by memory" (*CP*, 250). The ark fits suggestively with the metaphors of artistic representation that dominate the poem: a single pair of each species was rescued within it. Here, the pairing is the doubling of memory, each creature accompanied not by a flesh-and-blood mate but by a mental trace, and even the Noah of this ark will survive as "the image of a young man on a pier," not the young man incarnate. Ultimately, the ark-heart is

> a ship within a
> ship within a ship, a bottle
> where this wharf, these
> rotting roofs, this sea,
> sail, sealed in glass.
>
> (*CP*, 250)

The nesting of ships within ships suggests an infinite regression. And yet, somewhere within the concentric ships, everything to be left behind must be sealed in an inviolable core, safe from change, so that even the "rotting roofs" will remain as they are instead of crumbling away.

With thoughts of departure come temptations to disloyalty. "How often didn't you hesitate / between rose-flesh and sepia, / your blood like a serpent whispering / of a race incapable of subtler shadow, / of music, architecture, and a complex thought" (*CP,* 251). Leaving the island could be a first step toward a cultural "whiteness," a rejection of West Indian traditions for a Europeanized identity. To leave is also to leap into the unknown, and the only way to prepare for it is to "be happy / in every uncertainty" (*CP,* 251). In this restless mood, the young poet finds his friends "too preoccupied / with balance" (*CP,* 251), the very quality that his mother's house had sung so softly (*CP,* 157). It is time to leave the house, and the extended household that is the island. The surf's "monotonous scrawl" now seems to have been "for years trying to reach" him, with its message, "[g]o" (*CP,* 252).

Chapter 17 closes with the departure, incorporating lightly revised versions of a sonnet from the 1958 *Bim* version of "Tales of the Islands," dropped in the revision for *In a Green Night,* and the final sonnet of the sequence, embedded within a longer verse paragraph. As Walcott turns from the island, it turns away from him. Suddenly, "things . . . would not say what they once meant" (*CP,* 255). The materials of his art abandon him: "No metaphor, no metamorphosis, / as the charcoal-burner turns / into his door of smoke" (*CP,* 257). Once, "through the door of this landscape" (*CP,* 199), he had entered the fire of artistic inspiration. Now, the charcoal-burner, archetypal figure of St. Lucian folk culture, disappears behind a door not of fire, but of smoke, and along with him, "three lives dissolve in the imagination, / three loves, art, love and death, / fade from a mirror clouding with this breath" (*CP,* 257). The flesh-and-blood figures are gone, replaced by their immortal but incorporeal counterparts in imagination. The last line of Part Three, as if longing to return from art to life, calls the fictionalized characters "Gregorias" and "Anna" by their literal names: "Harry, Dunstan, Andreuille" (*CP,* 257).

Walcott titles the fourth part of his poem "The Estranging Sea," a phrase in its epigraph from Matthew Arnold's "To Marguerite." For Walcott, Arnold's phrase, "longing's fire," becomes not just his love for Anna, but everything else evoked by "fire" in his context: the blazing days spent painting with Gregorias, the first awakenings of artistic vocation and erotic desire. The poem, returning to Harry Simmons, shows us the grim result when longing's fire burns itself out.

Harry, like the young Walcott and Gregorias, had followed Gauguin's example, painting the unsophisticated beauty of "black lissome limbs" (*CP,* 261), while withdrawing on his houseboat to secluded parts of the coast. Despite his squalid housekeeping, Simmons persuades himself "that although it stank / this was the vegetable excrement of natural life," and

> that there on the ocean with his saints,
> Vincent and Paul, his yellowing *Letters to Theo*
> and *Noa Noa*, though the worms bored their gospel,
> he no longer wanted what he could become,
> his flame, made through their suffering, their flame,
> nightly by the brass-haloed lamp, he prayed
> whatever would come, come.
>
> (*CP*, 261–62)

In his very attempt to follow the uncompromising path of van Gogh and Gauguin, Simmons renounces "what he could become." The underlying motive appears to be loss of confidence in his own powers, a growing self-conscious "thought and the shadow of that thought" lying "across coarse canvas or the staring paper" (*CP*, 262). He is "a man used / to giving orders," but now "the surface would acquire its own ambition," fighting the artist much as it had resisted the young Walcott in Chapter 9. In a poignant twist on the imagery of Walcott's "golden year" of artistic and erotic flowering, Simmons discovers himself in "the legend of Midas and the golden touch"; his hand brings ruin instead of fulfillment, and "everything he touches breaks."

Walcott resists any suggestion that *Another Life* attributes Simmons's suicide to social causes.[41] But I am inclined to trust the tale and not the teller:

> And perhaps, master, you saw early
> what brotherhood means among the spawn of slaves
> hassling for return trips on the middle passage,
> spitting on their own poets,
> preferring their painters drunkards,
> for their solemn catalogue of suicides. . . .
>
> (*CP*, 265)

The idea that Simmons took his life because St. Lucian society could not or would not appreciate its artists runs strongly through Chapter 21, and some such notion seems implicit when Walcott follows his account of Simmons's breakdown with an angry chapter of invective against betrayers of the West Indian people.

Chapter 19 bears the subtitle "Frescoes of the New World II" (*CP*, 269). Gregorias's "heaven" of Chapter 10 ("Frescoes of the New World I") has become a Dantesque hell, with Anna as Beatrice (filling in for Virgil) guiding the tour, while the sulphur volcano of Soufrière is the final abode of Caribbean political hucksters, inflicting "their own sulphur of self-hatred" upon

> all o' dem big boys, so, dem ministers,
> ministers of culture, ministers of development,
> the green blacks, and their old toms,
> and all the syntactical apologists of the Third World
> explaining why their artists die
> by their own hands, magicians of the New Vision.
>
> (*CP,* 269)

The "green blacks" (i.e., inexperienced in government, but also newly re-invented as "blacks") are as reprehensible as the accommodating "old toms." Those who promise a New Vision nonetheless excuse the status quo as inevitable. Like "the academics crouched like rats" (*CP,* 269), the politicians worship the god of "history" (*CP,* 270), who justifies unacceptable actions in the present as the inevitable result of the past. "They are the dividers, / they encompass our history, / in their hands is the body / of my friend and the future, / they measure the skulls with calipers" (*CP,* 270). Instead of seeing all human beings as fundamentally alike, they divide according to races and ideologies. "Encompass," as the image of the measuring "calipers" confirms, evokes the image of Blake's famous plate of Urizen with his drawing compass, marking a boundary to the possible. The vulnerable body is not safe in these hands that worship an abstract god. Nonetheless, Gregorias will survive: "their vision blurs, their future is clouded with cataract, / but out of its mist, one man, / whom they will not recognize, emerges / and staggers towards his lineaments" (*CP,* 270). With the Blakean overtones of "lineaments," Gregorias becomes a sort of St. Lucian giant Albion struggling to free himself of his specters.

Despite Chapter 19's affirmative close, Chapter 20 strikes an elegiac tone. It combines Walcott's mourning for Harry Simmons with his celebration of Gregorias's narrow escape from a similar fate. Walcott has heard ominous reports of Gregorias "driven deep in debt, / unable to hold down a job, painting so badly / that those who swore his genius vindicated / everything once, now saw it as a promise never kept" (*CP,* 272). When they are reunited, at Piarco Airport in Trinidad, Gregorias tells of his own near-suicide. Moved by his story, Walcott "saw him brutally as Mayakovsky" (*CP,* 273) in Pasternak's *Safe Conduct.* The comparison again reinforces the suggestion that West Indian social conditions drive artists to despair, for Mayakovsky appears in Pasternak's account as a great poet tormented by Soviet culture's incomprehension of his art.

Gregorias has "entered life" (*CP,* 272), but Harry Simmons is not so resilient. News of Simmons's death comes during a long spell of rain, figured as a suicidal protest in its own right: "All day, on the tin roofs / the rain berates the poverty of life, / all day the sunset bleeds like a cut wrist" (*CP,* 275). The death of Simmons confirms premonitions hinted at even in the midst of the idyll with Anna. In Chapter 9, that youthful love "came / out of the Book of Hours," which included a pastoral "reaper with his scythe" (*CP,* 202); now the harvest's "autumnal fall of bodies" has been gathered, for "in the Book of Hours, that seemed so far, / the light and amber of another life, / there is a Reaper busy about his wheat" (*CP,* 275), as the picturesque reaper of Chapter 9 becomes the familiar personification of death.

In the elegy that ends the chapter, Simmons appears as the kind of artist he and Gregorias had aspired to be, one who has absorbed St. Lucian life and landscape completely and embodied them in all of his actions: "People entered his understanding / like a wayside church, / they had built him themselves" (*CP,* 276). Just as Pasternak eulogizes Mayakovsky as the personification of the emergent spirit of the new Russia, Walcott writes that although Simmons "is a man no more," he survives as "the fervour and intelligence / of a whole country" (*CP,* 277). As in a traditional elegy, Walcott summons the people of the countryside to join in the mourning. He evokes not stylized shepherds, but ordinary St. Lucians, whom Simmons knew, engaged in their everyday labors:

> Leonce, Placide, Alcindor,
> Dominic, from whose plane vowels were shorn
> odorous as forest,
> ask the charcoal-burner to look up
> with his singed eyes,
> ask the lip-cracked fisherman three miles at sea
> with nothing between him and Dahomey's coast
> to dip rainwater over his parched boards
> for Monsieur Simmons, *pour* Msieu Harry Simmons,
> let the husker on his pyramid of cocoanuts
> rest on his tree.
>
> (*CP,* 277)

The vowel-producing carpenter's plane, linking poetry to physical labor, recalls also Gregorias's depiction of the carpenter Joseph in the church at Gros Îlet (*CP,* 205), as well as the "tongues of shavings" that "coil from the moving pen" (*CP,* 216). The charcoal-burner, his eyes "singed" by his fire, and the fisherman, "lip-cracked" on the "parched boards" of his boat, are counterparts of Simmons's spirit, parched and singed by despair. The fisherman's clear path to "Dahomey" reminds us that Simmons, despite his worship of European art, was one of the first St. Lucians to value and study the African and Amerindian contributions to the island's culture. His example to Walcott and Gregorias was not only the discipline of European artistic tradition, but also the fusion of that tradition with the materials of West Indian common life. But his work remains incomplete: "Blow out the eyes in the unfinished portraits" (*CP,* 277), Walcott continues. The "simple flame" of the idyll with Anna, the "light of the world" kindled by artistic awakening, is extinguished in mourning. The lament closes with the wish that "His island forest, open and enclose him / like a rare butterfly between its leaves"[42] (*CP,* 277), completing the fusion of Simmons with the "whole country."

Chapter 21 poses the question "Why?" (*CP,* 278), and despite Walcott's objection to sociological explanations of Simmons's death, the poem takes such speculations quite seriously. We are instructed to "Go down to the shacks," or to "follow the path / of the caked piglet through / the sea-village's midden," to "smell the late, ineradicable reek / of stale rags like rivers / at daybreak, or the dark corner of the salt-caked shop where the cod / barrel smells of old women" (*CP,* 278). The answer has something to do with the constricting poverty of the island. After experiencing these sights and smells, "you can start then // to know how the vise / of horizon tightens / around the throat" (*CP,* 279). We recall Walcott's description of his own restlessness, just before his departure for Jamaica: "The horizon tightened round his throat" (*CP,* 253). He can guess how Simmons felt. But finally, he abandons the search for an answer and must settle for an "assent founded on ignorance" (*CP,* 280). Against the harsh fact of this death, and "the young deaths of others," there is still "something which balances" in the valedictory image of Simmons "bent under the weight of the morning, / against its shafts, / devout, angelical, / the easel rifling his shoulder, / the master of Gregorias and myself" (*CP,* 280).

As he looks back on the losses of Anna and Harry, Walcott recalls the self-forgetfulness of the hillside vision of his fourteenth year (*CP,* 184–85). In that moment, the depth of his pain and gratitude had erased the boundaries of identity, and the distinctions of man and woman, parent and child, even statement and its logical contradiction: "I knelt because I was my mother, / I was the well of the world, / I wore the stars on my skin, / I endured no reflections." His "sign was water," or "Janus,"[43] since he "saw with twin heads, / and everything I say is contradicted" (*CP,* 281). In this condition, he felt released from his egotism and indecisiveness: "I shared, I shared, / I was struck like rock, and I opened / to His gift!" (*CP,* 282). Now, in that spirit of generosity, he begs Simmons's pardon for using him as a character in the poem, which now seems an exploitation: "Forgive me, if this sketch should ever thrive, / or profit from your gentle, generous spirit" (*CP,* 282). Even in death the master changes the sketch, as he did so long ago in life (*CP,* 147): "When I began this work, you were alive, / and with one stroke, you have completed it!" (*CP,* 282). This closure, however painful, frees Walcott, who can now say, with Villon, that he has "swallowed all [his] hates." The chapter closes with a celebration of his marriage to "one whose darkness is a tree. . . . // Who holds my fears at dusk like birds." Her treelike stability gives an organic continuity to the rhythms of everyday life and the advance of generations; in her "leaves," their "children / and the children of friends settle / simply, like rhymes" (*CP,* 282). But this metaphor does not entirely convince as a resolution. The next chapter returns to the language of perpetual starting over that permeates the rest of the poem.

Chapter 22, set at Rampanalgas, on Trinidad's northwest coast, affirms the triumph of West Indian nature over "the Muse of history" (*CP,* 284). The landscape will refuse interpretation; beside its "water-coloured water, / let the historians go mad . . . / from thirst" (*CP,* 283).[44] The tautology of "water-coloured water" mocks the powers of language itself. Even the "astigmatic geologist" finds "not a sign" (*CP,* 284). Poets too may have nothing to add, for "[a]ll of the epics are blown away with the leaves" (*CP,* 284).

In this historyless landscape where time moves at the glacial pace of evolution itself, "while the lizards are taking a million years to change" (*CP,* 284), Walcott watches his son and two daughters at play. Each is "a child without history, without knowledge of its pre-world," and in this is "like his father." The children have a vague sense of their past as a fusion of diverse races and origins (Margaret Walcott is part East Indian, part Afro-Caribbean, while Derek Walcott, as his poetry often reminds us, has African, English, and Dutch ancestry): "That child who puts the shell's howl to his ear, / hears nothing, hears everything / that the historian cannot hear, the howls / of all the races that crossed the water" (*CP,* 285). This heritage is too tangled and extensive to be made articulate, unless through poetry; the shell is an "intricately swivelled Babel" (*CP*, 285) that speaks in a confusion of all languages. The past survives only as a primal knowledge beneath the level of language and memory, for "the crossing of water has erased their memories / and the sea, which is always the same, accepts them. / And the shore, which is always the same, / accepts them" (*CP*, 285–86). The ambiguous pronoun reference allows us to read that sea and shore have accepted the memories, or accepted the children. Both possibilities seem relevant. The earth we live on and by does not care what we remember but accepts us among its creatures. But the memories have been transferred to the sea and shore, which are the abode of an eternal present: "In the shallop of the shell, / in the round prayer, / in the palate of the conch, / in the dead sail of the almond leaf / are all of the voyages" (*CP*, 286).

With such an understanding of the past's life in the present, the historian's temptation to "gild cruelty," to "see a golden, cruel, hawk-bright glory / in the conquistador's malarial eye, / crying, at least here / something happened" (*CP*, 286), becomes inadequate. It forgets that all possibilities of human nature are latent in all settings. We "begin again, / from what we have always known, nothing" (*CP*, 286). The alternative to such a new beginning is determination by the past, which for art means "penitential histories passing / for poems" (*CP*, 287). The passage culminates in the outburst "*Pour la dernière fois, nommez! Nommez!*" (*CP*, 288), recalling the priest's attempt, in Chapter 4, to exorcise the demon that possessed Auguste Manoir (*CP*, 170). The modern demon is history-worship, which turns the living into *gens gajés* in thrall to the dead. Walcott affirms to his son the inviolable sacredness of the present, despite the "tortured" look of the almond trees (*CP*, 289). Not only "holy" but "holiest" of all is "the break of the blue sea below the trees, / and the rock that takes blows on its back / and is more rock" (*CP*, 289). He singles the rock out for praise because instead of capitulating to the blows it endures, it becomes even more itself. In praising the sea that strikes the blows along with the rock that endures them, Walcott figuratively confirms his ideal of the Caribbean present as a reconciliation of former oppressors and oppressed. He imagines himself merged, in old age, with both:

> I wanted to grow white-haired
> as the wave, with a wrinkled
>
> brown rock's face, salted,
> seamed, an old poet,
> facing the wind

and nothing, which is,
the loud world in his mind.

(*CP,* 290)

The closing lines, which recall the radical emptying of self in Wallace Stevens's "The Snow Man," leave the poet as a historyless consciousness among elemental presences.

Chapter 23 closes the poem in St. Lucia. Looking at the surf, Walcott sees an accelerated likeness of the passing of human generations, in the midst of which the island, like the sea-beaten rock, goes on being itself. But the landscape no longer resonates with his own subjectivity. The mimosa, instead of greeting him like an old friend, says "You mightn't remember me" (*CP,* 292). The poet cannot reenter the past: "I would not call up Anna. / I would not visit his [Harry's] grave." As he watches tourists on horseback galloping down the beach, he sees the scene as if it were a painting, a tarted-up version of the lonely, heroic art he had emulated with Gregorias. It is a canvas "out of Gauguin by the Tourist board." Things have changed more than he had noticed at first. He repeats the imagery of the opening lines, in which the "divided child" tries to read "the pages of the sea" (*CP,* 145). It is still the same "eternal summer sea" (*CP,* 292), but the human artifacts are mutable:

And what if it's all gone,
the hill's cut away for more tarmac,
the groves all sawn,
and bungalows proliferate on the scarred, hacked hillside,
the magical lagoon[45] drained
for the Higher Purchase plan,
and they've bulldozed and bowdlerized our Vigie,
our *ocelle insularum,* our Sirmio
for a pink and pastel NewTown where the shacks and huts stood
teetering and tough in unabashed unhope. . . .

(*CP,* 292–93)

In contrast, "the untroubled ocean" continues as before. "[T]he moon / will always swing its lantern / and evening fold the pages of the sea" (*CP,* 293).

The passage brings out a tension between the desire to keep the island's cultural integrity intact and the recognition that, after all, much of that culture is rooted in poverty, and that to resist development for aesthetic reasons is dangerously close to wanting the "folk" as a romantic backdrop. Walcott follows his elegy for the lost landscape by asking the "folk" to "forgive our desertions" (*CP,* 293). The plural suggests that his departure is only one desertion among others.

The last section of the poem is reserved for praise, not penitence, and its closing benediction alights on Gregorias. He is the hero of the poem because he sustains an art (and by his example, a poetry as well) grounded in St. Lucia: "you painted our first, primitive frescoes" (*CP,* 294). Returning to the imagery of fire and gold, Walcott calls his friend "A sun that stands back / from the fire of itself, not shamed, prizing / its shadow, watching it blaze!" Gregorias has both the intensity and the detachment of the artist, and he has exorcised the racial self-contempt instilled by colonialism: he is not ashamed of the fire's dark "shadow." Gregorias's energy, and Walcott's own, may have been a "destructive frenzy / that made our years one fire," but it was also a sacred fire. Walcott echoes his words from Chapter 12 (*CP,* 220):

> Gregorias, listen, lit
> we were the light of the world!
> We were blest with a virginal, unpainted world
> with Adam's task of giving things their names,
> with the smooth white walls of clouds and villages
> where you devised your inexhaustible,
> impossible Renaissance,
> brown cherubs of Giotto and Masaccio. . . .
>
> (*CP,* 294)

The Adamic moment, though shadowed by Harry's suicide, Walcott's "desertions," and St. Omer's struggles with despair, remains a source of possible renewal. In that "lit" state of inspiration, there was "nothing so old / that it could not be invented," and the fusion of St. Lucian culture and European art was "inexhaustible," producing "brown cherubs" that are also progeny of the European masters. The poem ends with a reaffirmation of the promise of Part Two, that the light of the world, once lit, never goes out entirely. For as the Master of "the master of Gregorias and [himself]" has said, "Just as long as I am in this world, I am the light of the world."

7

"Pulling in the Seine / of the Dark Sea": "The Schooner *Flight*"

"Well, when I finished 'The Schooner *Flight*,' I thought that maybe I had done something," Walcott said in 1989. And for the most part, readers (and readers with widely differing standards) have agreed. It has impressed custodians of the canon enough to be excerpted in the fourth edition of the *Norton Anthology of Poetry*, but the West Indian cultural nationalist Edward Kamau Brathwaite praised it too, as Walcott's "first major nation language effort."[1] The line "Either I'm nobody, or I'm a nation" may finally have replaced the ending of "A Far Cry From Africa" as Walcott's most quoted passage. Walcott struggled for a long time with "The Schooner *Flight*," which appeared in three different forms before its inclusion in *The Star-Apple Kingdom*.

The publication dates of the three preliminary versions span the period from winter 1977 through 1979.[2] Given the lead time between submission and publication, Walcott must have begun the poem in 1976, when his affair with Norline Metivier, later to become his third wife, was breaking up both his second marriage and the social cohesion of the Trinidad Theatre Workshop. Knowing the circumstances, one can hardly help reading the poem as grounded in autobiography, preoccupied as it is with the sundering of ties to marriage and nation and with a quest for self-transformation and rebirth. The revisions show Walcott increasing the artistic distance between himself and his persona, the sailor-poet Shabine, and shifting the center of gravity from Shabine's personal troubles toward his disillusionment with postcolonial Trinidad and his visionary struggle to free himself from the colonial past. Linguistically, the revisions move, as in "Tales of the Islands," down the register from standard to creole, as Walcott makes Shabine increasingly credible as a man of the folk, a sailor whose "common language go be the wind."

The first printed version (*Massachusetts Review,* winter 1977) acknowledges its incompleteness in a note explaining that the poem is "a work-in-progress about the travels of a West Indian sailor called Shabine, the St. Lucian creole name for a mulatto."[3] The narrative of Shabine's personal difficulties is already fairly complete in this draft: we learn of his affair with Maria Concepcion, his fear of taking the rap for his bosses in a whiskey-smuggling racket, his stint of salvage diving, and his inability to make love with other women after quarreling with Maria. Walcott would later add the story of the fight and subsequent friendship with the cook from St. Vincent, but Shabine's personal circumstances at the time of his departure are fully accounted for in the *MR* version. What's largely missing is the public and historical dimension of the poem: the critique of "the Revolution," the encounter with the ghost-ships of the Middle Passage, the dream identification with the fleeing Caribs in Dominica, the meeting with "History," and Shabine's aspiration to "give voice to one people's grief" do not yet appear. The first version seems especially concerned with justifying Shabine's desertion, as if Walcott felt obliged to defend his alter ego. Shabine accuses Maria of "horn[ing]" him, of having "pick up with a man." In the *Chant of Saints* version, these phrases remain unchanged, but they disappear in the *Trinidad & Tobago Review* and *Star-Apple Kingdom* texts.

If the sequence of revision implies a story of Walcott distancing Shabine from himself, and then connecting Shabine's personal troubles to a collective West Indian "grief," it also shows an increasingly earthy language. In the *Trinidad & Tobago Review* text, we read for the first time of Shabine's resolve that as he writes the poem, "each line must be soaked in salt." The marination of its language in the brine of Caribbean vernacular seems to have taken a few years, and even this line would drop "must be" for the creole "go be" when it appeared in *The Star-Apple Kingdom.* Perhaps the most striking instance of this linguistic transformation is the passage about Shabine's encounter with a personified "History." Absent from the initial *Massachusetts Review* text, it appears in the *Chant of Saints* version, thus:

I saw History once, but he didn't recognize me;
an old man with a parchment skin as mottled with warts
as a barnacled sea-bottle, he crawled crab-wise through the shade
of the Creole Quarter, from Castries to Christiansted,
through holes in the net that was cast by the thread
of ironwork balconies, in cream linen and Leghorn hat,
with blue, rheumy eyes and a neck pink as a buzzard's,
and, making history, I shouted with affection:
"Ay, sir! Is me, Shabine, your unhistorical
grandson; you remember Grandma, your black cook at all?"
The deaf bitch spat. It's worth a thousand words.
That's all those bastards left us anyway. Words.[4]

Here, creole is confined to the two-line self-quotation; Shabine's framing narrative adopts West Indian Standard throughout, except perhaps in its use of "bitch."[5] The code-switching for the quotation seems to register a firm distinction between Shabine as narrator of his autobiography and Shabine as character within the story—a distinction that works against the aspiration, explicitly avowed in later revisions, to fuse the roles of poet and representative common man.

In the *Trinidad & Tobago Review* text, Walcott tightens the syntax of the earlier version, with its baroque nestings of prepositional phrases, and uses creole throughout:

I met History once, but he ain't recognize me,
a parchment Creole, more mottle with warts,
than an old sea-bottle, crawling like a crab
through a net of sunlight cast by the shade
of a grillwork balcony, cream linen, cream hat,
I confront him and shout. 'Sir, is Shabine!
They say I'se your grandson, you remember Grandma
your young cook, at all?' The bitch hawk and spat.
A spit like that worth any number of words.
But that's all they left us, anyway, words.

Some of the changes are relatively small, like the omission of -ed endings, so that "mottled" becomes "mottle"; "The bitch hawk and spat" replaces "The deaf bitch spat." But there's a transforming difference between "he didn't recognize me" and "he ain't recognize me," the second of which releases a sardonic irony concealed by the first. "A spit like that worth any number of words" is also an inspired second thought. In both cases, the creolisms place the speaker's voice, socially, as belonging to the unrecognized and spat-at West Indian people. But also, because we have already heard Shabine speak a more elevated language, we understand his switch into this register as a deliberate choice, a way of claiming his place among that people while sarcastically deflating History's pretensions to superiority. As Walcott has remarked in discussing this poem, "[t]he basic language, out of which that dialect emerges, comes out of a dramatization through the medium of masks or faces or characters."[6] This dramatic function of creole becomes increasingly clear with each revision. The passage would undergo a bit more fine-tuning for *The Star-Apple Kingdom,* but the crucial transformation occurs between the two versions quoted above.

In "What the Twilight Says: An Overture," Walcott conceded that in mastering the English tradition, he "insisted on a formality which had nothing to do" with the lives of the West Indian actors who performed his scripts.[7] With "The Schooner *Flight*" he begins to integrate this dualism. In this respect, he both influenced and participated in a widespread change. As Laurence Breiner has observed, West Indian poets, under "the cultural imperatives associated with Independence and the high water mark of Black Power," at first dramatized "an opposition between 'alien' SE and indigenous nation language." But since the early 1970s, he maintains, "the notion of polarity has largely been supplanted by one of continuum. SE has come to be recognized again as a component of nation language."[8] This movement from polarity to continuum draws support from implicit continuities within Creole culture itself, which scholarship of recent years has rendered visible.

Sociological work on the Caribbean has been rethinking a related polarity, the opposition of the culture of respectability and the culture of reputation, influentially posited in Peter J. Wilson's *Crab Antics: The Social Anthropology of English-Speaking Negro Societies in the Caribbean* (1973). In Wilson's thesis, West Indian life negotiates between the codes of respectability, centered in the yard and school room, dominated by matriarchal authority and colonially induced values, and reputation, centered at the crossroads and the rum shop, dominated by the peer relations of rebellious young men. The first supports decorous behavior and SE speech, while the second encourages flamboyant performance and subversive play. The English literary canon, in this view, would be associated with colonized values of the respectability culture, stifling the vital idiom of the crossroads. As Walcott put it in his early poem, *Epitaph for the Young:* "We'll drink to any West Indian who / Strips speech of tie and socks" (*EY,* 31 [Canto X]).

Some important studies, such as Roger D. Abrahams's *The Man-of-Words in the West Indies* (1983) and Richard D. E. Burton's *Afro-Creole: Power, Opposition and Play in the Caribbean* (1997), have built on the idea of the two cultures but have treated them as less a dualism than a continuum. Abrahams argues that the "sensible" performing style of the respectability culture and the "nonsense" style of the reputation culture have need of each other: "The community recognizes the need, on certain occasions, to channel certain of the motives implicit in the nonsense behavior in predictable directions, in the form of performance occasions, even though this behavior is regarded as courting chaos and is therefore feared."[9] Accordingly, the Standard English found in the "sensible" performances of "sweet" talkers and the Creole "nonsense" performances of "broad" or "bad" talkers are integrated into "the speech economy of their community" (Abrahams, 91). Both styles can turn into their opposites: "A rite which starts with a formality (e.g. a wedding) is likely to end in masquerade; a rite which starts with masquerade (e.g. New Year's Eve, Carnival) is likely to end in formality" (E. R. Leach, quoted in Abrahams, 74). And "when a scandal song, written in creole, is judged especially successful because of its wit and economy of expression and its memorability, it may be praised as a sweet" (92).

Burton goes even further than Abrahams in describing the codes of respectability and reputation, sense and nonsense, as intermeshed. In discussing the disappearance of patois from Trinidadian calypso in the early twentieth century, he remarks that "as in the case of the altiloquent tea meeting or wedding reception speechifier, much more was involved than a simple, and ultimately sterile, attempt to mimic the language of the colonial master. It was just as much a question of appropriating the power felt to reside in the dominant language, of using that power as a way of enhancing one's own reputation and devaluing one's rivals."[10] So the "sweet" performances can serve reputation as well as respectability. He entertains the possibilities suggested in other recent scholarship that *both* respectability and reputation cultures are products of the colonial past, neither more indigenous than the other (Lisa Douglass, quoted in Burton, 167), and that just possibly, the respectability culture has more potential to generate effective resistance than does the reputation culture, for all its rebellious gestures (Daniel Miller, quoted in Burton, 168). The binary pairings of SE versus creole, European vs. African, European vs. creole, emerge as oversimplified, if deeply ingrained, frames of reference.

In assimilating canonical English poetic styles, then, Walcott was not turning his back on creole culture but following a pattern within creole culture itself, which itself adopts practices of European origin and evolves an "Afro-American style" in which to perform them. "Talking sweet," in its delight in elevated diction and rhetorical ornament, offers an indigenous counterpart to the "mighty line" of English verse. "European" forms are still alive within creole culture. Conversely, a look at the English canon through creole categories may reveal a West Indian Trojan Horse within the London wall. Christopher Marlowe, whose "mighty line" Walcott aspired to "prolong," was an Elizabethan badjohn, twice arrested for fighting and killed at twenty-nine in a tavern brawl. In *Tamburlaine,* the play that established Marlowe's reputation on the London stage, the hero rants like a Midnight Robber in Carnival. The "mighty line," within the English tradition itself, can be either a sense or a nonsense performance. It is associated with moral seriousness and the Miltonic sublime, but also with the pleasures of gorgeous language for its own sake and with the seductions of rhetoric. Like the speeches of a St. Vincent Tea Meeting, it can leave semantic reference behind, as Ben Jonson censured Marlowe's *Tamburlaine* for doing, along with other plays "of the late age, which had nothing in them but the scenicall strutting, and furious vociferation, to warrant them to the ignorant gapers."[11] Like the Mighty Sparrow, the mighty line can be serious and frivolous at once.

More could be done with comparison of the early drafts, and I shall have occasion to return to them in passing, but it is the text as Walcott finished it that concerns us most. The poem opens with Shabine's account of stealing away before dawn to ship aboard the *Flight.* His decision to leave sets the poem in motion. In the first version, he narrates his departure rather briefly, but in the process of revision, the opening expands into a nuanced foreshadowing of the conflicts to come. After the initial five lines describing his departure, Shabine continues:

> Out in the yard turning grey in the dawn,
> I stood like a stone and nothing else move
> but the cold sea rippling like galvanize
> and the nail holes of stars in the sky roof,
> till a wind start to interfere with the trees.
> I pass me dry neighbour sweeping she yard
> as I went downhill, and I nearly said:
> "Sweep soft, you witch, 'cause she don't sleep hard,"
> but the bitch look through me like I was dead.

> A route taxi pull up, park-lights still on.
> The driver size up my bags with a grin:
> "This time, Shabine, like you really gone!"
> I ain't answer the ass, I simply pile in
> the back seat and watch the sky burn
> above Laventille pink as the gown
> in which the woman I left was sleeping,
> and I look in the rearview and see a man
> exactly like me, and the man was weeping
> for the houses, the streets, that whole fucking island.
>
> (*CP*, 345)

Beginning with Shabine's immobile, stone-like stance, we sense that the moment of his departure is a death of sorts, a suggestion confirmed by the neighbor's staring through him as if he were not there, by the possible double meaning of the driver's "really gone," and by his own view of his reflection ("in the rearview," the mirror of the past) as that of another man, an old self still visible but no longer embodied. In leaving his house, he has left an entire way of life behind him, and his home now is "the sea rippling like galvanize," beneath "the nail holes of stars in the sky roof." It is hard to say (and is probably meant to be so) whether his tears are for the people of "that whole fucking island," including the poor of Laventille (identified through the dawn with the pink of Maria's gown, and therefore as another beloved), or for *his own loss* of the island and everything it has given him. Or, as seems most likely, for both. And since it is the *Doppelgänger* "in the rearview" and not the fleeing Shabine who weeps, this grief may be untrustworthy and nostalgic, itself one more thing to be left behind. With this last thought, we return to Walcott's often reiterated suggestion that the way to deal with an impossible past is by amnesia, by the annihilation of history. Shabine says "I taking a sea-bath, I gone down the road" (*CP*, 346); if his departure is a form of death, it is also, potentially, a baptismal immersion, a rebirth.

The old "witch," already awake outside the house where the young Maria Concepcion lies asleep, is in a sense Maria's double. The epithet "witch" may be suggested by the broom she uses to sweep the yard, but the seductive Maria, too, has exercised a sort of sexual witchcraft on Shabine. The poem, as it turns out, is replete with doublings. In this passage alone, there are at least two others: Shabine confronting his alienated reflection in the taxi "rearview," and the linking of Maria, through the pink nightgown of sunrise, to the island itself. There are also Shabine's abandoned home and his new home fashioned of sea and sky. Shabine, like Walcott "divided to the vein," envisions the world as a linked system of dualisms, choices, conflicting loyalties. As the poem unfolds, it plays not only on the familiar binarism of white and black, but on a series of others: poet and sailor, sea and land, flight and return, death and renewal.

Ned Thomas, in a brief but perceptive discussion of "The Schooner *Flight*," notes the degree to which unreconciled tensions are latent within the title itself. "One's first thought in the early stages of the poem," writes Thomas, "is that 'Flight' suggests escape from what Conrad calls land-entanglements." But by the end of the poem, "two other emphases have been found: that of "poetic Flight," as in the phrase "flight of the imagination," and that of a flight, like that of an arrow to its target, that is "not *from* but *to*," driven by "a purpose though that purpose is sensed rather than known," and simultaneously "emotional and sexual but also metaphysical."[12] At the point of Shabine's departure, he weeps for what he must leave behind, but by the end of the poem, what he has abandoned has been restored to him in a displaced form.

Shabine's tears "for that whole fucking island" turn his attention from his personal crisis to his disillusionment with the "bohbohl"[13] of postcolonial Trinidad. "[I]f loving these islands must be my load, / out of corruption my soul takes wings" (*CP*, 346). In this image, the spirit finds inspiration in the least promising sources, as a flying insect might be bred in "corruption" of a more literal sort. With "wings" comes another image of flight, and of love as a "load" or burden dragging the soul earthward. There is a similar moment in "The Gulf," where the speaker compares departure to the *via negativa:* "So, to be aware // of the divine union the soul detaches / itself from created things" (*CP*, 104). But whereas in the earlier poem, by a grave pun, "we leave Love Field," in "The Schooner *Flight*" Shabine carries his love with him, and he never stops seeking some form of reunion with what he has left behind, although literal return is impossible.

The most extreme instance of Shabine's aspiration to carry with—or within—him all that he has left behind comes in his celebrated words, "either I'm nobody, or I'm a nation." Through his racially mixed heritage and his knowledge of "these islands from Monos to Nassau,"[14] Shabine harbors within him a West Indies of the spirit. Similarly, he knows, even as he abandons her, that there will "be no forgetting" Maria. Nor, he swears, has he ceased to care for the family he left to pursue his affair with Maria: "I loved them, my children, my wife, my home; / I loved them as poets love the poetry / That kills them, as drowned sailors the sea" (*CP*, 347). The two analogies for his love reveal that for him, love is an almost unsustainable emotion, involving a choice between being killed by love's object or abandoning it.[15] That which constitutes the poet's vocation, what he labors to sustain and bring forth, ultimately destroys him, just as the sea, the medium of passage, drowns the sailor in the end. But no sooner are those words out than he vows to write "this poem," tightly rigged as the schooner *Flight* itself, "soaked in salt" of the sea. In so doing, the sailor-poet confronts literally the two destructive forces he has just likened to the love he has left behind. The voyage and the poem (which are perhaps the same thing, if one reads the voyage as a sustained metaphor for the making of the poem) become a quest not for oblivion but for transformation, a way of remaking what has been left behind as something that can be carried in the heart, and a way for Shabine to atone for abandoning those he has loved. Everywhere in this poem, there shall be no way out but through, no annihilation of the past except through its ritual reworking. The smallest descriptive details warn that this will be so: "the port side of dories, schooners, and yachts / was painted afresh by the strokes of the sun," but in the next line we learn that the sun's brushstroke, even as it Adamically renews the visible world, is "signing her [Maria's] name with every reflection" (*CP,* 346). Even the first light of morning is subject to "reflection," by which it reports to the eye the forms already waiting before it arrived, and Shabine, too, is engaged in "reflection," inscribing (or "signing") the present with his memories. And having pointed forward with his vow to shape a poem from the "common language" of "the wind," Shabine turns not to his outsetting voyage but to an account of "how this business began."

Before leaving the first section for the main body of Shabine's narration, we might pause for our own reflection on what his vow means. Ned Thomas has called attention to the vexed meanings of "my common language":

> In the first place, it must reflect a commitment to the salted vigour of ordinary speech. . . . However, compared to many West Indian poets, Walcott achieves that effect by a very few touches drawn mainly from West Indian syntax and verb-forms, devices that in no way lose Walcott his international audience. But the adjective "common" is grappled perplexingly to the possessive pronoun "my." "Our common language" would have proclaimed allegiance to Caribbean English while at the same time underlining its popular nature, but that, of course, is not Walcott's position on "nation language." So "common" must have a wider reference to the international currency of English, and "my" must represent the poet's in-

> div[i]dual attempt to wrest it to his own purpose, an ambitious, individualist undertaking.[16]

One may go even further: Shabine says that his common language is not to be any form of English but "the wind," which is indeed audible but is not linguistic. He invokes a Romantic poetics in which the authority of language is grounded not in convention but in nature itself, and in which the play of wind on an aeolian harp supplied an analogy for poetic inspiration. As we shall find later in the poem, Shabine's idea of poetry as a "weapon" against political power also recalls the Romantic poets, especially Shelley and Blake. Shabine's "common language," with which his voyage brings him into primal contact, is above all nature itself, the renewing source that the corrupt language of Trinidian politics no longer honors.

Shabine, drawn into smuggling to finance his gifts to Maria Concepcion, already makes his living on the sea, although the seven-mile run across the Serpent's Mouth "between Cedros and the Main" is landlocked seafaring. (The isolated and sparsely populated Cedros would indeed be a good place to conceal a smuggling operation.) When investigators catch up with the smugglers, Shabine knows that the indictments will land not on "O'Hara, big government man," since the "Commission of Enquiry" has been set up "with himself as chairman investigating himself," but on ordinary "khaki-pants niggers like you and me" (*CP*, 348). The introduction of a "you" of the same class and race as Shabine evokes a dramatic situation, in which Shabine is telling his story to men much like himself, fellow citizens of "this Trinidad, this Limer's[17] Republic." Walcott's international audience stands outside that circle, overhearing what is said within it.

Shabine's next line of work is salvage diving. Now he descends from the surface of the sea into its depths, and what he sees there frightens him. He learns, as another poem in *The Star-Apple Kingdom* puts it, that "the sea is History." The undersea trail of ground bones "from Senegal to San Salvador" obliquely evokes The Middle Passage, which he will encounter head-on during his voyage. Finally, Shabine succumbs to undersea "raptures":

> and I saw God
> like a harpooned grouper bleeding, and a far
> voice was rumbling, "Shabine, if you leave her,
> if you leave her, I shall give you the morning star."

After this incident, he does a stint in "the madhouse," then finds himself impotent when he tries to forget Maria with other women. This passage introduces the suggestion that hallucinatory madness (the promise of the morning star alludes to Revelation 2:28) is to prophetic genius near-allied. His resolve, in section 9, to defeat the "ministers" and "businessmen" of the postcolonial regime with "no weapon but poetry / and the lances of palms and the sea's shining shield" (*CP*, 357–58) will seem to others as Quixotic as Makak's quest for Africa. The fit of "raptures" also establishes the sea as an object of erotic desire, alternately threatening and alluring as he believes women to be. During his failed sexual encounters, Shabine sees the women's genitalia as "sea-eggs," oviform but infertile, "spiky" and so capable of wounding him.

As the second section closes, Shabine still hopes for some unifying perspective:

> Where is my rest place, Jesus? Where is my harbour?
> Where is the pillow I will not have to pay for,
> And the window I can look from that frames my life?
>
> (*CP*, 350)

He still hopes to replace the domestic stability he is about to abandon, to look from some other window as he once looked from that of his home. Less literally, that "window" is a narrative angle of vision, a point of view from which his life looks whole, "frame[d]" and composed like a painting, rather than like a desperately improvised series of isolated decisions. He hopes, too, for a stable and fulfilling sexual relationship—one may read "harbour" as a sexual metaphor, and presumably Shabine would like to share that "pillow" with someone who does not charge him for it. Or one might take "harbour" metonymically, as the harbor of some new homeland, with its own anchorage to replace the one at Carenage.

"I had no nation now but the imagination," the third section begins, and so memorably powerful is this statement that one may forget to ask how Shabine arrives at it. So far, we have learned something of his contempt for the corruptions of Trinidadian government and for the cynical lassitude of his fellow citizens of "the Limers' Republic," but nothing that would quite explain his sense of belonging to no community but the one he carries within himself. In a sense, as Benedict Anderson has argued, Shabine's aphorism on nationality applies to everyone else as well, but there is a great difference between a shared imagined community, reinforced by public institutions, and a community imagined by only one of its citizens. And yet, if nations begin with someone's belief that a nation latently exists, then Shabine may cling to the hope that some day there will be immigrants to his nation of one.

In an interview of 1990, Walcott commented, suggestively but self-contradictorily, on Shabine's statement:

> you could take this to mean that the nation of the imagination would be a nation in which the temperament and the spirit of the poet would enter the spirit of politics. . . . This other nation we are talking about is the nation that acts imaginatively in the higher sense of the imagination. And in the way that the imagination creates a work of art, a nation's ideal should be to be a work of art. . . . [I]t is inevitable to have a flawed nation, but the effort to create a nation as if it were an act of imagination would be more creative than the repetition of the usual clichés and conduct. Shabine is not going that far with his statement. I am simply saying that if I have no nation but in imagination, the artist is left out of the nation and therefore his recourse is to an imaginary nation which is his nation, his imagination. So by disaffection, he has become an artist.[18]

In the first part of this commentary, Walcott upholds the Shelleyan ideal of the poet as unacknowledged legislator whose vision, despite its apparent lack of social utility, offers an ideal toward which nations should aspire. By the end of it, he appears to accept the marginality of the poet: art begins with "disaffection," the artist's refusal of national community in favor of a solitary vocation. To some extent, however, this contradiction inheres in Shelley's own account, wherein the poet is "unacknowledged" and so must remain unseen in order to act at all. Similarly, Emerson enjoins the poet: "Thou shalt leave the world, and know the muse only. Thou shalt not know any longer the times, customs, graces, politics, or opinions of men, but shall take all from the muse." And yet, though "isolated among his contemporaries," the poet has "this consolation in his pursuits, that they will draw all men sooner or later."[19] In the late twentieth century, when most poets see the connection between the imagination and the public realm as historical and cultural, Walcott insists on an older view in which the poet participates in the public realm by turning away from it, by opposing to "History" the visionary imagination, Quixotically tilting at power with "lances of palms," speaking an elemental "common language" of the wind.

Looking back from the commentary to the poem, however, one sees not so much a rejection of social connection as an anxious shuttling back and forth between the intensely personal and the social. Unlike many of his U.S.-born contemporaries, who sought justification for treating personal experience as a microcosm of the social,[20] Walcott sees the two as disjunct, requiring the work of poetry to bring them together. The entire second section shifts back and forth between Shabine's anger at Trinidadian corruption and his troubles with Maria Concepcion. The window that can frame his life would be a point of view, not yet reached, that gives his personal history a place in a larger narrative.

In the third section, the social collides with the personal. Shabine's mulatto identity, like Walcott's, places him between "the white man," who "chain my hands and apologize, 'History,'" and the new ideologues of Black Power, who "said I wasn't black enough for their pride" (*CP,* 350). He is trapped in a dualism not of his own creation. History, as the colonizer's self-justifying narrative, is personified as a white planter in a tropical suit. His crab-like movement, sideways and backward, suggests evasiveness and inability to go forward into the future. His reply to Shabine's greeting goes deeper than any words: spitting, like the common language of the wind, is more primal than the earthiest creole. If nature is deeper than language, so too is the cultural embedding of historical pain, historical contempt. These will not be easily dislodged; Shabine's effort at exorcism pits one primal language against another.

Revolution, one means of exorcism, Shabine can no longer take seriously, having "seen that moment Aleksander Blok / Crystallize in *The Twelve*" (*CP,* 351). In Blok's poem, a revolutionary Christ figure leads his armed Bolshevik disciples through a driving blizzard wind that is "scouring God's world":

> Abusing God's name as they go,
> all twelve march onward into snow . . .
> prepared for anything,
> regretting nothing . . .
>
> Their rifles at the ready
> for the unseen enemy

Although "At arm's length you can only just / make out your neighbour's form,"[21] they are prepared to fire on anyone who stirs.

But if the rhetorical fury of the 1970 Trinidadian revolt reminded Walcott of the Russian Revolution, the outcome was of course different. The revolution failed, and its scale was minuscule beside the Russian events. Shabine's response to the call for "black power" is "Tell me, what power, on these unknown rocks— / a spray-plane Air Force, the Fire Brigade, / the Red Cross, the Regiment, two, three police dogs / that pass before you finish bawling 'Parade!'?" (*CP,* 350). The Trinidadian narrative totters between tragedy ("Young men without flags / using shirts, their chests waiting for holes") and farce:

> In the 12:30 movies the projector best
> not break down, or you go see revolution. Aleksander Blok
> enters and sits in the third row of pit eating choc-
> olate cone, waiting for a spaghetti West-
> ern with Clint Eastwood and featuring Lee Van Cleef.
>
> (*CP,* 351)

The 12:30 movie, a cherished entertainment in Port of Spain, becomes the opiate of the people, a low-budget neocolonial control imported from Hollywood. The hyphenated rhyme on Blok's name undercuts his dignity, while movie actors supplant him—and Shabine, and Walcott—as the artists of the people.

Section three might be seen as Shabine's catalogue of failed hopes. When he looks to the past, "History" spits at him in contempt, but when he places his hope in the future by trusting to "revolution," he sees either the pitiless brutality envisioned by Blok or, what is almost worse, a degradation of revolution to a craving for spectacle. He is even "losing faith in the love of" Maria Concepcion, which might have sustained him despite his lack of social connection. When the poem continues in section four, the *Flight* has weighed anchor and put to sea.

As the *Flight* skims along the northern coast of Trinidad, it passes the fishing village of Blanchisseuse. Shabine's last look at Trinidad grants him a pastoral moment, far from the Bohbohl and trouble of Port of Spain (*CP,* 346). This scene suggests that "paradise" survives beside the "slums of empire." The natural and the human interpenetrate and sustain each other, as

> lighthouse and star start making friends,
> down every beach the long day ends,
> and there, on that last stretch of sand,
> on a beach bare of all but light,

> dark hands start pulling in the seine
> of the dark sea, deep, deep inland.
>
> (*CP,* 351–52)

On that "beach bare of all but light," the corruptions of culture are washed away ("Blanchisseuse," fittingly, means "laundress"). Lighthouse and star, the dark sea and the dark hands, form a harmonious whole, and the fishermen haul the sea's elemental power "deep inland" to dwell in their abode. Shabine bids farewell to an ideal image of the island, unspoiled by the "things that would make a slave sick / in this Trinidad, the Limers' Republic" (*CP,* 348).

The first four parts of the poem have been a leave-taking. But instead of escaping into the open sea, Shabine immediately encounters the first of several reminders of his personal and historical past. However much he wishes to flee from history, history rises before him to bar his path. It exacts a ritual re-experiencing of its cruelties before it will let him pass. On the first morning out, "fog coil from the sea," bringing visions of phantom ships and their crews. The first apparitions are warships, commanded by "great admirals, / Rodney, Nelson, De Grasse," all three of whom figure prominently in the Caribbean battles between England and France for possession of the islands. When Walcott writes of "the hoarse orders / they gave those Shabines," he reminds us that a white eighteenth-century common seaman was also a "Shabine" in status, and that those celebrated battles were fought to maintain colonial sway over lucrative slave plantations. These ships of the line have a necessary connection to the "slave ships" that appear next.

The phantom warships' "forest / of masts sail right through the *Flight*" (*CP,* 352). History, as it so often is for Walcott, becomes apparitional, haunting us precisely because it is veiled in a mist of "amnesia," eluding narrative recovery, accessible only as nightmare. But in the moment of the apparition, Shabine feels himself a part of an unending cycle of ships and sailors,

> like this round world was some cranked water wheel,
> every ship pouring like a wooden bucket
> dredged from the deep; my memory revolve
> on all sailors before me, then the sun
> heat the horizon's rim and they was mist.
>
> (*CP,* 352–53)

Like the fishermen of Blanchisseuse, hauling "the seine / of the dark sea, deep, deep inland," the procession of ships brings the mysteries of the sea up into the human domain. Shabine's vision brings him closer not only to his befogged history, but to the "depths of the sea" (*CP*, 361) from which, at the poem's close, he claims to derive his song.

The still more traumatic encounter promised by the fourth section's title, "Shabine Encounters the Middle Passage," has been deferred until its last five lines. In contrast to the detailed, Gothic descriptions of the naval ships' ghost crews, with their "rusty eyeholes like cannons" and bodies so emaciated that "you traced their bones / like leaves against the sunlight," the occupants of the slave ships are not described at all. They remain below decks, invisible and inaudible. Even a supernatural vision cannot penetrate the veil of amnesia shrouding the Middle Passage. Shabine finally gives up his attempts to summon a response:

> our fathers below deck too deep, I suppose,
> to hear us shouting. So we stop shouting. Who knows
> who his grandfather is, much less his name?
>
> (*CP*, 353)

His genealogical amnesia remains intact.

As the *Flight* approaches Barbados, its first "Landfall," Shabine pauses for a meditation on colonial naming, reminiscent of "Names" and "Sainte Lucie" in *Sea Grapes*. The trees "on the low hills of Barbados" may be called "cedars, cypresses, or casuarinas," and while to an outsider one name may seem as good as another, "we live like our names and you would have / to be colonial to know the difference" (*CP*, 353). The section's title, "The Sailor Sings Back to the Casuarinas," gives that name priority over its two competitors, but the ensuing lines are more circumspect. The referent of "them" in the first remains suspended until the fifth, and even then the matter remains in doubt:

> You see them on the low hills of Barbados
> bracing like windbreaks, needles for hurricanes,
> trailing, like masts, the cirrus of torn sails;
> when I was green like them, I used to think
> those cypresses, leaning against the sea,
> that take the sea-noise up into their branches,
> are not real cypresses but casuarinas.
>
> (*CP*, 353)

When the trees are finally named, Shabine calls them "those cypresses," remarking that in his youth he "used to think" they were casuarinas. In his "green" thinking, moreover, casuarinas are not trees in their own right but imposters: these "are not real cypresses," but inferior colonial imitations. The captain of the *Flight* compounds the confusion, calling them "Canadian cedars." The *OED* explains that the name "cedar" is often "[a]pplied, with or without distinguishing epithet, to various trees more or less resembling the true cedar: including species of *Cedrela, Juniperas, Thuja, Cupressus* [the cypress], *Pinus";* among the varietal names are "Barbados cedar" and, suggestively for Walcott's theme, the "Barbados bastard cedar." (There is no entry for "Canadian cedar.") If a casuarina is a false cypress, then a cypress, in turn, is a false cedar.

For the trees as trees one name is indeed as good as another, "since they were trees with nothing else in mind / but heavenly leaping or to guard a grave." But they also have a symbolic role in Shabine's attempt to reconcile land and sea, culture and nature. Like the fishermen of Blanchisseuse pulling the sea inland, the trees "take the sea-noise up into their branches," and throughout the passage Shabine describes them in anthropomorphic language ("when I was green like them," "watching their wailing bodies wail like women," "their hair hangs down in rain" [*CP,* 353–54]). Naming is central to Walcott's claims for an "Adamic" New World poetics. The act of naming takes the natural into the cultural domain while grounding language in the domain of the natural. And the choice of a name reveals much about the consciousness of the namer, the degree to which it has become Adamic by exorcising "the pain of history words contain" (*CP,* 354). In this section of "The Schooner *Flight,*" Shabine still struggles with that pain.

In the first lines of section six, Shabine recalls that he "used to" suppose that the cypresses were actually casuarinas. By lines 13–14, he seems to have reversed himself: "Once the sound 'cypress' used to make more sense / than the green 'casuarinas'" (*CP,* 353)—once, but not any more. There are, then, three stages in Shabine's naming of the trees. In his green youth, he thought of them as casuarinas, but with the additional thought that they were "not real cypresses." To speak of them as casuarinas would admit their failure to be legitimate cypresses. At a later stage, the choice of cypress "used to make more sense": the first naïveté past, Shabine is ready to accede to the name "cypress." By the closing lines of the section, he has become aware of the unwitting colonial subservience in his earlier attempts at naming. Knowing, now, the historical pain contained in the words, he realizes that one had "to be colonial" in order

> to love those trees with an inferior love,
> and to believe: "Those casuarinas bend
> like cypresses, their hair hangs down in rain
> like sailors' wives. They're classic trees, and we,
> if we live like the names our masters please,
> by careful mimicry might become men."
>
> (*CP*, 354)

Shabine no longer thinks of his love as inferior, and he no longer wishes to turn the casuarinas into cypresses. Shabine "Sings Back to the Casuarinas" in more than one sense: he responds, as a namer, to the natural forms confronting him; he sings his way back to his first intuition, that the casuarinas are casuarinas and not an inferior form of something else; and he delivers a lyrical riposte (to sing back is also to answer back) to the linguistic impositions of the colonial past. Even though casuarinas are, like the human residents of the islands, imports, coming from Australia and the Pacific islands, they are now familiar parts of the landscape in Barbados (and St. Lucia); to call them by their right name is to claim them as one's own.

Sections seven and eight might be seen as a contrasting pair, through which Shabine establishes his simultaneous claim to be poet and lover, but also, in Whitman's phrase, "one of the roughs," a man among men who can settle a quarrel by force. He can rhapsodize on his first love's "young face washed by the wind" (*CP*, 354), but he can also relish a triage of violence: "Some case is for fist, / some case is for tholing pin, some is for knife" (*CP*, 355). In these sections, Shabine completes the fusion of his dual identity as poet and sailor, witness and voice of his "people's grief," but also a sharer of it, no more refined than the rest of the *Flight's* crew.

In section seven, "The *Flight* Anchors in Castries Harbor," Shabine's role as a mask for Walcott becomes especially obvious, for readers of *Another Life* will recognize that this section is addressed to "Anna," Walcott's fictional name for his first love, Andreuille Alcée. The section recalls a lost wholeness, the last time that Shabine knew, or thought he knew, an "island that heals with its harbour / and a guiltless horizon," which he now sees as the unreachable "target" of his "vain quest" for a haven of "the longing, the lunging heart" (*CP*, 361). "When the stars self were young over Castries, / I loved you alone and I loved the whole world" (*CP*, 354). It was possible then to love one woman only, and to love the entire world without division. We have seen, in contrast, how his present life has been shattered by the division of his love between two women, and by the racial divisions of white and black. And we are about to see the man who once loved the whole world throw a knife into his shipmate's calf.

Section seven is yet another instance of the way Shabine's flight keeps leading him back to origins, both personal and historical. His parting words to Anna reaffirm their connection even as he takes leave of her:

> I have kept my own
> promise, to leave you the one thing I own,
> you whom I loved first: my poetry.
> We here for one night. Tomorrow, the *Flight* will be gone.
>
> (*CP,* 354)

That last line can be taken literally: the *Flight* sails in the morning. But it is hard not to read it as a statement about human mortality as well: all anchorages, including the anchorage in life itself, are brief, and the journey presses on. So taken, the line adumbrates Shabine's acceptance, in the eleventh section, of his own life as a continuous voyage. In the second section, he could ask "Where is my rest place, Jesus? Where is my harbour?" (*CP,* 350), but he has begun to realize that rest places and harbors are temporary, "for one night" only.

In the eighth section, "Fight with the Crew," Shabine's language, which began section seven with the creole phrase "the stars self" only to modulate into standard thereafter, immediately dives back toward the basilect: "It had one bitch on board, like he had me mark" (*CP,* 354). Enough of the lover's courtly language; back to the argot of men at sea. The cook provides another instance of doubling in the poem. He is from St. Vincent, St. Lucia's immediate neighbor to the south. Racially, he is rather like Shabine, a mulatto with "red" skin and blue (as opposed to Shabine's "sea-green") eyes. He may be understood as Shabine's antiself or mask, like Yeats's fisherman: he considers poetry unmanly (he "start mincing me like I was some hen / because of the poems" [*CP,* 355]) and contemptible. Stealing the exercise book in which Shabine writes his poetry, the cook mockingly reads aloud for the crew: "'O my children, my wife'" (*CP,* 355). He chooses the passages dealing with Shabine's regret for his abandoned family because these show him to be weak, dependent on women, and missing the comforts of shore. When Shabine responds by throwing the knife, he passes a test of virility and so puts an end to the conflict:

I suppose among men
you need that sort of thing. It ain't right,
but that's how it is. There wasn't much pain,
just plenty blood, and Vincie and me best friend,
but none of them go fuck with my poetry again.

(*CP,* 355)

Shabine has proved himself a man's poet, someone nobody "go fuck with" anymore. At the same time, Walcott emphasizes that Shabine "beg him first, / but he keep reading." The violence was provoked, and the wound turns out to be minor. Shabine is tough, but he is not brutal.

The friendship of Shabine and Vince recalls the literary conventions of male friendship, often depicted as forged from initial hostility or violence. One might go back all the way to Gilgamesh and Enkkidu. Closer to Walcott's domain, one finds in American literature such pairings as Huck and Jim, Natty Bumppo and Hard Heart, Ishmael and Queequeg. In all of those examples, the friendship reconciles cultural conflicts by crossing racial barriers. But Shabine and Vince are racially alike: the boundary to be crossed is not between races, but between the West Indian man of letters and the sailor as instance of the unlettered West Indian common man.

The ninth section, "Maria Concepcion & the Book of Dreams," takes Shabine even further back than the middle passage. Again, the future and "progress" are juxtaposed with the backward look toward history: "The jet that was screeching over the *Flight* / was opening a curtain into the past. / 'Dominica Ahead!'" Ahead and behind, as it turns out, for Dominica is one of the last places where descendants of the first inhabitants remain: "'It still have Caribs there'" (*CP,* 355). Looking up at the plane and ahead to Dominica, but backward to the long history of the Caribs, Shabine and Vince are moved to meditate on "progress," which falls under the same suspicion that Shabine had turned on "the revolution" in section three:

"One day go be planes only, no more boat."
"Vince, God ain't make nigger to fly through the air."
"Progress, Shabine, that's what it's all about.
Progress leaving all we small islands behind."

To which Shabine replies,

"Progress is something to ask Caribs about.
They kill them by millions, some in war,

some by forced labour dying in the mines
looking for silver, after that niggers; more
progress. Until I see definite signs
that mankind change, Vince, I ain't want to hear.
Progress is history's dirty joke."

(*CP,* 355–56)

There may be material progress, but there has been none in human nature. Shabine's words link Afro-Caribbeans to the first inhabitants, and they unmask progress as the cynical work of that "parchment creole," History, who has already refused to acknowledge Shabine in section three.

In what remains of section nine (the longest in the poem), Shabine allies himself with the antagonists of "progress": dreams, prophecy, and poetry. On the night the *Flight* passes Dominica, Shabine dreams he is among the Caribs who leapt into the ocean rather than submitting to the enemy, "drowned at last / in big breakers of smoke" (*CP,* 356). The dream of death by drowning foreshadows the near-shipwreck of the *Flight* in the storm of section ten ("If we's to drong, we go drong, Vince, fock-it!" [*CP,* 358]). But, like the death by drowning of Phlebas in *The Waste Land,* it may be seen as a death fraught with the promise of rebirth. It is another image of Shabine's healing "sea-bath," his necessary immersion in the destructive element. For after this dream, and its literalization in the storm, Shabine is freed from his obsession with history, his longing for Maria, and his need for a final "rest place" that will resolve the tensions of his life.

To interpret his dream, Shabine goes not to Freud or some other modern guide, but to a folk manual of dream interpretation that Maria used to consult. He recalls that for one of her dreams, involving "'whales and a storm, / . . . the book had no answer"; the following night, he himself "dreamed of three women / featureless as silkworms, stitching my fate," and for this, too, "there was nothing" (*CP,* 357). Shabine's dream so clearly alludes to the three fates that one is tempted to suppose an allusion in Maria's also—perhaps to the fate of Jonah, who like Shabine was in "flight" when he put to sea, attempting to evade God's call to prophecy. It was after this dream that Shabine "broke— / they found me round the Savannah,[22] screaming" (*CP,* 357). From dreams and madness, from the breaking of his old, no longer tenable identity, comes Shabine's poetry and his authority as prophet. In Yeatsian fashion, Shabine's dreams bring new responsibilities. "All you see me talking to the wind, so you think I mad," he says, but those who think so are themselves "mad people," and they underestimate his strength:

The coconuts
standing by in their regiments in yellow khaki,
they waiting for Shabine to take over these islands,
and all you best dread the day I am healed
of being a human. All you fate in my hand,
ministers, businessmen, Shabine have you, friend,
I shall scatter your lives like a handful of sand,
I who have no weapon but poetry and
the lances of palms and the sea's shining shield!

(*CP,* 357–58)

If "I shall scatter your lives like a handful of sand" speaks the language of the Old Testament prophets, "the lances of palms and the sea's shining shield" are images of chivalric combat. Is Shabine an Isaiah or a Don Quixote? Or has Isaiah, in our skeptical age, been reduced to Don Quixote, his prophecy inescapably framed by irony? Or is prophecy Quixotic in the first place, inherently destined to fail—did God not command Isaiah to "tell this people, Hear ye indeed, but understand not; and see ye indeed, but perceive not," so that they will *not* "understand with their heart, and convert, and be healed"?[23] Maybe Shabine's prophecy, like Isaiah's, is effectual only as witness, not as warning. To inflict chastisement, Shabine must be "healed of being a human," transformed either to a god above the human level or to a pitiless avenger as subhuman as the "minister-monster" politicians he prophesies against. Neither transformation seems imminent.

The storm of the tenth section releases the accumulated tensions of the poem. As far back as *The Sea at Dauphin,* Walcott had written memorably of rough weather at sea, and the sailors' language recalls that of the early play: "Be Jesus, I never see sea get so rough / so fast! That wind come from God back pocket!" (*CP,* 358), says Shabine, sounding much like *Dauphin*'s Gacia: "this just half the wind. The next half in the sea back pocket" (*DMMOP,* 46). The restlessness of the sea creatures signals the coming storm: "A stingray steeplechase across the sea, / tail whipping water, the high man-o'-wars / start reeling inland, quick, quick an archery / of flying fish miss us!" (*CP,* 358). By seeing the flying fish as "an archery," Walcott foreshadows the eleventh section's characterization of the *Flight*'s own quest as "the arrow" sped toward "a target whose aim we'll never know" (*CP,* 361), as if to suggest that animals as well as humans are driven by the same inarticulate longing. The sea itself becomes a bestiary: "a black-mane squall pounce on the sail / like a dog on a pigeon, and it snap the neck / of the *Flight* and shake it from head to tail" (*CP*, 358), its quick metamorphosis from horse ("mane") to dog to mule ("Worse than the mule kick of Kick-'em-Jenny Channel")[24] appropriate to its protean nature.

Enjoined by Vince to "say [his] prayers," Shabine silently replies "I have not loved those that I loved enough" (*CP*, 358), taking the impending storm as a judgment on his abandonment of his family for Maria, and of Maria for the open sea. He sees himself as the drowned sailor in Maria's *Book of Dreams*, about to meet his predicted fate. Shabine is spared, not because he deserves to be, but because of his faith:

> Then a strength like it seize me and the strength said:
> "I from backward people who still fear God."
> Let Him, in His might, heave Leviathan upward
> by the winch of His will, the beast pouring lace
> from his sea-bottom bed; and that was the faith
> that had fade from a child in the Methodist chapel
> in Chisel Street, Castries, when the whale-bell
> sang service and, in hard pews ribbed like the whale,
> proud with despair, we sang how our race
> survive the sea's maw, our history, our peril,
> and now I was ready for whatever death will.
>
> (*CP*, 359)

The lines acknowledging the Lord's sovereignty over "Leviathan" recall the submission of Job after the Almighty rebukes him with a string of questions beginning "Canst thou draw out leviathan with a hook?" (Job 41:1). Shabine's religious submission is also, however, an affirmation of solidarity with his "backward people who still fear God," in contrast to the white inflicters of "progress" and the black cynics of postcolonial Trinidad. Recalling the survival of his "race," despite a perilous history, revives his courage. In this passage, too, Shabine virtually removes the mask that distinguishes him from Derek Walcott: how many Trinidadian sailors just happen to have attended Methodist services in the Chisel Street church of Castries, St. Lucia?

If Shabine is saved by faith, not works, then the *Flight*'s captain is his savior, a black Christ redeeming him, by heroic struggle, from a deserved death:

> But if that storm had strength, was in Cap'n face,
> beard beading with spray, tears salting the eyes,
> crucify to his post, that nigger hold fast
> to that wheel, man, like the cross held Jesus. . . .
>
> (*CP*, 359)

After that all-night vigil, "there was no more storm," either on the sea or within Shabine himself. It is not that he has achieved happiness—on the contrary, he will tell us toward the poem's close, he tries "to forget what happiness was" (*CP*, 361). Rather, he has learned to do without it, to accept uncertainty, yearning, and transience without asking for more: "I wanted nothing after that day" (*CP*, 360).

With Shabine's resignation comes a peace of sorts, as he transforms his passion for Maria into a more pantheistic, disinterested love:

> I saw the veiled face of Maria Concepcion
> marrying the ocean, then drifting away
> in the widening lace of her bridal train
> with white gulls her bridesmaids, till she was gone.
>
> (*CP*, 360)

At the moment of his departure, Shabine had never expected to reach such detachment: "there'd be no rest, no forgetting. / Is like telling mourners round the graveside / about resurrection, they want the dead back" (*CP*, 346). By the end of the poem, just as he has exorcised the historical past by his encounter with its horrors, Shabine has also gone past the need to retrieve the "dead" relationships of his personal past. "Resurrection" is no longer a fable told to comfort "mourners round the graveside," but something Shabine has actually experienced in surviving the storm.

To the extent that he still does "want" something, Shabine's desires are for his people. He asks the rain to "make these islands fresh / as Shabine once knew them!" and he asks for his poetry only that it give "voice to one people's grief" (*CP*, 360). His mood, quarrelsome and bitter earlier in the poem, has become serenely beneficent:

> and from this bowsprit, I bless every town,
> the blue smell of smoke in hills behind them,
> and the one small road winding down them like twine[25]
> to the roofs below. . . .
>
> (*CP*, 360)

Shabine has moved from a relentlessly sexual desire for Maria to a perception of her as a presiding spirit of the ocean, and from the desire for a resting place to a desire for the healing of the islands.

As Rei Terada points out, Walcott "expands the tension between individual and communal by pulling his perspective as far back as it can go" when Shabine likens the earth itself to "one / island in archipelagoes of stars" (*CP,* 361):

> The relation of earth to stars recalls and enlarges Shabine's nobody/nation pairing like a magnifying mirror. . . . The collected peoples of earth . . . make one, just as we can find a microcosmic "nation" in Shabine. But Walcott's line break shakes these human unities, and the earth's with the stars: when we pull back even further, the unities disappear in more disunities. From an already wide perspective, "This earth is one," but from an even wider perspective it is only "one / island in archipelagoes of stars."

Ultimately, Terada concludes, "[t]he equation works both ways; we have to keep in mind simultaneously that what we consider multiple can be seen as one, and that what we think single is multiple."[26]

Suggestive and even poetic as Terada's commentary is, it pushes a deconstructive self-consciousness onto Walcott's poem that the context will not entirely support. The underlying emotion is wonder, of a piece with the awe at the power and vastness of the ocean, the willingness to trust and "fear God" that sustained Shabine through the storm. It is the insignificance of human beings within the creation as a whole that Shabine's cosmic metaphor powerfully evokes, rather than the analytical undoing of a binary distinction.[27]

The closing of "The Schooner *Flight*" somewhat recalls that of *Dream on Monkey Mountain.* "I finish dream," says Shabine, as he moves to his benediction of the islands and his meditation on the archipelago of stars. And then, at the very end:

> Sometimes is just me, and the soft-scissored foam
> as the deck turn white and the moon open
> a cloud like a door, and the light over me
> is a road in white moonlight taking me home.
> Shabine sang to you out of the depths of the sea.
>
> (*CP,* 361)

Makak had to awaken from two dreams in order to be taken "home," and he had to stop following the goddess of "white moonlight" in order to remember his true name, Felix Hobain. But in the cosmically expanded context of "The Schooner *Flight*," the moon has lost the racialized significance it had in the play, appearing instead as a road to the transcendent, beyond the cloud's open "door" at the boundary between the sublunary and the eternal.

Where, though, can "home" be, when Shabine has so eloquently accepted a condition of transcendental homelessness in which the rest of his days are to be "the flight to a target whose aim we'll never know, / vain search for one island that heals with its harbour / and a guiltless horizon" (*CP,* 361)? Is it that Shabine remains suspended, always following a road that takes him toward home but never arrives there, finally getting no further than the elliptical "towards . . ." of *Epitaph for the Young,* written thirty years earlier? Or is home the deck of the schooner *Flight* itself, its voyage no longer a brief attempt at desperate escape but the condition of life itself? The last line, which insists that Shabine is not singing to us from a "home" safely arrived at but "from the depths of the sea," in the moment of crisis and near-destruction, saves the ending from valedictory complacency. It suggests that home is more like the direction North than like any earthly harbor. One can go toward it but one cannot go there. Shabine must settle for home in the more provisional sense that a ship is home: a frail stay against the elements, a small community that sustains him in transit.

8

Derek *Sans Terre:* The Poetry of the 1980s

In the 1980s, Walcott published three new volumes of poetry and *Collected Poems 1948–1984.* Published in 1986, the *Collected Poems* marked an important moment in Walcott's career, as it was widely reviewed and made early out-of-print work available again. However, since it contained no new poems, I shall not write of it here. As Robert Hamner remarks, "[t]he critical reception of this large, diverse work was not, as should be expected, unanimous"; assessments ranged from J. D. McClatchy's conclusion that "bulk does not serve Walcott well" to Lachlan Mackinnon's insistence "that *Collected Poems* is a triumph."[1] In 1986 Walcott also brought out a collection of three plays, the best of which is *A Branch of the Blue Nile* (1983), about the troubles of a West Indian theater company. Although he has written and staged other plays since, with the exception of *The Odyssey: A Stage Version* (1993), he has not published any. As we have seen, the plays until 1976 were written for West Indian companies and audiences. When Walcott cut his ties with the Trinidad Theatre Workshop, he lost an important anchorage, though he continued to stage plays with other companies in the region. As things stand I consider his best plays to have been written from 1954 (*The Sea at Dauphin*) to 1967 (*Dream on Monkey Mountain*), though *The Joker of Seville, Pantomime, Remembrance,* and *A Branch of the Blue Nile* are also strong works.

If "The Schooner *Flight*" is Walcott's "testament to a crisis in his relationship with the Caribbean," aptly described by Calvin Bedient as "a marriage, all blows and departures,"[2] *The Fortunate Traveller* (1981) inaugurates a restless decade of shuttling between the Caribbean and North America, with increasingly frequent trips to Europe as well. "I accept my function," he declares, "as a colonial upstart at the end of empire, / a single, circling, homeless satellite" (*FT,* 11). In "The Hotel Normandie Pool," he receives advice and comfort from the ghost of another exiled poet, Ovid. Although the poem is set in Trinidad, Walcott, so recently a resident, is now a guest in a "small, suburban tropical hotel" (*FT,* 69) at the northern edge of Port of Spain. In this book, as Paula Burnett remarks, "he seems to have sharpened his perspective of the particularity of his own region, the Caribbean, conscious of the values he misses, while reaching out to a wide-ranging engagement with what he sees as specifically northern problems."[3] The poems, grouped in sections titled "North" and "South," reveal, along with a quickened interest in North American landscapes, "problems," and speech, an uneasy sense of dislocation. Although in an interview of 1982 Walcott said he thought he had achieved a "*balance* between being in the United States and Trinidad,"[4] the dust jacket of *The Arkansas Testament* (1987) concedes that "for several years, Derek Walcott has lived mainly in the States."

The very title of the book evokes transience, and the adjective "fortunate" has its freight of irony. Walcott thought of appropriating Thomas Nashe's title, *The Unfortunate Traveller,* and he may have been thinking of the decisive moment in Nashe's narrative when a banished English earl scolds Jack Wilton for venturing abroad: "Let no man for any transitory pleasure sell away the inheritance he hath of breathing in the place where he was born."[5] In the title poem, the traveler, though he "flies first-class" and enjoys first-world comforts, is engaged in betraying a third-world client, uneasily aware of his wrongdoing even as he commits it. The poem is an indictment of how the "north" deals with the "south," but as Mervyn Morris has noticed, "the poet, more publican than pharisee, sees himself as part of the problem. . . . The poet-persona stands accused of privileged indifference."[6]

Walcott in the United States was indeed a more "fortunate" traveler than most, with prizes and teaching opportunities coming his way. The poems show him adapting to North American residency, even trying on North American identity for size. "I am falling in love with America," he declares in "Upstate" (*FT,* 6), and in "Old New England," he moves Bedient to object that "the 'our' in 'The crest of our conviction grows as loud / as the spring oaks' or 'our sons home from the East' is ersatz," since "Walcott is not in fact a New England poet."[7] The stylistic echoes of Robert Lowell have been widely noted.[8] (In the very first poem, "Old New England," Walcott appropriates not only Lowell's landscape, but two memorable end rhymes: "church" and "birch" from "Waking Early Sunday Morning," and "beast" and "east" from "The Quaker Graveyard in Nantucket" [*FT*, 4].) And yet, the experiment with assimilation is shadowed with mistrust and guilt, and as a result many of the poems have a tentative, provisional quality that differs from the self-division to be found in most of the earlier works, where the tensions between contraries, though not necessarily resolved, evolve slowly and remain stable enough for prolonged contemplation. They are like geological formations, whereas the states of consciousness in many of Walcott's poems of the 1980s resemble weather systems, ready to dissolve at a moment's notice.

Some critics find in *The Fortunate Traveller* a new self-reflexive quality. Robert Hamner goes so far as to claim that "such subversion of the text's hitherto inviolable surface makes *The Fortunate Traveller* crucial to an understanding of Walcott's evolving technique in the 1980s."[9] While the change strikes me as one of increased emphasis rather than sudden reversal—much earlier moments such as the textualization of nature in "Crusoe's Journal" are self-reflexive—there is more self-reflexiveness in *The Fortunate Traveller* than in the earlier works, and certainly more attention to it on the part of his critics from the mid-1980s onward, culminating in Rei Terada's portrait of Walcott as postmodernist in *American Mimicry* (1992). Several reasons for this perceived change converge: the growing vogue of deconstructive criticism in the United States in the early 1980s; Walcott's increased contact with U.S. writing and its intellectual ambience; and Walcott's attenuated relation to the Caribbean, which deprived him of the naturalizing trope of an Antaeus-like power derived from place. It is a change that his critics half perceive and half create.

Less widely noticed, however, is *The Fortunate Traveller*'s changed conception of relations between formerly colonial places and the metropole. In the earlier moment of decolonization, getting free of England meant independence. By 1981, Trinidad and Tobago had been an independent state for nearly twenty years, and even tiny St. Lucia had become a nation in 1979. If the islands remained oppressed, one could no longer locate the oppressor so easily. One first sees Walcott's awareness of the changed situation in the title poem of *The Star-Apple Kingdom*. In a mordantly satirical account of the disintegration of the West Indies Federation, Walcott does not blame any nation so much as a transnational cabal of cynical politicians and inscrutably structured corporations. The passage envisions empire as frustratingly elusive, rather like Pascal's sphere whose circumference is everywhere, its center nowhere. But instead of God, this power is only "seven prime ministers who bought the sea in bolts," selling it "at a markup to the conglomerates," who then "retailed it in turn to the ministers / with only one bank account, who then resold it / in ads for the Caribbean Economic Community, / till everyone owned a little piece of the sea" (*CP,* 390).

The blurring distinction between metropole and margin is parallel to the increasing sense, emerging in "The Schooner *Flight,*" of a continuum linking creole and metropolitan language. In *The Fortunate Traveller,* "The Spoiler's Return" includes italicized quotations from The Mighty Spoiler's most famous calypso, "The Bedbug," and John Wilmot, Earl of Rochester's "A Satyr against Mankind." The first quotation comes entirely from Spoiler (*FT,* 53), but in the second, Walcott grafts two lines from Spoiler onto four of Rochester's (*FT,* 54):

> Were I, who to my cost already am
> One of those strange, prodigious creatures, Man,
> A spirit free, to choose for my own share,
> What case of flesh and blood I wished to wear,
> I hope when I die, after burial,
> To come back as an insect or an animal.

Those last two lines replace Rochester's continuation—"I'd be a *Dog,* a *Monkey,* or a *Bear,* / Or any thing but that vain *Animal* / Who is so proud of being rational."[10] The calypso couplet, since it can be heard either as accentual tetrameter or iambic pentameter, slips unobtrusively into Rochester's frame, continuing not only his thought but to, a surprising degree, his manner—though Rochester would not have allowed the second-foot trochee in that last line. Spoiler's ghost summons the "Old Brigade of Satire, / . . . Martial, Juvenal, and Pope" to sing with him, and promises that these artists, along with Dryden, Swift, and Lord Byron, will appear "in Satan tent next Carnival." Shelley's *Peter Bell III* also makes an oblique appearance, as the tetrameter "Hell is a city much like London" conveniently gains a foot in Walcott's "Hell is a city much like Port of Spain." Among the stars of the English canon Walcott tosses in "Quevedo," better known by his Calypso name, "Atilla the Hun." The brigade of satire is international, as active in Port of Spain as in London.

In the title poem of *The Fortunate Traveller,* the speaker is English but has become an emissary of some unspecified transnational agency for the relief of poorer nations. He is one of the bureacrats who, when third-world governments begin to collapse, "are the first / to scuttle, radiating separately / back to Geneva, Bonn, Washington, London" (*FT,* 90). His briefcase harbors "Xeroxed forms to the World Bank," though it is not certain whether he is their employee or some kind of middleman. As the list of scattered cities implies, neither the World Bank nor the huge corporate "conglomerates" whose investments determine the economic fortunes of the poorer nations serve any national government. These are transnational powers unto themselves.

Striking, too, is the seemingly contradictory movement toward the self-reflexiveness noted by Hamner and a strong intimation of universality in human experience. Even as the poems increasingly acknowledge their own artifice and brood on the unstable identity of the poet as permanent traveler, they seek something everywhere the same. "Believe me," Nashe's banished Englishman tells Jack Wilton, "no air, no bread, no fire, no water, doth a man any good out of his own country."[11] But Walcott, by the time we come to *Midsummer* (1984), is ready to let his imagination "take its luck / on the roads," as "summer is the same / everywhere," and "light is plenty to make do with" (*M,* VIII). To "make do with" light may entail a renunciation of native soil, but in compensation it educates the imagination to resist illegitimate demands for national allegiance. For the old men of "Tropic Zone," "there is no ideology in the light"; "Their revolution is that things come in circles" (*M,* XLII, v).

In *The Fortunate Traveller,* however, Walcott has not yet resigned himself to making do, and the poems dwell on the stark difference between what the light falls upon in North America and in the Caribbean. The difference extends from physical environment—the "knife blade of cold air" and "smoke / from the far factories" in "Upstate" (*FT,* 5) versus "Trees with dust on their lips, cars melting down / in a furnace" in "Port of Spain"[12] (*FT,* 61)—to the equally extreme differences of wealth and power. Yet in both places, the political order crumbles. In the south, it's "*junta* and *coup d'état,* the newest Latino mood" (*FT,* 61), while in the north, the empire, in decline, drifts toward apocalyptic destruction, as "those in the north all wait for that white glare / of the white rose of inferno, all the world's capitals" (*FT,* 11).[13]

The title poem, with its epigraph from Revelation, catches this apocalyptic anxiety powerfully. It also envisions a cosmopolitan world in which the erosion of national sovereignty diffuses accountability, as power becomes amorphous, many-centered, and bureaucratic. The speaker of "The

Fortunate Traveller," a former Sussex Don specializing in "the Jacobean anxieties" (*FT,* 91), has moved from seventeenth-century cloak-and-dagger work to its contemporary counterpart, working as an intermediary between northern financial power and the impoverished Caribbean. But, as Bedient justifiably wonders, "who, exactly, does he represent?"[14] In the briefcase "manacled to [his] wrist," "small countries pleaded through the mesh of graphs, / in treble-spaced, Xeroxed forms to the World Bank / on which I had scrawled the one word, MERCY" (*FT,* 88). Does he work for the World Bank, or is he a go-between, recommending compassion for his clients? We know that two Haitians have obtained his promise to secure tractors for them, though they wonder "why are you doing this, sir?" (*FT,* 89), and that for reasons never described, he has failed to deliver. The negotiations that bring him to London and Bristol, and then to Walcott's St. Lucia,[15] are never explained. Everything is just as opaque to the reader as it is to the "small countries" whose fortunes rest on these deliberations.

The speaker of "The Fortunate Traveller" participates in a characteristically modern form of evil. As Walcott put it in our conversation of April 10, 1989:

> I think that is the peak of the idea of history, I think it climaxed, it apotheosized, it became a Goya-type demon after the Holocaust. I think something was shaped, a demon was made, a new demon was made in the twentieth century from that experience. If you can understand the refinement of science in the Holocaust, you can understand somebody smoking behind a glass chamber, a glass wall, and looking down and saying, I can blank this part out of my mind, I can do that. I am simply doing my job, I am simply doing something which will look horrible, and it'll be OK; you know, it looks horrible, but it is part of the process. Now that neutrality, without remorse, had never happened before, never happened.

In this new form of evil,

> there is a faceless clerk who does what he does, and that guy is working for History, that's his boss. He's not working for Stalin, he's not working for Hitler, he's working for will, the will that has to be performed, that has to be observed. So nobody's responsible.[16]

The most frightening thing about the speaker of "The Fortunate Traveller" is that he understands what he is doing. He himself says, "The heart of darkness is not Africa. / The heart of darkness is the core of fire / in the white center of the holocaust" (*FT,* 93). He recalls that his friend, "Jacob," dates the present era of the world "not Anno Domini: After Dachau" (*FT,* 94). And yet the man who speaks these words can coldly ask, "who cares how many millions starve?" (*FT,* 92). His moral judgment remains clear but has been strangely disconnected from his actions.

Mervyn Morris, answering Bedient's comment that "the poem perhaps errs in endowing the speaker—that beetle-like criminal—with the poet's own blazing conscience," suggests that "it is difficult to locate the controlling voice," implying that the moral judgment comes from one speaker, the callousness from another.[17] But it may be that the seemingly irreconcilable split between the speaker's conscience and his unconscionable actions is exactly the point. If so, that would explain why the crucial moral decision, the actual betrayal, occurs offstage, everywhere pointed to but nowhere visible.

Even the biblical imagery of apocalypse, inaugurated by the epigraph from Revelation, becomes implicated in the speaker's evasion, though it also provides metaphors of an absolute judgment from which his maneuvers cannot escape. For to envision the famines of the poor nations as an apocalyptic scourge, unleashed by an angel's opening of a seal in heaven, is to deny human responsibility for them. But Walcott, or his speaker's not-quite-silenced conscience, redirects the imagery of famine and devouring insects toward the uncharitable north: the impoverished become the locusts, driven to rush blindly toward the wealth they have been denied:

> Like lice, like lice, the hungry of this earth
> swarm to the tree of life. If those who starve
> like these rain-flies who shed glazed wings in light
> grew from sharp shoulder blades their brittle vans
> and soared toward that tree, how it would seethe—
> ah, Justice!
>
> (*FT,* 95)

In this passage, the poor themselves become the potential instruments of retribution. The imagery presents them as "vermin" (*FT,* 95) but also as flightless beings that once had wings and might sprout them again. They are, as it were, angelic vermin. Since the speaker has already likened himself and his colleagues to roaches, his airplane to a weevil (*FT,* 89), and famous colonizers such as Ponce de León to locusts (*FT,* 92), the insectile imagery seems the product of his own dehumanizing vision, reducing oppressors and victims alike to noisome, squashable bugs.

But if I am correct in crediting this speaker with moral self-knowledge and a desperate will to deny that knowledge, then it makes sense that his metaphors continually spin out of his own control, suggesting the very meanings he is keen to avoid. As Paula Burnett points out, the Nazis, in their propaganda, depicted Jews as vermin threatening the health of the Reich, and therefore best exterminated. So the speaker's use of dehumanizing imagery, though seemingly intended to allay his guilt, becomes a damning self-condemnation, since it replicates an infamous genocidal rhetoric to which his own words call attention. Similarly, the image of the crushable, expendable insect is shadowed by the nightmare of the insect as armored avenger, which takes over in the closing lines of the poem:

> still, through thin stalks,
> the smoking stubble, stalks
> grasshopper: third horseman,
> the leather-helmed locust.
>
> (*FT*, 97)

In the last two lines, the innocent "grasshopper" merges with the apocalyptic horseman as it becomes the harbinger of a divinely ordained scourge, like the plague of locusts in *Exodus*.

Burnett has persuasively argued that "The Fortunate Traveller" must be read in conjunction with the poem that follows it and concludes the volume, "The Season of Phantasmal Peace." She notes that the vision of humans as "wingless ones" in their "dark holes" revisits images of the wingless rain-flies and of roach-diplomats "entering the dark holes / of power" (*FT*, 90) in the title poem. To read these poems together, as a double vision of the same world, is to answer Calvin Bedient's charge that "The Season of Phantasmal Peace" is "effectively counter-political, distracting the reader from actual conditions."[18] Not only is this, as Mervyn Morris says, "[a]n oddly literal-minded way to read a lyric poem";[19] it is also a noncontextual way, forgetting the unsparing engagement with "actual conditions" that immediately precedes it.

In "The Fortunate Traveller," the speaker recalls that before his descent into cynical double-dealing, he "envisaged an Africa flooded with such light / as alchemized the first fields of emmer wheat and barley" (*FT*, 91). But now he inhabits a dreary world where "Rotting snow / flaked from Europe's ceiling" (*FT*, 88), where "gray mist [enfolds] the conspirator," and even in the Caribbean "the sky smokes like an ash heap" (*FT,* 95). In "The Season of Phantasmal Peace," the elusive light returns, but we know from the outset that it will not stay. Even the title concedes that this "peace" is seasonal, not permanent, though it also offers hope, because seasons eventually return. It has no more substance than permanence; it is "phantasmal."

Burnett observes that "phantasmal" connects to the word "phantoms," applied to the impoverished residents of the south in "Fortunate Traveller." That connection and the vision of a vanished light-flooded Africa support her argument that the redemptive qualities evoked in "Season" are those of the south's dispossessed, dark-skinned people, yet I take the poem to be ultimately universalist rather than culturally partisan. Not some, but "all the nations of birds," with their "multitudinous dialects," are needed to lift "the huge net of the shadows of this earth" (*FT,* 98). They are "stitching and crossing" the net, as the many cultures that converged in the Caribbean stitched together a common culture in their crossings. The images evoke Walcott's by now familiar conception of the Caribbean as a microcosm of the world's cultural encounters.

Having signaled the transience of its moment in the title and its first word, the temporal marker "Then," the poem arrives, by its ninth line, at the conviction that "there was no longer dusk, or season, decline, or weather," only to undercut itself in the tenth by continuing "only this *passage* of phantasmal light" (my emphasis). The poem evokes an intimation of the timeless within time, which, like the still point in Eliot's *Four Quartets,* can only last a moment in our inescapably temporal experience. But "passage," in addition to reasserting transience, can also be read as transcendence, the "passage" from one condition to another.

"[W]hat the wild geese drew" is the net of shadows, but "drew" has also its other meaning. The birds are drawing a sign in the sky, but the people below cannot see it, nor can they hear the "peaceful cries" of the starlings. The transcendent offers itself to us, but we are not able to receive it; at most, we have the intimation that it has been offered. The net, as the birds carry it higher, becomes a protective covering for "this world / like the vines of an orchard," or "the trembling gauze over the trembling eyes / of a child fluttering to sleep" (*FT,* 98). In order to protect, however, the net must recede from us into the sky, toward a transcendent but distant realm. The image of the "child fluttering to sleep" implies a likeness to the birds with their fluttering wings even as the image insists that humans are infantile and defenseless. The protected eyes and the protective gauze are both "trembling," as if to suggest a sympathy between protector and ward.

As the poem nears its ending, the "soundless cries" apparently become audible ("and no one *hearing* knew" [*FT,* 98]), but humans remain uncertain how to interpret what they hear. Before the fall, Adam and Eve could understand the language of the birds, but this poem, for all its yearnings, inhabits a fallen world. As if to emphasize the distance between that world and paradise, the poem ends by shrinking the scale of time:

> and this season lasted one moment, like the pause
> between dusk and darkness, between fury and peace,
> but, for such as our earth is now, it lasted long.
>
> (*FT,* 99)

The "season" has dwindled to a "moment"—and one, moreover, that marks a transition between two states, not an endpoint or goal. It is only the antechamber of peace, not yet peace itself.

Walcott's next collection, *Midsummer,* has intertextual links to *The Fortunate Traveller,* not only in the reuse of "Port of Spain" as the sixth poem of its sequence, but in its very first line, "The jet bores like a silverfish through volumes of cloud," language borrowed from the previous book's title poem. Though written for the most part during two summer returns to Trinidad, and responding at times to "a shelving sense of home" (*M,* I), it feels even more geographically detached than *Fortunate Traveller.*

A piece Walcott wrote for the *New York Times* in late 1983 sheds some light on the volume's peculiar tone. In the essay, Walcott describes "a short visit home to the island of St. Lucia," in which he stays at an upscale resort, "Hurricane Hole" on Marigot Bay. He objects to the picturesque name, one of those "rechristenings . . . given to places, as if they were lounges or suites, so the tourists can feel at home while the natives feel translated." He describes speaking creole "to the waitresses, to the waiters to show that nothing had changed me and I was still one of the boys." Nonetheless, he admits that "unless one lives where one is, all of us are tourists," which as of 1983 would include himself. He imagines that "Hurricane Hole" was chosen as "a fortifying name for courageous yachtsmen," whom he despises even as he admits that he once fantasized that he would sail, as they do, "sun-cracked and grizzled through all the channels of the archipelago, and put in at places called Hurricane Hole." Only after dealing with the weirdness of being native and tourist at once can he reach the lyrical climax of the essay, in which he goes out before dawn "onto the cool floorboards of the verandah," and can "feel, not see, the wetness of the flowers and the cool, even cold, dark green width of Marigot Bay, very dark green in the middle, and O! annihilation of the complaining self, the first wind with light in it."[20]

In its precision about the shade of green, its emphasis on the sensuous qualities of things as cherishable simply for what they are, and in its dissolution of the carping self in the "first wind with light in it," the passage anticipates the poems. They are, along with the recent *Tiepolo's Hound* and certain passages of *Another Life,* Walcott's most painterly work, not only in their strong evocation of the look of things, but in their interest in how the eye sees, and in their tendency to rest with the look of things as sufficient meaning, detached from intellectual interpretation or context in place. If "everything becomes / its idea to the painter with easel rifled on his shoulders" (*M,* XVIII), "idea" means composition, not intellectual proposition, so that "the identical carmine" will serve "for still life and for the slaughter / of youth."

Walcott juxtaposes poems with disparate settings, so that we leap from Trinidad in I to Rome in II and then, after returning to Port of Spain for III and IV, turn up in Greenwich Village for V, as if the pages were linked by jet travel. He also develops his metaphor of "midsummer" as a refining fire in which differences of place and history dissolve into a primal unity, though the heat is so intense it almost overwhelms the poet's powers of language: "Through the stunned afternoon, when it's too hot to think / and the muse of this inland ocean still waits for a name, / and from the salt, dark room, the tight horizon line / catches nothing, I wait" (*M,* XXV). The summer's energy, though generative, drives toward annihilation and stasis: in the north, "midsummer's leaves race to extinction" and "seethe toward autumn's fire" (XXIII), while, on a Caribbean beach, "noon jerks toward its rigid, inert center" (XXVIII).

As "one-dimensional as lust" (X), summer is a primal libidinal force, procreative and self-consuming. It is "the same / everywhere" (VIII), and its wordless speech is light and heat, its signature the flash of lightning, which momentarily leaps the gap between presence and sign: "Language never fits geography / except when the earth and summer lightning rhyme" (*M,* IX). Even then, the poet can never quite capture that rhyme in "one heraldic stroke":

Too rapid the lightning's shorthand,
too patient the sea repeatedly tearing up paper,
too frantic the wind unravelling the same knot,
too slow the stones crawling toward language every night.

(*M,* IX)

If the actions of the sea and the wind recall earlier figures of the Caribbean as a place of continual erasure, the difference is that in *Midsummer,* the history-annihilating immanence of the Caribbean has become portable. It can be found in north and south, New World and Old.

Walcott is also especially attuned in these poems to the treacherous entanglement of what is destructive with what is generative in human energies. So poem VIII, which ends joyously with the "[a]bounding grace" that arrives when "Midsummer bursts / out of its body, and its poems come unwarranted," begins with a grim omen: "A radiant summer, so fierce it turns yellow / like the haze before a holocaust." By the time we reach XLI, "a holocaust" has metamorphosed into *the* holocaust:

> But had I known then
> that the fronds of my island were harrows, its sand the ash
> of the distant camps, would I have broken my pen
> because this century's pastorals were being written
> by the chimneys of Dachau, of Auschwitz, of Sachsenhausen?

In these lines, we see the frightening obverse of Walcott's cosmopolitan universalism. Summer is the same everywhere, and light falling on objects behaves the same way everywhere, but by the same token, human brutality is the same everywhere, and even St. Lucia, which *Omeros* will call a "self-healing island," cannot separate itself from the evil done on the far side of the ocean. Nor can we North Americans distance ourselves from the meanings of "holocaust." At dawn by the Charles River, "Through the iron net of a bridge, / the sunrise climbs with the leisure of a nuclear blast" (XLV). Here, the fire of summer recalls the atomic bomb, a weapon only the United States has used.

In a book so concerned with the sensuous surface of things, it is not surprising that the poems are, as Robert Bensen justly observes, "frequently conceived and composed as verbal paintings—portraits, landscapes, seascapes, studies and sketches."[21] What strikes me as strange, however, is how the quickening of sensuous exactness in every description coexists with a detachment from place. It may be, as Bensen says, that "the artist is removed from his subject by the very act of creating"[22]—Walcott himself had described that removal in *Another Life.* But the detachment I refer to is not quite what Bensen, or Walcott, appear to have had in mind. It is instead a detachment in the location of the speaking "I," a little like the voice of the contemporaneous "Rediscovery of Islands," where the poet feels himself a tourist even at home. So in the first poem, where the jet bears him toward Trinidad, Walcott addresses Brodsky: "Our sunlight is shared by Rome / and your white paper, Joseph. Here, as everywhere else, / it is the same age." Staying at the Queen's Park Hotel, on Port of Spain's Savannah, he "reenter[s his] first local mirror" (*M*, III). But it shows only the estrangement wrought by time and distance: "Every word I have written took the wrong approach. / I cannot connect these lines with the lines in my face." Not only is home hard to reenter, but the dewy sweetness of a Port of Spain morning, reminiscent of those wet flowers at Marigot Bay in the *Times* essay, has been tinged with a foreign influence, as "dew has frosted the skins / of the big American taxis parked all night on the street." A hot day on the beach in Trinidad closes with the recognition that "In two more days my daughters will go home" (XXVIII)—that is, to his ex-wife Margaret, who still lives in Trinidad as he does not. In XLIII, "Tropic Zone," a sequence of eight poems set in Cuba, Walcott feels that he is and is not at home: "This is my ocean, but it is speaking / another language, since its accent changes around / different islands" (*M*, XLIII, i). When Bensen writes that the challenge for the artist, distanced by the abstraction of art, is nonetheless "to connect himself to his subject through the art, even if the subject is himself,"[23] I'm with him if we're speaking of *Another Life*. But in *Midsummer*, the attention to how light works, and the labors of paint and language that reveal its workings, yield an increased detachment from "the subject," at once a renunciation and a comfort.[24] If the senses and the play of light are in essence the same everywhere, the misfortunes of exile cannot come between the poet and his work. Where one happens to be, and what particular landscape the place offers, matter less than that which is constant in all places. The revisions to "Port of Spain" from *The Fortunate Traveller* that turn it into poem VI of *Midsummer* are instructive. Gone is the line about "*junta* and *coup d'état*, the newest Latino mood"; the first version is more focused on politics, the second on the look of things. The lines, "And one waits for lightning as the armed sentry / hopes in boredom for the crack of the rifle" become "And one waits for midsummer lightning as the armed sentry / hopes in boredom for the crack of a rifle." In the first version, where it resonates with "*junta* and *coup d'état*," the military vehicle of the metaphor has a literal force. The revision softens the political edge. As John Thieme remarks, in *Midsummer*, "lightning . . . is a vehicle for healing the post-Babel wound of the gap between 'language' and 'geography,'"[25] and not primarily an image of violence.

The detachment from subject, to be sure, is relative rather than absolute. Probably the most subject-centered poem of *Midsummer* is "Tropic

Zone," the sequence of eight poems set in Cuba. There, Spanish, like English elsewhere in the Caribbean, is fraught with history, so that "whether one chooses to say *"ven-thes"* or *"ven-ces"* / involves the class struggle as well" (*M,* XLIII, i). Yet even in this place, Walcott is looking for what remains the same: "history will pierce your memory like a migraine; / but however their flame trees catch, the green winds smell lime-scented, / the indigo hills lie anchored in seas of cane / deep as my island's" (*M,* XLIII, ii). True to his Adamic poetics, Walcott's "prayer is to write / lines as mindless as the ocean's of linear time." But in a country that has "nationalized Eden / in vehement acrylics" (*M,* XIII, iii), Walcott's poetics confronts its ideologically coarsened double. And so, "as is the case with so many revolutions, / the visitor doubts the murals and trusts the beer." To that extent, he shares that "hedonist's / idea of heaven" so dear to the French impressionists, for whom "art was *une tranche de vie,* cheese or home-baked bread" (*M,* XVIII).

Walcott criticizes the dismissive North American attitude, familiar from "colonial fiction" and the movies, wherein "evil remains comic and only achieves importance / when the gringo crosses the plaza, flayed by the shadow of fronds" (*M,* XLIII, iv). Meanwhile, "in the banana republics," beneath the north's threshold of attention, "techniques of camouflage / have taught the skill of slitting stomachs like fruits." But the effect of this critique is not so much to endorse hatred for "the Empire" (*M,* XLIII, i) as to hold Caribbean politicians responsible for evils of their own: "Tyranny brings over / its colonies this disorientation of weather. A new ogre / erects his bronzes over the parks" (*M,* XLIII, vii). Tyranny is a quasi-colonial oppression, and its new ogres are similar to the ones they have deposed. As often happens in Walcott, a natural image figures as a sign of resistance: despite the statues, "the senate / of swallows still arranges itself on benches / for the usual agenda," as if conducting a shadow government.

"Tropic Zone" ends with a retreat from politics and the particularities of history, back to the time-dissolving vision of the book as a whole. Walcott praises forgetful "sleep, which is midsummer's crown" (*M,* XLIII, viii), and returns us to "the furnace without fire," a gentled version of the recurring figure of midsummer heat as Heraclitian blaze or incipient holocaust. For sleep to perform its merciful deliverance, however, a new complication of Adamic amnesia is required: "Now the first gardener, under the tree of knowledge, / forgets that he's Adam." Not only must Adam forget the torments of history, he must forget his own role. He is beneath the tree of knowledge now; maybe he knows too much to sustain the Adamic pose.

This twist looks forward toward *Omeros,* in which St. Lucian fishermen are Adamic in large part because they lack the self-consciousness to think of themselves that way.

Enclosing the entire book are the opening and parting addresses to Brodsky. If, in the first poem, the two poets are bound by their shared fealty to "sunlight," which "[h]ere, as everywhere else, / . . . is the same age" (*M,* I), in the last, Walcott acknowledges the renunciations that have initiated him into this transnational republic of light. He evokes "these shacks that made me" (*M,* LIV), though he did not live in one, and he is reminded of "the faith I betrayed, or the faith that betrayed me." But there is no returning to the "child's hymnbook" or "the poems edged in gold leaf," recalling the golden year of youthful aspiration lovingly chronicled in *Another Life.* "Ah Joseph," he concludes, "though no man ever dies in his own country, / the grateful grass will grow thick from his heart." I take this memorable ending to suggest first of all that finally all are exiles, that even if one does not leave one's own country, it will have changed from the country of one's imagination and become strange. Second, that a generative seed from the place of origin travels with us, sending the grass of the heart's internalized home up from the grave. (The line looks back to the conclusion of Whitman's "Song of Myself," but also forward in Walcott's own poetry to the sea-swift of *Omeros,* which has borne the seed of a healing herb from Africa across the ocean to St. Lucia.) And finally, that the unavoidable departure causes the heart's death, or perhaps is a kind of death. "No man ever dies in his own country" primarily means that we cannot go home again, but it may also mean that if we could, we would be immortal; home is the place where "[n]o man ever dies." *Midsummer,* among Walcott's books, is the one that most severely tests the viability of Shabine's defiant assertion, "I had no nation now but the imagination." From this point on, the poems begin looking for home.

The desire to return to St. Lucia, along with a continuing sense of his estrangement from it, emerges in *The Arkansas Testament* (1987). Like *The Fortunate Traveller* with its dualism of "North" and "South," this collection divides itself between "Here" and "Elsewhere." As Bruce King notices, "Here" is not the Caribbean generally so much as St. Lucia in particular, since some of the poems in "Elsewhere" have settings in Martinique or Latin America.[26] *Arkansas Testament,* despite the U.S. place name in its title, begins a reassertion of St. Lucian identity without which it is impossible to imagine Walcott's next book, *Omeros.* As early as 1985, in his interview with Hirsch for *Paris Review,* Walcott said, "I've never felt that I belong anywhere else but in St. Lucia. The geographical and spiritual fixity is there," although he acknowledges a difference between himself, "a fortunate traveller, a visitor" who "can always leave" and the many St. Lucians who cannot.[27]

Not long after Walcott began spending most of his time in the United States, St. Lucia had become independent, which meant that he no longer had a British passport. He had to choose between St. Lucian and U.S. citizenship. King notes a connection between Walcott's sojourn in the American South, recounted in the title poem of *Arkansas Testament,* and his decision to remain a St. Lucian citizen. Although U.S. citizenship "would solve tax and other complications," it would mean that the American race problem would then become "his problem," consigning him to "second-class status."[28] It would seem that somewhere around the mid-1980s, Walcott began looking for a chance to end his "exile."

There are, to be sure, moments in *Arkansas Testament* that continue the cosmopolitan restlessness of the previous two volumes. "To have loved one horizon is insularity," the speaker of "Tomorrow, Tomorrow" declares; "it blindfolds vision, it narrows experience." Nonetheless, the appearance of the airport taxi provokes the rhyme of "upsetting" and "regretting," and the cab is "sidling to the curb like a hearse—so you get in" (*AT,* 79). Travel, like death, is necessary but odious. We encounter a very different taxi ride in the St. Lucian setting of "The Light of the World," where, instead of the North American cab with its private passenger, the poet rides a crowded sixteen-seat route taxi that becomes at once an emblem of transience and an image of community and home.

As Edward Baugh observes, "more than half of the poems in the book use quatrains. . . . Most, too, exploit the short line, almost always trimeter. This dominance of the quatrain is all the more noticeable when we come to *The Arkansas Testament* from its predecessor, *Midsummer,*" in which the poems use "long lines (variously pentameter and alexandrine, for the most part), and irregular rhyming."[29] One might suppose that the short lines enact a growing desire for definite boundaries and spatial closure, a sort of formal correlative of homecoming, just as the fluid lines of *Midsummer,* unconstrained by regular stanzas, are appropriate to poems of blurred distinctions and shifting location. Yet the line of *Midsummer* is rather like that of *Omeros,* Walcott's major poem of homecoming. There, however, the long line is gathered in tercets, providing a balance between fluid indeterminacy and bounded design, as the poem itself must undergo transatlantic wanderings in order to arrive at home.

In his *Paris Review* interview with Hirsch, Walcott had spoken of himself "as a carpenter, as one making frames, simply and well. . . . I find myself wanting to write very simply cut, very contracted, very speakable and very challenging quatrains in rhymes."[30] "Cul de Sac Valley" (named for a place just south of Walcott's beloved Vigie) begins with this analogy:

A panel of sunrise
on a hillside shop
gave these stanzas
their stilted shape.

If my craft is blest;
if this hand is as
accurate, as honest
as their carpenter's,

every frame, intent
on its angles, would
echo this settlement
of unpainted wood. . . .

(*AT,* 9)

As John Thieme says, this "and other poems in the first part of *Arkansas Testament* provide some of the most finely wrought expressions of Walcott's life-long goal of realizing St. Lucia on the printed page."[31] And yet the poem also reveals Walcott's recognition of the Quixotic impossibility of that goal. The passage is in the subjunctive, under the sign of "if." Less obviously, the referent of "their" in line 8 is elusive. It should refer to "these stanzas" in line 3, but if Walcott is not their carpenter, who is? One concludes instead that "their carpenter" is the local carpenter at Cul de Sac, whose work is displayed in the houses of "this settlement / of unpainted wood." In relation to these solid, inhabited constructions, the poet's quatrains can be at best an echo, corresponding to but not at one with what they depict.

In *Midsummer,* there are no conspicuous uses of creole, but beginning with the Rasta inscription, "MAN IS A BABYLON" in "The Lighthouse" (*AT,* 7), Walcott returns to it often, and one of the poems, "The Three Musicians," sustains creole English through most of its 120 lines. From the very first instance, however, Walcott's perspective on creole is double: the Rastas' sign laments diasporic exile from Africa, and "a" has its creole sense of "in." But in Walcott's context, the phrase also retains its meaning in SE: mankind is figuratively a Babylon ("a" functions as a determiner), and we experience the self as alien, a place of exile. In "Cul de Sac Valley," the poet's dream of making his verbal carpentry correspond to the wooden houses meets resistance from the building materials themselves, which warn him—in creole of course—that *"What you wish / from us will never be, / your words is English, / is a different tree"* (*AT,* 10).

Walcott's linguistic decorum in "The Three Musicians" enacts the tension between his wish to be folded back into the community and his sense of his troubling difference. The first seven quatrains are in quotation marks, and they turn out to be the words of Madame Isidor. When the poet's persona takes up the narration in stanza eight, he speaks SE, with rather formal syntactic nesting of modifiers:

> sings Madame Isidor,
> her front step scoured
> for her first visitor,
> Our barefoot Lord.
>
> (*AT,* 29)

But as he continues into the next stanza, his grammar slides from SE: "He was poorer than them," and by stanzas ten and eleven, his voice has virtually merged with the idiom of Madame Isidor:

> Whole week she practise
> her bow: "Pleased to meet you;
> this one here? That is
> Joseph, carpenter too."
>
> And that whole week self,
> if one vex, next one laugh;
> from the glass case Joseph
> sets the silver carafe. . . .

Without seeing the poem on the page, one might easily lose track of the quotation marks, the transitions from one voice to the other—except that if one were not reading the poem on the page, one would be hearing it spoken, and a good performer would dramatize the shift of voices. More than is usual in a Walcott poem, "The Three Musicians" modulates toward transcription of an oral performance, rather than language conceived as writing. But in the last four stanzas of the poem, something tolls the poet back to his sole self, for his voice returns to SE. One can hear the register shift between stanzas 26 and 27, even though the poet's persona speaks in both:

> she dream of white lace
> on soft ebony skin,
> but is somehow God's grace
> she cannot make children;
>
> the lifting curtains
> brighten the linoleum,
> they bring a child's presence
> to her varnished room.
>
> (*AT*, 31)

The poem ends with a moment of empathy between the speaker and the "Joseph" of the poem. Joseph and his wife are unable to have children, and so when the three musicians evoke the Nativity, the St. Lucian Joseph feels keenly the difference between his situation and that of Mary's husband in the Christmas story (and perhaps an ironic likeness as well, since Christ was not begotten by Joseph but by divine fiat). "[I]n the fiddler's screels," husband and wife "hunger and thirst / for the child. Joseph feels / that his heart will burst" (*AT*, 32). They hunger and thirst "for" the ill-lodged Christ child, empathizing with his deprivation, longing for the redemption he represents. But they also long for a child of their own. The speaker voices Joseph's feelings, although Joseph himself says nothing. But he voices them in SE, not as Joseph would speak them. The poem closes by disengaging the speaker from the identification with the characters prevailing in stanzas 10 through 26.

The book's powerful homing instinct comes into poignant conflict with its continuing awareness of Walcott's status as traveler even in his own country, never more so than in "The Light of the World," the poem Rei Terada chooses as representative instance of her decentered, postmodern Walcott. Her reading, intelligent and sensitive to linguistic nuance, tells half the truth about the poem with uncommon eloquence, but it's necessary to feel the contrary centripetal pull within the poem resisting its decentering impulses. Although she scrupulously concedes that Walcott's "Postmodernity trails behind it Modernism's tendency to universalize," she attempts to absorb that tendency into postmodern "perspectivism," as just one passing shake of the postmodern kaleidoscope.[32] In *The Other America*, J. Michael Dash follows her lead, declaring that the poem "enacts the drama of displacement and the impossibility of possessing any ultimate truth."[33] Walcott, according to Terada, "abstains from radically conspicuous forms of rhetoric not because he seeks transparency, but because of his conviction that any and all language depends upon rhetoric." And "The Light of the World," in her reading, "assumes that poetry is based upon figuration, and inquires whether poetry's reliance upon figuration divorces it from other linguistic forms."[34] It is tempting to question the assumption that "Walcott abstains from radically conspicuous forms of rhetoric"—he seems to me, for better and worse, one the most rhetorical poets now writing in English. But better to entertain her thesis and watch what happens when "The Light of the World" passes through its prism.

Terada begins by noting that the title recalls memorable lines in *Another Life:* "Gregorias, listen, lit / we were the light of the world!" Since that poem "comprehensively narrates Walcott's choice of [poetic] vocation," the return to its language implies a self-reflexive turn, an attempt to "revaluate [*sic*] Walcott's poetics."[35] The self-allusion is indeed important, but before turning the light of the world into the mirrored light of the word, it's well to recall two additional meanings, one "lower" and the other "higher" than Terada's. First of all, "lit" means drunk not only with inspiration but with alcohol. Nor should one forget that Walcott's use of the phrase "the light of the world" in *Another Life* is itself an allusion to the Gospels. Versions of the phrase occur in several places, but two are especially pertinent. In John 8:12 Jesus says: "I am the light of the world: he who follows me will not walk in darkness, but will have the light of life." And in the Sermon on the Mount as given in Matthew, he tells his listeners: "You are the light of the world. A city set on a hill cannot be hid. Nor do men light a lamp and put it under a bushel, but on a stand, and it gives light to all in the house. Let your light so shine before men, that they may see your good works and give glory to your Father who is in Heaven" (Matthew 5:14–15). The second of these statements confirms the promise of the first: whoever follows the light of the world will acquire and become that light, which is the God-term latently present in all people, made actively present by faith.

In an essay published two years after *The Arkansas Testament,* Walcott enjoins critics to judge poets by their approach toward the subject of "God, or the gods," and to recognize that "the source of this subject is chaos, ignorance, and its emblem is (how sweet Latin sounds in such contexts) *Dominus illuminatio mea,* Lord, who art the light of my life."[36] A poet who takes the idea of "God, or the gods" this seriously would appear to be seeking a transcendent center, or at least a pantheon of multiple centers.

The question for both *Another Life* and "The Light of the World" is what Walcott is doing with the scriptural allusion: is he secularizing the language of the sacred, or is he recovering the sacred within the secular? Does art replace religion or become a religion? And is the longing for a transcendent center related to the longing for an earthly center, for "home"?

The poem is set in a "transport," the term in St. Lucia for the vans, holding fifteen or twenty passengers, that serve as inexpensive route taxis between towns. Like the one in the poem, they typically herald their approach by the reggae or zouk pumping from the stereo. The poem's opening must be quoted in full, since it establishes the poet's relationship to the scene around him and leads up to the title phrase:

> Marley was rocking on the transport's stereo
> and the beauty was humming the choruses quietly.
> I could see where the lights on the planes of her cheek
> streaked and defined them; if this were a portrait
> you'd leave the highlights for last, these lights
> silkened her black skin; I'd have put in an earring,
> something simple, in good gold, for contrast, but she
> wore no jewelry. I imagined a powerful and sweet
> odour coming from her, as from a still panther,
> and the head was nothing else but heraldic.
> When she looked at me, then away from me politely,
> because any staring at strangers is impolite,
> it was like a statue, like a black Delacroix's
> *Liberty Leading the People,* the gently bulging
> whites of her eyes, the carved ebony mouth,
> the heft of the torso solid, and a woman's,
> but gradually even that was going in the dusk,
> except the line of her profile, and the highlit cheek,
> and I thought, O Beauty, you are the light of the world!
>
> (*AT,* 48)

For Terada, the salient features of this passage are the poet's attempt at "seeing [the woman] as art, manipulating her image in a series of framings and figurations," and the paradox that "in the moment before she becomes Beauty, nothing remains but a 'profile' and a highlight. It is entirely possible that in the moment Walcott apotheosizes her, she completely disappears."[37] The poem, in this reading, deconstructs the illusion of presence.

The attractions of the woman's figure, as it were, are supplanted by the seductions of figuration.

It's true that the speaker tries to see the woman as art, or as an artist's model. But he also notices her noncompliance: instead of sitting as he would pose her, she turns away. In the one part of the passage that Terada does not discuss, he imagines the "powerful and sweet / odour coming from her." This language insists on a carnality that resists visual representation: how might the painter suggest "odour"? When the fading twilight leaves visible only the outline of the woman's face, one might infer as Terada does an acknowledgment of the inevitable vanishing of presence in artistic representations. But that inference rests on the assumption that "O Beauty" in line 19 addresses "the beauty" of line 2, and not, in addition or even instead, the quality of Beauty. If one takes the exclamation in this second way, "Beauty" may shine out from this particular "beauty" (lowercase), but transcends its embodiment in her. That may partly explain why the speaker's erotically charged admiration soon expands to an *agape* that includes "the others, too. // Because I felt a great love that could bring me to tears" (*AT,* 50).

The poet offers a series of mediating analogies to evoke the "Beauty" of this beauty for the reader. But these comparisons fall short, so that he is compelled to discard each in its turn, replacing the portrait with the statue, then seizing on Delacroix's allegorical painting, which itself must be revised, only to revert to the sculptural analogy with "carved ebony mouth." All representations come short of the ineffable essence of Beauty itself. They are too sunken in the particular; they clutter the representation with ornaments (earrings), with allusion (to Delacroix) and allegory (Delacroix's title). In the gathering darkness, all inessential particulars become invisible, and only the eidetic "line of her profile" remains, lit as much from within as by the fading twilight—lit by "Beauty" itself, the light of the world. Read in this way, the passage implies not that figuration is all we have, but that something palpably real eludes the representational power of art. This is the language of Platonism, not postmodernism. The poet is left with the hope of making language point beyond itself, reaching toward that which it cannot enclose.

Elsewhere in the poem are other images of light imperfectly glimpsed or shining through darkness: the "bright doors" of the rum shops; the "wandering gas lanterns / hung on poles at street corners" in the Castries market of Walcott's childhood; "the orange lights / from the Vigie headland" glimpsed from the transport; the "brass lamp / with a kerosene lamp" by the imagined bed where the speaker wishes to take the "beauty"; the actual "lamps in the houses on the small hills / and thickets of stars"; the "beams of the lamps" of the transport itself, in which departing passengers say their good-nights; the "fireflies" guiding them "up to the lit door" of their houses (*AT,* 48, 49, 50, 51). These scattered lights are signs of human or natural presence, while the darkness evokes the separation across which a glance of mutual recognition passes. The transport itself is a moving spark of light, carrying a temporary, ad hoc community.

Walcott engages in conspicuous wordplay on the name "transport," which becomes more than the idiomatic word for a St. Lucian route taxi. An old woman, afraid the transport will leave without her, cries out "*Pas quittez moi à terre,*" which Walcott renders as "'Don't leave me on earth,' or, by a shift of stress: / 'Don't leave me the earth' [for an inheritance]" (*AT,* 50; square brackets Walcott's). Then he turns the phrase into a prayer for deliverance: "'*Pas quittez moi à terre,* Heavenly transport, / 'Don't leave me on earth, I've had enough of it'" (*AT,* 50). Terada's commentary emphasizes, though not exclusively, implications that pertain to writing: "'transport' is . . . a synonym for 'metaphor,' whose etymology includes the notion of 'carrying'"; the poet asks, in her reading, "whether metaphorical transport, in its ecstasy, either leaves its supposed subjects behind to unecstatic life and death, or carries them to oblivion while sweeping them up with it."[38] Again, this account attends most acutely to part of what needs to be noticed. But it thins out the social complexity of the poem and deflects emphasis from the speaker's yearning to reenter the community from which he has become estranged.

What the poet finds transporting on the transport, apart from the beauty of the woman he encounters on it, is its sense of community: "the bus felt warm with their neighbourliness, / their consideration, and the polite partings" (*AT,* 51). Those who live along the route know each other, but their "neighbourliness" extends to strangers, even to tourists. But once off the bus, the stranger steps back into the separate world of a hotel or guest house. If the "transport" is that of Walcott's own poetry, it is so only by a borrowed authority, in that he wants to ground his poem, which cannot be entirely *of* that community, on his emotional allegiance to it. More immediately, it is the "transport" of momentary reintegration with the community that he has abandoned, as the woman who cried "*Pas quittez moi à terre*" had feared the transport would abandon her.

The delicacy of Walcott's social placement of himself, as one both grounded in and estranged from his St. Lucian origins, becomes obscured if his "abandonment" is connected primarily to his writing, as in Terada's remark that "'abandon[ment]' in the negative sense invariably accompanies figuration, since writing—substituting figuration for presence—marks the site of perpetually abandoned presence."[39] But if Walcott's writing leads him to abandon his people, that seems less because all writing is the abandonment of presence than because "[a]n artistic generation in this part of the world [the Caribbean] is about five years. Five years of endurance. After that, I think people give up."[40] It is the problem that has troubled him from the outset: the culture that inspires the writing cannot or will not sustain the writer.

The gap between the speaker and others in the poem is the darkness across which "the light of the world" must shine. The poem defines that gap with full social particularity. When the speaker gets off at the Halcyon Hotel, he compares himself to the tourists there:

> but I came to my stop. Outside the Halcyon Hotel.
> The lounge would be full of transients like myself.
> Then I would walk with the surf up the beach.
>
> (*AT,* 51)

But if the Halcyon is his stop, it doesn't seem to be his hotel. He doesn't quite belong with the tourist crowd in the lounge, any more than he wholly belongs with the St. Lucians on the transport. He walks up the surf to an unspecified destination.[41] Walcott inhabits a liminal realm. He is still St. Lucian enough to understand the idiom "*pas quittez moi à terre*" and to feel a bond with the other passengers, but he knows the distance between their lives and his own. At the same time, he is not much like the vacationers at the Halcyon, for whom the "neighbourliness" of the transport passengers might be casually charming, but hardly the occasion for ecstasy and tears.

The uneasy bond between poet and folk can also be traced in the poem's allusions to Bob Marley, to whose "songs of sadness as real as the smell / of rain on dry earth" (*AT,* 51) the speaker has abandoned his countrymen. Terada notes that Marley is a competitor of sorts, a folk poet closer to the people whose prominence in the poem reveals Walcott's "jealousy toward another artisan."[42] But I am not sure Walcott's Marley-envy stems from the sense of him as a rival poet (who, incidentally, had been dead for five years in 1986). Marley's song, suffusing the transport long after his death, has become the unselfconscious music of the community, the sign of its wholeness and authenticity, which has to be translated somehow into the more "literary" music of Walcott's poem. Is he any more jealous of Marley than he would be of a gifted *conteur* or folk musician? He pays tribute to Marley but does not seem shy before him.

In the version of "The Light of the World" published in *Partisan Review,* Walcott's epigraph mishears the words as "Got to have Zion-ah," which was corrected to "Got to have Kaya now" in *The Arkansas Testament.* "Kaya" is the title cut of a Wailers LP that came out in 1978, with the song lyrics printed on the album cover. That he could make this mistake in 1986 suggests that he was not an avid Marley listener. Moreover, the word Walcott chooses to replace "Kaya" may be taken as evidence of his predisposition. If so, it would confirm my sense that despite its decentering gestures, this poem harbors a longing for an earthly and transcendent center, a "Zion."

The poem's ending, to be sure, is undeniably self-reflexive. The speaker gets off the transport, and

> Then, a few yards ahead, the van stopped. A man
> shouted my name from the transport window.
> I walked up towards him. He held out something.
> A pack of cigarettes had dropped from my pocket.
> He gave it to me. I turned, hiding my tears.
> There was nothing they wanted, nothing I could give them
> but this thing I have called "The Light of the World."

Terada argues that "Walcott's description of the poet's diminished powers sounds characteristically Postmodern, if we understand Postmodernism as a folding back from Modernism's totalizing ambitions." But even the diminution is rhetorical, since

> Walcott's last small "but" opens a floodgate through which poetic grandiosity and linguistic transcendence stream. Even by calling his poem "this thing," he simultaneously metaphorizes and reifies it. By further calling "this thing" (already metaphorized by being called a thing) "The Light of the World," Walcott enters the realm of undecidability. On the one hand, this last line is figurative and glorious; poems are, after all, the light of the world. On the other, it is merely literal and tautological. The title of the poem is, inarguably, "The Light of the World"; the phrase is a citation, referring us only to itself, and distances itself by its quotation marks from the notion of poetic glory.[43]

My own sense is that a decision does finally occur, in which transcendence emerges as credible. The self-reflexive irony is there, as Vernon Shetley says of the irony in Elizabeth Bishop, "to shield the poetry from skeptical deflation."[44] To be sure, one reason the speaker has nothing the people on the transport want is that his poems, including this one, are not what that community asks of art. But another is suggested in Lloyd King's remark that for the "Caribbean intellectual," return to the West Indian folk "is a return to a stage of grace, of wholeness."[45] In Walcott's eyes, that grace and wholeness is itself "the Light of the World"; the other passengers need not take it from him because they have it already. As in the Gospels, to say "I am the Light of the World" is also to say "You are the Light of the World." To have it is to perceive it in others. What his fellow passengers have given the poet, they have given without knowing it, and what he gives in return they might not want. But in calling to him by name, the man in the transport has extended recognition[46] with the same "neighbourliness" and "consideration" that he would give to someone who rode with him every day; and in writing the poem, Walcott has extended recognition back to him in his own way. That exchange, however oblique and limited, is a momentary flash of "the Light of the World."

9

Epic Amnesia: Healing and Memory in *Omeros*

From very early in his career, Walcott aspired to write a West Indian counterpart of Homeric epic. But it would be strange if the sixty-year-old author of *Omeros* thought of the Greek parallels in the same way as the nineteen-year-old author of *Epitaph for the Young*. Not only Walcott, but the Caribbean as well, had changed greatly during the intervening years. In 1949, the islands were anticipating independence and federation; by 1990, the federation had long since come and gone, and individual islands were struggling to survive, in an era of global capitalism, with isolated and dependent economies. Moreover, in the interim, Walcott had developed his paradox of the forgetful Adam, which places a new strain on his relation to Homer.

The Homeric epic is a genre devoted to cultural memory. As Martin Mueller observes, "One may well ask whether the Greeks, who during the dark centuries colonised much of the eastern and some of the western Mediterranean, would have resisted the centrifugal tendencies of such geographical dispersion had it not been for the common past, the common religion, and the common set of values that the *Iliad* 'created,' if only by putting traditional materials in canonical form."[1] Walcott's way of dealing with the past, however, encourages a necessary forgetting. In *Omeros*, this forgetting extends to the Homeric texts themselves. Encountering the spirit of Homer, the Walcott persona says of

The Odyssey: "I never read it, / . . . not all the way through" (*O*, 283). And yet, he claims, "I was the freshest of all your readers"—impudently fresh, perhaps, but Adamically fresh as well. The question of how a poetics of Adamic pastlessness can appropriate the memorious genre of epic leads to the deepest tensions, flaws, and glories of Walcott's poem.

Omeros and Epic

By the time we reach *Omeros,* the claim of universality for West Indian experience is no longer the only, or even the most important, implication of Homeric allusion. "Sea Grapes" (1976) opens by speculating that "a schooner beating up the Caribbean // for home, could be Odysseus, / home-bound on the Aegean." But "[t]his"—and in the absence of a particular referent, the pronoun gestures backward toward the parallel developed in the first three stanzas—"brings nobody peace." As the last line memorably puts it, "The classics can console. But not enough" (*CP,* 297). The sense, emerging in this poem, that the pain and unruliness of experience break the frame of classical parallel goes farther in *Omeros,* to the point where a reader may question whether the parallels are not to be renounced by the end of the poem, as the characters' recovery from historical alienation reveals the Homeric allusions as symptoms of alienated consciousness rather than as guarantors of meaning.

In a remarkable impromptu lecture, transcribed for *South Atlantic Quarterly,* Walcott claimed that "the last third" of *Omeros* "is a total refutation of the efforts made by two characters." The first is the English expatriate Dennis Plunkett's attempt to ennoble "the maid, Helen, who has worked for him" by comparing her to Helen of Troy; this obsession leads him to pursue every possible verbal coincidence linking St. Lucia to the Homeric narrative. But "the second effort is made by the writer, or narrator (presumably me, if you like), who composes a long poem in which he compares this island woman to Helen of Troy. The answer to both the historian [Plunkett] and the poet/narrator—the answer in terms of history, the answer in terms of literature—is that the woman doesn't need it." Indeed, the parallel, in its attempt to ennoble, actually demeans. If *Omeros* were, as some critics have said, "a reinvention of the *Odyssey,* but this time in the Caribbean," that would be "to humiliate the landscape and say to the Caribbean Sea, 'You must think of yourself as a second-rate Aegean, or, on a good day, you can look like the Mediterranean.'" The result of such "stupid historicism" is that "nobody takes the last part of the book seriously," refusing to see that *Omeros* "pivots on itself and accuses itself of vanity, of the vanity of poetry, of the vanity of the narrator." His critique seems of a piece with his rejection of our literary culture's obsession with echoes and derivations, the poststructuralist sense that everything is always already embedded in a text not of our own making. He seeks an unmediated art where there is no "history of the noun" between the poet and the object, only "the clarity of the thing being itself, without being clouded or even having a shadow. When you get to Dante, to the *Paradiso,* the poet is saying that this is a world without shadows, a timeless world. . . . To get beyond art is the ideal of the artist."[2]

Despite Walcott's eloquent complaint that "nobody" has noticed the book's turning against itself, a number of people have, most notably Rei Terada, who as early as 1992 justly remarked that "*Omeros* gradually frustrates one's hope of defining the connections between St. Lucian and Greek characters. The persona of the poet strives to release the poem's Homeric tier—to shed 'art' and henceforward to perceive 'life' only in relation to 'life.'"[3] But if the poem frustrates this hope, it also invests an enormous amount of rhetorical energy in raising it. Plunkett continues to elaborate his pseudohistory for many hundreds of lines, rehearsing the same speculations again and again. It is hard not to feel that Walcott takes Plunkett's quest seriously.

Noting that Walcott has said that his poem is not an epic, and that the narrator of *Omeros* undercuts the Homeric analogies repeatedly but does not abandon them, Gregson Davis invokes the epic convention of the *recusatio.* "What," he asks, "does the narrator gain from invoking Homer while disowning the Homeric genre?" The answer, he says, is to allow Walcott to "have his cake and eat it too," by the "reintegration of a disavowed term." Thus Plunkett's analogies, though they are in Walcott's own words "forced coincidences," remain "an integral part of the polyphonic composition." Walcott "is not actually renouncing 'epic' so much as redefining it and, in the process, demonstrating the fundamental fluidity of the whole concept of genre."[4]

If *Omeros* has uneasy relations with the epic genre, there may be political as well as literary reasons. Joseph Farrell argues that readers who "deny *Omeros* any meaningful connection with the epic genre" are motivated by a recognition that "[w]hen it comes to the assessment of postcolonial literature, the critical discourse of epic poetry acquires a racist tinge." It is more comfortable, therefore, to think of the poem as a novel in verse rather than a putatively monologic, imperial epic. Farrell argues, however, that the canonical epics contain a countervoice of self-criticism, as modern readings of the *Aeneid* and the Homeric poems have shown. Moreover, he contends, "traditional definitions" of the epic have been challenged by recent scholarship, which reveals them to be "wholly inadequate to describe even such poems as *The Aeneid* and *Paradise Lost.*" The epic, in this view, was never the font of orthodox authority that critical accounts from Hegel through Bakhtin claim it was. Carol Dougherty, in a similar attempt to dislodge the epic from the associations of cultural authority surrounding it, argues that Walcott's poem reminds us that before the *Iliad* and *Odyssey* were written down and enshrined in a literary canon, they were oral poems, malleable and not yet analyzed according to formal codifications of genre.[5] To return to the Homeric poems after reading *Omeros* is to see that they were once more like Walcott's text than we had supposed, improvisational and capricious, not yet encrusted with tradition. Thus Walcott's poem "opens up the ancient and authoritative Homeric texts and gently chides us for our previous lack of imagination about them."[6]

Davis, Farrell, and Dougherty offer subtle and elegant arguments by which I am partially convinced. And yet one is still left with the frustrations of reading *Omeros*. Why does it lavish so much tortured ingenuity, so much grandiose rhetoric, on analogies it ultimately condemns as pointless or even pernicious? Why does the poet so obsessively devoted to forging parallels with the Homeric epics end up confessing, to the spirit of Homer himself, that he has never read them "all the way through" (*O*, 283)? Can one ever really have one's cake and eat it too in literary matters? (Davis's examples of classical *recusatio* leave a great deal more of the poets' rhetorical edifice standing than a denial of the Homeric parallels would leave of Walcott's.) And I wonder how well these accounts, emphasizing literary self-reflexiveness, describe a poet who aspires "[t]o get beyond art" and who dismisses as "stupid historicism" the habit of seeing every text as derived from the already written. Granted, his cross-cultural nourishment of poetic forms can be understood as an instance of postmodern decentering and pastiche. But his quest to transcend the already given of history and textuality is at odds with such assumptions, as is his desire for formal and thematic resolution, his insistence on tying the disparate strands of the poem together. His characters shed false identities and recover true ones, rather than unmasking coherent selfhood as an illusion. Throughout *Omeros*, the sea-swift shuttles tirelessly across the Atlantic, stitching the poem's diverse subplots and scattered settings together. It is not merely Walcott's own account of the poem that warns us off a completely postmodernist reading. The self-undoing impulse in the tale itself, though undeniably present, seems countered by an equally strong impulse to bind together and unify all the parts, not only by the mythical parallels but also, and perhaps more importantly, by an extensive set of recurring motifs.

What shall we make of this tension between fluidity and closure? Does the poet, by throwing suspicion on his own analogies, also implicitly retract his other methods of unifying the narrative? Or does the pressure of his characters' experience, the refusal of their suffering to submit to analogical representation, break the coherence apart despite the author's best efforts? And if so, is his failure a fortunate defeat, allowing the poem's materials to assert their own energies, or simply a failure? Or, yet again, does the poem disavow one kind of coherence in the process of discovering another? Or does Walcott's futile persistence in the Homeric parallel enact the frustration of his own search for a form that harmonizes with his experience? The rhetorical excesses of the poem's epic analogies may be something like Odysseus' wanderings in the Aegean, as he is blown this way and that before at last finding his way home.

Robert Hamner, unlike Davis or Farrell, finds the genre of *Omeros* relatively unproblematic. Although it treats the epic models freely, as "catalysts for . . . innovative treatment of indigenous material," the poem is "largely an 'establishment epic,' in the sense that homecoming and the establishment of roots are paramount themes," and thus continues the tradition of the *Odyssey* and the *Aeneid*.[7] If Davis and Farrell are perhaps too keen to find in *Omeros* a postcolonial subversion of the epic, Hamner may underestimate the tension between postcolonial realities and epic conventions. For Walcott, living in a creole culture, there must be multiple and tentative probes for origin, and accordingly, the European poetic models he invokes often jostle unstably with each other. This instability is nowhere more evident than in what he calls his "combination of a Homeric line and a Dantesque design."[8] The line may approximate an Englishing of Greek hexameters, but it does so very flexibly, sometimes contracting to a loose pentameter or even an accentual tetrameter, thereby blurring Homer's meter with Shakespeare's and that of folk ballads and hymns. The tercets, too, are a loose approximation of Dante's tightly woven *terza rima*. Walcott often rhymes the first two or the second two lines instead of the first and third, and there is no consistent pattern of linking rhyme to bind the tercets together. Moreover, some of Walcott's rhymes evoke Byron's *Don Juan* more than Dante's *Comedia:* occasionally a word splits in two at the line break to accommodate a rhyme, and quite often Walcott rhymes feminine or double-feminine endings. Both rhyme and meter have the homemade texture of creole traditions, stretching to accommodate many influences both high and low.

The Significance of Philoctetes

Just as Dante is superimposed on Homer, the story of Philoctetes, told in a play by Sophocles but only briefly in the *Iliad,* takes on an importance at least as great as the more familiar stories of Achilles, Hector, and Helen. Carol Dougherty remarks that Philoctetes "lurks at the edges of the *Iliad* and the *Odyssey,* denied a central role." He is, she argues, "[a] Caliban figure within the Greek poetic tradition," embodying "the themes of isolation, suffering, and the power of the primitive." So, by returning "the wounded hero to the center in his Caribbean epic," Walcott is interpreting "from a postcolonial point of view," making the suffering, isolated, and allegedly "uncivilized" Philoctetes as important as the warring heroes.[9]

I would add only that whereas all the other parallels come under skeptical attack from the narrator himself, the Philoctetes analogy does not. It is the only parallel that does not trip the reader up with inconsistent matching of St. Lucian characters to their Greek counterparts. And it is the only one that succeeds as a fully imagined metaphor rather than a "forced coincidence." In his merging with Philoctetes, the amnesiac Adam-Crusoe acquires a visible wound, as if Walcott were now acknowledging openly the formerly tacit ironies of his Adamic stance.

Walcott had already engaged with the story of Philoctetes years earlier. Bruce King notes that in 1975 there were plans to produce "a new Walcott play called *The Isle Is Full of Voices* (eventually produced as *The Isle Is Full of Noises* in 1982 in the United States)."[10] The unpublished script of *The Isle Is Full of Noises*[11] shows the myth of Philoctetes emerging from the composite figure of Adam and Robinson Crusoe. (The obvious point of contact with Crusoe is Philoctetes' ten years of solitary island existence after Odysseus abandons him.) Whatever the play's value in its own right, it illuminates *Omeros* as a first sketch of Walcott's West Indian Philoctetes. In the play, Walcott is still sorting through the possibilities suggested by the myth.

The Isle Is Full of Noises is set on an imaginary West Indian island, variously referred to in the script as "Santa Maria," "Saint Matthew," and (in the last sentence of the play) "Saint Marta,"[12] where the most cynical pandering to foreign capital has long since quelled the idealism of the Federalist experiment. The figure in whom the Crusoe and Philoctetes narratives join is Sir Lionel Robinson, "first Prime Minister of the West Indies Federation, also known as Crusoe, aged 70, a hermit" (*IFN,* 1). Sir Geoffrey Thwaite, the English ambassador to Barbados, compares Sir Lionel to the actual first (and only) Prime Minister of the Federation, Sir Grantley Adams, but he also places the fictional PM in the company of Nehru and

Michael Manley. Sir Lionel is now living in solitude on "Pigeon Island," which is the name of the islet off St. Lucia that figures prominently in *Omeros.* Lionel Robinson can hardly be taken as a literal portrait of any historical figure, any more than his island can be literally equated with St. Lucia.

Sir Geoffrey offers the Sophoclean parallel early in the play: "Sir Lionel, the great and glowing orator, the lone black wolf of Magdalen College, the author of several books, had lived on Pigeon Island for years as an embittered recluse because, to put it brutally, he stank. He stank like Philoctetes from a boil, a suppurating wound that drove him into a huge, church-vaulted cave on the lee of Pigeon Island, spear-fishing with the bow of Philoctetes" (*IFN,* 5). In this phase of his life, the statesman has become a fisherman, like Philoctete and his colleagues Achille and Hector in *Omeros.*

In Sophocles' account, Philoctetes has been put ashore on an uninhabited island on the way to Troy because the stench of his wound and his cries of distress have disturbed a religious rite. But toward the end of the war, an oracle reveals that Philoctetes and his infallible bow must return to Troy if the Greeks are to win. So Odysseus, who had deceived and abandoned him, is dispatched with Achilles' son Neoptolomus to bring him back. In Walcott's play, it is not the recluse but the land he occupies that is needed. The Odysseus role falls to "the volatile, powerful and capricious Sir Ernest Henry," Robinson's successor as chief minister, known among his people by the Duvalier-like epithet "Papa." With the financial assistance of "New Aegean Enterprises" (represented by two foul-mouthed, cynical Americans), "Papa Henry" wants to build a hotel and tourist shopping complex, and he can hardly allow Sir Lionel's wound to spoil the tourist experience. As he explains, "tourists don't want to see reality" (*IFN,* 6), much less smell it. James the son of Achille, like Neoptolomus the son of Achilles in the myth, is dispatched to disarm the hermit, who carries a spear-gun instead of bow and arrows.

In the prologue, Achille suggests the metaphorical significance of Philoctetes' weapon when he says of Sir Lionel: "It is he whose power drew this archipelago tight as a bow" (*IFN,* 3). The bow, then, is the unifying spirit of the Federation. Sir Lionel, in a conversation with James, stresses that he was helped by a collective will: "It wasn't I alone who drew this bow. / I drew this bow with all the strength of the party" (*IFN,* 55). This language begins to recall not the bow of Philoctetes but the bow of Ulysses, which only its owner could bend (and which gave J. A. Froude the metaphorical subtitle for his book on the West Indies).[13]

In Walcott's play, James acquires the speargun from Sir Lionel as he rechristens himself with the Yoruba name "Ajamu," "he who fights for what he wants." As we have seen, renaming often figures in Walcott's poetry as liberation from historical paralysis, a way of claiming Adamic freedom. In the conversation with Sir Lionel that leads to his decision to break with Papa Henry, he says "My skin's on fire. / My skin is a shirt of fire" (*IFN,* 55), alluding to the shirt of Nessus. And he too dies by fire. Rather than surrender after his attack on the corrupt Babsie Hercules, he burns himself alive, in a martyrdom that triggers the island's revolt against Papa Henry.

Through James's sacrifice, Sir Lionel is finally healed of his wound. Rejuvenated, he ignites the crowd with a eulogy for James that stresses not politics but a bond to place, to "the ochre roads," "the companionable rivers," "the green quiet of the forest," "the faces of the old people" (*IFN,* 75). Its language aspires to Walcott's "Adamic" ideal of direct relation to one's physical environment, unmediated by cultural or political entanglements. Yet its lyrical sincerity has a political effect: it exposes by contrast the hollowness of Papa Henry's rhetoric, and a revolt swiftly follows. The people hail Sir Lionel as a delivering "JOSHUA!"[14] (*IFN,* 76) and return him to power.

The meaning of Philoctetes' wound evolves during the play. It is implicitly connected to recurring images of filth and corruption throughout. Sir Geoffrey refers to the odor of the wound as "the stench of a dying past" (*IFN,* 5). Sir Lionel himself does not offer interpretive hints until the first scene of the third act, when he says "Job flagellates his sores with a sea-grape branch for all these islands" (*IFN,* 53), implying that his agony is endured for the sake of the archipelago. He goes on to attribute his affliction to a divided identity from which James also suffers:

> You're a sundered man. I've seen rocks split by the sea's action, as the Atlantic split history. There is no bridge that arcs it, but you must fuse those halves: the present with the past. When I was Sir Geoffrey Thwaite's colleague at Magdalen we amused ourselves comparing archipelagoes, the Aegean and this one, I taught him African mythology, he taught me Greek, and we discovered what any schoolboy knows, the universalities of myth. He believes in reincarnation, I believe unless we can join these halves we aren't yet born. I got my sores that way, despite all their real agony their origin is psychic, when I left public office with your father, and, after your father in shame took his own life, after I saw corruption

> on the increase, the ulcers budded and flowered into mouths that sang
> in memory of Philoctetes. (*IFN*, 54)

The corruption of postcolonial politics here emerges as a symptom of a cultural trauma,[15] the inability to connect present with past or to join the disparate pasts of Europe and Africa.

This motif of cultural trauma links Philoctetes to Adam, the figure of Walcott's conundrum of remembrance and forgetting. When he blesses young James in the prologue, Sir Lionel performs a baptismal rite at the edge of the sea:

> I dip your head into
> an ocean of memory.
> Once. For the bones
> of your ancestors under
> the ribbed sea-floor.
> (HE ducks the BOY's head once.)
> Twice. To forget them,
> for their bones are like chains
> hanging round your neck,
> and the future is a whole
> burden in itself.
> (HE ducks the BOY's head again.)
> Thrice, to remember them.
> Three times, for the promise.
> (HE ducks the BOY's head again.)
>
> (*IFN*, 1)

Here is the tension, which we have seen in Walcott's account of Adamic poetics, between the senses of "amnesia" as psychic scar of historical violence and as release from historical burden. One remembers so that the bitterness of the past, no longer evaded, loses its power to encumber the present. In Crusoe, Walcott found his Caribbean second Adam, whose shipwreck so radically separates him from his past that he seems to have none. But his Philoctetes still suffers from the sundering violence of the Middle Passage; only when that wound heals can he be Adamic.

The Distribution of Mythical Roles in *Omeros*

The mythical analogies in *The Isle Is Full of Noises* are tangled together. In *Omeros,* Walcott distributes some of the qualities conflated in the play to distinct characters, so that distinctions become more readable by contrast. But that which *Omeros* untangles soon becomes tangled once more, as characters begin to play more than one mythical role at once. Plunkett is both Crusoe and an Odysseus figure seeking his long-lost Telemachus. He is also linked to Philoctetes through the metaphor of the wound. Hector and Achille in effect double as Paris and Menelaus, Helen's lovers. Walcott also reverses Homer's characterization of a hotheaded Achilles and a steady, responsible Hector. Ma Kilman, the obeah woman who cures Philoctete, is something of a Sibyl or Cassandra figure. But, since she must find the moly-like herb that heals him, she doubles as Athena freeing Odysseus from Circe. The pairing of the Walcott persona, Odyssean poet-wanderer, with the rooted oral poet Seven Seas competes with the simultaneous parallel between the Walcott persona and Achille, whose dream voyage to Africa is the counterpart of the poet's travels to Europe.

If the idea of Philoctetes as wounded New World Adam is the one mythical analogy that remains intact after the rest have been undercut, then it makes sense that a literal or figurative wound appears in almost all of the characters and subplots. As the narrator openly tells us, Plunkett "has to be wounded, affliction is one theme / of this work" (*O,* 28). In addition to giving affliction its visible sign, the wound also betokens the loss of unalienated work, through which the varying powers of each person, however modest, can be integrated into a community. Hector deserts the sea to drive tourists around the island. "He was making money, // but all of that money was making him ashamed" (*O,* 231). When Achille "[runs] out of money" (*O,* 47), he takes a job on Plunkett's pig farm, sweeping up after "swine matted with their shit" (*O,* 48). Plunkett's obsessive research on the Battle of the Saints distances him from the world outside his study and from Maud. Helen quits her job at the Halcyon Hotel because it subjects her to sexual harassment from white tourists (*O,* 33–34). Ma Kilman has begun to forget the bush medicine that will give her the power to cure Philoctete, who spends much of his time idling in her No Pain Café, unable to fish because of his wound (*O,* 10). And the Walcott persona, forced by his work as poet to go abroad, is separated from the very culture that sustains him.

During Achille's imagined return to Africa, Walcott comments that "The worst crime is to leave a man's hands empty. / Men are born makers."

The worst torment of the Middle Passage was that "The chained wrists couldn't forget // the carver for whom antelopes leapt, or / the bow-maker the shaft, or the armourer / his nail-studs." Deprived of the bond between imagination and environment (both social and natural) their work had given them, the enslaved Africans become only "coals, firewood, dismembered / branches, not men" (*O*, 150). The branches must be literally re-membered through an act of imaginative recovery of the past, breaking through the amnesia of diaspora and enslavement. That is the role of memory. Once this act of recovery has been accomplished, the past as "history," a crippling deformation of the present, falls away, allowing an Adamic consciousness of the present as open, facing toward the future. That is the role of forgetting. So it is Ma Kilman's ability to remember, at last, the name and hidden location of the curative herb that enables Philoctete to be healed of his wound of history and emerge as "Adam" in "Eden," "its light the first day's" (*O*, 248). With the cure of Philoctete's wound, "The bow leapt back to the palm of the warrior" (*O*, 247), filling the hand left empty since the sundering from Africa. To experience the present as the beginning of creation rather than the grimly determined outcome of a brutal past requires above all recovery of agency, the power to transform, through one's work, both oneself and the community in and for which the work is done.

The opening scene of the poem, in which Philoctete narrates for tourists the story of "how, one sunrise, we cut down them canoes" (*O*, 3), is an account of communal, unalienated labor, as the fishermen gather to chop down trees to be shaped into fishing boats for their own use. But the narration itself is alienated work of a kind, a potentially degrading performance that contrasts with the Homeric bard's narration, for Achaeans, of a tale that confirms their collective identity. The tourists "try taking / his soul with their cameras" (*O*, 3), and only Philoctete's refusal to explain the "cure" of his wound, which is one of those "'things . . . worth more than a dollar'" (*O*, 4), preserves his privacy from their intrusion. Since Philoctete is already healed at the time of his narration, we infer that this performance occurred *after* the events of which we are about to read. But the tree-cutting he describes occurred *prior* to those events. Between the ritual of a communal wholeness, about to be shattered, and the restoration of wholeness through the cure of the wound, the events of the plot will unfold.

The term "wound" first enters the poem as a verb, when Philoctete recalls: "I lift up the axe and pray for strength in my hands / to wound the first cedar." The cutting of the trees is portrayed as violent yet sanctioned by nature. Before Philoctete strikes the cedars, "the axe of sunlight" has already hit them. And the ferns, which "sound like the sea that feed us / fishermen all our life . . . nodded 'Yes, / the trees have to die'" (*O*, 3). Even so, the action becomes a metaphorical deicide: "These were their pillars that fell, leaving a blue space / for a single God where the old gods stood before. / The first god was a gommier" (*O*, 5).

French creole names (*"laurier-canelles,"* *O*, 3; "La Sorcièr," *O*, 4) remind us of the French colonization of St. Lucia; the description of the logwood as "red-skinned" identifies it with the Aruacs (Walcott's spelling, in *Omeros*, for "Arawaks"), whose "patois" is linked to that of their creole successors. In the closing lines of the passage, the Afro-Caribbean fishermen resemble the "barbarian" conquerors of Rome. Even as the passage commemorates the historical violence that has placed the fishermen in their present situation, it celebrates them as conquerors, not victims. Their labor has brought down the old gods and taken agency back into their own hands. If all had remained as it was in that moment, there would be no wound and no story. But like "the pause / between dusk and darkness, between fury and peace" in "The Season of Phantasmal Peace," this dawn can last but "one moment" (*CP*, 465). By the end of Chapter Two, we are plunged into "the prose / of fishermen cursing over canoes" (*O*, 15).

The figure of wounding or disease, though pervasive throughout, nonetheless takes different forms according to the differing situations of the main characters. It is most of all to be found in the men: Helen, in particular, seems ultimately unwoundable. The men suffer from their longing for her, but the poem does not dwell on her unspoken pain, although it hints at a "hole in her heart" (*O*, 152) opened by her estrangement from Achille. Her reconciliation with Achille is both a sign and a partial cause of his cure. Ma Kilman, too, is more comforter than sufferer: she looks after Philoctete until her recovery of the forgotten herb allows her to heal him.

Walcott makes a strong contrast between the visible wound of Philoctete and Plunkett's invisible wound. Philoctete's wound is in the shin, Plunkett's in his head, at nearly opposite extremes of the body; Philoctete's pain is mostly somatic, whereas Plunkett's is mostly psychological. The Afro-Caribbean fisherman and the English expatriate, then, are alike in suffering from a wound that refuses to heal, but the contrasts imply that they are complementary opposites. The development of the poem suggests that the healing of black and white, ex-colonized and ex-colonizer, are mutually implicated but not identical. In Achille, Philoctete, and Hector, we see the historical wound as it afflicts the descendants of slaves; in Dennis Plunkett, we see its less obvious corrosion in the descendants of masters. In the Walcott persona, we see a third variant of historical affliction: the effect of the colonial legacy on the vocation of poetry, and even on the style of *Omeros* itself, with its metastasis of proliferating analogies that finally require radical surgery if the poem is to live.

The Wound and Cure of West Indian Consciousness

Philoctete has been severed from his past, and his cure requires Ma Kilman to recover its African component: the herb she must rediscover crossed the Atlantic as a seed brought by the sea-swift, just as the enslaved Africans carried their ancestors as "seeds in [their] stomachs" (*O,* 149). Plunkett, expatriate descendant of the former colonizers, has been severed from his future: he has no son to carry on his name, no daughter either, and no illusions about the legacy of the vanishing empire. That severance from past and severance from future belong to the same larger historical trauma, the poem suggests by its vision of a "reversible world" (*O,* 207), in which time can move in either direction, opposites can change places, and whatever has happened can be lived again. Not only does Philoctete's cure, which reopens his future, require Ma Kilman's retrieval of the past, but Achille's readiness for his future with Helen and her child requires his vision of a reunion with his African ancestors. Plunkett, for his part, seeks a "son" in the figure of one Midshipman Plunkett who died in the Battle of the Saints, roughly a hundred and fifty years before he was born. Sometimes the successful recovery of the past opens the future, as in the cure of Philoctete; sometimes, however, the quest for the past turns out to be as futile as Makak's in *Dream on Monkey Mountain.* And sometimes it is a half success. In his vision, Achille is thwarted when he tries to change the past by preventing the capture of slaves, and his meeting with Afolabe ends in a mutual recognition that they are but shadows to each other. Yet he returns with a quickened sense of St. Lucia's link to Africa, as when he explains that the traditional cross-gendered dance on Boxing Day is done "for something older; something that he had seen / in Africa . . . / where he had been his own father and his own son" (*O,* 275). He wants to give Helen's child "an African name" and believes "[t]hat Helen must learn / where she from" (*O,* 318). He has partly succeeded in retrieving the past, while recognizing the limit of that success. Plunkett's obsession with naval history proves more sterile. After Maud's death, he comes to regret that his researches kept him apart from her, and only when he abandons them can he embrace the island as his adopted home. The usable past is never irrevocably lost but always latently available in the present. But Plunkett, in seeking to make the Midshipman into a son, is like Achille in his attempt to rescue the slaves. He asks the past to be other than it was, and that is a futile wish.

Although Philoctete's wound has come "from a scraping, rusted anchor" (*O*, 10), it is ultimately, like Sir Lionel Robinson's, as much "psychic" as somatic. Philoctete himself "believed the swelling came from the chained ankles / of his grandfathers" and that "the cross he carried" was also "that of his race" (*O*, 19). Plunkett received his wound serving in the British Army in North Africa during World War II; the choice of the African theater may be significant, since the end of the British empire, whether in Africa, India, or the Caribbean, will preoccupy him in later years: "It will be rewritten / by black pamphleteers, History will be revised, // . . . and when it's over, / we'll be the bastards!" (*O*, 92). After being hit, Plunkett "could remember nothing / for months, in casualty" (*O*, 27)—his wound, no less than Philoctete's, entails amnesia. He is wounded in the last "good war," and once that war had ended, Britain began divesting itself of colonial possessions.

Since Walcott's cure of the Caribbean psyche requires the reconciliation of black and white, descendants of slaves and descendants of masters, Plunkett's disaffection with the ideology of empire and eventual integration into St. Lucian society are as important to the plot as Achille's recovery of African origins. When we first meet him, he already has no use for his fellow expatriates, "middle-clarse farts" who bask in the attentions of "black, white-jacketed servitors" (*O*, 25) and affect upper-class accents, "[e]very one of them a liar / dyeing his roots" (*O*, 26). Whites, no less than Afro-Caribbeans, can be prisoners of masks. He is acutely sensitive to the beauty of the island, taking Maud out for long drives in clear weather, as "harbour after crescent harbour closed his wound" (*O*, 61). His kindness to Achille, who gets work on his pig farm when the fish give out, also disposes us well toward him, although his attitude toward his employees remains patronizing, and for his part, he supposes their "view of him would always remain / one of patronage" (*O*, 55). His wife, Maud, remarks that "they start to behave // as if they owned you" (*O*, 63). Both are well aware that tensions of race and class divide them from the people of the island. Even as he looks from a high vantage point across the Edenic landscape, Plunkett thinks: "[t]here's too much poverty below us" (*O*, 63).

Although he has lived in St. Lucia for twenty years, Plunkett cannot entirely surrender to its eternal present: "After a while the happiness grew oppressive. / Only the dead can endure it in paradise, / and it felt selfish for so long" (*O*, 63). He still has the metropolitan craving for activity, drama, and plot, and he confuses this need with altruism. Perhaps because he feels selfish, he decides "that what the place needed / was its true place in history" (*O*, 64), which, through tireless researches, he will generously give it. He appears to forget that he chose St. Lucia after the war because it was "somewhere . . . / . . . where what they called history could not happen" (*O*, 28). Having encountered excoriations of "history" in Walcott's previous works, we immediately regard Plunkett's offer with suspicion.

The suffering of Achille and Hector is related to the racial wound of Philoctete, though less overtly connected to historical causes than either Philoctete's or Plunkett's. When we meet Achille and Hector at the opening of Chapter Three, they attribute their quarrel to a disagreement over a bailing tin rather than jealousy over Helen. Such displacement of anger from its occasion might be taken as a sign of free-floating historical rage: after all, to say that they fight over "a shadow, and its name was Helen" (*O*, 17) is to imply that they fight as much over the idea of her as over the living woman. Since she is identified with the island itself, the anger arises in part from the fear that losing Helen would also mean dispossession, placelessness.

As Hector flings insults at Achille in patois, his theme is that Achille inflates his own importance. "'[O]us croire 'ous ni choeur campêche?" he asks, and "'Ous croire 'ous c'est roi Gros Îlet?" Or, as he repeats in English: "Who do you think you are? Logwood Heart?" and "You think you're king of Gros Îlet . . .?" (*O*, 16). So in a sense, the first challenge to the epic treatment comes from one of the characters, not from the narrator. It is ridiculous for a fisherman to behave as if he were a king or a hero, and yet the Homeric parallel to Hector and Achilles endorses the claim. By the end of the poem, Achille has become—without benefit of Homer—a most plausible, if uncrowned, "roi Gros Îlet."

Early in the poem, Achille runs out of money and has to take work on Plunkett's pig farm. Formerly self-employed, he is reduced to dependence, although he is "glad that Plunkett still gave him a break" (*O*, 48) after Helen's dismissal from her job as the Plunketts' housemaid. His situation undermines his self-confidence, and when Helen, goaded by his jealousy, returns to Hector, he begins "to lose faith in his hands" (*O*, 116). He regains Helen only after his return to fishing. His roles as worker, as suitor for Helen, and as secure possessor of the land Helen symbolically represents are intermeshed so that success in one entails success in the others.

Hector leaves fishing for transport-driving as a result of his intervention in Achille's quarrel with Helen. "[H]e had bought this chariot // and left the sea" because "[h]e believed she still loved Achille" (*O*, 118). In flight from this fear, he seeks "wide horizons" and more money, specializing in the long runs from Castries to Vieux Fort and "making four trips a day when most transports made one" (*O*, 118). The visceral thrill of speed and the lure of profits mask his pain but ultimately increase it. His career as transport driver, like Plunkett's obsessive plunge into historical research, is a futile attempt at escape. Walcott interprets Hector's death as the tragic "penalty of giving up the sea" (*O*, 231): "He was making money, // but all of that money was making him ashamed." Gradually, "Castries was corrupting him," but his recognition that "the sea was a love // he could never lose made every gesture violent." His death is an accident tinged with suicide.

If Caribbeans are, as Benítez-Rojo would have it, "people of the sea," then the exile of Hector and Achille to land work becomes an alienation from identity as well as livelihood. When Philoctete attempts "to make peace between" Hector and Achille, he argues "that they had a common bond / between them: the sea" (*O*, 47). That bond includes the knowledge of historical pain. Achille, diving illegally for conch shells, discovers (like Shabine) that the floor of the Caribbean is an unofficial history of the region in "corpses / that had perished in the crossing" (*O*, 45), the "deep evil" (*O*, 46) of the Middle Passage. But if the sea is a shared past, it is also a shared workplace. "[W]hatever a woman does, / that is her business," says Philoctete, "but men are bound by their work" (*O*, 47). If rivalry over Helen is one cause of Achille and Hector's unhappiness, the necessity of leaving the sea is another.

As one familiar with Walcott's poetry would expect, political organization offers no balm to the wounds of his characters. Hector and Philoctete support the protest candidacy of "Maljo," with Hector's Comet serving as campaign vehicle while Philoctete distributes pamphlets. But this is a comic subplot, although Walcott's satire is uncharacteristically gentle and even affectionate. The ruling party is led by "Compton," the actual name of St. Lucia's first prime minister, and the opposition by "the barber's son" (*O*, 104), who has moved from his father's Garveyism to Marxism. "Maljo," whose name means "evil eye" in East Caribbean creole,[16] operates on a shoestring budget, renting Hector's van and speaking through a battery-powered "hand-held megaphone" (*O*, 104). His primitive sound system, along with "the short-circuit prose / of his electrical syntax in which he mixed / Yankee and patois" (*O*, 105), earns him the nickname "Statics." It is fitting that Philoctete, embodiment of his people's cultural wound, distributes the handouts for this doomed candidacy, for Maljo is the candidate of the wounded: "[h]e, who was once / fisherman-mechanic, felt newly empowered / to speak for those at the backs of streets" (*O*, 105), for dwellers in "shacks on twilight ridges // in the wounding dusk" (*O*, 106).

Maljo's speech to the crowd, laced with wordplay, French and English creole phrases, and an occasional Yankeeism, is at once comic and linguistically inventive, a bit like robber-talk or the "talking sweet" of tea meetings, both of which ambiguously celebrate and poke fun at the extravagant mixtures of West Indian language. His promise to his followers, "Nous kai rock / Gros Îlet" [We'll rock Gros Îslet] (*O*, 108), catches its flavor succinctly. He invokes his own Homeric analogy, seeing the major parties as Greeks and Trojans, "both fighting for Helen"; but only his own party, United Love, "can give you the answers" (*O*, 107). His "Blocko" fundraiser is rained out, he loses the election, and he leaves "as a migrant-worker for Florida" (*O*, 109). The reader is left to balance respect for the core of truth in his diatribes with suspicion of his demagoguery and sudden exit. At no point, however, does the reader expect his campaign to deliver anything more than an amusing subplot.

Although the figurative wound is most evident in the men, who take up the nationalist quest of possessing "Helen" as symbol of the island, the women have their own hurts. Moreover, women are somewhat more fully characterized than is usual in Walcott's work, especially in the case of Maud Plunkett and to a lesser extent Ma Kilman. Helen, laboring under a crushing burden of conventionally gendered symbolism, remains vague, but then, the poem admits that she is obscured by the accretions of fantasy that gather around her, emerging only toward the poem's end from her "Homeric shadow" (*O*, 271).

Dennis Plunkett's wife, Maud, is Irish, so the marriage already crosses a boundary between colonizer and colonized, establishing both of them as likely candidates for assimilation into St. Lucian identity. If the Major has to make peace with the demise of the England he knew before the war and his own diminished sense of Englishness, Maud suffers from nostalgia for her County Wicklow childhood and, still more, the growing withdrawal of her husband into his historical speculations. Just as he was once sexually tempted by the flesh-and-blood Helen when she worked in his household, he is now tempted by the romance of the island as Helen; in these indulgences, he has been unfaithful to his wife in spirit, if not in body. Like Penelope, she feels abandoned but waits patiently; like Penelope, she absorbs herself in making a tapestry. But Maud's choice of motif for her embroidery, "all the horned island's / birds" (*O*, 267), can be read as her acceptance of St. Lucia as her home, and as her counterpart to her husband's quest for the spirit of the place. Like Walcott, she thinks that nature finally takes us farther into its truth than "history" can. And like Walcott, both in *Omeros* and in such earlier poems as "The Season of Phantasmal Peace," she chooses the birds as emblems: they are of the place but connect it, across the space between islands, or even, in the case of the sea-swift, with lost origins across the sundering Atlantic.

Like Maud, Ma Kilman is a motherly woman with no children to mother, and in this lack, both might be likened to Achille and Hector, fishermen who no longer fish. In a sense, the incapacitated Philoctete becomes Ma Kilman's child, reaching manhood when she effects his cure. The only childbearing woman in *Omeros* is Helen, with paternity shared by Hector, the biological father, and Achille, who is reconciled with Helen after Hector's death. The poem ends with Helen still pregnant, and since the child will be born of one dead and one living parent, one might compare this resolution with the ambiguous birth-in-death that closes "Laventille." Nonetheless, in context, the expected child provides a more affirmative resolution than the "swaddling cerements" of the earlier poem. If Helen represents the spirit of the island, her child represents its future, a much more promising one than Plunkett's desperately conjured "son." To the extent that the Plunketts have been gathered into a St. Lucian identity by the time of Maud's death, they figuratively belong to this child's extended family. If the men in *Omeros* suffer an alienation from work and from mastery of the physical world, the corresponding privation for the women is childlessness. The impending birth of Helen's child promises, in metaphorical terms, the end of a cultural impasse, the West Indian birth-in-death that Walcott could not resolve in "Laventille."

Ma Kilman has "the oldest bar in the village" (*O*, 17), a place where communal memory is gathered, the haunt of the fishermen and the local bard, Seven Seas. But although she is known as "a *gardeuse,* sybil, obeah-woman" (*O*, 58), her recollection of the old ways remains incomplete. Her Catholicism competes with her faded ancestral links to African deities: "She took Holy Communion / with Maud sometimes, but there was an old African / doubt that paused before taking the wafer's white leaf." The old gods are "waiting to be known by name; but she / had never learnt them, though their sounds were within her, / . . . Erzulie // Shango, and Ogun; their outlines fading, thinner / as belief in them thinned" (*O*, 242). In "Laventille," Walcott had lamented the loss of "customs and gods that are not born again" (*CP*, 88), but in *Omeros* they are resurrected, albeit as metaphors rather than objects of belief.

Ma Kilman recovers the lost herbal cure by learning to understand "the ants talking the language of her great-grandmother" (*O*, 244). Ants—like vines, smoke, the sea-swift, and other recurring motifs —acquire symbolic resonance in the course of the poem. In the initial scene of tree-cutting, the men, "like ants," haul logs to be made into canoes (*O*, 7). Anonymously laboring Caribbean people repeatedly evoke the insects' persistence and disproportionate strength. The most memorable instance occurs when the poet, accompanied by the ghost of his father, sees a line of women unloading coal in Castries harbor as an "unending / line crossing like ants" (*O*, 74) in their movement up and down the gangplank. When Philoctete's wound at last heals, Walcott exclaims, "See her there, my mother, my grandmother, my great-great-/ grandmother. See the black ants of their sons, their coal-carrying mothers" (*O*, 245). Although both men and women may appear as ants, the motif usually occurs in conjunction with matriarchal figures such as the coal-bearers or Ma Kilman.

The folk muse of *Omeros*, in contrast to Dante, Homer, and other mostly white, male, and European writers evoked as literary heroes, is a black Afro-Caribbean woman, steeped in an unofficial, unwritten lore passed on from mothers to daughters. The coal-carriers provide an image of the vanishing past: as the poem notes, Derek as a child still "watched them from [his] grandmother's house" (*O*, 76). Each one "climbed with her hundredweight basket, every load for / one copper penny, balanced on their necks / that were tight as the liner's hawsers from the weight." Managing the operation were "two tally clerks in their white pith helmets" (*O*, 74). With this *tableau vivant* as text, Warwick preaches an application. "Kneel to your load, then balance your staggering feet / and walk up that coal ladder as they do in time, / one bare foot after the next in ancestral rhyme" (*O*, 75). If the father, as ghost, is "only the shadow of that task" (*O*, 74), so too is the son's work of writing, motivated by "the language's / desire to enclose the loved world in its arms" (*O*, 75). The best writing, then, seeks to "enclose" the physical world, and to bring its physicality into language itself. The poet's lines ultimately derive from the labors of unlettered St. Lucians such as these women.

Jonathan Martin objects to this "morally distasteful comparison between the work of poetry and the crushing labor of Caribbean slave women," which inflates "the poet's role to that of savior."[17] But a closer look at the passage raises the question of who is saving whom. The poet describes his writing as a shadow-like doubling of physical work, a secondary mimesis of labor. Warwick asserts that the form of his son's poetry emerged from the rhythm of the women's steps: "the couplet of those multiplying feet / made your first rhymes" (*O*, 75). As a child, he was "wounded by their power and their beauty" (*O*, 76): through them, the wound of Philoctete enters his own consciousness, leaving him the responsibility to give the women's "feet a voice" (*O*, 76). If that last aspiration seems grandiose (as well as metaphorically ill-advised), the self-aggrandizement diminishes when we remember that what the poet gives is finally only given *back*, having been first acquired from the women his verse will celebrate. We can see the analogy as one of reciprocity rather than unmitigated appropriation. Whether one finds it convincing or not, its structural importance to the poem is crucial, for it provides the connection between the wounded characters and the wounded consciousness of the poet, and between the cure of Philoctete and the poem's self-corrective cure of its own language and form.

For Ma Kilman, Achille, and Philoctete, memory heals, but Helen's inviolable innocence requires a clean break with the past. Plunkett may feel that she needs a history, but when she sings, she chooses the Beatles' "Yesterday" (*O*, 34), a song about capricious change ("Why she had to go / I don't know, / she wouldn't say") in which memory brings regret but not insight. History has no narrative; today replaces yesterday as tomorrow will presumably replace today, as Hector replaces Achille who had replaced Hector in Helen's affections. There is, to be sure, that "hole in her heart," but it seems less a grief for something lost than an inarticulate yearning for a completeness not yet found. She vacillates between her two men, often "vexed with both of them" (*O*, 124), and when she becomes pregnant, she does not "know for who" (*O*, 34). She abandons herself to the pleasure of the dance at the Gros Îlet Friday Night Jump-ups, despite Achille's disapproval; she goes from job to job, unwilling to display the expected subservience. She follows her own desire where it leads and, until her reconciliation with Achille at the end of the poem, does not look back. And perhaps she does not look back even then, for Helen's advancing pregnancy and Achille's return to fishing have matured the surviving couple, and Hector's death has narrowed Helen's choice.

At the end of the poem, two of its central characters, Maud and Hector, are no longer alive. The survivors commemorate the fallen with due ceremony, but they move on, and the prevailing mood of the last pages is forward-looking, although looking forward includes the Walcott persona's glance ahead to his own eventual death. The last words of the poem belong to the ocean: "the sea was still going on" (*O*, 325). It was already going on long before human beings appeared on the earth and will likely continue after we have disappeared. As we shall find in considering Walcott's metaphorical connections between the sea and writing, the ocean is the central trope of memory-as-forgetting, hoarding the past in its depths, but erasing, with each surge of generative energy, the marks of human presence on the shore.

Metaphor and Metastasis: Analogy as Disease and Cure

In turning from the characters of *Omeros* to the authorial persona and the style to which he commits the poem, we might begin with his insistence that "[t]here was no difference / between me and Philoctete" (*O*, 245), that "we shared the one wound, the same cure" (*O*, 295). The wounded poet produces a wounded poetry: "Like Philoctete's wound, this language carries its cure, / its radiant affliction" (*O*, 323). If the source of Philoctete's wound—historical trauma and the amnesia that results from it—is also its cure, to be sought in a paradoxical remembering of history in order to forget it again, this time by choice rather than necessity, then the "cure" of the poem's wounds must proceed by a similar path. As to what the poem's wounds are, my experience as its reader and its own testimony roughly agree. Walcott admits a parallel between his own analogical effort and Plunkett's: if "Plunkett, in his innocence, // had tried to change History to a metaphor / in the name of a housemaid" (*O*, 270), Walcott has "altered her opposite." The two have adopted "opposing stratagems / in praise of her and the island" (*O*, 271). The opposite of changing history to a metaphor would be changing a metaphor to history: if Plunkett begins with an actual incident in St. Lucian history and ends up with a flimsy Homeric allegory, Walcott begins with a poetic conceit and nearly allows it to become literal, displacing the evidence of his own senses: "when would I not hear the Trojan War / In two fishermen cursing in Ma Kilman's shop? / When would my head shake off its echoes . . .?" He would instead "see Helen // as the sun saw her, with no Homeric shadow." When echoes and shadows displace direct perception, literature becomes as "guilty as History" (*O*, 271).

When Walcott speaks of "this language" carrying a "radiant affliction," he means not only that the affliction is a source of light as well as pain, but also that it radiates outward. At one point, he refers to Philoctete's wound as a "cancer" (*O*, 274), and the spread of cancer by metastasis gives an apt figure for the proliferation of analogies in Walcott's language. As the pain of Philoctete's wound affects every part of his body, the wound of the poem affects its diction, its syntax, its use of metaphor. The poem must cure itself of its rage for comparison, which is shadowed throughout by Plunkett's Quixotic effort to make Homer's epics prophesy the literal events of St. Lucian history. In the early pages of his poem, Walcott's invocation of Omeros interposes the Greek master between the world and his own imagination: "Only in you," he says, "can I catch the noise / of the surf lines wandering" (*O*, 13). By the end of the poem, the primacy of Homer and the sea has been reversed. By then, the poem's own analogical project has come to crisis in Books IV and V, where Walcott extends his wanderings to North America and Europe, seeking to make every event rhyme with a Caribbean counterpart.

As the poem moves into the Walcott persona's wanderings in the United States and Europe, juxtaposed with the story of Catherine Weldon and the Sioux taken up in the last chapters of Books IV and V, the moral parallelisms grow ever larger and vaguer. The narrative pace, already unhurried, slows to a crawl, while the West Indian islands almost disappear in the vast scale of Walcott's catalogue of diplacements and genocides. Robert Hamner justly remarks that "[s]uch inclusiveness obviously threatens the integrity of the central narrative. As many critics have already complained, Walcott's attempts to incorporate the disparate stories of North American natives and then Europeans are the least defensible aspects of the poem," most of all when Walcott's juxtaposition of his divorce with the obliteration of the Sioux opens him "to charges of self-aggrandizement."[18]

Although the divagations to North America and Europe seem to me, as to Hamner, the weakest stretch of the poem, one can recognize in them an attempt to touch all the endpoints of arrival and embarkation that frame the Caribbean diaspora. Walcott's European itinerary emphasizes the cities from which the colonial powers set out to explore and conquer. But the expulsion of the Sioux from North Dakota in the late nineteenth century, or of the Cherokee and Choctaw from Georgia some fifty years earlier, seems connected to the Caribbean only as a parallel example of imperial violence against native peoples. Walcott also frames these stories in another context: that of his own uprooted wanderings in the United States, including his encounters with contemporary American racism. It is in the juxtapositions of his own difficulties with cataclysmic historical events that the poem most painfully overreaches itself.

Just possibly, however, it knows that it overreaches itself, for soon after his return from these wanderings, the Walcott persona begins to criticize his own obsession with Homeric parallels. But if there are hints of disavowal in the tone of Books IV and V, they are faint indeed. Only framing these passages between the beginning and the end of the poem will allow such a reading, and my own sense is that Walcott's own degree of commitment to the analogies he offers remains uncertain to the end.

The American sojourn turns toward Walcott's own "abandonment in the war of love" (*O*, 171). He has become a Philoctetes or Crusoe figure himself, one of the "castaways" who "make friends with the sea; living alone / they learn to survive on fistfuls of rainwater / and windfall sardines" (*O*, 171). One might balk, however, at his attempt to link his own pain with that of the displaced Sioux. The spike that completed the Union Pacific was "hammered / into the heart of their country as the Sioux looked on"; and it

> had entered
> my heart without cheers for her far gentler weapon.
> I could not believe it was over any more
> than they did. Their stunned, anachronistic faces
>
> moved through the crowd, or stood, with the same expression
> that I saw in my own when I looked through the glass,
> for a land that was lost, a woman who was gone.
>
> (*O*, 175)

Not only does this equation seem overextended, it casts doubt on the notion of Helen as an embodiment of St. Lucia. If the metaphor of land as woman leads, by its own figurative logic, to analogies like this, maybe it needs to be pursued with more skepticism, or perhaps abandoned altogether.

Elsewhere, Walcott explicitly connects North American Indians with the St. Lucian coal carriers when he describes "women moving in ragged bands" along the Trail of Tears as "like those on the wharf" (*O*, 177). In a further attempt to link the U.S. setting to the Caribbean plot line, Walcott leaps from the Sioux in the Dakotas circa 1890 to Georgia, where, some fifty years before, the Cherokee, Choctaw, and several other nations had been dispatched to Oklahoma on the Trail of Tears. The Georgia landscape has also been the site of lynchings, with "Afolabes hung like bats" (*O*, 178) on its trees. As the analogies begin to acquire a life of their own, Walcott resorts to unpersuasive descriptive similes: "Negro shacks // moved like a running wound, like the rusty anchor / that scabbed Philoctete's shin" (*O*, 178). The visual appearance of the shacks gets lost as the language strains after parallels.

Walcott explains his fascination with Catherine Weldon and the Sioux as arising from an attempt to escape his own troubles. "When one grief afflicts us we choose a sharper grief / in hope that enormity will ease our affliction"; thus Catherine Weldon's story can make "a fiction / of [his] own loss" (*O*, 181). One might read this remark as a self-criticism, correcting the conflation of the destruction of the Sioux with Walcott's divorce. If so, it sets in motion questions that the poem does not fully engage. If one writes about the Ghost Dance or the Trail of Tears because it is therapeutic to dwell on an "enormity" that dwarfs one's own problems, has compassionate witness given way to something less scrupulous, a desire to confer borrowed dignity on private pain? Or is such a process, in which one's own "sorrow" is "replaced" by something larger, a laudable sublimation—the only means, however impure, by which imaginative identification with another's grief can happen at all? One might apply the observation to Catherine Weldon as well: does her compassion for the Sioux stem from her desire to eclipse her sorrow for her dead child with a "sharper grief"? The poem, however, is not in a questioning mood; rather, its rhetorical machinery is in high gear, asserting the connection of all its elements with heightened vehemence just where the claim is least sustainable. Much as I admire Walcott for insisting, in a time of identity politics, on common ground in human experience, the metamorphosis of Sioux into Cherokee into African Americans who are also Afro-Caribbeans who in turn are like Homeric Greeks proceeds so rapidly, and with so little interest in the particular qualities of any of these peoples, that the universal becomes a blank category.

There are, however, two kinds of figurative proliferation in *Omeros*. Most obvious are the large-scale analogies: Hector and Achille to Homeric warriors, their rivalry for Helen to the Trojan War, North American tribes to the Caribs and Arawaks, European contenders for empire to the Greeks and Trojans. The poem returns to these analogies over and over again, to the point of heavy-handed insistence. When Walcott finally begins to cross-examine them toward the end of the poem, one's reaction is relief mixed with an irritation that it has taken him so long. But at a more descriptive and local level, the figuration is more subtle, and eventually the second kind of metaphorical language emerges as an alternative to the first. My analogy to metastasis applies most to the large-scale analogies. Just as spreading cancer destroys organs with differentiated functions by substituting its own amorphous, undifferentiated cells, the attempt to sustain the Homeric analogies and their corollaries becomes destructive because it overwhelms the poem's delicacy, its responsiveness to particularity and difference. Even Walcott's painterly eye goes blank in passages like his run-on metaphorical description of the shacks in Georgia.

The other kind of metaphor is implied rather than overtly announced, and instead of emphasizing a reductive equivalence, the parallelism of one action or situation to another, it emphasizes fluidity, metamorphosis, the gradual convertibility of one thing into another. That sense of fluidity underlies the poem's vision of a "reversible world," in which time can run backward, things can turn into their opposites, and historical damage can be undone. Although the thematic implications emerge slowly, such metaphors are present throughout the poem. In Chapter IX, for instance, Walcott links Hector's two occupations, fishing and transport-driving, through a natural description: "The wind changed gear like a transport with the throttle / of the racing sea" (*O*, 49). The figurative progression of this passage is typical of Walcott's logic of metaphor: the wind is the tenor of a simile whose vehicle is a transport; then the transport's throttle is the tenor of another analogy in which the vehicle is the sea. So nature is like machinery, which in turn is like nature. This circular figure suggests that Hector remains with the sea, or the sea with him, even though he has left it. One might also connect it to the "self-healing" powers of the island, which, as the poem would have it, can absorb the discord of modernity into its organic wholeness.

Temporal and spatial reversals occur when characters return to the Old Worlds across the Atlantic. In Africa, Achille finds that "the future reversed itself in him" (*O*, 141). The poet's journey to Europe parallels Achille's voyage to Africa and similarly emphasizes the language of temporal and spatial reversal. "I crossed my meridian" (*O*, 189), Book V begins. Swifts, those same birds that provided Achille with his guide, fly "in reverse," and the "clouds read backwards" (*O*, 189). "My meridian," as readers of "The Caribbean: Culture or Mimicry?" will recognize, evokes Walcott's challenge, in that essay, to the notion that there is some line of demarcation between Europe and its inferior New World derivative, the latter doomed to futile mimicry of the Old World original. It also alludes to Pope Alexander's decree (*O*, 191), by which a longitudinal line divided the empires of Spain and Portugal; here, too, the "meridian" is a demarcation not only in space but in a field of political power. In crossing his meridian, the poet has also transgressed the distinctions of power and authority they represent, and so taken a step toward their erasure. Likewise Achille, in his voyage to Africa, has crossed a "parallel," and in so doing, "cancels the line of master and slave" (*O*, 159). One might read the metaphor of meridian-crossing as the beginning of the poem's turn toward self-criticism. For if meridians and hierarchies can be erased, parallels become the wrong mode of connection. Fluidity, metamorphosis, the imperceptible shading of one thing into another, become more appropriate to the poet's revised conception of his world. Coming home to St. Lucia, he declares: "I smelt with my eyes, I could see with my nostrils" (*O*, 224), a synesthesia appropriate to the arabesque of descriptive metaphor that has quietly survived beside the devouring Homeric parallels. Finally, "all those parallels" are "pointless," since "names are not oars / that have to be laid side by side" (*O*, 312–13). And parallels, in the other sense of meridians of demarcation, are pointless as well, given the indivisibility of the ocean connecting all parts of the world, constantly changing and flowing.

The obsessive proliferation of Homeric comparisons might be seen as a lingering wound of colonized consciousness, motivated by an insecure longing to claim the founding authority of the European canon. One can understand the temptation, however, in the light of Achille's conversation with Afolabe about names. The most extended discussion of language in *Omeros* occurs not between the Walcott persona and Omeros, but between an illiterate St. Lucian fisherman and his African ancestor. The sundering from Africa has left not only empty hands but empty words as well.

The dialogue reveals a split between Afolabe's sense of linguistic transparency and Achille's acceptance of that gap between the signifier and the signified which, according to poststructuralist theory, is inescapably produced by the relation of words and things. In *Omeros*, words become severed from their signifieds only in diaspora, as the result of a historical fall into alienation. The "father" introduces himself as "'Afo-la-be,' / touching his own heart" (*O*, 137). The gesture implies an inviolable connection between the name and the man who bears it, with all the conventional attributes of the "heart" as center of emotion, intention, and identity. He wants to know what the name "Achille" means. But Achille cannot answer: "The deaf sea has changed around every name that you gave / us; trees, men, we yearn for a sound that is missing" (*O*, 137). Without the lost sound that corresponds to essence, Achille has had no choice but to "accept the sounds we are given"; his name is a "sound whose meaning [he] still do[es] not care to know" (*O*, 138). For Afolabe, "every name is a blessing," and if its "sound means nothing," then its bearer "would be nothing. / Did they think you were nothing in that other kingdom?" (*O*, 137). The link between name and person is the social objectification of the person's very existence; without it, one undergoes a social death akin to that of slavery itself:

if you're content with not knowing what our names mean,

then I am not Afolabe, your father, and you look through
my body as the light looks through a leaf. I am not here
or a shadow. And you, nameless son, are only the ghost

of a name.

(*O*, 138–39)

This passage is crucial if we are to balance the senses in which Walcott is a self-reflexive, postmodern writer, as Rei Terada portrays him, with the ways in which he remains committed to language as a quest, however difficult, for the recovery of a transparent correspondence between word and thing. Like so much else in his art, Walcott's address to the problem of language is paradoxical: through the metamorphic fluidity of his metaphors, arbitrary and self-reflexive though they seem at first, he redescribes and renames, until word and thing once more align themselves in a right relation.

The poem begins, then, with an untenable choice: it must either conscript itself to the Homeric analogy in order to acquire significance, or accept a severance of language from meaning as a consequence of diasporic estrangement. Walcott's fluidity of descriptive metaphor sets in motion a process of renaming, of adjusting the relations of words to things. It continues throughout the poem, but the degree to which it supplants the Homeric scaffolding remains open to question. To make a fair estimate, we need to look more closely at how the metamorphic language works, and then at the way the poem ends.

Nowhere is the metamorphic language more apparent than in Walcott's recurring descriptions of the shape-shifting sea itself. We first encounter it in the seventh line of the poem, where wind through the ferns sounds "like the sea that feed us / fishermen all our life" (*O*, 3). Already it is part of a transformation, air as water, and already associated with the communal source of life. At the end of Chapter One, earth also becomes ocean, as "the ground / shuddered under the feet in waves" (*O*, 5). We have been prepared from the outset for bolder transformations to follow: the island's "elements," as the poet notices upon his return from his wanderings, "changed places," so that "[t]he grooved sea was Achille's garden, / the ridged plot of rattling plantains carried their sense // of the sea," while at night, instead of falling, "rain rose upwards" (*O*, 234).

Throughout the poem, but especially toward its end, the sea is associated both with the history of the Caribbean and with the erasure of historical particularity in a primal whole, "the one element that had made them all // fishes and men" (*O*, 156). When Achille walks back from Africa under the Atlantic, three hundred years of history pass over his head, but on the ocean floor time has stopped. Describing the Plunketts' drive down the coast of the island, Walcott speaks of "a white, amnesiac Atlantic" and "harbour after crescent harbour" that "closed his wound" (*O*, 61). The ocean, here, is the element of healing and benign forgetting. "Our only inheritance," the poem declares, is "that elemental noise / of the windward, unbroken breakers, Ithaca's / or Africa's, all joining the ocean's voice" (*O*, 130).

In one sense, the sea for Walcott is history, as the title of a poem in *The Star-Apple Kingdom* explicitly says. In *Omeros,* the displaced slaves "felt the sea-wind tying them into one nation / of eyes and shadows and groans, in the one pain / that is inconsolable" (*O*, 151). He speaks of "our wide country, the Caribbean Sea" (*O*, 320), envisioning not the islands but the ocean itself as the West Indian's home. The sea, then, is nationhood, with the Atlantic crossing as the one common past, the displacement to the Caribbean as a shared destiny. But it is also poetry, in which particular identities dissolve and transcend themselves.

The local Homer figure's very name, Seven Seas, associates the art of poetry with ocean. When the Walcott persona encounters Omeros by the Thames in London, the Greek bard is "naming the ships," reading "the inverted names of boats in their element" (*O*, 195). "Inverted" literally describes the reflection of the name in the water, but it also links up with Walcott's figure of reversibility: it is in the element of water that reversal, metamorphosis, and renaming take place. The climactic second encounter with Omeros, in which he and Walcott share a song in praise of the island, depicts Homer as a Protean figure, going from a white bust to a shadow, a driftwood log, and finally "a foam-headed fisherman in his white, torn // undershirt" (*O*, 280–81) like Achille or Philoctete, as "the shapes metamorphosed" (*O*, 280). Walcott greets him, saying "I have always heard / your voice in that sea, master" (*O*, 283), even as he concedes that he has never read the *Odyssey* "all the way through."

At this point, we may return to the question with which we began: what to make of Walcott's astonishing confession. To subvert, strongly misread, or swerve, to refract or recontextualize, these are all recognizable ways for a poet to respond to a great canonical influence; but to ignore, to erase, not to read it at all, even while claiming to be "the freshest of all" its "readers"—what can Walcott's response mean? It would seem that

Homer the historically particular poet has become the voice of ocean itself. Walcott says he has always heard the poet's voice in the sea's, not the sea's voice in the poet's. What makes Homer Homeric is the oceanic power in his voice; Walcott makes him a force of nature whose poems are unmediated by history or language. The ocean is its own poem; it has "no memory of the wanderings of Gilgamesh, / or whose sword severed whose head in the *Iliad.* / It was an epic where every line was erased // yet freshly written in sheets of exploding surf" (*O*, 296). In the Homeric texts, "whose sword severed whose head" is a matter of some importance, and the difference between the wanderings of Gilgamesh and those of Odysseus might be thought a wide gulf indeed, in language, time, and cultural tradition. But "Homer" becomes for Walcott not the author of certain texts in Greek, but a permanently available power of imagination quickened by the power of the natural world. Poems are not written to be enshrined in libraries and revered forever; they must be erased and remade, much as the ocean reshapes itself in every wave that strikes the shore.

The epic, as noted above, has served as the genre of cultural memory, but in the depths of the sea, "the true element, / water . . . commemorates nothing in its stasis" (*O*, 297). Similarly, Walcott identifies his own writing with the sea; he goes to his work "like a fisherman walking towards the white noise / of paper" (*O*, 241). Walcott's oceanic epic celebrates the emergence of a culture in the present rather than a heritage gathered from the past. Most of all, it celebrates the power of imagination to reshape its world, to heal old wounds and reverse historical damage. The poem achieves its resolution by erasures and undoings. The cure of Philoctete's wound figuratively reverses the Middle Passage. As Achille has "learnt" (*O*, 241) and "Ma Kilman taught" (*O*, 242), Philoctete's wound "was given by the sea, but . . . the sea could heal / the wound also." As Philoctete sits in the healing bath, it figuratively expands to become the sea washing the archipelago: "The lime leaves leeched to his wet / knuckled spine like islands that cling to the basin / of the rusted Caribbean" (*O*, 247). The curative herb is homeopathic: it has a foul odor, like that of the festering sore it cures, and "its pronged flower" (*O*, 237) is shaped like the "anchor" that inflicted the wound.

The sea-swift, in bringing the flower's seed across the Atlantic, "aimed to carry the cure that precedes every wound; the reversible Bight / of Benin was her bow" (*O*, 239). If the cure precedes the wound, then it is always latently available once the wound has been given. To history's timeline, drawn by a determinism of cause and effect, Walcott answers with a vision of an oceanic eternal present to which temporal movement always returns, cyclical rather than linear. As Warwick's ghost instructs him, "in its travelling all that the sea-swift does / it does in a circular pattern" (*O*, 188). The swift binds together the worlds on either side of the Atlantic by shuttling back and forth between them, retracing the routes of the triangular trade and rejoining what the Middle Passage had sundered: "Her wing-beat carries these islands to Africa, / she sewed the Atlantic rift with a needle's line, / the rift in the soul" (*O*, 319).

Having absorbed Homer into the voice of the sea, Walcott aspires to disappear into it as well. He compares his own quest as writer to a sea voyage, in which "the 'I' is a mast," and

> The right journey
> is motionless; as the sea moves round an island
>
> that appears to be moving, love moves round the heart—
> with encircling salt, and the slowly travelling hand
> knows it returns to the port from which it must start.
>
> (*O*, 291)

This journey of circular return, fulfilling Warwick's injunction to "simplify / your life to one emblem, a sail leaving harbour // and a sail coming in" (*O*, 72), is in effect motionless, for though it spans Old and New Worlds, all that it encounters there must be carried home to the place of origin, enriching and transforming its present. As Walcott steers his poem toward closure, regretting "so much left unspoken // by my chirping nib!" (*O*, 321), he imagines his own funeral and prays, "let the deep hymn // of the Caribbean continue my epilogue," as if to say that everything his poem would say, the sea will continue to utter when he falls silent. The poem's last line, "When he left the beach, the sea was still going on" (*O*, 325), refers to Achille, but it could be said of anyone, fisherman or poet: when we are gone, the sea will go on as it always has.

Walcott's ending is a little bit like the astonishing conclusion of Whitman's "Song of Myself," except that if we want him, we must look for Walcott under the breakers rather than under our boot-soles. In claiming kinship with the sublime power of the ocean, to which he has already commended Homer, he may seem stunningly arrogant; in subordinating his own voice to that of the sea, as if his poem were only a borrowed strain from "the deep hymn // of the Caribbean," he may seem remarkably humble. In either case, what startles is the literalness with which he presents art as natural energy, in an age acutely aware of the artificiality of language, and in a poem whose own Homeric analogies could hardly be more flagrantly artificial.

In closing, I return to the question of how to integrate the obsessive, long-winded excess of the Homeric parallels into one's experience of the whole poem. Surely Maud is not alone in her exasperation when Plunkett "roar[s] out Breen's encomium by heart" (*O*, 99),[19] or informs her and us that "[']near sunset, on April 12, hear this, the *Ville de Paris* // struck her colours to Rodney. Surrendered. Is this chance / or an echo? Paris gives the golden apple, a war is / fought for an island called Helen?'" (*O*, 100). In one passage of just six lines, he compares the St. Lucian Helen not only to her Greek namesake, but to Judith and Susanna as well (*O*, 97). Walcott puts the same desperate will to analogy in the mouths of other characters as well; Catherine Weldon, after a disastrous defeat of the Sioux, says "I walked like a Helen among their dead warriors" (*O*, 216). During his North American wanderings, the Walcott figure laments that after too much time in art museums, "[o]utside becomes a museum," until "every view is a postcard signed by great names" (*O*, 183), and sometimes *Omeros* becomes similarly encumbered with allusion.

It is true that, as a rule, Walcott assigns the most obsessive Homer-hunting to Plunkett, but as the maker of the poem, he has responsibility for adjusting its proportions. If so much of our time must be spent with Plunkett's speculations and Walcott's eventual dismantling of them, then they should represent a serious temptation that needs to be understood and resisted. But from fairly early in the poem, Walcott subjects Plunkett's musings to rather broad satire. How should one respond when the Major, noting that the island's Amerindian name means "where the iguana is found," begins haranguing an actual iguana with rhetorical questions such as:

> Was the greatest battle
>
> In naval history, which put the French to rout,
> fought for a creature with a disposable tail
> and elbows like a goalie? For this a redoubt
>
> was built? And his countrymen died? For a lizard
> with an Aruac name?
>
> (*O*, 92)

To which one might reply, No, of course not; could we please move on? In Book IV, Walcott's own voice begins to resemble Plunkett's in its rage for resemblance, so that "The wandering smoke below me was like Achille's / hallucination" (*O,* 175), slaves in the United States are "Hectors and Achilleses" (*O,* 177), towns in the southern United States are "named Helen, // Athens, Sparta, Troy," while displaced Choctaw and Creek women "headed for Oklahoma" are like the coal carriers on the wharf in Castries.

Though I have made the case for the poem's critique of its own analogical method, it is finally impossible, after multiple rereadings, to feel that the whole poem is built with that critique in mind. Too many parts of it seem sincerely invested in the Homeric analogy critiqued elsewhere or simply unaware that their reaching for analogies is strained. My guess is that the self-critique emerged in the course of composition, and that Walcott could not (or would not) integrate the portions he had already completed into his belated insight. *Omeros* remains a great poem, large in scope and sympathies, with much unforgettable writing. But sometimes the Homeric figure it most reminds me of is Laocoön, tangled in serpentine coils of dubious analogy. Still, it has the strength to break its bonds and compel us to keep reading. When Walcott and the rest of us have left the beach, this poem, like the sea itself, will still be going on.

10

Post-Homeric Derek: *The Bounty* and *Tiepolo's Hound*

Seven years elapsed between the publication of *Omeros* and Walcott's next volume, *The Bounty* (1997). For such a prolific poet, that was a long interval, but given the scope and ambition of *Omeros,* a fallow period might have been expected. In 1992, Walcott received the Nobel Prize, and as Bruce King observes, for some time afterward he "appeared a bit directionless."[1] Suddenly people who had never cared about his work before were besieging him with requests. There were other distractions as well: a sexual harassment charge in 1994, the death of his mother, Alix Walcott, in 1992 and of his close friend Joseph Brodsky in 1996. And there had been the planning and building of the house in St. Lucia, and the disruption, however welcome, of moving into it.

The restlessness and weariness of these years can be sensed in *The Bounty.* Though winning the Nobel Prize is a lovely problem to have, it seems to have given Walcott an oppressive sense of closure. In his sixtieth year, he had published his most expansive, ambitious poem; then, with his mother's death, no parent stood between him and the end. The Nobel, great honor though it was, also marked an ending of sorts, a magnificent tombstone acknowledging the crowning work of a career. After *Omeros* and the Nobel Prize, what remained for him to do?[2] Haunted by the death of his mother and his friend and by the poet's own advancing age, *The Bounty* is his most melancholy book. As John Thieme puts it, "Death . . . casts a longer shadow over this volume than any of Walcott's collections since his very earliest work."[3] After reading from the poems in advance of publication, at The Poetry Center of the 92nd Street YMHA in New York on November 18, 1996, Walcott "told a friend that he could feel death coming off the page."[4] Bruce King and William Logan[5] both find a resemblance to *Midsummer,* another book that belongs to a period of rapid change and uncertainty in Walcott's circumstances. Like *Midsummer,* the book offers a long sequence of untitled poems, roughly twenty to thirty lines long, in elastic pentameter to hexameter lines, with sudden globe-crossing leaps from one setting to another. Despite Walcott's return to St. Lucia, he still had his teaching in Boston and an even busier travel schedule after the Nobel created an international demand for his appearances. But one need not read the poems through biographical context to sense the restless, unsettled tone of voice.

The Bounty begins with an elegy in seven sections for Alix Walcott. One may guess that it was painful to write, and some of it is painful to read, in that Walcott's rhetorical habits seem to defend him from its occasion at least as much as they enable him to respond to it. By the time we hear, in line 17, of "the beach road near which my mother lies" (*B,* 17) we have been armed with allusions to Isaiah, Dante, John Clare, the folkloric figure of Tom O'Bedlam, Captain Bligh, and John the Baptist. By the time the speaker addresses "Mamma" in line 2 of the fourth section, he has already addressed "Mad Tom" and asked forgiveness of John Clare. The reading of the famous mutiny as an allegory in which "the God-captain is cast adrift / by a mutinous Christian" (*B,* 9) parallels one of Alix's "earliest lessons, how the Christ-Son / questions the Father, to settle on another island, haunted by Him" (*B,* 10). It sounds a little too much like the exegesis of some Dennis Plunkett who has gone in for theology. There are lingering echoes of *Omeros* in the use of irregularly rhymed tercets and the metaphor of ants to suggest the heroic but anonymous labors of the Caribbean people ("I am moved like you, mad Tom, by a line of ants; / I behold their industry and they are giants" [*B,* 4]).

The sixth and seventh sections, in their unflinching contemplation of mortality, are the core of the poem. Section six presents the beauty of the St. Lucian landscape as simultaneously a self-renewing field of energies and a *memento mori.* "The mango trees serenely rust when they are in flower" (*B,* 13), it begins: they rust and flower at once, in imperturbable serenity. Other trees drop their blossoms: the cedar's "bell-flowers fall, the pomme-arac purples its floor." As the day ends, "the firefly keeps striking matches," each flash burning out in its turn. Just as nature's energies prodigally spend and renew themselves, so nightfall brings stirrings of human energy: "Buckets clatter under pipes, villages begin at corners." Nonetheless, "The earth smells of what's done," as "day dies and its mourners / begin, the first wreath of gnats," and the scene reminds the poet that "this was when we sat down // on bright verandahs watching the hills die." The death of the hills was cyclical, renewed each evening, but not the death of the woman who made up part of the "we" who watched. The dead are no longer watchers of nature's deaths and renewals, but gathered up into nature itself,

> part of earth's vegetal fury; their veins grow
>
> with the wild mammy-apple, the open-handed breadfruit,
> their heart in the open pomegranate, in the sliced avocado;
> ground-doves pick from their palms; ants carry the freight
>
> of their sweetness, their absence in all that we eat,
> their savour that sweetens all of our multiple juices,
> their faith that we break and chew in a wedge of cassava,
>
> and here at first is the astonishment: that earth rejoices
> in the middle of our agony, earth that will have her
> for good: wind shines white stones and the shallows' voices.
>
> (*B*, 13–14)

These lines have a curiously mixed affect, both affirmative and terrifying. The dead enter nature and generously offer their bounty, as it were, to the living: the breadfruit is "open-handed," the pomegranate "open" to reveal "their heart." At the same time, the sense of human identity dissolved in "vegetal fury," the dead belonging to the earth "for good," denies any conventional Christian idea of an individual afterlife, and the evocative depiction of physical decay and transformation is unsettling: to eat the breadfruit, pomegranate, or cassava is also to eat the dead, in a sort of metaphorical cannibalism. It is a sort of reverse Kélé, in which the ancestors feed the living. It inverts the lament of Wallace Stevens's speaker in "Madame La Fleurie," whose "grief is that his mother should feed on him, himself and what he saw."[6] If the poem were to end here, it would lack the elegy's traditional turn toward consolation.

As usual in Walcott, however, the poem includes conflicting impulses. In the fifth section, addressing his mother, the speaker concedes that "there are inexplicable instincts that keep recurring / not from hope or fear only" (*B*, 11), so that even "though we no longer believe in the shining ones" (*B*, 12), and even though he must resign the hope of seeing her again "ever," he "felt something less than final at the edge of [her] grave." His seventh section opens with images of natural renewal after winter in northern climates: "In spring, after the bear's self-burial, the stuttering / crocuses open and choir, glaciers shelve and thaw, / frozen ponds crack into maps, green lances spring // from the melting fields" (*B*, 15). Such imagery has been associated with the idea of resurrection in many an elegy before Walcott's. But in his native island, and hers, "there is one season, our viridian Eden / is that of the primal garden that engendered decay." Moreover, his mother, in dying, "took time with her," leaving "no climate, no calendar except for this bountiful day." The temporal narrative, suggested by the turning seasons, of death followed by resurrection, gives way to Walcott's familiar Edenic myth of an eternal present that will be "bountiful" to those who are receptive to its gifts. From this attitude toward the world springs his "business and duty," the vocation that is, he says to his departed mother, "the lesson you taught your sons" (*B*, 16):

> to write of the light's bounty on familiar things
> that stand on the verge of translating themselves into news:
>
> The crab, the frigate that floats on cruciform wings,
> and that nailed and thorn-riddled tree that opens its pews
> to the blackbird that hasn't forgotten her because it sings.
>
> (*B*, 16)

In the closing lines, Christian motifs return to the poem, emphasizing the crucifixion as a bond of suffering but also a support and haven: the "nailed and thorn-riddled tree" on which Christ died becomes the tree that shelters the blackbird. If the pronoun "her" implicitly refers to Alix Walcott, then Walcott implicitly projects himself into the bird, and rests on the faith evoked by the "nailed and thorn-riddled tree" (*B*, 16).

The Bounty has two unequal parts: the fourteen-page title poem, and a sixty-page untitled sequence. Thieme finds that the book is still "worrying away at possible parallels between Caribbean and Greek cultures," ultimately emphasizing "the Odyssean traveller" as the only still relevant mythical figure, whether Greek or Yoruba,[7] but although the Greco-Caribbean analogy still appears from time to time, most notably in the final poem evoking Oedipus at Colonus, Walcott's handling of it has become more casual, less obsessed with confirming or denying its validity. It has taken a more modest place, as a familiar *topos* available for use, not requiring a Plunkett-like commitment to its historical truth. Nor does he continue to imagine the Aegean as an authorizing precedent for Caribbean aspirations. The archipelagoes are equals, for "In maps the Caribbean dreams / of the Aegean, and the Aegean of reversible seas" (*B*, 62).

The sequence opens with the words "I cannot remember the name of that seacoast city," as if Walcott's Adamic namer were lamenting his declining powers. This poem establishes a valedictory tone sustained through much of what follows. The city (or was it just a "town"?) was only a brief stopping place in the poet's wanderings through the European Elsewhere, preserved in the "good watercolour" he managed to do there, whose "stroke and tint have eluded time" (*B*, 19).[8] Despite the permanence of the painting, "it estranges," as the poet thinks back on "so many deaths" of those he has loved. The seaside city in Europe recalls "the seaside city of graves" at Vigie in St. Lucia, the cemetery in which Alix Walcott lies buried. Even painting and poetry are losing their power to console, as "the only art left is the preparation of grace," in anticipation of one's own death. The poem ends with the poet's "own epitaph, 'Here lies / D. W. This place is good to die in.' It really was." The switch from present to past tense sounds posthumous, as if Walcott had indeed verified the statement by dying in that town, far from his beloved St. Lucia. Or is "this place" St. Lucia after all, from which the poem speaks, rather than the place it so imperfectly remembers? Or even earth itself, all of whose creatures die eventually?

There is a similar deathbed tone in Walcott's prediction, "I foresee myself as blessedly invisible," followed by the recognition that

> All of this will soon
> be true, but without sorrow, the way stones allow
> everything to happen, the way the sea shines in the sun,
> silver and bountiful in the slow afternoon.

As elsewhere in the sequence, Walcott lifts the "sorrow" from mortality by envisioning it as part of natural processes that are unfailingly "bountiful" in their sheer abundance of being.

In "Where I Live," written for the January 1997 Caribbean Perspective issue of *Architectural Digest*, Walcott remarked that since his move to the dry uplands of Cap Estates, his "palette has altered from viridian green, scarlet, and cobalt to the ochers, siennas, and umbers of a Braque reproduction, the hues of a semidesert, the greens those of spiky agave and heraldic cactus."[9] The landscape vocabulary of *The Bounty* has changed as well, so that the Caribbean scenes are less lush than formerly, replete with thorns, earth brown colors, and dry hills.

Much of the imagery, despite the altered landscape, comes from a stock quite familiar to a reader of Walcott's other poetry. An uncharitable judge might conclude that the poems, lacking inspiration, simply recycle effects that have worked before. But on closer acquaintance, one finds that familiar images often take on different emphases in this elegiac book, so preoccupied with preparing for the end. Consider, for instance, the ending of the second section of "Parang":

> the running stream's bliss
> contradicts the self-importance of despair,
> by these glittering simplicities, water, leaves, and air,
> that elate dissolution which goes beyond happiness.
>
> (*B*, 27)

The appeal to the elements as a source of stability amid human turmoil is familiar, and especially to water as the solvent of history and rigid boundaries of identity. But "dissolution," in this context, carries intimations of mortality: this is not the "elate dissolution" of Adamic erasure of history, but something closer to a mystical acceptance of one's own dissolution, through which one is returned to nature, as Alix Walcott was in the sixth section of the title poem. Or, to cite another example, there is the interplay between the end of "Six Fictions," ii, in which the speaker declares "I myself am a fiction" (*B*, 50), and the end of poem 35:

> and in Vieuxfort continuous whitecaps
> that are not fiction, as the Atlantic is not, but nothing
> is as fresh as the salt wind that comes off its lines.
>
> (*B*, 76)

The elemental force of the Atlantic is a sign that the world will go on after the "fiction" of the self has dissolved. Walcott's familiar wordplay on "nothing," through which it becomes suffused with latent creative energies, retains its ironically positive undertones, but also becomes in context a reminder of the extinction of consciousness at death, which in turn points to the difference between the ocean's "lines" and those a mortal, conscious poet writes.

In "Parang," i, Walcott returns to the old question of his relationship to the people and places of the island to which he has at last returned: "Can you genuinely claim these, and do they reclaim you / from your possible margin of disdain, of occasional escape[?]" (*B,* 26). He concludes that they do indeed "reclaim you in a way you need not understand," and that does not necessarily involve their personal solicitude for him. In questioning his own side of the exchange, he asks: "the deprived but resigned ones / whom you have exalted: are they utterly your own / as surely as your shadow is a thing of the sun's?" The simile cuts two ways. It may imply a monstrous arrogance: as the poet's shadow is "a thing of the sun's," so they would be things of his, shadows cast by the light of his poetry. Or are they the sun casting the poet's shadow, so that they can be utterly his only if he becomes a thing of theirs?[10] The ambiguity seems appropriate in dramatizing Walcott's lifelong fear that his art, even in its homage to the Caribbean, may exploit or betray the very culture that sustains it.

The impulse to claim and be reclaimed continues through poem 6, where Walcott remembers a section of "the old town," no longer extant, where poor fishermen lived, and declares that "from its shacks and their fishnets these lines are made" (*B,* 30), only to be questioned by the very trees of St. Lucia themselves, who reject his claim that he has "tried to serve both" (*B,* 32) St. Lucian vernacular and English. "And there's your betrayal," they reply. They will have none of his universalist certainty "that all the trees of the world shared a common elation / of tongues, gommier with linden, *bois-campêche* with the elm." Twisting a biblical phrase, they insist that his "right hand forgot its origin . . . / but kept its profitable cunning," and that despite his poetry, they "remain unuttered." But the poet has the last word in the quarrel in the section following, where

> the sun and the rain contend for the same place
> like the two languages I know—one so rich
> in its imperial intimacies, its echo of privilege,
> the other like the orange words of a hillside in drought—
> but my love of both wide as the Atlantic is large.
>
> (*B,* 33)

The choice of the Atlantic as the measure of love's width is not arbitrary, for it is the transatlantic peopling of the island that created the language conflict; a love that would reconcile it must be wide enough to connect the sundered shores.

Although *The Bounty,* like any mature book of Walcott's, contains much beautiful writing, it seems, like *Midsummer,* a transitional, unsettled collection. But whereas the earlier volume's central metaphor evokes a willing surrender to the furnace-like energies of the season, which promise a transformative fusion of the self with some larger power, in *The Bounty* natural process hastens toward dissolution and death. Its elegiac and drifting mode hardly points to the return to narrative in *Tiepolo's Hound,* which comes as a bracing change of direction. And yet *Tiepolo's Hound* began as a project undertaken as Walcott was finishing *The Bounty.* In June 1996, when he turned the *Bounty* manuscript over to Farrar, Straus and Giroux, he and Sigrid "also signed a contract . . . for a book of about a hundred Walcott paintings and drawings which Walcott said he would introduce with a ten-page essay."[11] By November 1997, the essay had become a poem in progress,[12] and what finally emerged was a novella-length poem, accompanied by reproductions of twenty-six Walcott paintings.

One might instead call it "Tiepolo's Decoy," for although Walcott's obsession with a depiction of a hound in a feast scene by Tiepolo (or was it Veronese?) sets the poem in motion, the painter most on his mind is Camille Pissarro, whose "inexact and blurred biography" (*TH,* 101) dominates its pages. And yet the curious displacement of the title reveals the poem's concern with the elusive: the vanishing flash of inspiration that haunts poets and painters; the uncertain location of "home"; the disparity between a life's meaning and its narrative form; the deceptions of memory. During an early visit to the Metropolitan Museum of Art in New York, he

> caught a slash of pink on the inner thigh
> of a white hound entering the cave of a table,
>
> so exact in its lucency at *The Feast of Levi,*
> I felt my heart halt.
>
> (*TH,* 7)

Haunted by that moment, he never succeeds in finding the painting again, uncertain whether it is by Tiepolo or Veronese. So confident was the painter's technique that "one stroke caught / the bright vermilion of the white hound's thigh" (*TH,* 115). Such unerring grace recalls the exuberance of Gregorias in *Another Life,* whose painting expressed "one muscle in one thought," in contrast to Walcott's own "poor crab" of a hand (*CP,* 201). It establishes a similar contrast between the Renaissance master, whether Veronese or Tiepolo, who caught the hound's thigh in one flick of the wrist, and Pissarro the gifted but insecure Jewish colonial, plagued by self-doubt and struggle for technical mastery. Walcott's Pissarro wonders "[w]ho would want / 300 versions of visions of Pontoise // when Claude would need just one to get it right?" (*TH,* 68). He is prone to moments of lacerating despair, when "all his work revealed itself / as a betrayal," his restlessly developed technique "no more than a Sunday amateur's" (*TH,* 80). The same doubt strikes Walcott himself, struggling with "a canvas whose rudderless sail drifts from its course // to morose resignation" (*TH,* 98).

By the time we reach Book Four, the last section of the poem, Walcott is convinced that his painting is *The Feast at the House of Levi* by Veronese, but when he makes the pilgrimage to Venice and stands before it, the magical brushstroke does not appear. "Research" could clear the matter up, "but I refused. Faith was a closed church" (*TH,* 117). He leaves the matter, like Pissarro's life, "inexact and blurred," preferring "the exact perspective of loss" (*TH,* 8) to the cold light of fact. "Tiepolo's Hound" is finally not the thoroughbred dog in the painting but Walcott and his fellow Caribbean artist Pissarro, each hot on the traces of the European tradition, each, like a "mongrel" uneasily aware of "the doors it could not enter" (*TH,* 27).

Though Walcott never finds his painted hound, actual dogs cross his path, and Pissarro's, throughout the poem. In Walcott's St. Lucia or Pissarro's St. Thomas, "ochre pot hounds forage, not at the Feast // of Levi, but for scraps of garbage. None / has the arched white grace of a whippet / or wolfhound" (*TH,* 37). Although these beasts are less glamorous than those of the Venetian painting, they finally replace the painted dog as the goal of his quest. After his vain quest for the hound in the museum in Venice, he finds "the parody of Tiepolo's hound" in his own island, "requiring no research, / but something still unpainted, on its own ground" (*TH,* 138). This dog, who "shook with local terror," compassionately rescues "a starved pup," and Walcott concludes that

> this was the mongrel's heir, not in a great
> fresco, but bastardy, abandonment, and hope
>
> And love enough perhaps to help it live
> like all its breed, and charity, and care,
>
> we set it down in the village to survive
> like all my ancestry. The hound was here.
>
> (*TH,* 139)

The hound becomes, as it were, a family emblem, standing not, like the purebred dogs of European heraldry, for noble ancestry, but for a heritage of cultural "bastardy" ennobled by "hope // and love."

The quest for Tiepolo's hound is in one sense a quest for admission on equal terms to the European canon of painters and poets. Just as the island pot hounds are seen as inferior to the purebred animals of the painting, Jews or Blacks from the overseas provinces will not find themselves represented, apart from occasional "turbanned Moors at the edge of a feast" (*TH,* 37). Like the young Walcott, who had been "Stunned" as he "studied the exact expanse / of a Renaissance feast" (*TH,* 7), Pissarro in the Louvre studies "tiring colonnades of masterpieces," painfully aware that "None, none are his!" (*TH,* 35). Not only is he a young painter who has yet to prove his mettle, he is an outsider from whom "marbles turn their heads away." And yet, Walcott needs to believe that Pissarro's Caribbean heritage contributed to his European eminence. In an imagined conversation, the shade of Pissarro replies to Walcott's reproach that he "could have been our pioneer" with an affirmation: "'My history veins backwards / to the black soil of my birthplace'" (*TH,* 142). "Surely," Walcott insists, "he recalled how the remorseless March / sun scorched the hills, the consoling verandahs, // the family afternoons on the fretwork porch / in the infinity of Antillean Sundays" (*TH,* 144). Although "France will translate him" (*TH,* 50), some of his Caribbean identity survives the translation.

Like Walcott, Pissarro was a racial outsider: born in 1830 to Sephardic Jews, he grew up in St. Thomas as Jacob Pizarro, but changed the name when he set up as an artist in France. Like Walcott, Protestant in a Catholic island, he was part of a minority even at home. His family had sent him to school in Paris from 1841 to 1847, with a request from his father to the headmaster to discourage the boy's love of drawing. But unbeknownst to Pissarro's parents, the master was himself an enthusiastic amateur artist and encouraged the very thing he had been asked to quash. When school ended, Pissarro chafed at returning to the island to clerk in the family store. In his spare hours, he painted Charlotte Amalie with the encouragement of Fritz Melbye, who had been sent by the Danish government to do botanical sketches of New World species. With Melbye in tow, he bolted to Venezuela in 1852, returning after two years of intense artistic activity. At last, with the reluctant blessing of his parents, he set out for France in 1855 to pursue a career in painting. He would never cross the Atlantic again.

Born a hundred years before Walcott, Pissarro figures in the poem as both an alter ego and a master. What might have happened, Walcott speculates, if Pissarro had stayed in St. Thomas? Would he have given the Caribbean a major nineteenth-century artist, changing the entire cultural history of the region? Or could he have become a major artist only by going to France, nourishing his gift in the company of Monet, Gauguin, Degas, and Cézanne? (And nourishing the gifts of others, too; Cézanne's "dingy palette" acquired "colours / brightened by his tropical tutor's eyes" [*TH*, 56].) "What would have been his future had he stayed?" Walcott asks, but he knows the question is unanswerable. For "He was Art's subject as much as any empire's, // he had no more choice than the ship that steered / with its black chimneys and volcanic fires" (*TH*, 29). Pissarro departs from the island, watched by accusing eyes: "'We know you going. / We is your roots. Without us you weak'" (*TH*, 25). This, the one creole-English passage in the poem, ties Pissarro forever to the place of his origin, which haunts and sustains his career in France. Yet it is hard to imagine Pissarro, without the stimulus of the extraordinary artistic circle he joined in France, becoming as great a painter as he was. He may have had the best of both worlds, for the Old World was for him the New: "He paints in dialect, like an islander, / in a fresh France" (*TH*, 53); even though the Old World "is subtler, varied, with more breeding" (*TH*, 30), Pissarro sees it with Adamic eyes, as "fresh." In his career, we see in practice what Walcott hints at, in *Omeros*, by the phrase "reversible world."

Once arrived, Pissarro falls in with the young painters rejecting the standards of the Salons. His independence, Walcott imagines, owed something to his origins. Pissarro may have thought so too. Joachim Gasquet recalled the painter's claim that "he had the good fortune to be born in the Antilles; there he learned to draw without a teacher." And Pissarro's great-grandson Joachim finds it "remarkable . . . how much of the artist's future visual concerns" could be found in his early sketches of the St. Thomas years. He also notes the juxtaposition of disparate styles and techniques within a single painting; one might add that such an amalgamation, "in an idiosyncratic manner,"[13] of multiple styles is a hallmark of Caribbean aesthetics. In France, Pissarro is almost at home with "the Academy's outcasts, its niggers / from barbarous colonies" (*TH*, 45). For "all the others // in the Salon des Refusés, weren't they also Jews?" (*TH*, 61). At the same time, he never quite loses his awareness of colonial difference. The others "were still citizens, / Frenchmen, for all their mockery of the centre" (*TH*, 46). Later in his life, the Dreyfus affair painfully reminded him both of his Jewishness and of his suspicion that "all his canvases were forgeries" (*TH,* 102). Dreyfus's punishment also reminds him that the region he calls home is a remote netherworld of exile to a Frenchman: "Dreyfus was sentenced to his own paradise— / the Caribbean, off the coast of Cayenne, // on Devil's Island, where, if he dies, he dies / in sea and sunshine, luckier than most men" (*TH,* 105). Despite the admiration and friendship of the great painters of France, this interloper from the island named for the "patron saint" of doubt never feels entirely at home in his adopted country.

Despite the high regard in which the other impressionists held him, Pissarro had to persist in the face of rejection by the Academy and by art buyers and the poverty such rejection brought. Walcott depicts him as triumphing through sheer patience and hard work in the face of adversity. He had to provide for a wife and children but persisted with his art even though it did not earn much money. He lost almost all of the 1,500 paintings he left behind at Louveciennes while abroad in England during the Franco-Prussian War, when invading Prussian troops ransacked the studio. There were personal losses as well: his second daughter Adèle-Emma died three weeks after she was born in 1871, and his first daughter, Jeanne, died at the age of nine in 1874.

What saves Walcott's Pissarro, for all his self-doubt and discouragements, is his faith that "the paint is all that counts, no guilt, no pardon, // but the sense of narrative time / annihilated in the devotion of the acolyte," since "page and canvas know one empire only: light" (*TH,* 58). His art takes him to a place where "There is no history now, only the weather" (*TH,* 71). The sadness of his life if viewed as biographical chronicle cannot darken his art. And the great strength of Walcott's poem, committed to the proposition that "Time is not / narrative" (*TH,* 94) but an unfinishable process of trial and error, is its power to do in words what it admires in painting. Not in the passages that advance narrative or theme—some of which recall analogies more freshly used in other poems—but in extraordinary evocations of seeing, we find its most remarkable moments. In St. Lucia, "lights in the shacks bud orange across the Morne, / and are pillared in the black harbour" (*TH,* 163). In Pontoise, the light falls on "a reaper / [who] flails with a scythe to raise contentious crows, // abandoned aqueducts, tree-hidden stations, / cloud puffs of steam over a toy-sized train" (*TH,* 68). The poem's form, too, serves its evocation of an unfinishable struggle toward mastery. It is written in loose pentameter couplets, rhymed across their boundaries *ab ab,* as if each couplet were half of a quatrain. It is Gray's Elegiac Stanza broken in half, and the breakage matters more than one might expect. The verse movement, its restlessness accentuated by Walcott's frequent enjambment, undermines the orderly look of the couplets on the page. It is an appropriate gait for a poem that knows the old masters, "with arthritic fingers and shovel-wide beards," are "still learning," leaving behind "their disasters" that become "our masterpieces" (*TH,* 94).

Though I am no art critic, it is impossible to resist discussing Walcott's own paintings. Twenty-six of these, handsomely reproduced watercolors and oils, adorn *Tiepolo's Hound,* making it the most strikingly beautiful new book of poems to appear in many years. Walcott the painter is not the peer of Walcott the poet, and certainly not of Pissarro, but the watercolors, especially, give great pleasure: the colors are bold yet harmonious, the brushstrokes deftly evocative. Walcott has been regularly working in oils only since about 1993,[14] and, perhaps for that reason, the oils lack the technical assurance of the watercolors. Some of the watercolors (e.g., "St. Lucian Fisherman") look as if they might have been better as oils—there are large spaces in the background with little variation of color, and these might have gained texture from the thicker brush marks that can be obtained with oils. And a few of the oils (e.g., "Headland in Drought") seem technically similar to the watercolors. But as long as one does not demand that they be on the same level as his poems, or challenge comparison with Pissarro, Veronese, and Tiepolo, the paintings can evoke only pleasure and admiration.

As Paula Burnett remarks, "though they don't illustrate the poem in any direct sense," the paintings "are crucial to its meaning."[15] So, for instance, "Gauguin's Studio" and "Gauguin in Martinique" pay tribute to one of his two youthful heroes, "St. Paul, St. Vincent" (*TH,* 17). He calls Gauguin "our creole painter of *anses, mornes,* and *savannes*" (*TH,* 16). One might see Gauguin's flight from Paris to Tahiti as a "reversible" counterpart of Pissarro's contrary movement from island to metropolis. There is a garden scene in Stratford-on-Avon, in Warwick Walcott's namesake shire, in which a white marble statue, its face blank of features, seems to gaze away to the right, like one of those in the Louvre that avert their eyes from Pissarro. There's one older painting done in Port of Spain ("Savannah, Early Morning," c. 1982), but most are recent and depict St. Lucia: not only long-familiar places such as the sea wall at Choc Bay (featured on the cover of *Collected Poems*) or the Church of St. Joseph the Worker in Gros Îlet, but the dry, upland pastures of Cap (where Walcott's house is), the sea at Becune Point, or the beach at Vieux Fort, on the south end of the island. There are scenes of St. Lucian everyday life, with fishermen, musicians, domino players in a rum shop. There are also portraits: of himself, of Sigrid Nama as "The Chess Player," and of his daughter Anna. This last appears next to lines describing Pissarro's grief for his daughter. But in this book so preoccupied with the image of an elusive hound, the only painting to include one is "St. Malo," the "good watercolour" mentioned in *The Bounty.* A black dog, about knee-high, heels on a short leash, its nose thrust eagerly forward.

EPILOGUE

Toward a Just Evaluation of Walcott

Obviously, I would not have spent eleven years on a book about Derek Walcott if I did not believe, as he might put it, that he had "done something." Equally obviously, Walcott has received many of the highest honors poets can receive, including the Nobel Prize. But time does not always endorse the judgments of contemporaries, as a look at the roster of past Nobel Prize winners in literature will confirm. Moreover, as Paula Burnett has pointed out, "the awarders" of major prizes

> are usually associated with the old centres and institutions of imperial hegemony, not noted for their lively attention to art from the margins; therefore the selection of a winner from outside the circle of power can be read either as a welcome indication of growing enlightenment, in that the honour is going to a hitherto unacknowledged quarter, or as yet another manifestation of neo-colonialism, in that once again the north acts as global arbiter of quality and manipulator of power.[1]

Without presuming to settle the question of Walcott's stature, I shall briefly address the main arguments that have been made for—and against—his eminence, and offer my own assessment.

First of all, some have argued that Walcott's success in

carrying off the prizes of the metropole has been won by a betrayal of the Caribbean common people—a charge, as we have seen, that he has frequently brought against himself. This argument was heard frequently in the Black Power era of the 1970s, so that one finds Paul Breman introducing his Walcott selections for a 1973 anthology of poetry by black authors with the rather sour remark that

> by 1961 (when he received the Guinness award for poetry) he had emerged as a firm favourite of what Walter Lowenfels would call "the white poetry syndicate." Blessed by Robert Graves and generally hailed in much the same patronizing manner as the French used to kill their own literate colonials like Senghor or Césaire, it is hardly surprising that Walcott carried off a succession of coveted prizes and distinguished reviews; it is more of a tribute perhaps that he was a very persistent second in the Dakar Festival of Negro Arts in 1966.[2]

As recently as the mid-1980s, the Trinidadian-born writer Dionne Brand attacked Walcott's politics in a review of *Midsummer,* and as recently as 1994, Susan Gingell, writing about Brand's response, was still doing the obligatory cringe: "what Brand's insider's critique goes on to say makes decidedly uncomfortable reading for a white Canadian middle-class feminist academic like myself, who has read and taught Walcott's poetry with enthusiasm for years."[3] But I think we may safely dismiss such bullying. I hope that my discussion of Walcott in this book suffices to show Brand's assertion that "Walcott's figure in the Caribbean plays to the belief that colonization brought civilization, brought culture" to be crudely reductive, as one might expect from someone who thinks that "poetry is ideology and politics."[4] Poetry certainly manifests an implicit ideology and politics—sometimes insistently and centrally, sometimes only tangentially—but if it were in essence these things, a topical pamphlet or a revolutionary uprising would have a better claim to be "poetry" than, for instance, the Odes of John Keats.

I can share some of Brand's distaste for Walcott's "ideology," especially on matters of gender, and still think of him as a great poet. As Elaine Savory has argued, Walcott's "macho attitudes" limit the valid domain of his art, although "[f]ortunately, given his attitudes to women, Walcott's creative world is a predominantly male one."[5] But in 1993, when I tried to draw out Velma Pollard and Lorna Goodison on the question of sexism in Walcott's writing, they would have none of it. "I think Derek loves women," said Pollard; "We're so damn proud of him," said Goodison, "that you're not going to find anybody to say a word against him."[6]

Other Caribbean critics find a thin line at times between Walcott's embrace of paradox and something that smacks of double standards or double talk. Thus Victor Questel, whose sharply perceptive dissertation I have cited earlier, noted that "For Walcott, the whole 'folk' concept is based on a sentimental notion of some original 'pure' or genuine state from which urban stereophonic man has fallen. Walcott himself attacks the 'pastoralism' implicit in this point of view, particularly when such pastoralism is married to ideas about the 'African presence' in the Caribbean, or Black Power, its political corollary." And yet, "Walcott shares in this pastoralism in so far as he does believe in 'green beginnings,' or the 'primal' or concepts of 'Adamic man.'"[7]

Other skeptics of Walcott have criticized not his ideology but his language, either for its diction or for its form. To the extent that these critiques involve a demand for more use of "nation language," they are closely related to the ideological objections noted above. Less reductive, and less dismissable, is Gerald Guinness's criticism of Walcott's elevated diction and ornate syntax as motivated by an "Anxiety of Elsewhere." He notes that "Walcott often writes strongly and simply," but "at other times turgidly and with a numbing air of pretension." He suggests that

> The metamorphic overdensity, overly "high" diction, and bouts of portentousness in Walcott's poetry have their source in the poet's ambition to beat the writers of the West—particularly the *difficult* writers—at their own game. It's as if Walcott feels that he has to make a special effort to overtake them from his backward starting-point in St. Lucia and that he is unduly conscious of their favored positions at the gate. Disadvantaged by a position at the back, Walcott guns his engine and flashes by on two wheels and in overdrive. Often the spectacle is magnificent, but at times all the spectator becomes conscious of is the squeal of tires and the smell of overheated oil.[8]

While I agree that Walcott sometimes overwrites, I am skeptical of Guiness's ungracious surmise about the motive. Most metropolitan critics have been queasy about high diction for some while now, as is shown by the many British and U.S. reviewers who have objected to the same sort of thing that bothers Guinness. If Walcott is trying to make a statement by using elevated diction, I suspect it is less "I can beat you at your own game" than "I refuse to accept your diminished, timid conception of poetry."

In the United States, critics have objected to Walcott's rhetorical excess as a fault of proportion: the parts overwhelm the whole; heterogeneous materials do not combine to make a unity. In her review of *The Fortunate Traveller,* Helen Vendler found "patois poems" such as "The Spoiler's Return" "unconvincing" and generalized that "A macaronic aesthetic, using two or more languages at once, has never been sustained in poetry at any length." Elsewhere, she noted an "uncertainty in diction" and a lack of "psychic coherence" in the details of descriptive passages. Although each detail "is made carefully to resemble a literal portion of the landscape, taken together they do not resemble a soul in act."[9]

Vendler's proscription of a "macaronic aesthetic" has been ably answered elsewhere, most concisely by Laurence A. Breiner: "Such code-switching, which quite accurately reflects West Indian speech habits, is chronically misunderstood by critics outside the region. Convinced that no one could actually speak like this, they find the texts artificial and 'macaronic' because they do not abide by the decorum that segregates poetry in creole from that written in SE."[10] The argument about "psychic coherence" takes us onto more difficult ground; it raises the question of what we recognize as coherence in poetry. What Vendler means by "psychic coherence" seems, on the simplest level, a sense of unified perspective, such that the landscape can be assembled in an imagined space: in questioning Walcott's comparison of dry boulders to "the calcareous molars of a Cyclops," she asks, "where . . . is the rest of the Cyclops, and why are his discarded molars lying around the landscape?" "A soul in act" presumes a consciousness assimilating outward correlatives to its process of meditation. So when Walcott describes "the maniacal frothing of a cave," she asks, "why should an innocent cave seem to be frothing at the mouth like the proverbial madman (since nothing is subsequently made of the 'maniacal' cave)?"

These are good questions, of a kind I ask too, and they are not so readily answered as her objection to the "macaronic." Although maniacal frothing visually evokes the ocean's surf breaking at the cave mouth, so might other analogies; what motivates this choice? In objecting to an excess and arbitrariness in the relation between image and affect, she has identified a pervasive fault in Walcott's poetry. One might defend the passage she criticizes by saying that the rest of the Cyclops has been dispersed over the millennia, leaving the molars as fossil traces; that the choice of the Cyclops and the sinister frothing cave reveal something frightening or uncanny in this landscape for this speaker, an ex-colonial confronting the haunted origin of Western cultural authority. But she has a point.

Calvin Bedient (also reviewing *The Fortunate Traveller*) voices similar reservations. He finds "something like genius" in "The Schooner *Flight*," when Walcott "sailed, so it seemed, by the last breath of Romantic quest." But by some accelerated recapitulation of literary history, Walcott has mutated from Romantic, bypassing the modern, to the antiheroic "incertitude" of the contemporary, "a rolling stone, not a landscape of a mind."[11] It is striking that, independently of Vendler, he asks landscape to become landscape of a mind (or soul); the demand presumes both a unity of consciousness and the possibility of a seamless joining of mind and world, so that nothing remains heterogeneous, random, or stubbornly contrary. Vernon Shetley, in a similar vein, argues that Walcott is "prone to revel in the excess of language over matter," overwhelming the reader with "an enormous, bountiful profusion," without often supplying "the sense of struggle that seems necessary to authenticate the act of writing in the world of distractions that we all inhabit."[12] For all of these critics, Walcott's opulent surfaces don't cohere.

The most unsparing review Walcott has received comes from William Logan, who like Shetley finds an "easy, careless abundance" in Walcott, but also a literary "vanity" in his style: "he is so busy with seduction he sometimes forgets the poem has somewhere to get to." *Omeros*, he complains, "attempted to shrink the *Iliad* and the *Odyssey* into the tiny sins and squabbles of some Caribbean fishermen and bewildered colonials." In *The Bounty*, "the lines are heavy with habitat, never one image when half a dozen will do." Walcott's "rhetoric is as powerful as a trumpet, but every line has the same emphasis—you scarcely know where the crescendos are, because they're all crescendos." He prefers the "briefer lyrics" to "the rambling sequences or ambitious epics," though he makes a partial exception for *Another Life*.[13] Again, it is a matter of disproportion and disunity: the Homeric characters are too small, the long poems too long, the images too many. Even Logan concedes that Walcott's "verbal gift" is "not matched in his generation by anyone but Robert Lowell." But "what you remember in Walcott is the texture, never the text": the dazzling writing doesn't create "poems memorable as poems."

Why should a Caribbean poet whose entire lifework attests to a sense of multiple origins, identities, languages, and allegiances be expected to produce poetry that subordinates all its profusion to unity? This conception of poetic form might be seen as Romantic (the organic ideal of Coleridge) or modernist (Yeats's aspiration to "unity of being"). As I have argued in discussing "The Schooner *Flight*," there is a strand of Shelleyan romanticism in Walcott (as Shetley also maintains), and he has always acknowledged the influence of Yeats along with other high modernists such as Joyce, Pound, and Eliot. But between the Romantics and the modernists came the Victorians, and after modernism comes the "postmodernism" we are still groping to define. What is strange, wonderfully inclusive, and maddeningly contradictory in Walcott is that all four period styles are alive simultaneously in his work. And such transhistorical simultaneity accords well with the intuitions of Edouard Glissant and Wilson Harris that Caribbean history, having occurred as a series of sudden reversals, disruptions, and abandoned schemes of development, requires a nonlinear narrative. If that is true of political and cultural history, why shouldn't it be true of literary history as well?

Andrew Marr, reviewing *Tiepolo's Hound,* laments that "[a]mong the fading arts is the long narrative poem, the kind of thing the Victorians did so well. . . . In the century just past, readers and poets went more for intensity and compression, private-space poetry. People seemed to lose affection for lengthy, looser-limbed verse that cried to be read aloud." He sees *Omeros* as Walcott's "first rebuke to compression" and *Tiepolo's Hound* as a poem in the same mold.[14] One might argue, then, that Vendler, Bedient, and Shetley are judging Walcott by modernist standards of compression, whereas his work evokes the standards of another age.

Is writing with Victorian amplitude at the dawn of the twenty-first century a flight backward, or is it an instance of postmodernist polystylistics, like the allusions to Palladio in the architecture of Robert Stern, or the quotations of earlier music in Schnittke or Berio? Among those who would place Walcott with the postmodernists are Rei Terada and J. Michael Dash. Dash claims that "Walcott's aesthetic is translational and intertextual rather than essentialist and foundational."[15] In discussing "The Light of the World," I pointed out its lingering religiosity and Platonism, which force the conclusion that Walcott's aesthetic is somehow translational and intertextual yet also to some extent essentialist and foundational. If, as I suggested at the outset, his truest mythical persona is Proteus, then postmodernism is just one of his many shapes.

The critic I find most useful on the vexed question of Walcott's relation to postmodernism is Antonio Benítez-Rojo, whose speculations on Caribbean aesthetics in *The Repeating Island* not only seem apt for Walcott but cut through the sterile debate about whether or not the postcolonial and the postmodern are the same thing. Benítez-Rojo points out that "Caribbean discourse is in many respects prestructuralist and preindustrial," so that we face a difficult conundrum:

> supposing, in short, that we live within the psychology of postmodernity, then what thinking and what canons are we going to follow when we try to conclude some things about any economic or cultural phenomena that appear in the Caribbean, a part of the world that the very philosophies of postmodernism exclude from their field of play, a part of the world that hardly brushes against modernity and whose culture has doggedly held on to such things as blood sacrifice and voodoo, *santeria, pocomania,* and *macumba?*[16]

For Benítez-Rojo, a fertile contradiction between the premodern and postmodern implications of Caribbean experience is the hallmark of the region's cultural style. Certainly, the self-reflexive gestures Terada and Dash find in Walcott are part of his stylistic repertory. But even though Walcott did not grow up among the folk in the Haitian countryside practicing voudoun, he has always seen his art as drawing sustenance from folk culture. And some of his own beliefs—his religious faith, his insistence that poetry at its highest moments attains to the universal and transcendent—are hard to square with the antifoundational skepticism of postmodern thought and aesthetics. One might say that for Walcott, postmodern skepticism itself becomes absorbed in a larger dialectic of faith and doubt. What Benítez-Rojo says of the Caribbean novel is true of Walcott's poetry as well: "[t]he ordinary thing, the almost arithmetical constant in the Caribbean is never a matter of *subtracting,* but always of *adding,* for the Caribbean discourse carries . . . a myth or desire for social, cultural, and psychic integration to compensate for the fragmentation and provisionality of the collective Being."[17] If so, then the Caribbean notion of unity, rather than seeking the purifying exclusions demanded by Vendler or Bedient, seeks wholeness by including everything; it is not surprising that so many Caribbean readers, from José Martí to Walcott himself, have forgiven Walt Whitman his journalistic cheerleading for the Mexican War and admired him as the North American poet of inclusion.

I too find Walcott excessive at times. But, as one of Blake's Proverbs of Hell tells us, the road of excess leads to the palace of wisdom. Walcott's greatest weakness, his tendency to pile metaphor upon metaphor, image upon image, is inseparable from his greatest strength: his curiously fluid, metamorphic handling of figurative language. He is much like Hart Crane in this respect: Crane, like Walcott, wrote many dreadful lines, which no amount of cultural contextualization or theoretical ingenuity can palliate. And yet, it is hard to imagine Crane writing his best poems without having enough courage in his convictions to write his worst. Walcott, of course, has managed to stay alive and productive for much longer than Crane did, so even once we winnow the dross, there is a great deal left. More than this: as I hinted earlier, Walcott's elevated style can be read as a principled, even defiant claim about the poet's role. For postmodernists, that role is deflated. As Benítez-Rojo puts it, "for the poststructuralist critic, looking at the literary task from the postmodern standpoint, the author, far from being a creator of worlds, is a technician or artisan whose job is controlled by a preexisting practice or discourse; he is, simply, a writer."[18] Walcott will not accept this job description. In an essay praising Les Murray's verse as "rooted in its sacredness," he rebukes "this age of muttering soliloquys, of mildly tormented asides," in which "contemporary verse . . . averts its face from awe."[19]

What moves me in Walcott is his refusal of simplifications—and postmodernism as a literary program, it seems to me, is a simplification, in that it proposes a cool ironic comfort with the impossibility of truth or transcendence that too easily becomes the self-congratulation of the undeceived. Walcott includes in his work a longing for unity, authoritative truth, and poetic transcendence, but also a knowledge of all the reasons why those things may turn out to be illusory. In his combat with "history," too, he does not underestimate his antagonist: if Caribbean history is a dragon, he cannot strike at it before showing us its every scale, the beast alive and breathing. If he sometimes waxes sentimental about the folk, or about the redemptive powers of art, or about creole synthesis, a corrosive countervoice will usually speak up before long. I cannot agree with Shetley that there is a "lack of struggle" in his poetry. When he overwrites, he seems to me not glib but desperate, as if he were flinging metaphors at an elusive world that won't be caught in any of them.

What is sometimes caught, and I shall close with this observation, is the interconnectedness of things. As a concise instance, consider once more the statement in *Omeros* that "The wind changed gear like a transport with the throttle / of the racing sea" (*O*, 49). The metaphorical excess at first seems self-canceling (first the wind is figuratively a transport, then the throttle of the figurative transport is the literal sea). In context, however, it pulls together a number of intuitions: that Hector's betrayed love of the sea propels his reckless driving; that he can't really escape the sea even when he tries; that modern artifacts like the transport and other machinery ultimately are integrated into the organic culture of the island. Walcott sees the world as "reversible" and metamorphic, and if sometimes he appears too facile in turning everything into everything else (as I have objected, for instance, to some of the sweeping comparisons between Caribbean and Native American experience in *Omeros*), his fluid metaphors can powerfully evoke what it feels like to believe, amid a skeptical world, in the possibility of transcendence.

NOTES

Introduction

1. Interviewing Walcott for the first time on April 10, 1989, I asked him if he had a favorite among his own poems. "Well," he replied, "when I finished 'The Schooner *Flight*' I thought maybe I had done something."

2. Derek Walcott, *Collected Poems 1948–1984* (New York: Farrar, Straus & Giroux), 346.

3. James Anthony Froude, *The English in the West Indies; or, The Bow of Ulysses* (New York: Charles Scribner's Sons, 1897 [1887]), 347; V. S. Naipaul, *The Mimic Men* (New York: Vintage, 1985 [1967]), 146. Naipaul used the passage from Froude as an epigraph to *The Middle Passage: Impressions of Five Societies—British, French and Dutch—in the West Indies and South America* (New York: Vintage, 1981 [1962]), in which he seconded the verdict: "History is built around achievement and creation; and nothing was created in the West Indies" (29).

4. Edward Hirsch, "An Interview with Derek Walcott," *Contemporary Literature* 20, no. 3 (1979): 281.

5. "What the Twilight Says: An Overture," in *Dream on Monkey Mountain and Other Plays* (New York: Farrar, Straus & Giroux, 1970), 4.

6. Robert Pinsky, "American Poetry and American Life, I: Freneau, Whitman, Williams," in *Poetry and the World* (New York: Ecco, 1988), 111–14.

7. Victor Questel, "Derek Walcott: Contradiction and Resolution; Paradox, Inconsistency, Ambivalence and their Resolution in Derek Walcott's Writings, 1946–1976" (Ph.D. dissertation, University of the West Indies, St. Augustine, 1979), ii, 14.

8. Gordon Rohlehr, "The Problem of the Problem of Form," *Caribbean Quarterly* 31, no. 1 (1985): 31–32.

9. Edward Brathwaite, *The Development of Creole Society in Jamaica 1770–1820* (Oxford: Oxford University Press, 1971), 309.

10. As Laurence Breiner points out, Brathwaite takes the term "Great Tradition" from F. R. Leavis, who was "very influential in the Anglophone Caribbean." *An Introduction to West Indian Poetry* (Cambridge: Cambridge University Press, 1998), 10.

11. Edward Hirsch, "The Art of Poetry XXXVII: Derek Walcott [interview, June 1985]," *Paris Review* 101 (1986); reprinted in Robert D. Hamner, *Critical Perspectives on Derek Walcott* (Boulder, Colo.: Lynn Rienner, 1997), 71.

12. Edouard Glissant, *Caribbean Discourse: Selected Essays* (*Le Discours Antillais* [1981]), trans. J. Michael Dash (Charlottesville: University of Virginia Press, 1989), 61–62.

13. "The Muse of History: An Essay" (1974); reprinted in *What the Twilight Says: Essays* (New York: Farrar, Straus & Giroux, 1998), 39.

14. Walcott, *Collected Poems 1948–1984,* 88.

15. Walcott, "What the Twilight Says: An Overture," in *Dream on Monkey Mountain and Other Plays* (New York: Farrar, Straus & Giroux, 1970), 5.

16. Indeed, some important traits of Walcott's style seem neither modernist nor postmodernist, but Victorian: the unabashed delight in highly rhetorical language, reminiscent of formal oratory; the sense of being "between two worlds" that Matthew Arnold (whom Walcott in the first notebook for *Another Life* calls his favorite Victorian poet) described; or the eagerness to expand in figurative or narrative passages, rather than seeking the compression of the Poundian vortex.

17. Questel, "Derek Walcott: Contradiction and Resolution . . .," 201–2.

18. Walcott, "The Schooner *Flight,*" in *Collected Poems 1948–1984,* 350.

Chapter One

1. Derek Walcott, "A Far Cry From Africa," in *Collected Poems 1948–1984* (New York: Farrar, Straus & Giroux, 1986), 18. *Collected Poems* cited hereafter as *CP.*

2. "Leaving School," *The London Magazine* 5, no. 6 (September 1965): 7.

3. John Robert Lee, interview of July 1989, at Sir Arthur Lewis College, The Morne, St. Lucia.

4. Walcott, "Leaving School," 7.

5. Edward Baugh gives "under 80,000" in his *Derek Walcott: Memory as Vision: Another Life* (Norfolk, U.K.: Longman, 1978), 5. But the St. Lucian priest Rev. C. Jesse notes that "[b]y the end of 1931, the population of St. Lucia was estimated to have attained almost 60,000." *Outlines of St. Lucia's History,* 4th ed. (St. Lucia: Voice Publishing Co., for the St. Lucia Archeological and Historical Society, 1986), 54.

6. Mervyn C. Alleyne, "Language and Society in St. Lucia," *Caribbean Studies* 1, no. 1 (April 1961): 1.

7. Sidney W. Mintz, "From Plantations to Peasantries," in *Caribbean Contours,* ed. Sidney W. Mintz and Sally Price (Baltimore: Johns Hopkins University Press, 1985), 145.

8. Jesse, *Outlines,* 52.

9. Alleyne, "Language and Society," 4.

10. Carl Stone, "A Political Profile of the Caribbean," in *Caribbean Contours,* ed. Mintz and Price, 27.

11. Baugh, *Derek Walcott,* 9.

12. Baugh, *Derek Walcott,* 10.

13. "A Critique of the Art Exhibition of Dunstan St. Omer & Derek Walcott," *Voice of St. Lucia,* 9 September 1950, 2.

14. According to Walcott, Simmons's eccentricity was not Bohemian sloppiness but overfastidiousness: "he dressed like an Englishman in the tropics." Conversation of March 24, 1995.

15. Baugh, *Derek Walcott,* 14.

16. Simmons, "West Indian Artists Need Better Colour Combination," *Voice of St. Lucia,* 18 March 1944, 3.

17. Simmons, "The Need for an Arts and Crafts Society," *Voice of St. Lucia,* 21 April 1945, 3.

18. Simmons, "Arts and Crafts Society Inaugurated," *Voice of St. Lucia,* 27 April 1945, 1.

19. Simmons, "Co-Operation, What It Is? [sic]," *Voice of St. Lucia,* 25 April 1946, 2–3; "The Riddle of Dauphin," *Voice of St. Lucia,* 31 March 1945, 4.

20. *Another Life,* chapter 7, ii; *Collected Poems,* 184–85.

21. *Voice of St. Lucia,* 2 August 1944, 3.

22. Walcott, First notebook, 79, archive at UWI, Mona. (Also quoted in Baugh, *Derek Walcott,* 8.)

23. Rev. C. Jesse, F.M.I, M.B.E., "The Agreed Syllabus," *Voice of St. Lucia,* 2 September 1944, 3.

24. Walcott, "Leaving School," 13.

25. Samuel Omo Asein, "The Growth and Reputation of Derek Walcott as a Playwright" (Doctoral Thesis, University of Ibadan, Nigeria, 1974), 112–13.

26. Asein, "Growth and Reputation," 183–93.

27. Baugh, *Derek Walcott,* 8–9.

28. Edward Hirsch, "An Interview with Derek Walcott," *Contemporary Literature* 20, no. 3 (1979): 288.

29. Baugh, *Derek Walcott,* 8.

30. Quoted in Baugh, *Derek Walcott,* 10.

31. Hill no longer has the scripts.

32. Edward Hirsch, "The Art of Poetry XXXVII: Derek Walcott" [interview, June 1985], *Paris Review* 101 (1986); reprinted in Robert D. Hamner, ed., *Critical Perspectives on Derek Walcott* (Boulder, Colo.: Lynne Rienner, 1997), 71.

33. Irma Goldstraw, *Derek Walcott: An Annotated Bibliography of His Works* (New York: Garland, 1984), 5, 43.

34. Gregor Williams, "The St. Lucian World of Derek Walcott," *The Crusader* [Castries] 29, no. 42 (17 October 1992): 25.

35. Rev. C. Jesse, F.M.I, M.B.E., *Outlines of St. Lucia's History,* 4th ed. (St. Lucia: Voice Publishing Co., for the St. Lucia Archeological and Historical Society, 1986), 58–59.

36. Gregor Williams, "St. Lucian World of Walcott," 25.

37. Jesse, *Outlines,* 59.

38. Walcott, First notebook for *Another Life,* Archive at UWI, Mona, 73.

39. Earl Gooding, *The West Indies at the Crossroads* (Cambridge, Mass.: Schenckman, 1981), 3–31.

40. J. H. Parry and P. M. Sherlock, *A Short History of the West Indies,* 3d ed. (London: Macmillan, 1971), 295.

41. Peter Alter, *Nationalism,* trans. Stuart McKinnon-Evans (London: Edward Arnold, 1989), 28–34, 55–91.

42. Norman Manley, "West Indian Federation: A Cause Vital to Our Progress," in *Manley and the New Jamaica: Selected Speeches and Writings 1938–1968,* ed. Rex Nettleford (Trinidad and Jamaica: Longman Caribbean, 1971), 166.

43. Jesse, *Outlines,* 63.

44. Walcott, *25 Poems* (Port of Spain: Guardian Commercial Printery, 1948), 23; reprinted in *Collected Poems,* 6.

45. Walcott, *Another Life,* chap. 13, ii; *Collected Poems,* 226.

46. Walcott, "Leaving School," 9, 13–14.

47. S. O. Asein, "Walcott's Jamaica Years," *The Literary Half-Yearly* [Mysore, India] 21, no. 2 (July 1980): 24.

48. Mc[Donald] Dixon, "The St. Lucia Arts Guild," in the program for the Guild's "Statehood Production" of *The Sea at Dauphin* and Roderick Walcott's *A Flight of Sparrows* (St. Lucia: Litho Press, 1968), no page numbers. From the archive of the St. Lucia National Trust.

49. Quoted in Philip Sherlock and Rex Nettleford, *The University of the West Indies: A Caribbean Response to the Challenge of Change* (London: Macmillan Caribbean, 1990), 21.

50. Eric Williams, "W. I. University Must Provide Solution to W. I. Problems," *Voice of St. Lucia,* 19 April 1944, 2.

51. Before the federation of the English-speaking Caribbean, there had been a similar nationalist movement among the Spanish territories, late in the nineteenth century, the most famous proponent of which was José Martí. See J. Michael Dash, *The Other America: Caribbean Literature in a New World Context* (Charlottesville: University of Virginia Press, 1999), 10; and Silvio Torres-Saillant, *Caribbean Poetics: Toward an Aesthetic of West Indian Literature* (Cambridge: Cambridge University Press, 1997), 48–49. Anticipations of an interracial, pan-Caribbean unity can be traced back at least as far as the early eighteenth-century statement by the French visitor Père Jean-Baptiste Labat that "you are all together, in the same boat, sailing on the same uncertain sea . . . citizenship and race unimportant, feeble little labels compared to the message that my spirit brings to me: that of the position and predicament which History has imposed upon you. " Quoted in Antonio Benítez-Rojo, *The Repeating Island: The Caribbean and the Postmodern Perspective,* 2d ed. (Durham, N.C.: Duke University Press, 1996), 35.

52. Asein, "Walcott's Jamaica Years," 28.

53. Asein, "Walcott's Jamaica Years," 28.

54. Asein, "Walcott's Jamaica Years," 30.

55. Conversation with the author, July 16, 1993, Kingston, Jamaica.

56. Interview of July 16, 1993, Kingston, Jamaica.

57. The Federal Theatre Company gave the first performances of *Ione* at the Ward in 1957. According to Irma Goldstraw, Ronald Llanos rather than Errol Hill directed the production (*Annotated Bibliography,* 60), but Hill presumably directed some of the rehearsals. The published script of *Ione* contains an acknowledgment thanking "Errol Hill once more for his technical advice with the script"—and dedicating the play to Archie Hudson-Philips, Leith Thompson, and Harold Simmons.

58. Bruce King, *Derek Walcott and West Indian Drama* (New York: Oxford University Press, 1995), 12.

59. Asein, "Growth and Reputation," 114–15.

60. Walcott, "Letter from the Editor," *The Pelican,* 11 February 1951, 2.

61. Eric Williams, "Historical Background of Race Relations in the Caribbean," lecture delivered in Woodford Square, Port of Spain, August 16, 1955, in *Forged from the Love of Liberty: Selected Speeches of Dr Eric Williams,* ed. Dr Paul K. Sutton (Trinidad: Longman Caribbean, 1981), 210.

62. Walcott, "Letter from the Editor," *The Pelican,* 11 February 1951, 2.

63. Walcott, *The Pelican,* 25 February 1951, 2.

64. Walcott may be alluding here to the motto of UWI: *Oriens ex Occidente Lux.*

65. Walcott, "The Land of Look Behind," *Money Index,* 27 April 1993, D [pagination by letters rather than numbers].

66. Walcott, "The Land of Look Behind," E.

67. Walcott, "The Land of Look Behind," F.

68. Anderson, *Imagined Communities,* 19; Eric Hobsbawm, "Introduction: Inventing Traditions," in *The Invention of Tradition,* ed. Eric Hobsbawm and Terence Ranger (Cambridge: Cambridge University Press, 1983), 13.

69. Mervyn C. Alleyne, "A Linguistic Perspective on the Caribbean," in *Caribbean Contours,* ed. Sidney W. Mintz and Sally Price (Baltimore: Johns Hopkins University Press, 1985), 157–58. Alleyne is speaking of the Caribbean's linguistic diversity, but much else in Caribbean culture might also be called the "result" of the same causes.

70. Edward Kamau Brathwaite, "Caribbean Man in Space and Time," *Savacou* 11/12 (September 1975): 1: "The unity is submarine / breathing air, our problem is how to study the fragments/whole."

71. Robert Hamner, "Conversation with Derek Walcott," *World Literature Written in English* 16, no. 2 (November 1977): 416.

72. Sherlock and Nettleford, *University of the West Indies,* 1. It should be noted that this history, published in 1990, like Brathwaite's essay from 1975, invokes the authority of the past more than most federalist writing of the 1940s and 1950s did.

73. E. J. Hobsbawm, *Nations and Nationalism since 1780: Programme, Myth, Reality* (Cambridge: Cambridge University Press, 1990), 104.

74. Walcott, "Federal Art Exhibition," *Public Opinion,* 23 March 1957, 7.

75. Walcott, "The Institute of Jamaica," *Public Opinion,* 11 May 1957, 6.

76. Walcott, "Emerging Young Painters," *Public Opinion,* 16 February 1957, 7.

77. Walcott, "Artist of the Week," *Public Opinion,* 2 March 1957, 6.

78. Walcott, "Some Jamaican Poets 2," *Public Opinion,* 10 August 1957, 7.

79. Walcott, "Some Jamaican Poets 2," 7.

80. For a concise, informative account of Trinidadian writing in the 1930s, see Reinhard W. Sander, *The Trinidad Awakening: West Indian Literature of the Nineteen-Thirties* (New York: Greenwood Press, 1988).

81. Walcott, "West Indian Writing," *Public Opinion,* 26 January 1957, 7.

82. Walcott, "West Indian Writing," 7.

83. Goldstraw, *Annotated Bibliography,* 8.

84. Goldstraw, *Annotated Bibliography,* 58–63.

85. Asein, "Walcott's Jamaica Years," 37. I have reluctantly corrected the inspired but distracting typo, "Old Vice Theatre."

86. Goldstraw, *Annotated Bibliography,* xv; Walcott, "Meanings," *Savacou* 2 (September 1970): 45.

87. Walcott, "Derek's Most West Indian Play," *Sunday Guardian Magazine* [Trinidad], 21 June 1970, 7.

88. Walcott, "Leaving School," 45–46.

89. *Voice of St. Lucia,* April 1958; quoted in Asein, "Growth and Reputation," 152–53; Asein gives no more precise date. Derek had reviewed Roderick with similar cool objectivity. He found that *The Harrowing of Benjy,* Roderick's first play, "suffers somewhat from his affection for the leading character, so that it stays in one place, and hits one note. . . . The dialogue is pithy but could do with paring." *Public Opinion,* 22 June 1957, 6.

90. Walcott, "On Choosing Port of Spain," in *David Frost Introduces Trinidad and Tobago,* ed. Michael Anthony and Andrew Carr (London: André Deutsch, 1975), 14, 15, 20.

91. King, *Walcott and West Indian Drama,* 15.

92. Walcott, "Meanings," 46.

93. Victor Questel, "History of the Trinidad Theatre Workshop," unpublished typescript, 1981 [?], in Box 10, Walcott archive, West Indiana Collection, UWI, St. Augustine, 8.

94. Walcott, "Meanings," 46.

95. Questel, "History," 8.

96. Quoted in Questel, "History," 8.

97. Questel, "History," 8.

98. Questel, "History," 28–34. Ulric Mentus, "The Little Workshop's Mammoth Task of 5 Plays a Year. From the Basement to the Summit in Drama," *Sunday Mirror,* 8 May 1966, quoted in Questel, "History," 33.

99. Goldstraw, *Annotated Bibliography,* 95–173.

100. Questel, "History," 6.

101. Questel, "History," 6.

102. Box 1, Walcott Archive, West Indiana Collection, UWI, St. Augustine, Trinidad.

103. Box 1, Walcott Archive, West Indiana Collection, UWI, St. Augustine, Trinidad.

104. Walcott, "*Seven Year Itch* Not Up to Scratch," *Trinidad Guardian,* 14 November 1959, 5; "*Our Town* Beyond the Players," *Sunday Guardian,* 6 December 1959, 7.

105. Walcott, "Spiritual Purpose Lacking: Derek Walcott Appraises the Arts," *Sunday Guardian,* 5 January 1964, 3.

106. Walcott, "Encouraging Turn," *Trinidad Guardian,* 29 December 1965, 6; "Writer's Cramp on a Stage," *Trinidad Guardian,* 8 June 1966, 5.

107. Walcott, "Here They Come, Ready or Not," *Trinidad Guardian,* 26 May 1965, 5.

108. Frantz Fanon, *Toward the African Revolution (Political Essays),* trans. Haakon Chevalier (New York: Grove Press, 1967), 24, 17, 27.

109. Walcott, "Playing the Old Race Game," *Sunday Guardian,* 29 November 1964, 21.

110. Walcott, "Time to Separate Politics from Good Verse," *Trinidad Guardian,* 17 March 1966, 5. P. M. Sherlock is Philip M. Sherlock, better known as a historian than as a poet.

111. Walcott, "The Theatre of Abuse," *Sunday Guardian,* 3 January 1965, 4. Walcott remarks, in characteristically universalist fashion, that Jones, "unlike Burroughs or Joyce or Genet[,] is not a great hater. Great haters like Pope, Swift, Voltaire, Baudelaire, spit on the whole concept of mankind. It is the entire race that[,] at moments, moves them to such a cold, articulate contempt, and not a single section of it."

112. Walcott, "His Is the Pivotal One about Race," *Sunday Guardian,* 1 December 1963, 23.

113. Walcott, conversation with the author, April 10, 1989.

114. *The Crusader,* 28 August 1993, 1.

115. Breiner, "Walcott's Early Drama," in *The Art of Derek Walcott,* ed. Stewart Brown (Mid Glamorgan, Wales: Seren Books, 1991), 71.

116. Questel, *History of the Trinidad Theatre Workshop Part III: Questel Interviews Key Members of the Trinidad Theatre Workshop* [24 August, 1980] (Ph.D. dissertation, University of the West Indies, Box 10, Walcott Archive, UWI St. Augustine, Trinidad), 3–4.

117. Box 5, Walcott Archive, West Indiana Collection, UWI, St. Augustine, Trinidad.

118. Conversation with the author, October 30, 1994, at Arena Stage, Washington, D. C.

119. See King, *Walcott and West Indian Drama,* 128–37.

120. Box 2, Walcott Archive, West Indiana Collection, UWI, St. Augustine, Trinidad.

121. Bruce King, e-mail message, February 7, 1999.

122. My account of Walcott's activities in this period is drawn from Bruce King, *Derek Walcott: A Caribbean Life* (Oxford: Oxford University Press, 2000), chap. 22.

123. King, *Derek Walcott,* 401.

124. The 1975 visit is described in King's *Derek Walcott: A Caribbean Life,* 327. In addition, King says that Richard Montgomery recalls seeing Walcott at a play in London in 1968 or 1969, and he says that Walcott stopped in England while returning from the 1964 Berlin festival (e-mail, August 28, 2000).

125. King, *Derek Walcott,* 396.

126. Asked about "Steel," he said, "That one still needs a lot of work" (conversation with the author, March 26, 1995).

127. Conversation with the author, July 1993.

Chapter Two

1. The version published in *Dream on Monkey Mountain and Other Plays* (New York: Farrar, Straus & Giroux, 1970) tones down the St. Lucian creole of the earlier version published in *Tamarack Review* 14 (1960), and Archie Hudson-Phillips told me that Jamaican audiences had trouble understanding early productions of this play (interview, Kingston, Jamaica, July 16, 1993).

2. Walcott, "Meanings," *Savacou* 2 (September 1970): 51.

3. Walcott, "What the Twilight Says: An Overture," in *Dream on Monkey Mountain,* 11.

4. Hirsch, "The Art of Poetry XXXVII: Derek Walcott" [interview, June 1985], *Paris Review* 101 (1986); reprinted in Robert D. Hamner, ed., *Critical Perspectives on Derek Walcott* (Boulder, Colo.: Lynne Rienner, 1997), 73.

5. Walcott, "Meanings," 51.

6. Hirsch, "The Art of Poetry XXXVII," 73.

7. "What the Twilight Says," 4.

8. W. J. Bate, *The Burden of the Past and the English Poet* (New York: Norton, 1970), 4.

9. Walcott, "What the Twilight Says" 31.

10. Harold Bloom, *The Anxiety of Influence: A Theory of Poetry* (New York: Oxford University Press, 1973), 152.

11. Homi Bhabha, *The Location of Culture* (London: Routledge, 1994), 86.

12. In *Dream on Monkey Mountai,* 4.

13. "The Caribbean: Culture or Mimicry?" *Journal of Interamerican Studies and World Affairs* 16, no. 1 (February 1974): 9, 12.

14. Hirsch, "An Interview with Derek Walcott," *Contemporary Literature* 20, no. 3 (1979): 282.

15. Hirsch, "The Art of Poetry XXXVII," 81.

16. 6. David Montenegro, *Points of Departure: International Writers on Writing and Politics* (Ann Arbor: University of Michigan Press, 1991), 96, 95.

17. Walcott, conversation with the author, April 10, 1989, Milwaukee, Wisconsin.

18. Laurence Breiner, "Tradition, Society, the Figure of the Poet (North American Theory of Influence and the Situation of West Indian Poetry)," *Caribbean Quarterly* 26, nos.1 and 2 (March-June 1980): 5.

19. Breiner, "Tradition," 9, 11.

20. Helen Vendler, "Poet of Two Worlds" [review of *The Fortunate Traveller*], *New York Review of Books,* 4 March 1982, 23.

21. Montenegro, *Points of Departure,* 96.

22. "Discourse in the Novel," in *The Dialogic Imagination: Four Essays by M. M. Bakhtin,* ed. Michael Holquist, trans. Caryl Emerson and Michael Holquist (Austin: University of Texas Press, 1981), 276.

23. Bakhtin, "Discourse in the Novel," 347.

24. Bakhtin, "Discourse in the Novel," 277.

25. Robert Pinsky, "American Poetry and American Life, I: Freneau, Whitman, Williams," in *Poetry and the World* (New York: Ecco Press, 1988), 113–114.

26. Walcott, "What the Twilight Says," 11.

27. 7. Renato Poggioli, *The Theory of the Avant-Garde,* trans. Gerald Fitzgerald (New York: Harper & Row, 1971), 31.

28. Aimé Césaire, *The Collected Poetry,* trans. Clayton Eshleman and Annette Smith (Berkeley: University of California Press, 1983), 34, 62; translated as: "sprawled-flat" and "Lying down like this town in its refuse and mud" (35, 63).

29. Conversation with the author, November 1989, Oneonta, New York.

30. Carl G. Rosberg Jr. and John Nottingham, *The Myth of 'Mau Mau': Nationalism in Kenya* (New York: Praegar/Hoover Institution, 1966), 283–84.

31. Walcott appears to have taken a phrase from the last line of Crane's "Black Tambourine," which describes the American black man as torn between his present situation "[a]nd, in Africa, a carcass quick with flies."

32. Walcott, *Collected Poems 1948–1984,* 17.

33. "The Muse of History: An Essay" [1974], reprinted in *What the Twilight Says: Essays* (New York: Farrar, Straus & Giroux, 1998), 63.

34. Robert Hamner, "Conversation with Derek Walcott," *World Literature Written in English* 16, no. 2 (1977): 411.

35. Conversation with the author, April 10, 1989, Milwaukee, Wisconsin.

36. "The first food offered at death rituals, which are conducted under the loa Ghede, is for Legba, guardian of the cross-roads [hence *carrefour*], and for the Marassa [the Divine Twins]"; Damballa, the serpent-god adapted from Dahomean worship, is "the ancient, the venerable father," the "lofty evidence of a just and eternal good." Maya Deren, *Divine Horsemen: The Living Gods of Haiti* (Kingston, N.Y.: McPherson & Co./ Documentext, 1970), 39, 115–16. One of the Petro divini-

ties has the name "Carrefour" and is associated, as the name suggests, with the crossroads, as the counterpart to Legba among the Rada *loa* (62–63).

37. "The Muse of History," 43, 47.

38. St. Lucia has its own "lady on the promontory," the statue of the Virgin in front of the Convent School, Vigie.

39. Benedict Anderson remarks that "all communities larger than primordial villages of face-to-face contact (*and perhaps even these*) are imagined." *Imagined Communities: Reflections on the Origin and Spread of Nationalism* (London: Verso, 1983), 15, emphasis added.

40. Conversation with the author, April 10, 1989.

41. Although the sequence is called "Tales of the Islands," the local allusions are mostly traceable to St. Lucia: the tale of the loupgarou (Chapter IX) reappears in a Castries setting in *Another Life;* Franklin, the stranded expatriate of Chapter VII, is also the protagonist of an unpublished play, *Franklin: A Tale of the Islands,* set in St. Lucia's "Quarter of Dauphin"; the reenacted kélé ritual of Chapter V and the obeah murder "Of a young child" in Chapter VI allude to St. Lucian events; there is in fact a mission school on the Dorée River near Choiseul; while Rue St. Louis (Chapter II) and Grass St. (Chapter VIII) are to be found in Castries.

42. Quoted in H. W. Janson (with Dora Jane Janson), *History of Art: A Survey of the Major Visual Arts from the Dawn of History to the Present Day* (Englewood Cliffs, N.J./New York: Prentice-Hall/Harry N. Abrams, 1962), 410.

43. Janson, *History of Art,* 410.

44. "College boys," in the West Indian sense, would be of high school rather than "college" age.

45. The rite described is kélé, of African derivation and still practiced, until the mid-1980s, by a small number of families in the Babonneau area of St. Lucia. The kélé sacrifice feeds the spirits of the ancestors.

46. Father C. Jesse, the dogmatic attacker of Walcott's first poem and of his play, *The Sea at Dauphin,* had an anthropological interest in "black customs"; this passage is, among other things, a subtle jab at him.

47. "Walcott and the Audience for Poetry," *Caribbean Quarterly* 14, nos. 1 and 2 (March-June 1968): 17.

48. As a look at the 1958 text (*Bim* 7, no. 26: 67–70) reveals, Walcott was revising "downwards," from relatively standard to more distinctively creole language. The text of both versions of Chapter VI is quoted in Morris, "Walcott and the Audience for Poetry," 18. As Morris says, the poem "has been completely transformed."

49. I have been unable to discover what this "chap" is quoting, or misquoting. In the 1958 version, he refers to Keats rather than Shelley, so perhaps the search for an actual source is pointlessly literal.

50. *Malfinis or the Heart of a Child* (*A Trial in Purgatory*) (Trinidad & Tobago: UWI Extra-Mural Department, 1967). In St. Lucian creole, "malfinis" means "chicken-hawk." I met St. Lucians of Walcott's generation who vividly recall hearing the story from their elders during childhood.

51. Reprinted in *English Romantic Writers,* ed. David Perkins (New York: Harcourt, Brace & World, 1967), 1102.

52. "West Indians Score Success with West Indian Play in London," *P. O. G. Gazette,* January 1952; "Errol Hill Overcomes Obstacles in Way of *Henri Christophe,*" *Evening News* (Port of Spain), 11 January 1952, quoted in Samuel Omo Asein, "The Growth and Reputation of Derek Walcott as a Playwright" (Ph.D. thesis, University of Ibadan, Nigeria, 1974), 114–15.

53. "What the Twilight Says," 11.

54. Walcott, "What the Twilight Says," 13.

55. Hubert Cole, *Christophe, King of Haiti* (New York: Viking, 1967), 218.

56. Cole, *Christophe,* 220.

57. Césaire, *La tragédie du Roi Christophe* (Paris: Présence Africaine, 1963), 90–94.

58. Walcott, "Caligula's Horse," in The Emperor Writes Back: Theory and Practice in Post-colonial Literatures, ed. Bill Ashcroft, Gareth Griffiths, and Helen Tiffin (London: Routledge, 1989), 141; T. S. Eliot, "Four Elizabethan Dramatists" [1924], in *Selected Essays* (New York: Harcourt, Brace, 1950), 98.

59. Eliot, "The Metaphysical Poets," in *Selected Essays,* 247.

60. All the scripts of earlier plays are lost. But Walcott says that none of the plays written before *Henri Christophe* made use of creole (conversation of March 23, 1995).

61. As his use of an epigraph from *Richard III* to preface "Part II" (scenes 5–7) suggests, Walcott may have modeled his murderers on the two in Shakespeare's play.

62. James, *The Black Jacobins: Toussaint L'Ouverture and the San Domingo Revolution* (New York: Vintage, 1963 [1938]), 371, 373–74.

63. J. S. Barker, *Trinidad Guardian,* 30 November 1954. Quoted in Samuel O. Asein, "The Growth and Reputation of Derek Walcott as a Playwright" (Ph.D. thesis, University of Ibadan, Nigeria, 1974), 118.

Chapter Three

1. Laurence A. Breiner, "Walcott's Early Drama," in *The Art of Derek Walcott,* ed. Stewart Brown (Mid Glamorgan, Wales: Seren/Dufour, 1991), 71. If there is an early version of *Dream on Monkey Mountain* from this period, I was unable to find it either in Mona or in Trinidad. Leroy Clarke, of the Trinidad Theatre Workshop, told Victor Questel that what Walcott initially brought in to the Workshop "was not a script just yet. The script of *Dream on Monkey Mountain* was written in the theatre" (Questel, "History of the Trinidad Theatre Workshop," Part II [unpublished, c. 1981, Walcott Collection, UWI, Trinidad], 3). See also Bruce King, *Derek Walcott and West Indian Drama* (New York: Oxford University Press, 1995), 82.

2. William Butler Yeats, "J. M. Synge and the Ireland of His Time" (1910), in *Essays and Introductions* (New York: Collier, 1968), 336. But he had been saying so since the play was newly written. He praised it in those terms to Joyce—see Richard Ellmann, *James Joyce* (New York: Oxford University Press, 1965), 128–

29—and, as Padraic Colum recalled, to just about anyone who would listen: "'A play that is like one of Aeschylus's' William Butler Yeats announced when he had read *Riders to the Sea.* 'Who is Aeschylus? Oh, he's the man who writes like John Synge.' In that characteristic way Dublin countered the claim Yeats set up." "My Memories of John Synge," in *J. M. Synge: Interviews and Recollections,* ed. E. H. Mikhail (London/New York: Macmillan/Barnes & Noble, 1977), 63.

3. Robin Skelton, *J. M. Synge and His World* (Norwich, U.K.: Jarrold & Sons, 1971), 46.

4. Nicholas Greene, *Synge: A Critical Study of the Plays* (London: Macmillan, 1975), 56.

5. Edward Hirsch, "An Interview With Derek Walcott," *Contemporary Literature* 20, no. 3 (1979): 288–89.

6. Hirsch, "An Interview With Derek Walcott," 286.

7. Slade Hopkinson, "So the Sun Went Down," *The Daily Gleaner,* 15 April 1956, 17; quoted in Bruce King, *Derek Walcott and West Indian Drama,* 14.

8. *DMMOP,* 46; "The Sea at Dauphin: A Play in One Act," *Tamarack Review* 14 (winter 1960): 77.

9. Yeats, "Synge and the Ireland of His Time," 336.

10. *The Complete Plays of John M. Synge* (New York: Vintage, 1960), 93.

11. *The Complete Plays of John M. Synge,* 89.

12. David H. Greene and Edward M. Stephens, *John Synge 1871–1909,* revised edition (New York: New York University Press, 1989), 296.

13. Informal conversation (not in taped interview), St. Lucia, March 1995. Bruce King also mentions this anecdote in *Derek Walcott and West Indian Drama,* 13.

14. Jane C. Beck, *To Windward of the Land: The Occult World of Alexander Charles* (Bloomington: Indiana University Press, 1979), quotations, respectively, from 103, 85, 86, 115, 109. For Charles's prior occupations, see 9–10, 57–83.

15. Hirsch, "An Interview with Derek Walcott," 288.

16. Hirsch, "An Interview with Derek Walcott," 286.

17. Most of Walcott's creole words can be readily traced to cognates in standard French; indeed, *garce* appears in *The New Cassell's French Dictionary* (New York: Funk & Wagnalls, 1962), but not in Jones E. Mondesir's *Dictionary of St. Lucian Creole* (Berlin: Mouton de Gruyter, 1992), which, in its zeal to present creole as a dignified language, omits most of the saltier vocabulary.

18. *The Complete Plays of John M. Synge,* 97.

19. "The Street Scene" and "The Modern Theatre Is the Epic Theatre," in *Brecht on Theatre: The Development of an Aesthetic,* ed. and trans. John Willett (New York: Hill & Wang, 1964), 122, 37.

20. Derek Walcott, "Derek's 'Most West Indian Play,'" *Sunday Guardian Magazine,* 21 June 1970, 7.

21. *Brecht on Theatre,* 122.

22. Bruce King, *Derek Walcott and West Indian Drama,* 25.

23. Walcott, "Derek's 'Most West Indian Play,'" 7.

24. "Preface" to the Second Edition of *Lyrical Ballads* (1800), in *The Complete Poetical Works of Wordsworth*, ed. Andrew J. George (Cambridge, Mass.: The Riverside Press, 1932), 797.

25. As he put it in conversation: "A culture can expend its spirit in anger. That anger can be provoked. But generally, it creates bad poetry." Interview, April 10, 1989.

26. *Drums and Colours, Caribbean Quarterly* 7, nos. 1 and 2, Special Issue (March-June 1961): 3; hereafter cited in text as *DC*.

27. C. L. R. James, "Preface to the First Edition," in *The Black Jacobins: Toussaint L'Ouverture and the San Domingo Revolution* (New York: Vintage, 1963 [1938]), ix.1nb

28. Ivar Oxaal, *Black Intellectuals Come to Power* and *The Dilemmas of Race and Class in Trinidad* (Cambridge, Mass.: Schenkman, 1982), 23. The most famous of the Calypsonians, the Mighty Sparrow, contributed to the festivities a Federation calypso much in the same spirit as Walcott's play: "Let us join together and love one another / We all is one." Keith Q. Warner, *Kaiso! The Trinidad Calypso* (Washington, D.C.: Three Continents Press, 1982), 70.

29. The scene alludes to John Millais's painting, "The Childhood of Raleigh."

Chapter Four

1. "Their [the great poets'] vision of man in the New World is Adamic." "The Muse of History: An Essay" [c. 1973], reprinted in Derek Walcott, *What the Twilight Says: Essays* (New York: Farrar, Straus & Giroux, 1998), 37.

2. In his *Puritan Origins of the American Self* (New Haven: Yale University Press, 1975).

3. "What the Twilight Says: An Overture" [1970], in *Dream on Monkey Mountain and Other Plays* (New York: Farrar, Straus & Giroux, 1970), 5.

4. R. W. B. Lewis, *The American Adam: Innocence, Tragedy, and Tradition in the Nineteenth Century* (Chicago: University of Chicago Press, 1955), 104.

5. *What the Twilight Says: Essays*, 37.

6. *What the Twilight Says: Essays*, 37–38.

7. "The Figure of Crusoe" in Robert Hamner, *Critical Perspectives on Derek Walcott* (Boulder, Colo.: Lynne Rienner, 1997), 37.

8. Unlike the other two pieces, this poem does not mention the name "Crusoe" (or, for that matter, the name Adam). But in its treatment of "the theme of isolation" and its metaphor of the West Indian artist as solitary "castaway," it is closely akin to the others and has often been discussed in connection with them.

9. Walcott may here be implicitly critiquing his own contemporaneous poem, "Crusoe's Island." Cf. the lines: "The rotting nut, bowled in the surf, / Became his own brain rotting from the guilt / Of heaven without his kind" (*CP*, 69).

10. Crusoe's ship is bound from Brazil to Barbados when the storm strikes it at the latitude of 12E 18′ north, which would actually place it closer to Grenada than Tobago. But other details of the narrative suggest that early accounts of To-

bago were Defoe's source. See V. S. Naipaul, *The Loss of Eldorado: A History* (New York: Vintage, 1984), 41.

11. *Stevens: Collected Poetry and Prose,* ed. Frank Kermode and Joan Richardson (New York: Library of America, 1997), 105.

12. Coleridge, *Biographia Literaria,* ed. James Engell and W. Jackson Bate (Princeton, N.J.: Princeton University Press, 1983), I.304.

13. The name means The Windmill (*La Ventille*).

14. "Tradition and the Individual Talent," in *Selected Essays of T. S. Eliot* (New York: Harcourt, Brace & World, 1964), 4.

15. *The Gulf: Poems by Derek Walcott* (New York: Farrar, Straus, Giroux, 1970), 17. Hereafter cited as *G.*

16. "The Art of Poetry XXXVII: Derek Walcott," *Paris Review* 101 [1986]; reprinted in *Critical Perspectives on Derek Walcott,* ed. Robert D. Hamner (Boulder, Colo.: Rienner, 1997), 74.

17. A version of this poem first appeared in *New Writing in the Caribbean,* ed. A. J. Seymour (Georgetown, Guyana: Guyana Lithographic Co., 1972), just two years after the 1970 revolt.

18. Kimberly W. Benston has written perceptively on the significance of name changes in African-American literature. That literature, he claims, has a central need "to resituate or displace the literal master/father by a literal act of unnaming," as Malcolm Little famously did in becoming Malcolm X. Walcott's poem evokes a more gradual process of unnaming, in which the black speaker does not reject the old name but appropriates it, giving it a new context and a new meaning. "I Yam What I Yam: The Topos of (Un)Naming in Afro-American Literature," in *Black Literature and Literary Theory,* ed. Henry Louis Gates Jr. (New York: Routledge, 1984), 151–72.

19. Dunstan St. Omer, conversation with the author in the Jacmel Church, St. Lucia, July 20, 1989.

20. Literally true: at the lower right corner, a man is seated playing a drum, and on the drum St. Omer has signed and dedicated the painting.

21. "The Art of Poetry XXXVII: Derek Walcott," 214–15.

22. Christopher Gunness, "White Man, Black Man," *People,* June 1978; reprinted in *Critical Perspectives on Derek Walcott,* 290.

23. Patrick Taylor, *The Narrative of Liberation: Perspectives on Afro-Caribbean Literature, Popular Culture, and Politics* (Ithaca, N.Y.: Cornell University Press, 1989), 206–7.

24. Bruce King, *Derek Walcott and West Indian Drama* (Oxford: Clarendon, 1995), 298.

25. King, *Derek Walcott and West Indian Drama,* 298. The quotation within the quotation is from Judy Stone, "What Corsbie Did to Walcott's 'Pantomime,'" *Trinidad Guardian,* 5 February 1981, 13.

26. Similarly, familiar racial stereotypes trade places when Jackson says that Harry is "like a blasted child" and Harry retorts that "You people are such prudes" (*R & P,* 104).

27. Albert Memmi, *The Colonizer and the Colonized,* trans. Howard Greenfeld, with an introduction by Jean-Paul Sartre (Boston: Beacon Press, 1965), 45–76.

28. Eve Kosofsky Sedgwick, *Between Men: English Literature and Male Homosocial Desire* (New York: Columbia University Press, 1985), 20.

Chapter Five

1. See Laurence Breiner, "Walcott's Early Drama," in *The Art of Derek Walcott,* ed. Stewart Brown (Mid Glamorgan, Wales: Seren/Dufour, 1991), 77–78; and Bruce King, *Derek Walcott and West Indian Drama* (Oxford: Clarendon, 1995), 78. Walcott recalls beginning the play "in the States in '59," but getting down to the writing much later, as the Trinidad Theatre Workshop prepared for its first tour. "Meanings," *Savacou* 2 (September 1970): 47. In a letter to Tom Maschler of Jonathan Cape Publishers, June 23, 1961, Walcott referred to a play "which I am re-writing called 'The Dream on Monkey Mountain'" (Walcott Archive, UWI, Trinidad, Box 1).

2. Victor Questel, "History of the Trinidad Theatre Workshop," Part II (Unpublished manuscript, Walcott Archive, UWI Trinidad, Box 10), 3–4 (the sections are each individually paginated).

3. Sharon Ciccarelli, "Reflections Before and After Carnival: An Interview with Derek Walcott," reprinted in *Conversations with Derek Walcott,* ed. William Baer (Jackson: University Press of Mississippi, 1996), 43.

4. Walcott, "Meanings," 50.

5. Conversations with Gregor Williams, July 1990 and June 2, 2000; with Cuthbert Charles, June 1, 2000.

6. "Man of the Theatre," *New Yorker,* 26 June 1971; reprinted in *Conversations with Derek Walcott,* 19.

7. Since Walcott's handwriting is remarkably clear, there can be no doubt that the name in the notebook is "Augier," and several St. Lucians, including Cuthbert Charles, confirm that "Makak" worked for the Augiers.

8. Entry for November 1, 1966, first notebook for *Another Life,* UWI, Mona, Jamaica, 74–75. For those who, unlike the judge, are not content to "understand enough," Makak says: "Ask the magistrate if it's in his mother's hole that I will find the five pounds." Gregor Williams explains that "chou-choute" is "one of the mothers of all curse words. . . . It is very comprehensive and takes in all orifices together." "Gourd" is "the money equivalent of pounds," though "the term is of French origin. . . . Dollars were not in circulation in Makak's time. E. C. dollars came in only after 1960" (e-mail message, May 14, 1997). Apparently, Walcott has settled on an exchange rate of three dollars to one gourd.

9. Patrick Taylor, *The Narrative of Liberation: Perspectives on Afro-Caribbean Literature, Popular Culture, and Politics* (Ithaca, N.Y.: Cornell University Press, 1989), 215, 214.

10. Tejumola Olaniyan, *Scars of Conquest/Masks of Resistance: The Invention of Cultural Identities in African, African-American, and Caribbean Drama* (New York: Oxford University Press, 1995), 108.

11. Frantz Fanon, *Black Skin, White Masks,* trans. Charles Lam Markmann (New York: Grove Press, 1967), 14, 36; *The Wretched of the Earth,* trans. Constance Farrington (New York: Grove Press, 1968), 38, 42, 94.

12. Taylor, *Narrative of Liberation,* 204.

13. Errol Hill, "Emergence of a National Drama in the West Indies," *Caribbean Quarterly* 18, no. 4 (December 1972): 33.

14. Fanon, "West Indians and Africans," in *Toward the African Revolution (Political Essays),* trans. Haakon Chevalier (New York: Grove Press, 1969), 27.

15. Robert Hamner, *Derek Walcott,* updated edition (New York: Twayne Publishers, 1993), 70.

16. Osy Okagbue, "Identity, Exile and Migration: The Dialectics of Content and Form in West Indian Theatre," *New Literatures Review* [New South Wales] 19 (summer [southern hemisphere] 1990): 19.

17. Quoted in Fanon, *Black Skin, White Masks,* 39; Fanon remarks that "there is no reason" why Breton should speak of Césaire in this way.

18. Robert Graves, *The White Goddess: A Historical Grammar of Poetic Myth,* 3d edition (London: Faber & Faber, 1952), 24.

19. Breiner, "Walcott's Early Drama," 80.

20. Graves, *White Goddess,* 122.

21. Fanon, *Black Skin, White Masks,* 129. Fanon quotes from "Que m'accompagnent kôras et balafong" in *Chants d'ombre* (1945): "Mais voici l'intelligence de la déesse Lune et que tombent les voiles des ténèbres, / Nuit d'Afrique ma nuit noire, mystique et claire noire et brillant."

22. Fanon, *Wretched of the Earth,* 38.

23. Walcott, "Meanings," 47.

24. Theodore Colson, "Derek Walcott's Plays: Outrage and Compassion," *World Literature Written in English* 12, no. 1 (April 1973): 95.

25. "To (prepare to) deprive yourself of many needs in difficult times; to tighten your belt for a long time to achieve a family aim." *Dictionary of Caribbean English Usage,* ed. Richard Allsopp (Oxford: Oxford University Press, 1996).

26. Edward Hirsch, "An Interview with Derek Walcott," *Contemporary Literature* 20, no. 3 (1979): 286.

27. And perhaps also of John 1:1: "In the beginning was the Word."

28. In at least one production, this symbolism has been visually reinforced. When the Trinidad Theatre Workshop took *Dream* on a tour to five other islands in 1968, the set, as Ulric Mentus noted in his review, "epitomise[d] the hopelessness of the situation—a towering dark mountain flanked on either side by giant spider webs." Quoted in King, *Derek Walcott and West Indian Drama,* 90.

29. "On" here seems to mean "in"; the *Dictionary of Caribbean English Usage* notes that "on" is "[w]idely used in C[aribbean] E[nglish] instead of several different prep[osition]s in S[tandard] E[nglish] idiom." "In" is one of the meanings given and illustrated in the entry.

30. Laurence Breiner notes the glancing allusion to Hopkins's "That Nature Is a Heraclitian Fire, and of the Comfort of the Resurrection." "Walcott's Early Drama," 79.

31. Hill, "Emergence of a National Drama in the West Indies," *Caribbean Quarterly* 18, no. 4 (December 1972): 33.

32. His first name, mentioned in the prologue, is Caiphas, recalling the High Priest who presided over the betrayal of Christ.

33. Cf. George Lamming, *In the Castle of My Skin* (Ann Arbor: University of Michigan Press, 1991 [1953]), 26–27: "The enemy was My People. My people are low-down nigger people. My people don't like to see their people get on. The language of the overseer. The language of the civil servant."

Chapter Six

1. Edward Hirsch, "The Art of Poetry XXXVII: Derek Walcott," *Paris Review* 101 (1986); reprinted in *Critical Perspectives on Derek Walcott,* ed. Robert D. Hamner (Boulder, Colo.: Rienner, 1997), 81.

2. "An Interview with Frederick Seidel," reprinted in *Robert Lowell: Collected Prose,* ed. Robert Giroux (New York: Farrar, Straus & Giroux, 1987), 241.

3. Robert Lowell, "91 Revere Street," in *Life Studies* [1959] and *For the Union Dead* (New York: Farrar, Straus & Giroux, 1964), 13.

4. Robert Lowell to Derek Walcott, February 19, 1973. Walcott Archive, Box # 1, UWI, St. Augustine.

5. Conversation with the author, April 10, 1989, Milwaukee.

6. Walcott, "Contemplative Is Word for His Genius," *Trinidad Guardian,* 15 October 1966, 5.

7. First notebook for *Another Life,* 1 (March 28, 1966). I have not found the translation Walcott used.

8. Boris Pasternak, *Safe Conduct, an Autobiography and Other Writings,* trans. Beatrice Scott (New York: New Directions, 1958), 146.

9. Pasternak, *Safe Conduct,* 28.

10. Pasternak, *Safe Conduct,* 60.

11. Pasternak, *Safe Conduct,* 72.

12. Pasternak, *Safe Conduct,* 28.

13. Rei Terada argues that the concept of "reversibility" emerges fully in Walcott's essay of 1974, "The Caribbean: Culture or Mimicry": "All of Walcott's poetry after 1974 builds upon its conclusions, and Walcott never lets go of the 'reversible' map of the world he defines there." *Derek Walcott's Poetry: American Mimicry* (Boston: Northeastern University Press, 1992), 25. Cf. also Wilson Harris, "Tradition and the West Indian Novel" [1964]: "one relives and reverses the 'given' conditions of the past." Reprinted in *Tradition the Writer & Society* (London: New Beacon Books, 1967), 36.

14. "Tradition and the West Indian Novel," 28, 30, 31.

15. Paul Breslin, "'I Met History Once, but He Ain't Recognize Me': The Poetry of Derek Walcott," *TriQuarterly* 68 (1987): 178.

16. Pasternak, *Safe Conduct,* 31.

17. First notebook for *Another Life,* 13.

18. Edward Baugh, *Derek Walcott: Memory as Vision: Another Life* (London: Longman, 1978), 36 n. 10.

19. Baugh, *Derek Walcott,* 21.

20. Goya's accompanying gloss, it is only scrupulous to point out, continues in good Enlightenment fashion: "La fantasia abandonada de la razon, produce monstruos imposibles: unida con ella, es madre de las artes y origen de sus mirabillas." ["Imagination abandoned by reason produces impossible monsters: united with her, she is the mother of the arts and the source of their wonders."] But Philip Hofer remarks in the introduction to his Dover edition of *Los Caprichos* on the "elusive nature of the captions beneath each plate," regarding this one in particular as "deliberately deceptive," disguising Goya's debt to a pictorial frontispiece in Rousseau's *Philosophie.* That allusion could have got him in trouble in the reactionary Spain of 1799. Francisco Goya y Lucentes, *Los Caprichos,* with an introduction by Philip Hofer (New York: Dover, 1969), 3, 2.

21. This phrase, too, is an allusion, to Pound's "what whiteness? what candor" (Canto 74); as with Graves's "white goddess," Walcott's appropriation adds a racial irony not suggested in the source.

22. Baugh comments on this juxtaposition; *Derek Walcott,* 22.

23. Baugh, *Derek Walcott,* 33.

24. Baugh, *Derek Walcott,* 19.

25. According to Baugh, Walcott was also thinking of Dylan Thomas's *Under Milkwood* and Galway Kinnell's "The Avenue Bearing the Initial of Christ into the New World." *Derek Walcott,* 28.

26. In West Indian usage, "clear-complexioned" means light-skinned, white or nearly white.

27. *Gens gajés* are persons who serve the devil in exchange for power or wealth.

28. Walcott, *Midsummer* (New York: Farrar, Straus & Giroux, 1984), xiv.

29. *The Lost Steps* [1953], trans. Harriet de Onís (New York: Farrar, Straus & Giroux, 1989), 72–73.

30. *Dear Theo: The Autobiography of Vincent van Gogh* [through an arrangement of the letters] [1937], ed. Irving Stone, with Jean Stone (New York: Penguin/Plume, 1995), 391, 361, 362. Harry Simmons's "yellowing *Letters to Theo"* (*CP,* 262) was probably this book; my net searches of library catalogues turned up nothing for the title *Letters to Theo.*

31. Baugh, *Derek Walcott,* 39.

32. Dunstan St. Omer, conversation with the author, July 1989.

33. St. Joseph the Worker is a very large church; local tradition has it that the priest responsible for its construction misread the plans, doubling both height and width. Dunstan St. Omer, conversation with the author, July 1989.

34. Baugh, *Derek Walcott,* 27.

35. Second notebook for *Another Life,* 87. [The entry is typed and pasted into the exercise book; the typed insert is number "91," but it is the eighty-seventh page of the manuscript.]

36. This name, which has been bestowed on the airport at Vieux Fort, derives from the Arawak name for the island, which Walcott renders in *Omeros* as "Iounalo," meaning "where the iguana is found."

37. See Pasternak, *Safe Conduct,* 16.

38. Malraux, *The Psychology of Art,* 1.109.

39. Randall Jarrell, *Poetry and the Age* [1953] (New York: Vintage, 1959), 234–35.

40. Baugh, *Derek Walcott,* 53.

41. Walcott, conversation with the author, March 23, 1995, Cap, St. Lucia.

42. In addition to his many other pursuits, Simmons also collected butterflies.

43. Walcott's birthday, January 23, makes him an Aquarian, and the month of January is named for Janus.

44. Perhaps a glance at Villon again (his "Ballade du concours de Blois," which begins with Charles D'Orléans's line, "Je meurs du soif auprès de la fontaine").

45. Cf. Chapter 13, section iv (*CP,* 228): "Magical lagoon, stunned / by its own reflection!"

Chapter Seven

1. *History of the Voice: The Development of Nation Language in Anglophone Caribbean Poetry* (London: New Beacon Books, 1984), 10.

2. *The Massachusetts Review* 18, no. 4 (winter 1977): 795–800; *Trinidad & Tobago Review* 2, no. 9 (May 1978): 11–14; and *Chant of Saints,* ed. Michael S. Harper and Robert B. Stepto (Urbana: University of Illinois Press, 1979), 166–74. Although the *Trinidad & Tobago Review* version appeared before the one in *Chant of Saints,* the *Trinidad & Tobago* text is much closer than the *Chant of Saints* version to the poem as printed in *The Star-Apple Kingdom* (1979) and reprinted without further change in *Collected Poems: 1948–1984* (1986). Moreover, the production of a book, especially a large anthology such as *Chant of Saints,* takes longer than the production of a serial issue. I therefore assume that the versions in order of composition are: *Massachusetts Review, Chant of Saints,* and *Trinidad & Tobago Review.*

3. The *Dictionary of Caribbean English Usage,* ed. Richard and Jeannette Allsopp (New York: Oxford University Press, 1996), defines shabine or "chaben" as a derogatory term for "a person of mixed African and European descent who has a dull sort of pale brown skin, coarse reddish hair and sometimes freckles and greyish eyes." (The word derives from French *chabin,* a thick-wooled variety of sheep "once thought to be a cross between a sheep and a goat.")

4. *Chant of Saints,* 170.

5. Many words and sentences are idiomatic in both West Indian Standard and creole. When I argue that one version is more creolized than another, I mean simply that one contains more words and phrases that are idiomatic in creole *but not in West Indian Standard.*

6. Charles H. Rowell, "An Interview with Derek Walcott" (1987), reprinted in *Conversations with Derek Walcott,* ed. William Baer (Jackson: University Press of Mississippi, 1996), 130.

7. Walcott, *Dream on Monkey Mountain and Other Plays* (New York: Farrar, Straus & Giroux, 1970), 31–32.

8. Laurence Breiner, "Walcott's Early Drama," in *The Art of Derek Walcott,* ed. Stewart Brown (Mid Glamorgan, Wales: Seren/Dufour, 1991), 180.

9. Roger D. Abrahams, *The Man-of-Words in the West Indies: Performance and the Emergence of Creole Culture* (Baltimore, Md.: Johns Hopkins University Press, 1983), 90.

10. Richard D. E. Burton, *Afro-Creole: Power, Opposition and Play in the Caribbean* (Ithaca, N.Y.: Cornell University Press, 1997), 191.

11. Ben Jonson, *The Complete Poems,* ed. George Parfitt. (New Haven: Yale University Press, 1982), 398.

12. Ned Thomas, "Obsession and Responsibility," in *The Art of Derek Walcott,* ed. Stewart Brown (Mid Glamorgan, Wales: Seren/Dufour, 1991), 86–87.

13. The *Dictionary of Caribbean Usage* defines bohbohl or "bobol" as "fraud or corrupt practices organized, usu[ally] on some scale, by well-placed persons in authority in a company or in government administration." The editors speculate that the word "may be a modification . . . of Fr[ench] Cr[eole] *Vaval,* an early (1920s) masque king of *StLu*[*cian*] carnival"; Walcott suggested, when I interviewed him in 1989, that the word may derive from "bubble."

14. Nassau, the capital of the Bahamas, is on the island of New Providence, near the northern end of the archipelago; Monos is one of the "Five Islands" off Carenage, Trinidad, at the southeastern end of the chain.

15. Not my favorite moment in this on the whole superb poem. Can Shabine believe that the sincerity of his emotions undoes the harm he has inflicted on others by acting on them?

16. Thomas, "Obsession and Responsibility," 88.

17. The *Dictionary of Caribbean Usage* defines a "limer" as "an idler; a time-waster; one (usu[ally] a man) who stands around with others on the sidewalk or in some other public place watching people go by, and sometimes being mischievous," from the verb *lime,* "to sit, loaf, or hang about with others." In *Street Life: Afro-American Culture in Urban Trinidad* (Cambridge, Mass.: Shenkman, 1981), Michael Lieber gives a subtler definition (followed by detailed accounts from limers themselves): "Liming may be best glossed as 'just hanging around,' but hanging around with eyes and ears keenly tuned to the flow of action and the recognition of advantage. The limer is attuned to making something eventful of street life" (60).

18. J. P. White, "An Interview with Derek Walcott," in *Conversations with Derek Walcott,* ed. Baer, 160.

19. "The Poet," in *Selected Writings of Ralph Waldo Emerson*, ed. William H. Gilman (New York: New American Library, 1965), 326, 308.

20. This development is the subject of my study, *The Psycho-Political Muse: American Poetry since the Fifties* (Chicago: University of Chicago Press, 1987).

21. Aleksander Blok, "The Twelve," in *The Twelve and Other Poems*, trans. Jon Stallworthy and Peter France (New York: Oxford University Press, 1970), 141, 157, 156.

22. The Savannah is the large open park at the north end of Port of Spain, with facilities for horse racing and cricket; it is also where Calypso tents are pitched during Carnival.

23. Isaiah 6:9–10.

24. Shabine makes good on his claim to "know these islands from Monos to Nassau." Kick 'Em Jenny, or Diamond Island, is a tiny islet just north of Ronde, itself a small island just north of Grenada. "Nobody knows where the name comes from. Maybe it's a corruption of the French, cay que gêne, 'the troublesome cay,' because the currents around it gave the old sailing ships such a hard time. Some say it's Kick 'em Jenny because it kicks like a mule." Laddie McIntyre, a Grenadian yachtsman quoted by Carleton Mitchell, *Isles of the Caribbees* (Washington, D.C.: National Geographic Society, 1966), 29–30.

25. As Ned Thomas notes, "[t]he road like twine recalls an earlier use of the image with a similar structure of feeling, when in the last of 'Tales of the Islands' the young Walcott records leaving his island by plane." *The Art of Derek Walcott*, 89. Moreover, though Thomas does not mention it, the image had already been recycled once when Walcott embedded the sonnet in Chapter 17, IV of *Another Life* (*CP*, 257).

26. Rei Terada, *Derek Walcott's Poetry: American Mimicry* (Boston: Northeastern University Press, 1992), 114–15.

27. Knowing of Walcott's longstanding admiration for James Joyce, I suspect that his magnificent lines, "There are so many islands! / As many islands as the stars at night / on that branched tree from which meteors are shaken / like falling fruit around the schooner *Flight*" (*CP*, 361) have their taproot in the gorgeous phrase that fairly leaps from its drab surroundings in the catechism section of *Ulysses*: "The heaventree of stars hung with humid nightblue fruit." *Ulysses* (New York: Random House, 1946), 683. Terada (*Derek Walcott's Poetry*, 240–41 n. 11) hears the same phrase from *Ulysses* behind Walcott's "Dusk, the tree of heaven, broke in gold leaf" in *Another Life* (*CP*, 205).

Chapter Eight

1. Robert D. Hamner, *Derek Walcott*, updated edition (New York: Twayne, 1993), 136.

2. "Derek Walcott: Contemporary," reprinted in Robert D. Hamner, *Critical Perspectives on Derek Walcott* (Boulder, Colo.: Lynne Rienner, 1997), 317.

3. Paula Burnett, "Appropriating Heirlooms: 'The Fortunate Traveller' and Its Intertexts," in *Derek Walcott: Politics and Poetics* (Gainesville: University of Florida

Press, 2000). I quote from an unpaginated advance copy I received as an e-mail attachment. Other citations of Burnett in my ensuing discussion of *The Fortunate Traveller* also refer to this source.

4. *Trinidad Express,* 14 March 1982, quoted in Richard Dwyer, "One Walcott, and He Would Be King," reprinted in Hamner, *Critical Perspectives,* 325.

5. Thomas Nashe, *The Unfortunate Traveller and Other Works,* ed. J. B. Steane (Middlesex, U.K.: Penguin, 1971), 346.

6. Mervyn Morris, "The Fortunate Traveller," in *The Art of Derek Walcott,* ed. Stewart Brown (Mid Glamorgan, Wales: Seren/Dufour, 1991), 105.

7. Bedient, "Derek Walcott: Contemporary," 314.

8. E.g., by Bedient, "Derek Walcott: Contemporary," 314; and Helen Vendler, "Poet of Two Worlds," *New York Review,* 4 March 1982.

9. Hamner, *Derek Walcott,* 122.

10. John Wilmot, Earl of Rochester, *Poems,* ed. Vivian de Sola Pinto (Cambridge, Mass.: Harvard University Press, 1953), 118.

11. Nashe, *Unfortunate Traveller,* 346.

12. A revised version of this poem appears as VI in *Midsummer.*

13. Antonio Benítez-Rojo considers the Caribbean imaginary to be inimical to apocalyptic visions. See *The Repeating Island: The Caribbean and the Postmodern Perspective,* 2d ed., trans. James E. Maraniss (Durham, N.C.: Duke University Press, 1996), 10. If so, this poem marks an exception, unless one can attribute its apocalyptic bent to its engagement with the north.

14. Bedient, "Derek Walcott: Contemporary," 320.

15. Identifiable, as Paula Burnett remarks, by the place-name "Canaries," *FT* 93.

16. Derek Walcott, conversation with the author, Milwaukee, Wis., April 10, 1989.

17. Bedient, "Derek Walcott: Contemporary," 320; Morris, "The Fortunate Traveller," 105.

18. Bedient, "Derek Walcott: Contemporary," 320.

19. Morris, "The Fortunate Traveller," 107.

20. Walcott, "A Rediscovery of Islands," *New York Times,* 13 November 1983, Section XX (travel), 13.

21. "The Painter as Poet: Derek Walcott's *Midsummer,*" in Hamner, *Critical Perspectives,* 338.

22. "The Painter as Poet," 345.

23. "The Painter As Poet," 345.

24. As Sven Birkerts observes, "Walcott writes poem after poem with little differentiation of subject. His settings and descriptions are, in a sense, pretexts. He would like to throw out as much as possible in order to clear a path to his real subject: language becoming poetry." "Heir Apparent," in Hamner, *Critical Perspectives,* 333.

25. John Thieme, *Derek Walcott* (Manchester: Manchester University Press, 1999), 171.

26. Bruce King, *Derek Walcott: A Caribbean Life* (Oxford: Oxford University Press, 2000), 467.

27. Edward Hirsch, "The Art of Poetry XXXVII: Derek Walcott," *Paris Review* 101; reprinted in Hamner, ed., *Critical Perspectives on Derek Walcott*, 79.

28. *Derek Walcott: A Caribbean Life*, 468.

29. Baugh, "The Arkansas Testament," 123.

30. Hirsch, "The Art of Poetry XXXVII," 71.

31. Thieme, *Derek Walcott*, 177.

32. Rei Terada, *Derek Walcott's Poetry: American Mimicry* (Boston: Northeastern University Press, 1992), 225.

33. J. Michael Dash, *The Other America: Caribbean Literature in a New World Context* (Charlottesville: University of Virginia Press, 1998), 105.

34. Terada, *Walcott's Poetry*, 215.

35. Terada, *Walcott's Poetry*, 215. Terada quotes lines from *Another Life*, Chapter 23, iv, which repeat almost verbatim lines in Chapter 12, iii (*CP* 294, 220).

36. Walcott, "Caligula's Horse," in *After Europe*, ed. Stephen Slemon and Helen Tiffin (Sydney: Dangaroo Press, 1989), 141.

37. Terada, *Walcott's Poetry*, 217.

38. Terada, *Walcott's Poetry*, 219.

39. Terada, *Walcott's Poetry*, 220; square brackets are Terada's.

40. Hirsch, "The Art of Poetry XXXVII," 112.

41. The Villa Beach Cottages, where Walcott usually stayed during returns to St. Lucia in the 1980s, are a few hundred yards north of the Halcyon.

42. Terada, *Walcott's Poetry*, 223.

43. Terada, *Walcott's Poetry*, 224–25.

44. Vernon Shetley, *After the Death of Poetry: Poetry and Audience in Contemporary America* (Durham, N.C.: Duke University Press, 1993), 28–29.

45. Lloyd King, "Caribbean Literature: Aspects of a Nationalist Process," in *Perspectives on Caribbean Regional Identity*, ed. Elizabeth M. Thomas-Hope (Liverpool: Centre for Latin American Studies, University of Liverpool, 1984), 100.

46. One is left to wonder how this man came to know Walcott's name: did they introduce themselves to each other during the ride, or did he recognize him? Just how much of a stranger would the most famous living St. Lucian be on his frequent returns to the island?

Chapter Nine

1. Martin Mueller, *The Iliad* (London: Allen & Unwin, 1986), 4.

2. Derek Walcott, "Reflections on *Omeros*," *South Atlantic Quarterly* 96, no. 2 (spring 1997): 232–34.

3. *Derek Walcott's Poetry: American Mimicry* (Boston: Northeastern University Press, 1992), 185.

4. Gregson Davis, "'With No Homeric Shadow': The Disavowal of Epic in Derek Walcott's *Omeros,*" *South Atlantic Quarterly* 96, no. 2 (spring 1997): 322, 327, 328.

5. Joseph Farrell, "Walcott's *Omeros:* The Classical Epic in a Postmodern World," *South Atlantic Quarterly* 96, no. 2 (spring 1997): 247–73.

6. Carol Dougherty, "Homer after *Omeros:* Reading a H/Omeric Text," *South Atlantic Quarterly* 96, no. 2 (spring 1997): 356.

7. Robert Hamner, *Epic of the Dispossessed: Derek Walcott's* Omeros (Columbia, Mo.: University of Missouri Press, 1997), 23, 29.

8. J. P. White, "An Interview with Derek Walcott," *Green Mountain Review* 4, no. 1 (1990): 36. Quoted in Hamner, *Epic of the Dispossessed,* 4–5.

9. Carol Dougherty, "Homer after *Omeros,*" 339, 341, 342, 347.

10. *Derek Walcott and West Indian Drama: 'Not Only a Playwright but a Company': The Trinidad Theatre Workshop 1959–1993* (Oxford: Clarendon Press, 1995), 220.

11. I shall cite a typed script, from the Walcott Archive of the West Indiana Collection, UWI, St. Augustine, as *IFN.* Since it is riddled with errors, I have taken the liberty of correcting them in cases where the intended word seems obvious, so as to avoid a distracting outbreak of *sics*.

12. At one point in the manuscript (p. 5), the name of the island is simply represented by a blank space, as if Walcott meant to fill it in after he had decided.

13. As Rei Terada explains, "In Froude's allegory Britain is a weak-kneed Odysseus which cannot live up to its imperial past," no longer capable of stringing the bow. *Derek Walcott's Poetry,* 241 n. 1.

14. If, as former Prime Minister of the Federation, Robinson recalls Sir Grantley Adams, this epithet alludes to the career of another West Indian leader, Michael Manley. Leading a strike against the Jamaican Broadcasting Company, Manley "faced the walls of the station and called the structure 'Jericho,'" at which point "the workers rechristened him, changing his nickname from 'Young Boy' to 'Joshua,' and the name stuck." Rachel Manley, *Drumblair: Memories of a Jamaican Childhood* (Kingston, Jamaica: Ian Randle Publishers, 1996), 306.

15. Jahan Ramazani goes so far as to claim that in the play, "the wound signifies indigenous political corruption, not inherited colonial injury." "The Wound of History: Walcott's *Omeros* and the Postcolonial Poetics of Affliction," *PMLA* 112, no. 3 (May 1997): 415 n. 2. That simplification may stand for the purposes of his argument, but colonial injury and postcolonial corruption are historically intertwined, and the play does not make a sharp distinction between them.

16. The word is more widely used in Trinidad than in St. Lucia. Some St. Lucians have thought that "Maljo" may be partly modeled on George Odlum, but Odlum is a more thoughtful and sophisticated man than the politician in the poem, and unlike "Maljo," he remains in St. Lucia.

17. "Nightmare History: Derek Walcott's *Omeros*," *Kenyon Review* 14, no. 3 (fall 1992): 203–4. Coaling in St. Lucia began only well after emancipation, in 1885, and lingered into the 1940s. To be sure, it was ill-paid, as the poem's reference to wages indicates. The Moyne Commission report of 1945, investigating conditions of work in the West Indies, confirms that women were "required to carry very heavy weights," up to fifty pounds in each load, for "only a few shillings a week." Exploited workers, yes, but not slave women. Martin's assumption that they were slaves, even though the poem clearly tells us that both Walcott and his father had seen them firsthand, suggests that he is looking for a melodrama of slave-drivers and brutalized victims, and then grows impatient when Walcott refuses to supply one.

18. Hamner, *Epic of the Dispossessed*, 95.

19. He is quoting, with only slight alteration, Henry H. Breen's *St. Lucia: Historical, Statistical, and Descriptive* [1844] (London: Frank Cass & Co., 1970), 72–73.

Chapter Ten

1. Bruce King, *Derek Walcott: A Caribbean Life* (Oxford: Oxford University Press, 2000), 629.

2. St. Lucians, well aware of Walcott's single-minded devotion to his work, joke that his new goal is to become the first writer to win the Nobel Prize twice.

3. John Thieme, *Derek Walcott* (Manchester, U.K.: Manchester University Press, 1999), 194.

4. King, *Derek Walcott*, 601.

5. King, *Derek Walcott*, 597; William Logan, "The Fatal Lure of Home," *New York Times Book Review*, 29 June 1997, 11. Logan considers both books to be Walcott at his worst.

6. Wallace Stevens, "Madame La Fleurie," in *Collected Poetry and Prose*, ed. Frank Kermode and Joan Richardson (New York: Library of America, 1997), 432.

7. John Thieme, *Derek Walcott*, 194, 196.

8. The poem never does name the town, but the watercolor titled "St. Malo," reproduced in *Tiepolo's Hound*, is clearly the one described here, complete with "the man walking his dog."

9. "Where I Live," *Architectural Digest* 54, no. 1 (January 1997): 30.

10. The analogy of the shadow recalls Makak's dilemma: "I was a king among shadows. Either the shadows were real, and I was no king, or it is my own kingliness that created the shadows" (*DMMOP*, 304).

11. Bruce King, *Derek Walcott*, 598.

12. King, *Derek Walcott*, 608.

13. Joachim Pissarro, *Camille Pissarro* (New York: Abrams, 1993), 19, 22, 43.

14. Bruce King, *Derek Walcott*, 570.

15. Paula Burnett, "An Ordinary Miracle or Two," *The Independent*, 2 September 2000, Features, 9.

Epilogue

1. Paula Burnett, "Hegemony or Pluralism? The Literary Prize and the Post-Colonial Project in the Caribbean," *Commonwealth Essays and Studies* 16, no. 1 (1993): 1–2.

2. Paul Berman, ed., *You Better Believe It: Black Verse in English from Africa, The West Indies and the United States* (Middlesex, U.K.: Penguin, 1973), 239.

3. Susan Gingell, "Returning to Come Forward: Dionne Brand Confronts Derek Walcott," *Journal of West Indian Literature* 6, no. 2 (May 1994]): 44.

4. Quoted in Gingell, "Returning to Come Forward," 44.

5. Elaine Savory [Fido], "Value Judgements on Art and the Question of Macho Attitudes: The Case of Derek Walcott," *Journal of Commonwealth Literature* 21, no. 1 (1986): 110.

6. Interviews with Velma Pollard (Mona, July 16) and Lorna Goodison (Kingston, July 17), Jamaica, 1993.

7. Victor A. Questel, *Derek Walcott: Contradiction and Resolution; Paradox, Inconsistency, Ambivalence and their Resolution in Derek Walcott's Writings, 1946–1976* (Ph.D. dissertation, UWI St. Augustine, 1979), 201–2.

8. Gerald Guiness, *Here and Elsewhere: Essays on Caribbean Literature* (Río Piedras: Universidad de Puerto Rico Press, 1993), 152.

9. Helen Vendler, "Poet of Two Worlds," *New York Review of Books,* 4 March 1982, 26.

10. Laurence A. Breiner, *An Introduction to West Indian Poetry* (Cambridge: Cambridge University Press, 1998), 184.

11. Calvin Bedient, "Derek Walcott: Contemporary," reprinted in *Critical Perspectives on Derek Walcott,* ed. Robert D. Hamner (Boulder, Colo.: Lynn Rienner, 1997), 313, 315, 313.

12. Vernon Shetley, "Review of *The Arkansas Testament,*" reprinted in *Critical Perspectives,* ed. Hamner, 395, 394.

13. William Logan, "The Fatal Lure of Home," *New York Times Book Review,* 29 June 1997, 11.

14. Andrew Marr, "A Small Square of Colour," *The Daily Telegraph* (London), 19 August 2000, 3.

15. J. Michael Dash, *The Other America: Caribbean Literature in a New World Context* (Charlottesville, Va.: University of Virginia Press, 1999), 100.

16. Antonio Benítez-Rojo, *The Repeating Island: The Caribbean and the Postmodern Perspective,* 2d ed. (Durham, N.C.: Duke University Press, 1996), 23, 151–52.

17. Benítez-Rojo, *The Repeating Island,* 189.

18. Benítez-Rojo, *The Repeating Island,* 153.

19. Walcott, "Crocodile Dandy: Les Murray" [1989]; reprinted in *What the Twilight Says: Essays* (New York: Farrar, Straus & Giroux, 1998), 184, 186.

INDEX